INUYASHIKI 5

HIROYA OKU

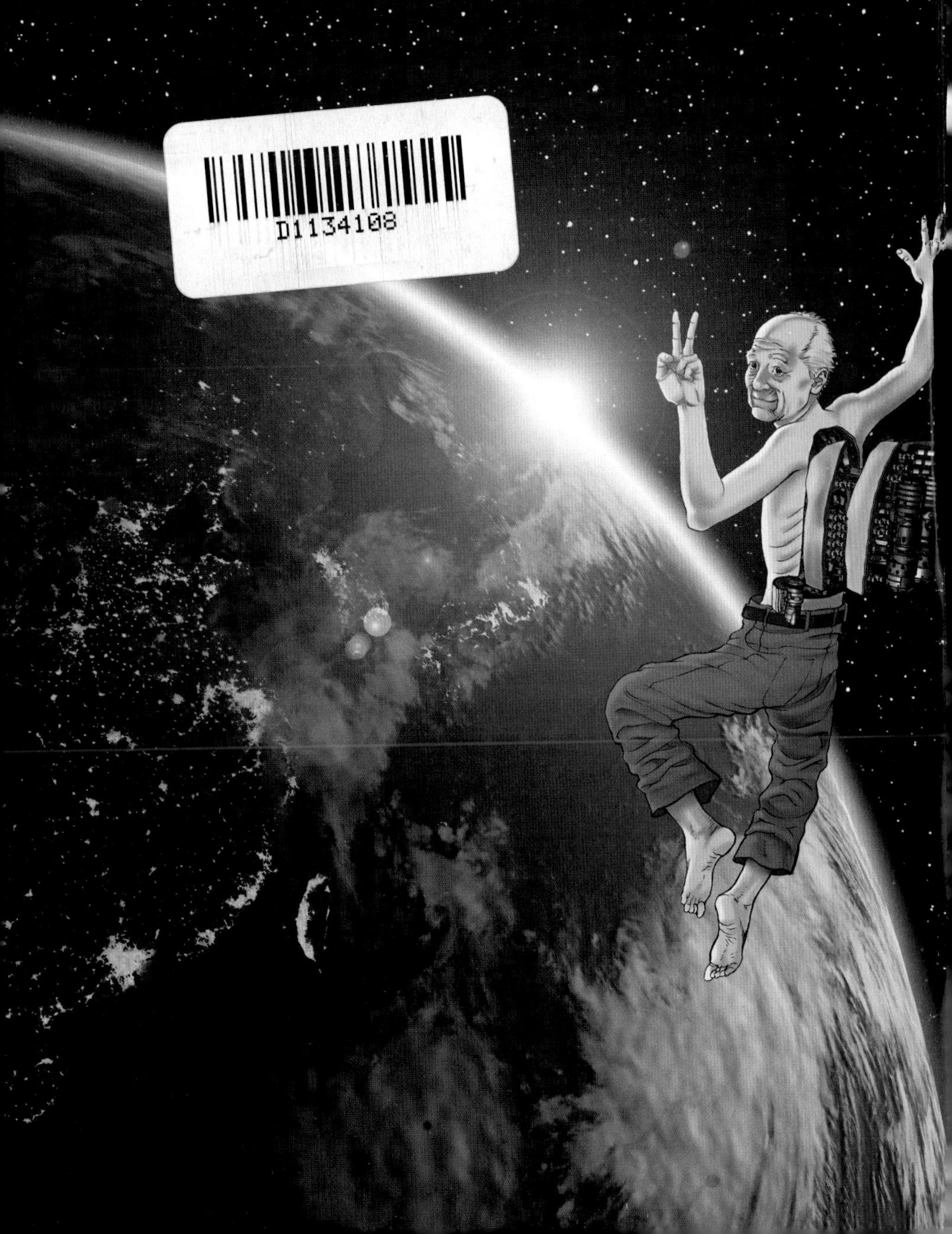

INUYASHIKI 5 CONTENTS

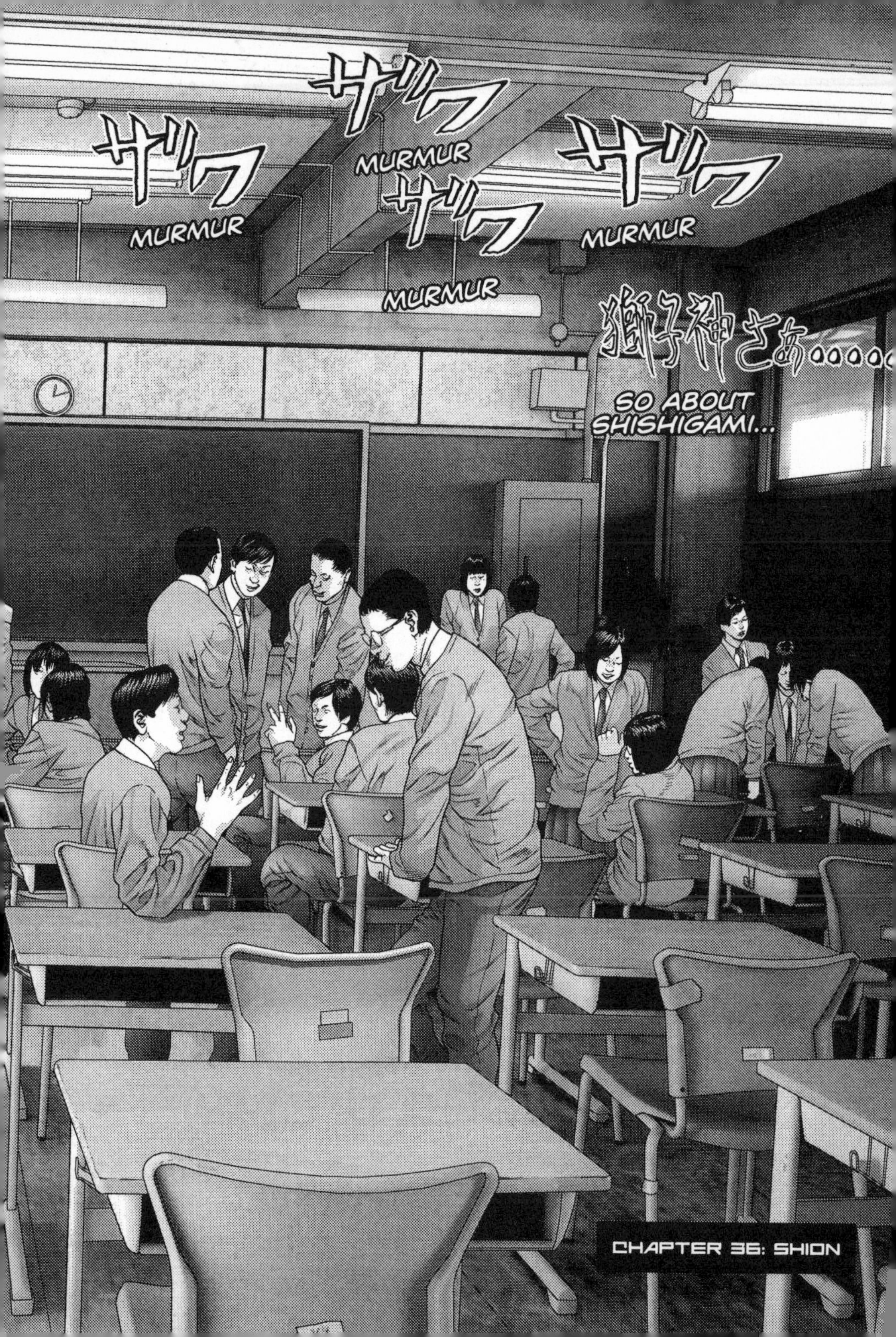
ザワ
MURMUR
ザワ
MURMUR
ザワ
MURMUR
ザワ
MURMUR
獅子神さあ……
SO ABOUT SHISHIGAMI...
CHAPTER 36: SHION

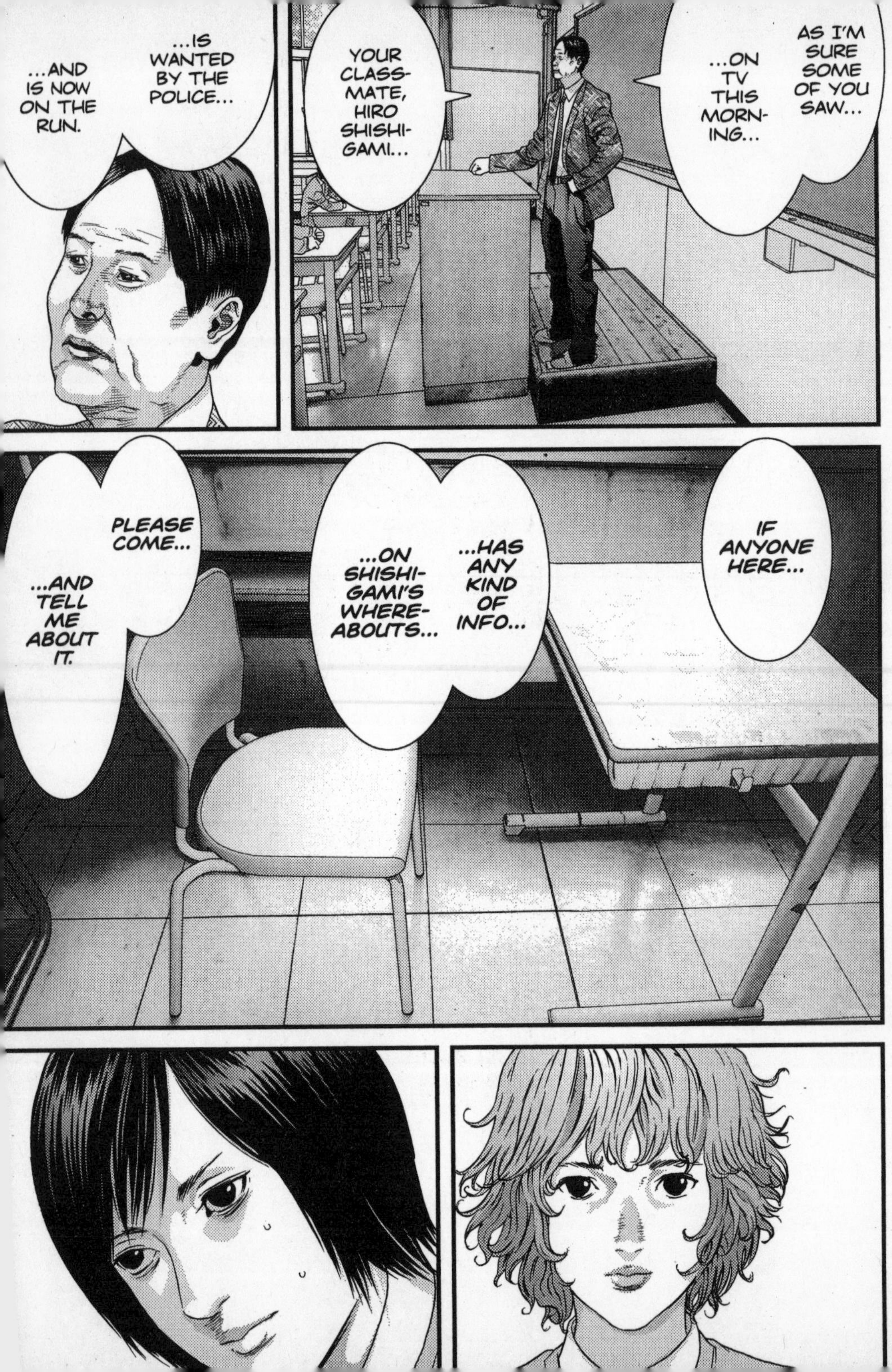
AS I'M SURE SOME OF YOU SAW...
...ON TV THIS MORNING...
YOUR CLASSMATE, HIRO SHISHIGAMI...
...IS WANTED BY THE POLICE...
...AND IS NOW ON THE RUN.
IF ANYONE HERE...
...HAS ANY KIND OF INFO...
...ON SHISHIGAMI'S WHEREABOUTS...
PLEASE COME...
...AND TELL ME ABOUT IT.

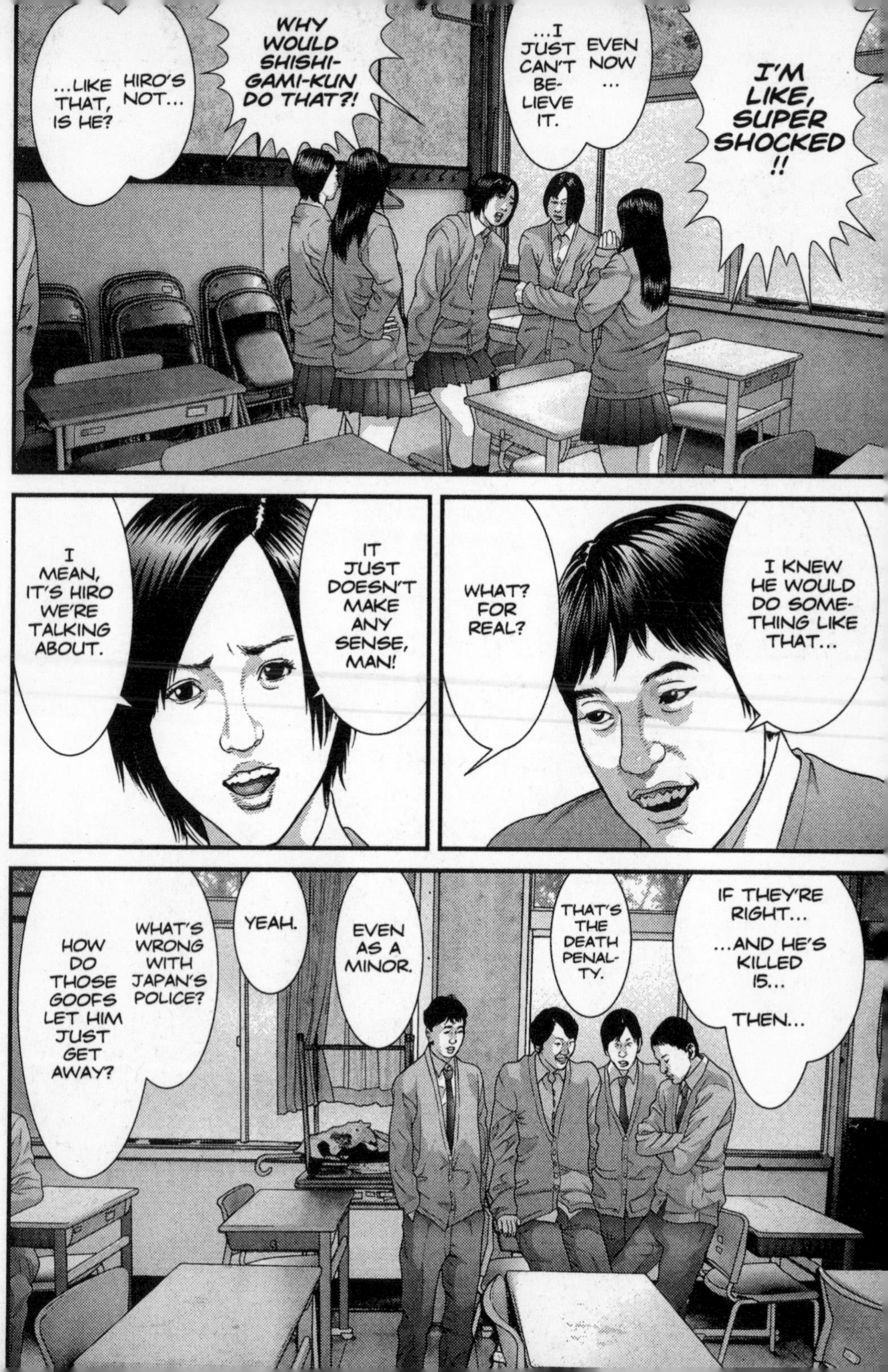
I'M LIKE, SUPER SHOCKED!!
EVEN NOW...
...I JUST CAN'T BELIEVE IT.
WHY WOULD SHISHIGAMI-KUN DO THAT?!
HIRO'S NOT...
...LIKE THAT, IS HE?
I KNEW HE WOULD DO SOMETHING LIKE THAT...
WHAT? FOR REAL?
IT JUST DOESN'T MAKE ANY SENSE, MAN!
I MEAN, IT'S HIRO WE'RE TALKING ABOUT.
IF THEY'RE RIGHT...
...AND HE'S KILLED 15...
THEN...
THAT'S THE DEATH PENALTY.
EVEN AS A MINOR.
YEAH.
WHAT'S WRONG WITH JAPAN'S POLICE?
HOW DO THOSE GOOFS LET HIM JUST GET AWAY?

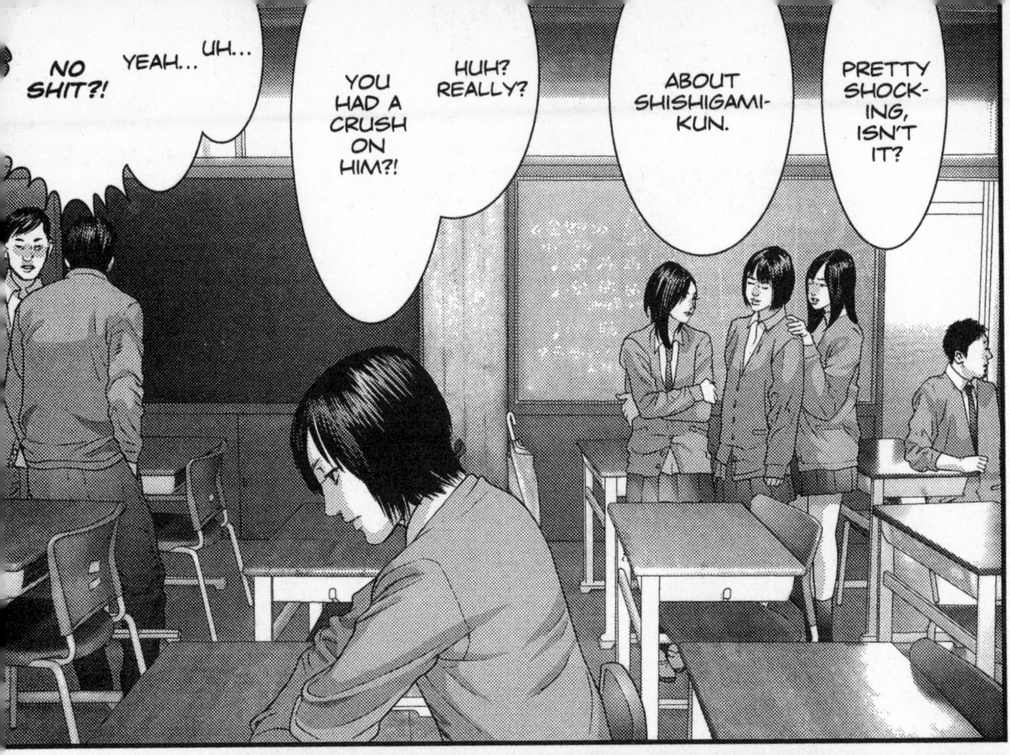
PRETTY SHOCKING, ISN'T IT?
ABOUT SHISHIGAMI-KUN.
HUH? REALLY?
YOU HAD A CRUSH ON HIM?!
UH...
YEAH...
NO SHIT?!

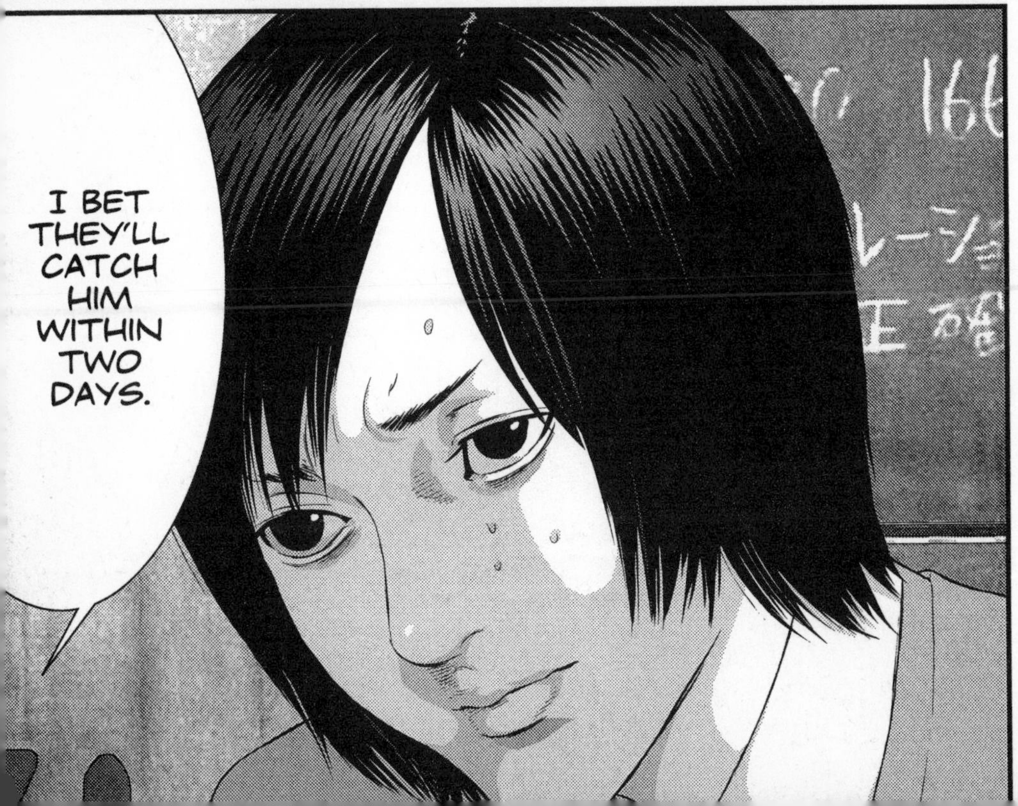
I BET THEY'LL CATCH HIM WITHIN TWO DAYS.

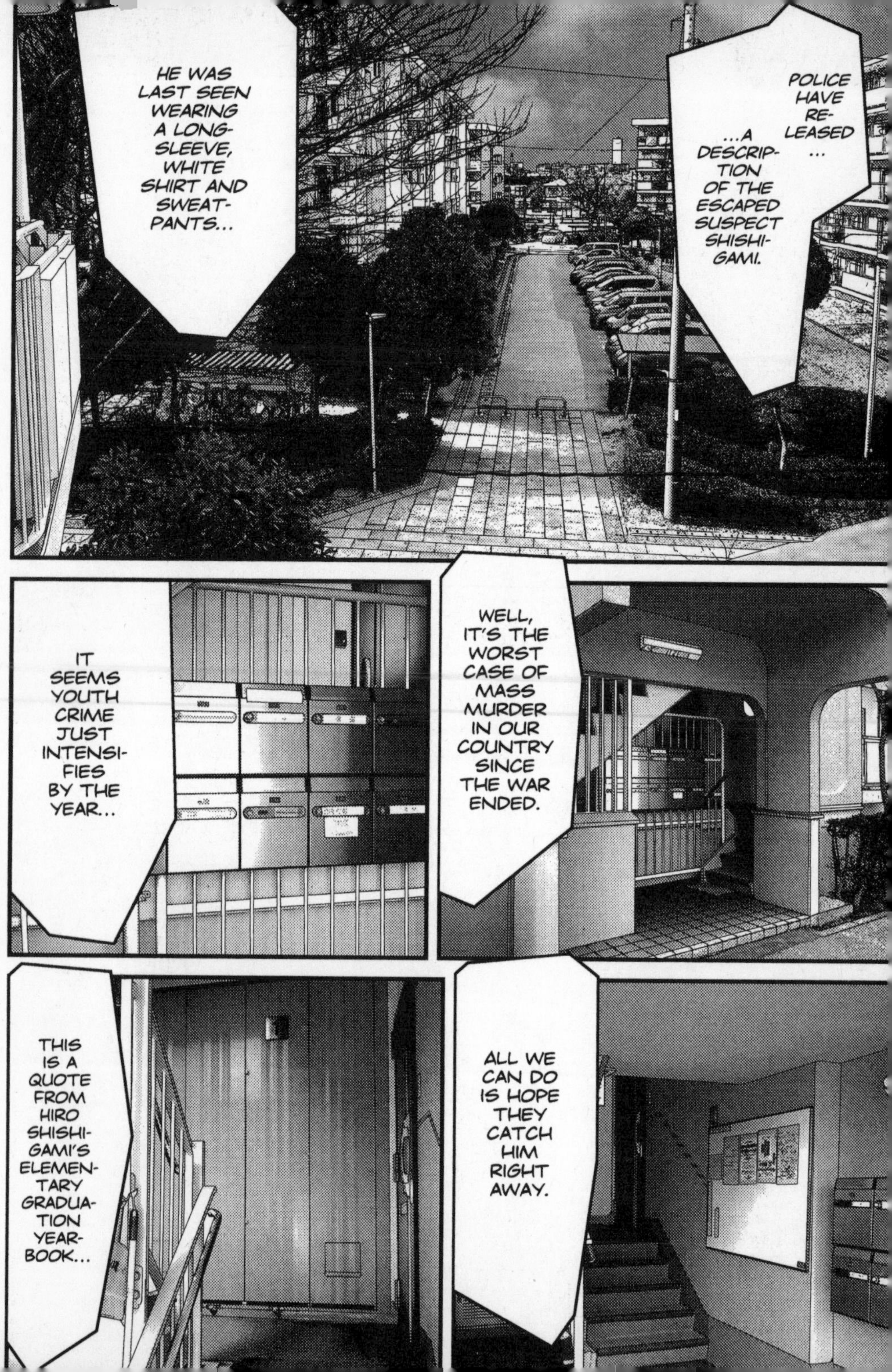
POLICE HAVE RELEASED...
...A DESCRIPTION OF THE ESCAPED SUSPECT SHISHIGAMI.
HE WAS LAST SEEN WEARING A LONG-SLEEVE, WHITE SHIRT AND SWEATPANTS...
WELL, IT'S THE WORST CASE OF MASS MURDER IN OUR COUNTRY SINCE THE WAR ENDED.
IT SEEMS YOUTH CRIME JUST INTENSIFIES BY THE YEAR...
ALL WE CAN DO IS HOPE THEY CATCH HIM RIGHT AWAY.
THIS IS A QUOTE FROM HIRO SHISHIGAMI'S ELEMENTARY GRADUATION YEARBOOK...

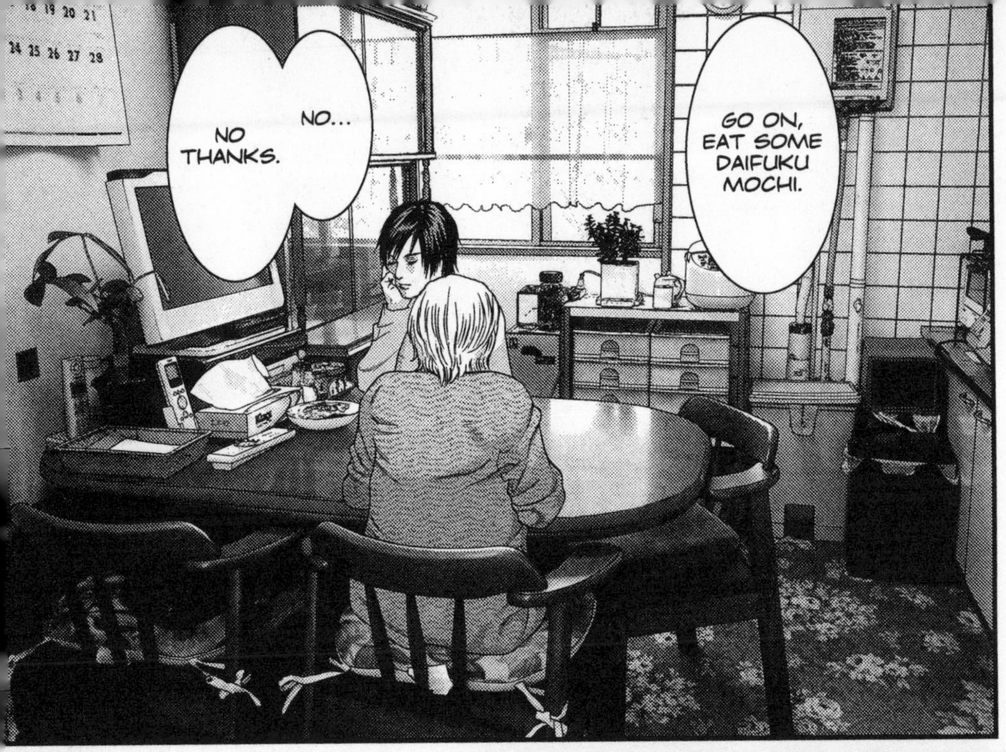
GO ON, EAT SOME DAIFUKU MOCHI.
NO...
NO THANKS.

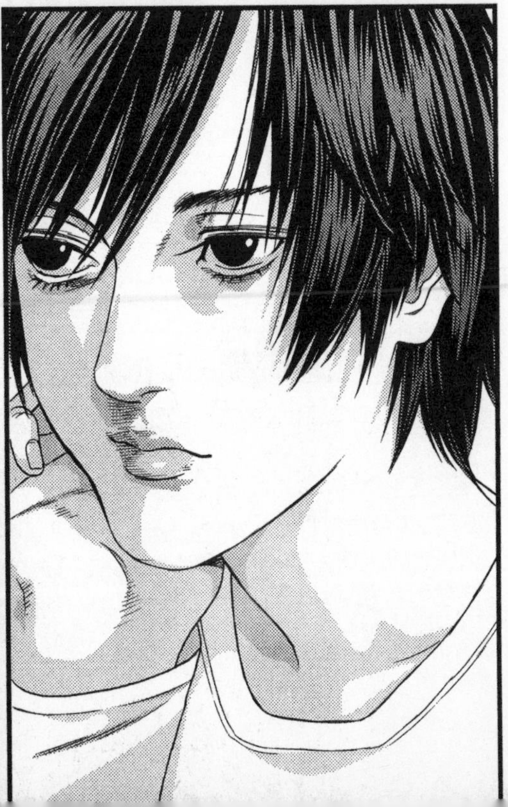

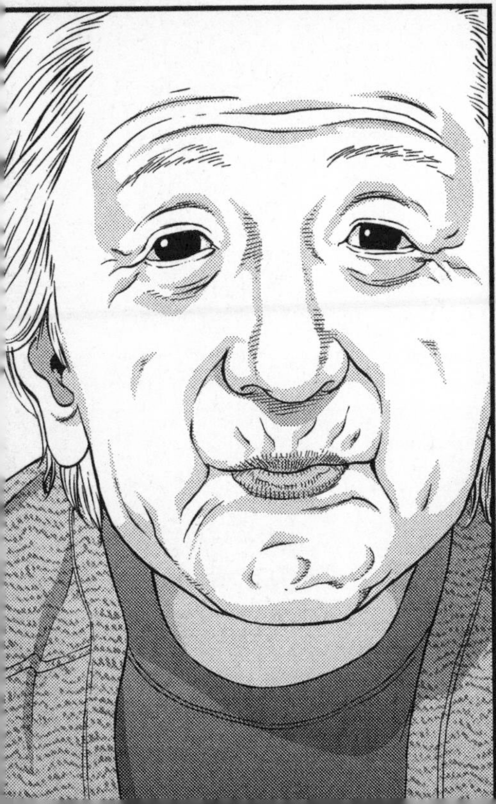

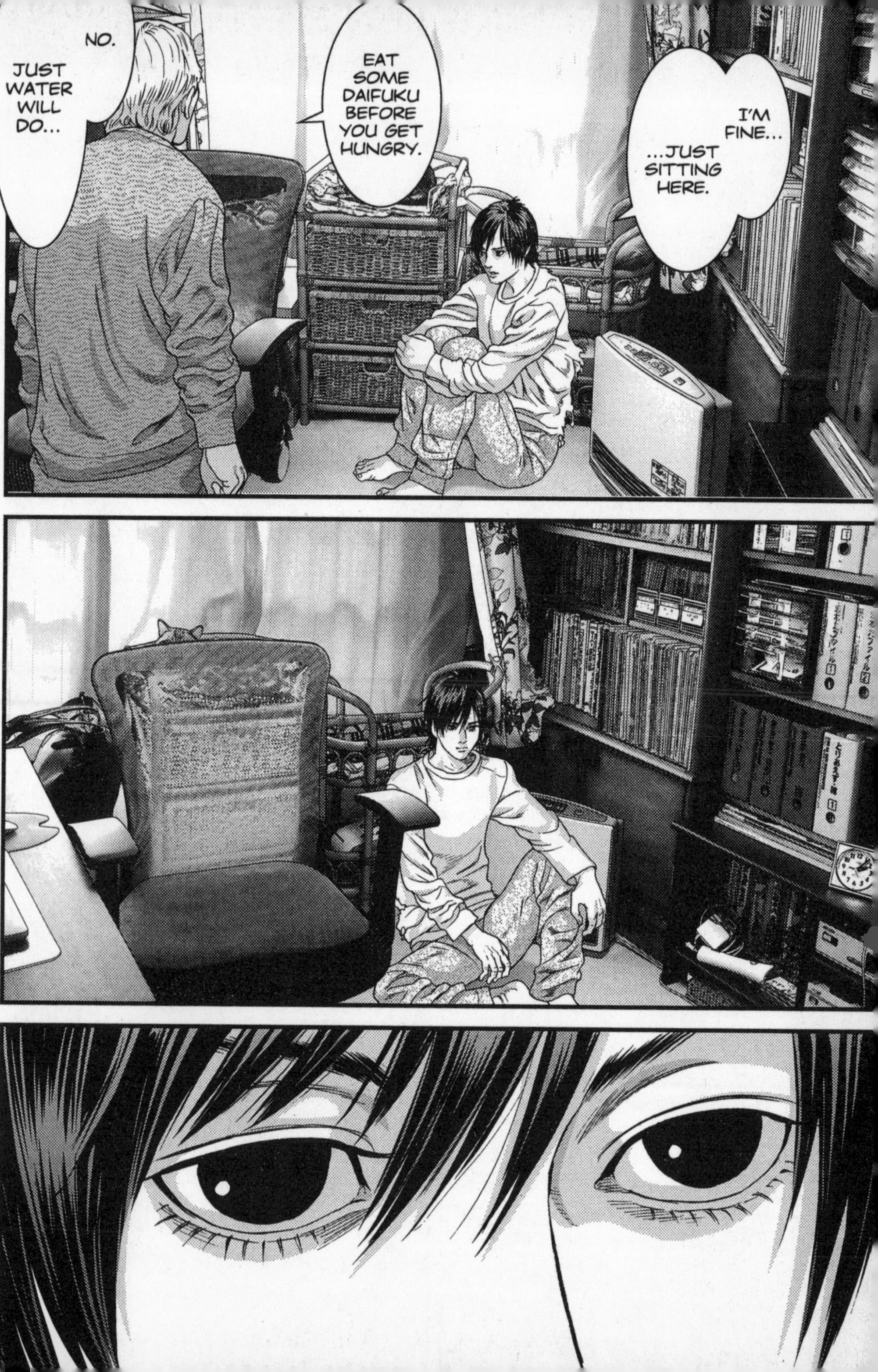
I'M FINE... ...JUST SITTING HERE.
EAT SOME DAIFUKU BEFORE YOU GET HUNGRY.
NO. JUST WATER WILL DO...

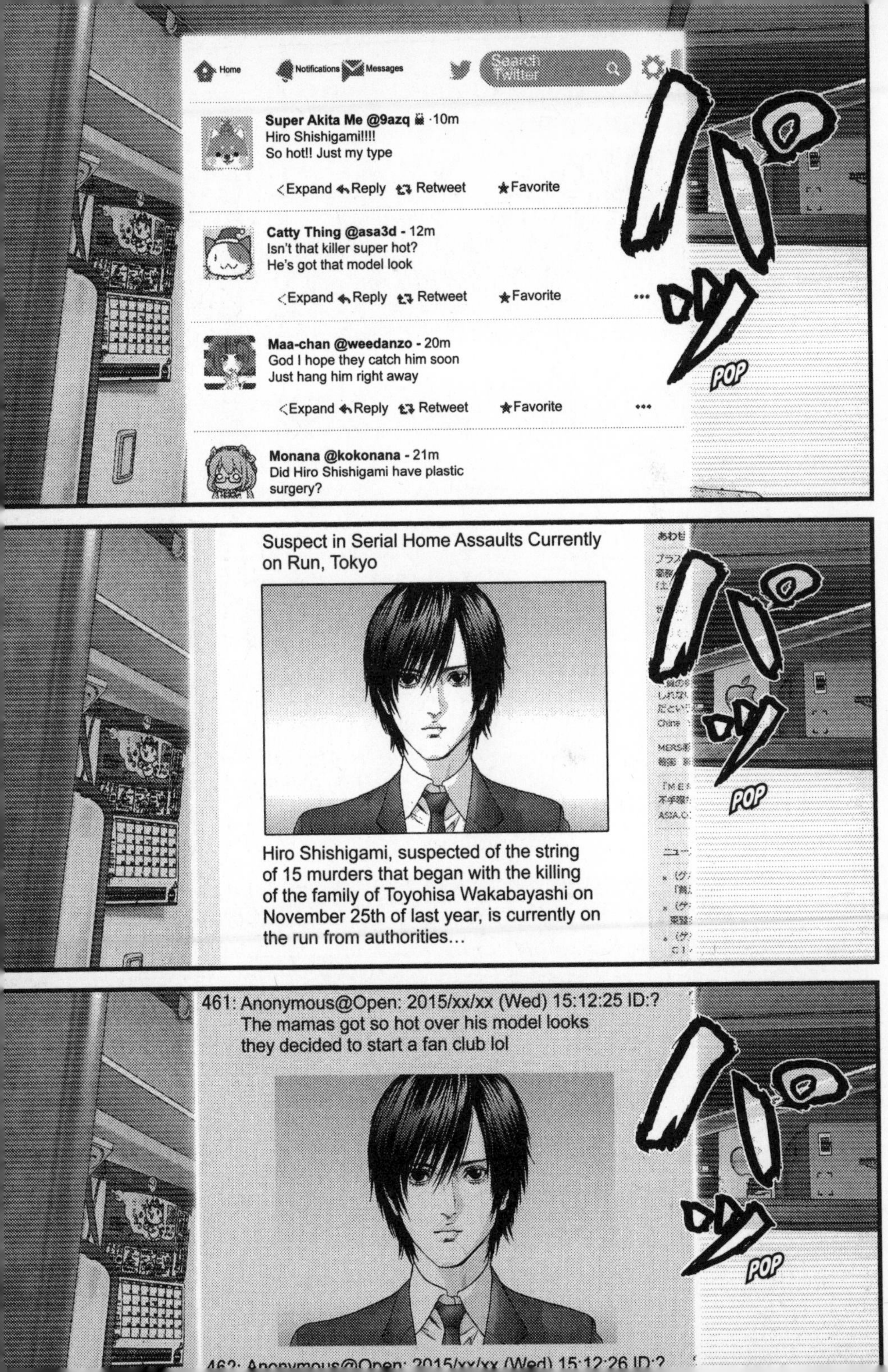
POP
Home
Notifications
Messages
Search Twitter
Super Akita Me @9azq · 10m
Hiro Shishigami!!!!
So hot!! Just my type
Expand Reply Retweet Favorite
Catty Thing @asa3d - 12m
Isn't that killer super hot?
He's got that model look
Expand Reply Retweet Favorite
Maa-chan @weedanzo - 20m
God I hope they catch him soon
Just hang him right away
Expand Reply Retweet Favorite
Monana @kokonana - 21m
Did Hiro Shishigami have plastic surgery?
POP
Suspect in Serial Home Assaults Currently on Run, Tokyo
Hiro Shishigami, suspected of the string of 15 murders that began with the killing of the family of Toyohisa Wakabayashi on November 25th of last year, is currently on the run from authorities…
POP
461: Anonymous@Open: 2015/xx/xx (Wed) 15:12:25 ID:?
The mamas got so hot over his model looks they decided to start a fan club lol
462: Anonymous@Open: 2015/xx/xx (Wed) 15:12:26 ID:?

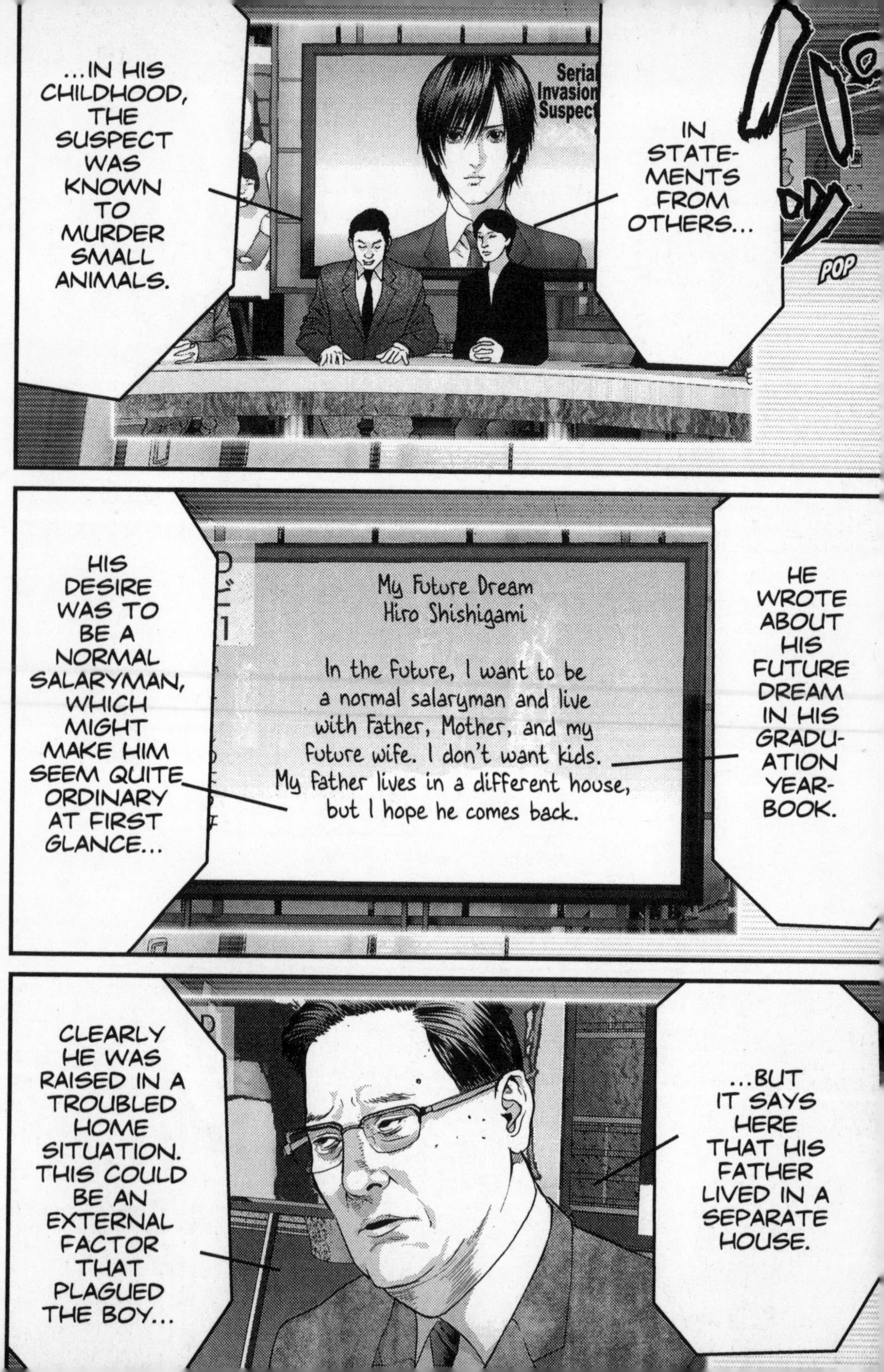
POP
Serial Invasion Suspect
IN STATEMENTS FROM OTHERS...
...IN HIS CHILDHOOD, THE SUSPECT WAS KNOWN TO MURDER SMALL ANIMALS.
HE WROTE ABOUT HIS FUTURE DREAM IN HIS GRADUATION YEARBOOK.
My Future Dream
Hiro Shishigami
In the future, I want to be a normal salaryman and live with Father, Mother, and my future wife. I don't want kids. My father lives in a different house, but I hope he comes back.
HIS DESIRE WAS TO BE A NORMAL SALARYMAN, WHICH MIGHT MAKE HIM SEEM QUITE ORDINARY AT FIRST GLANCE...
...BUT IT SAYS HERE THAT HIS FATHER LIVED IN A SEPARATE HOUSE.
CLEARLY HE WAS RAISED IN A TROUBLED HOME SITUATION. THIS COULD BE AN EXTERNAL FACTOR THAT PLAGUED THE BOY...

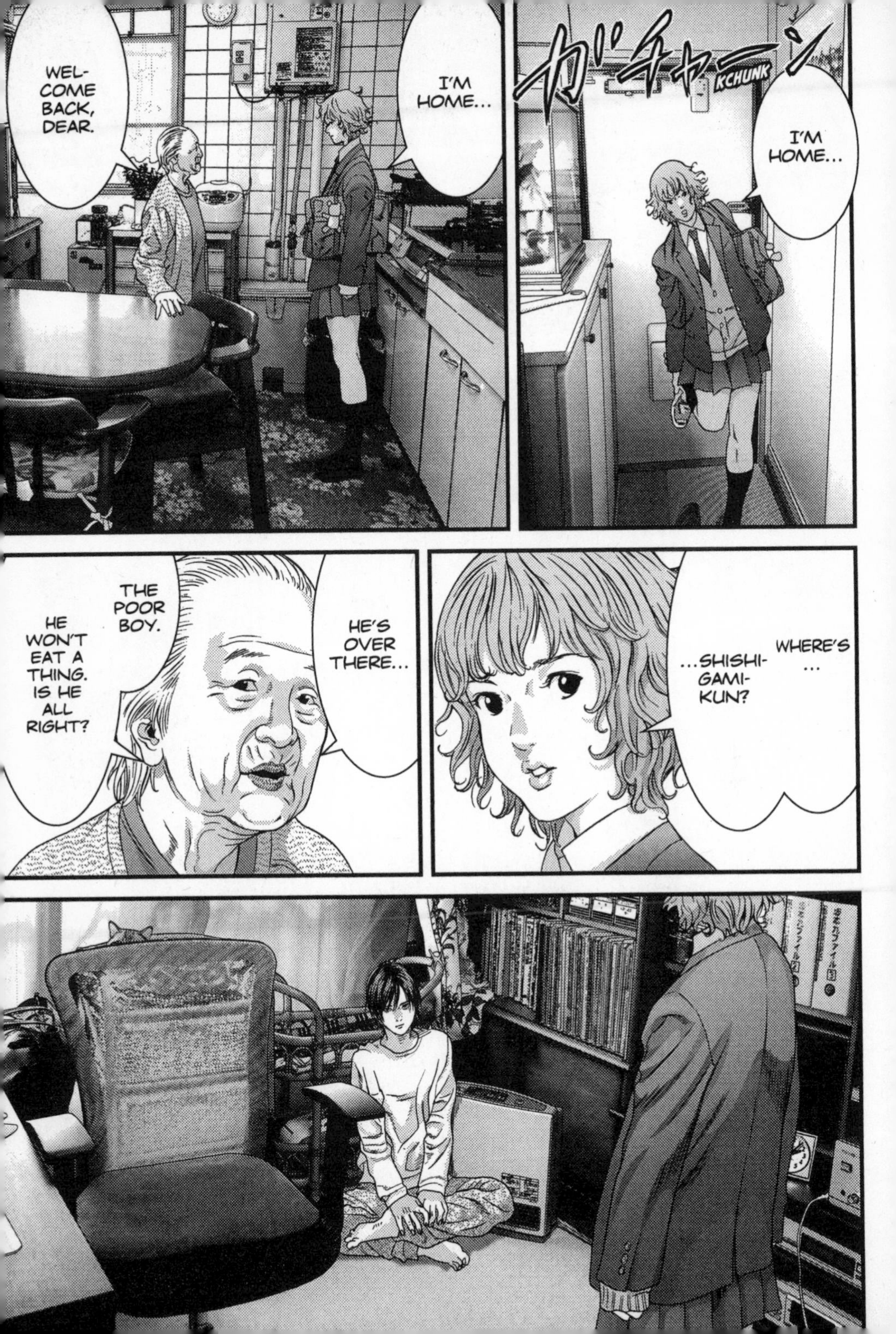
ガチャーン
KCHUNK
I'M HOME...
I'M HOME...
WEL-COME BACK, DEAR.
WHERE'S ...
...SHISHI-GAMI-KUN?
HE'S OVER THERE...
THE POOR BOY.
HE WON'T EAT A THING. IS HE ALL RIGHT?

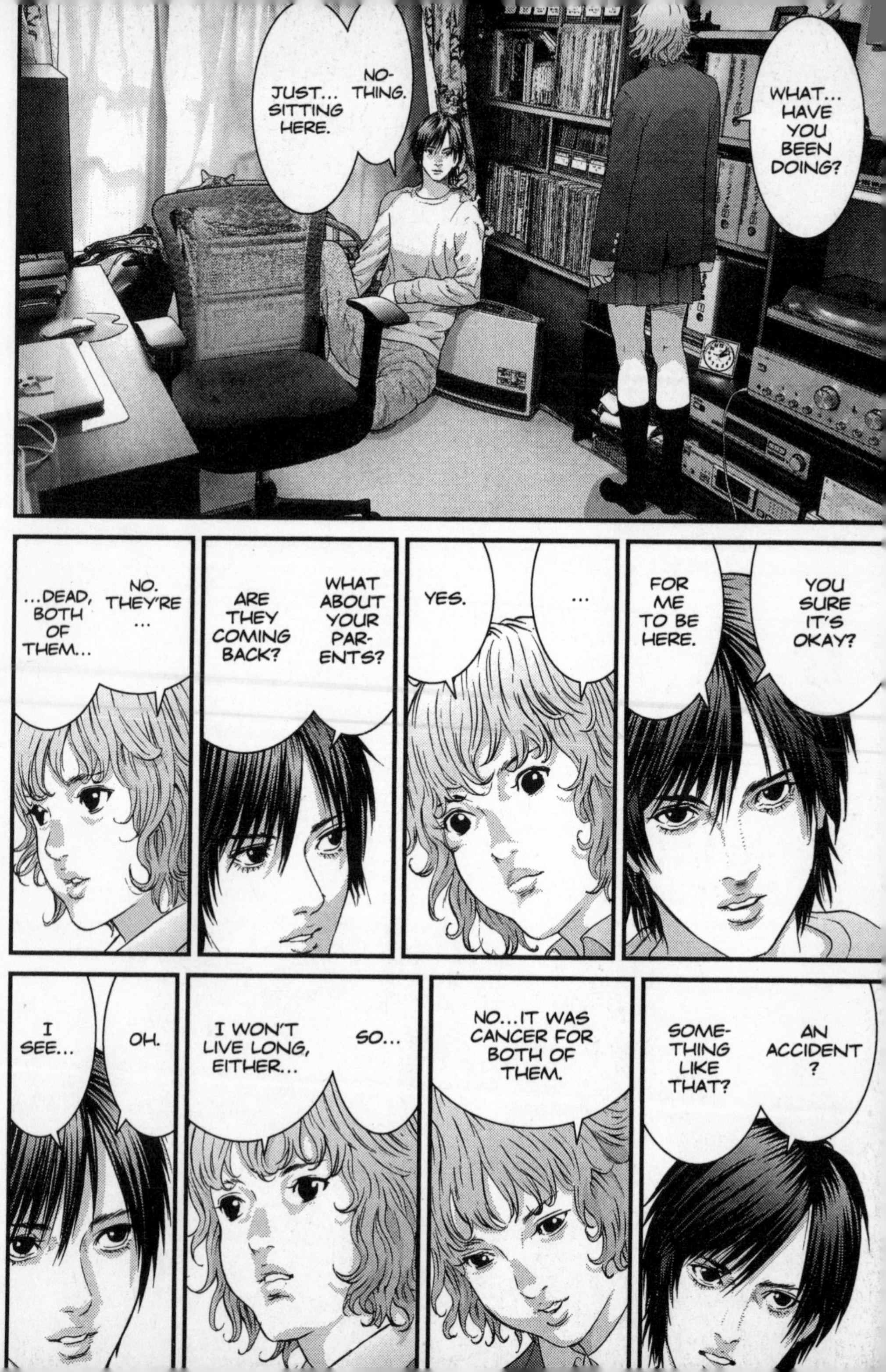
WHAT... HAVE YOU BEEN DOING?
NOTHING. JUST... SITTING HERE.
YOU SURE IT'S OKAY?
FOR ME TO BE HERE.
...
YES.
WHAT ABOUT YOUR PARENTS?
ARE THEY COMING BACK?
NO. THEY'RE ...
...DEAD, BOTH OF THEM...
AN ACCIDENT?
SOMETHING LIKE THAT?
NO...IT WAS CANCER FOR BOTH OF THEM.
SO...
I WON'T LIVE LONG, EITHER...
OH.
I SEE...

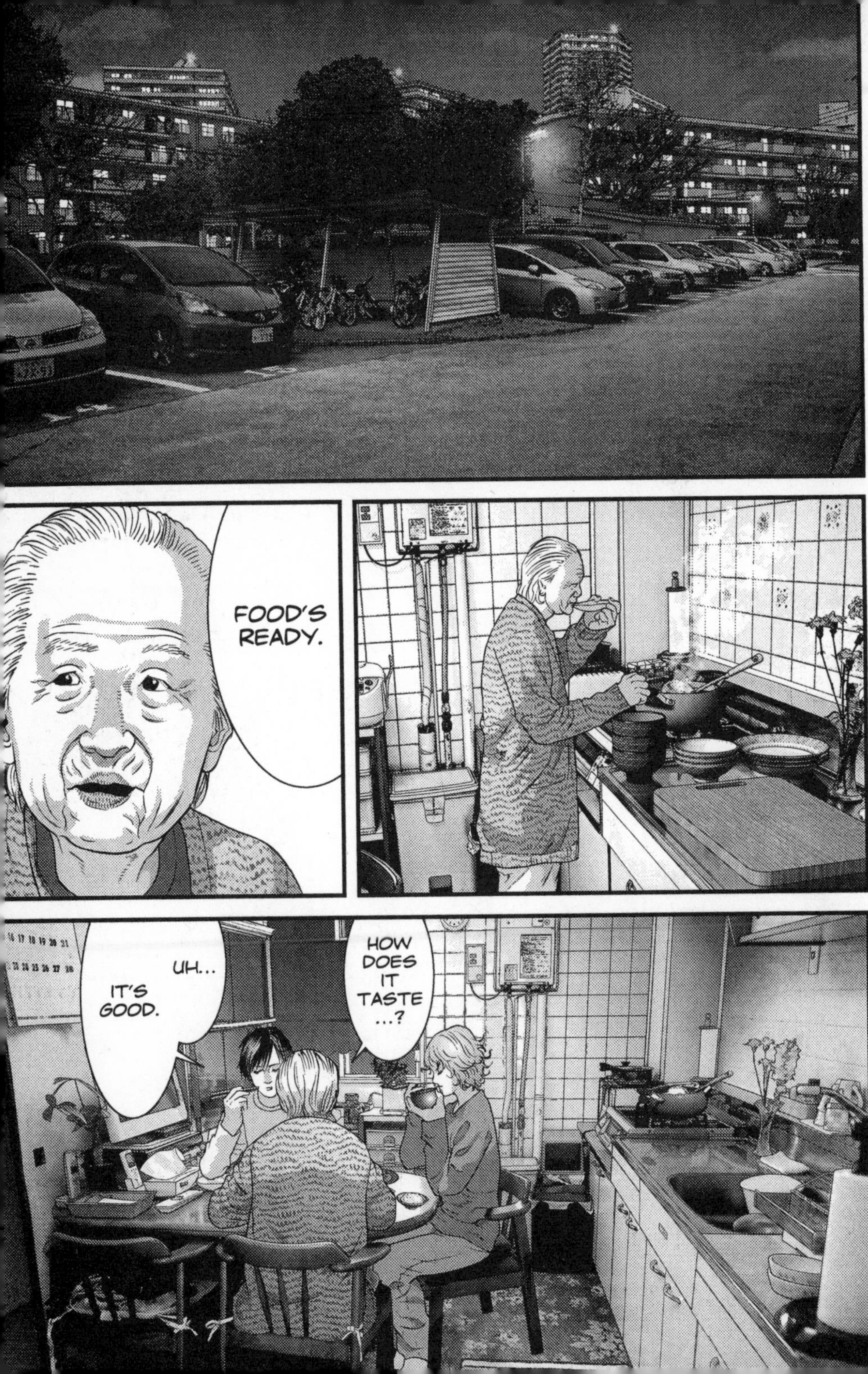
FOOD'S READY.
HOW DOES IT TASTE ...?
UH...
IT'S GOOD.

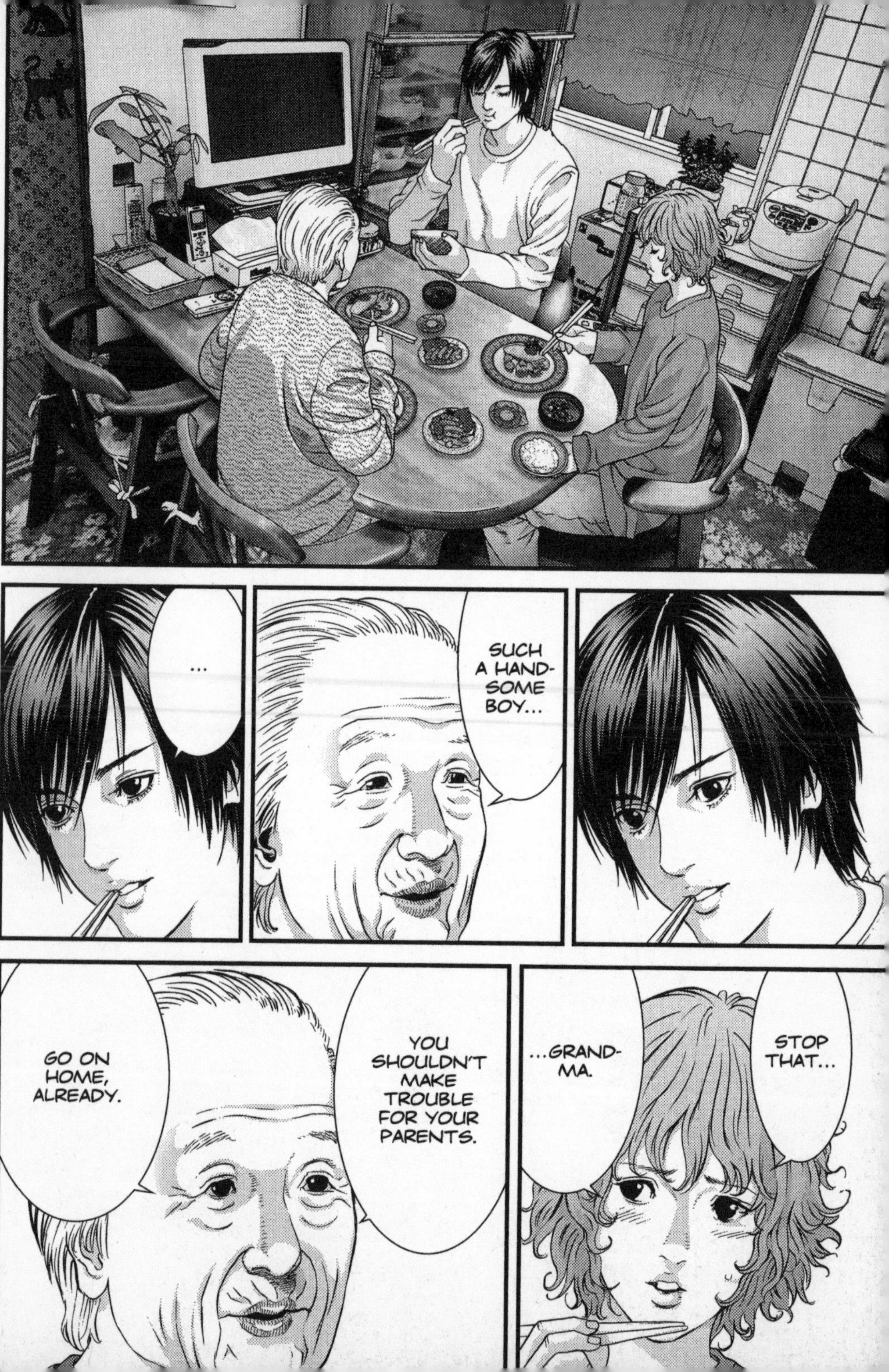
SUCH A HAND-SOME BOY...
...
STOP THAT...
...GRAND-MA.
YOU SHOULDN'T MAKE TROUBLE FOR YOUR PARENTS.
GO ON HOME, ALREADY.

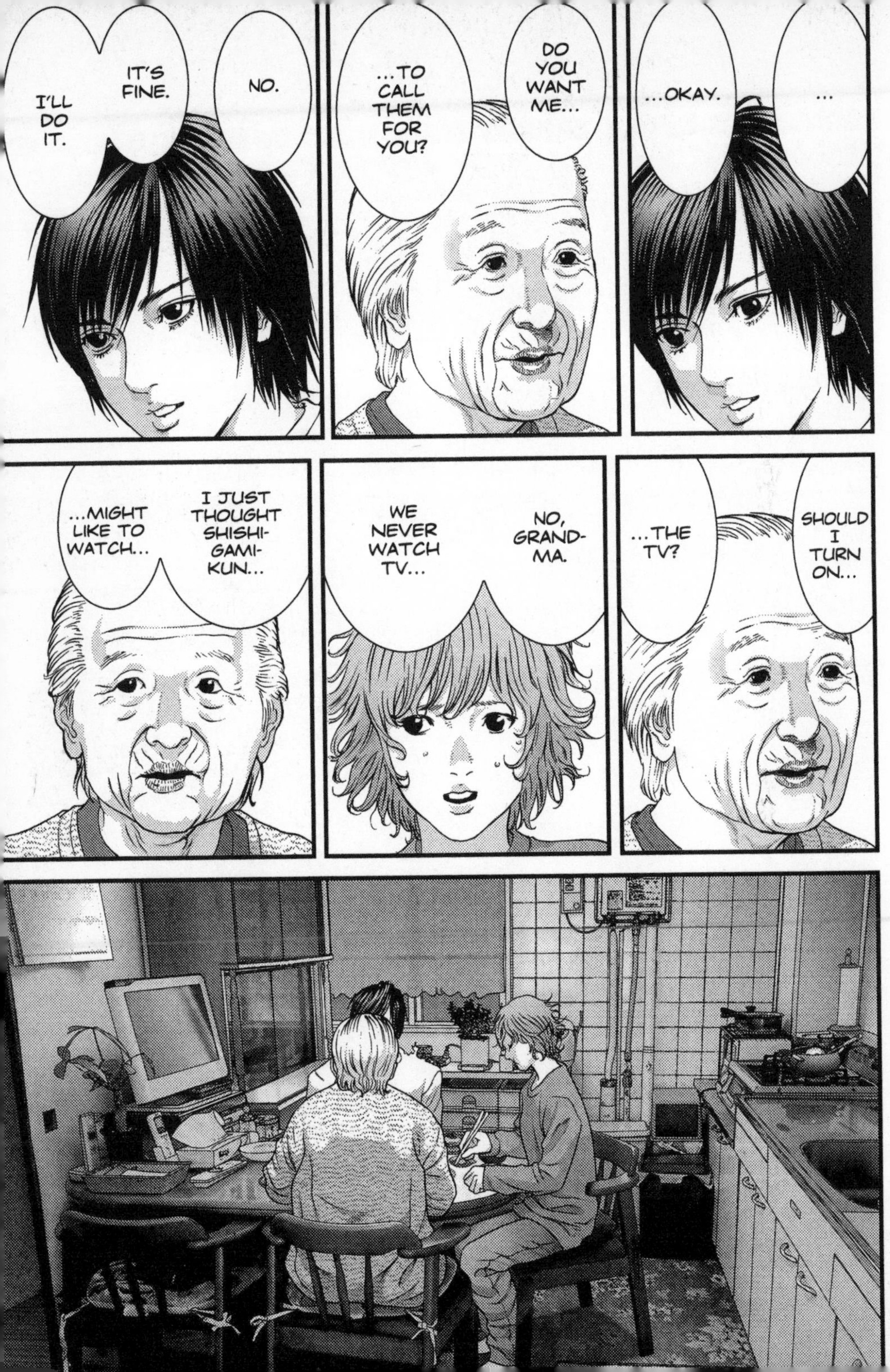
...
...OKAY.
DO YOU WANT ME...
...TO CALL THEM FOR YOU?
NO.
IT'S FINE.
I'LL DO IT.
SHOULD I TURN ON...
...THE TV?
NO, GRANDMA.
WE NEVER WATCH TV...
I JUST THOUGHT SHISHIGAMI-KUN...
...MIGHT LIKE TO WATCH...

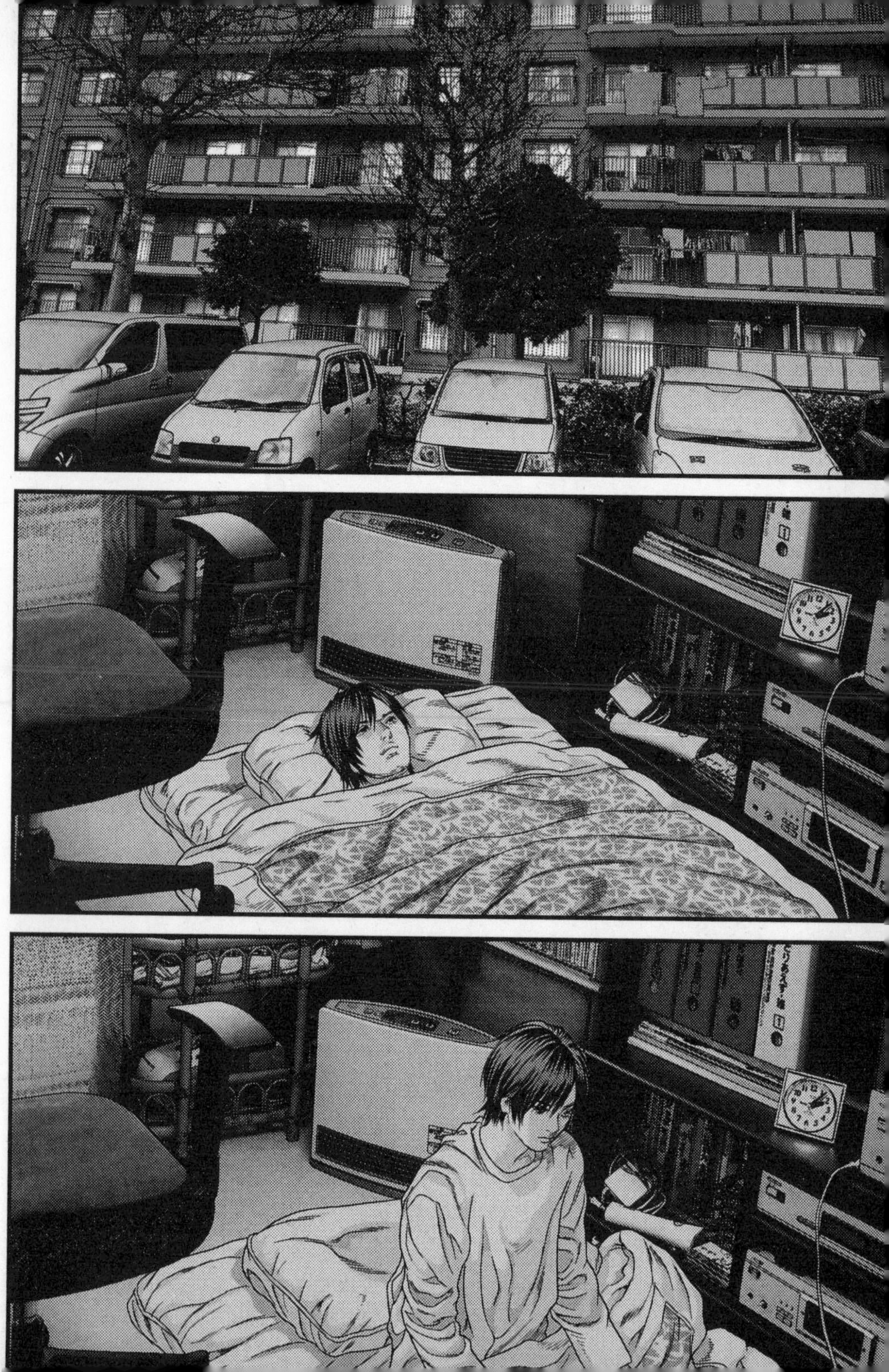

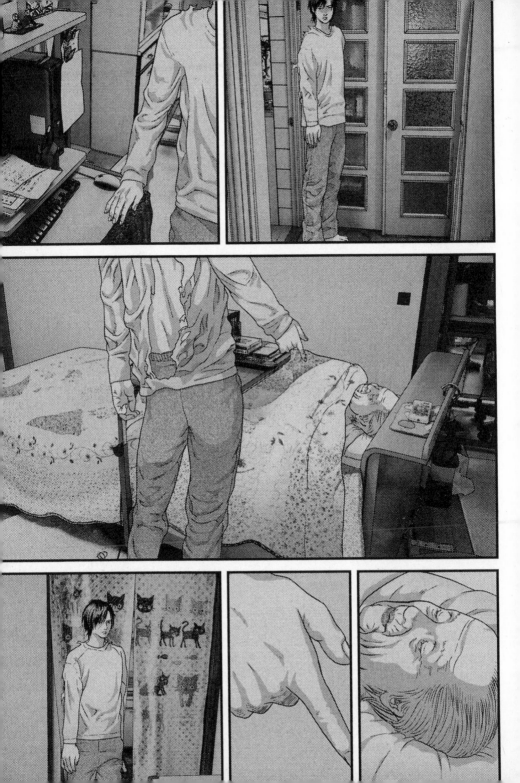

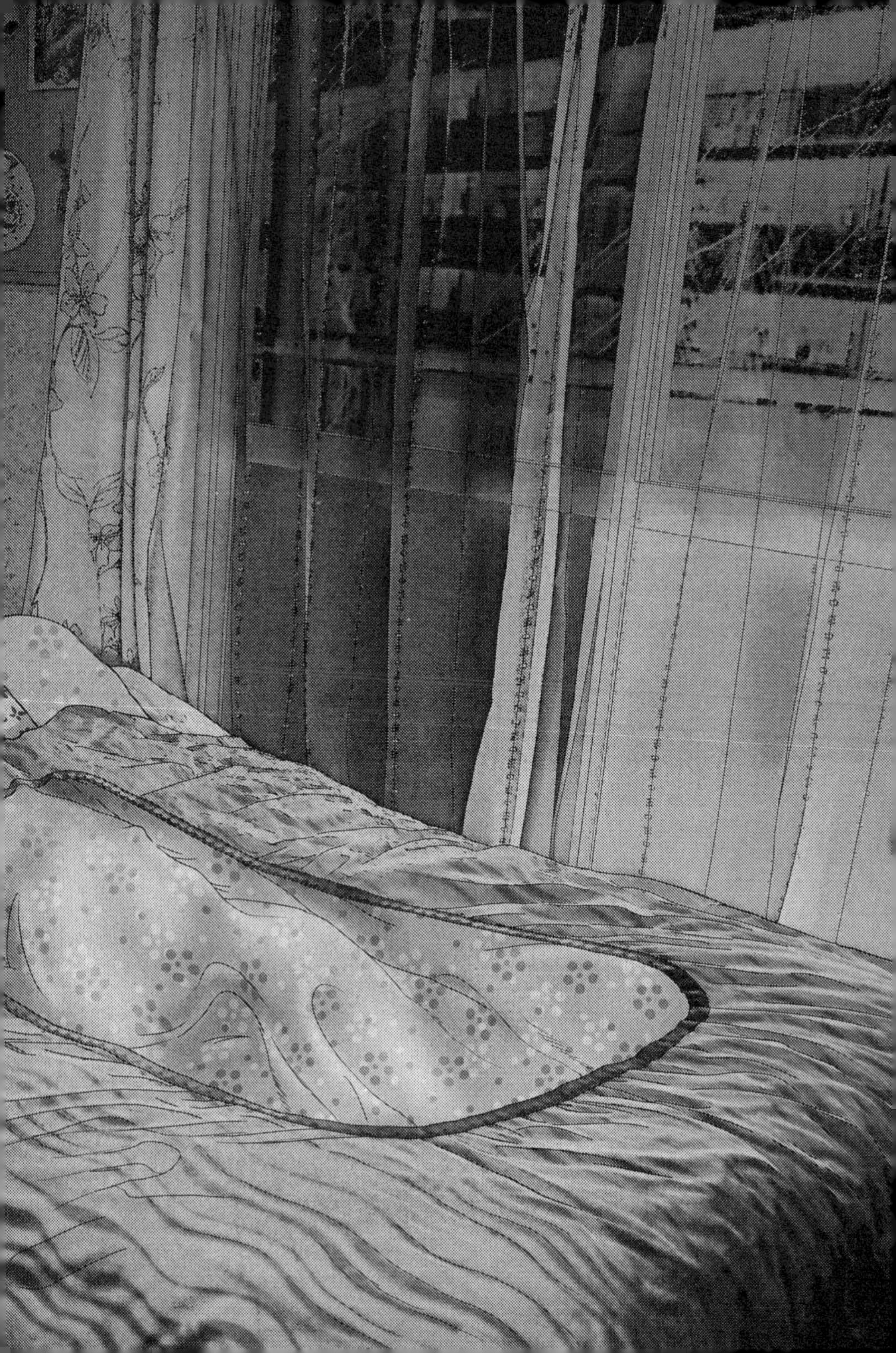

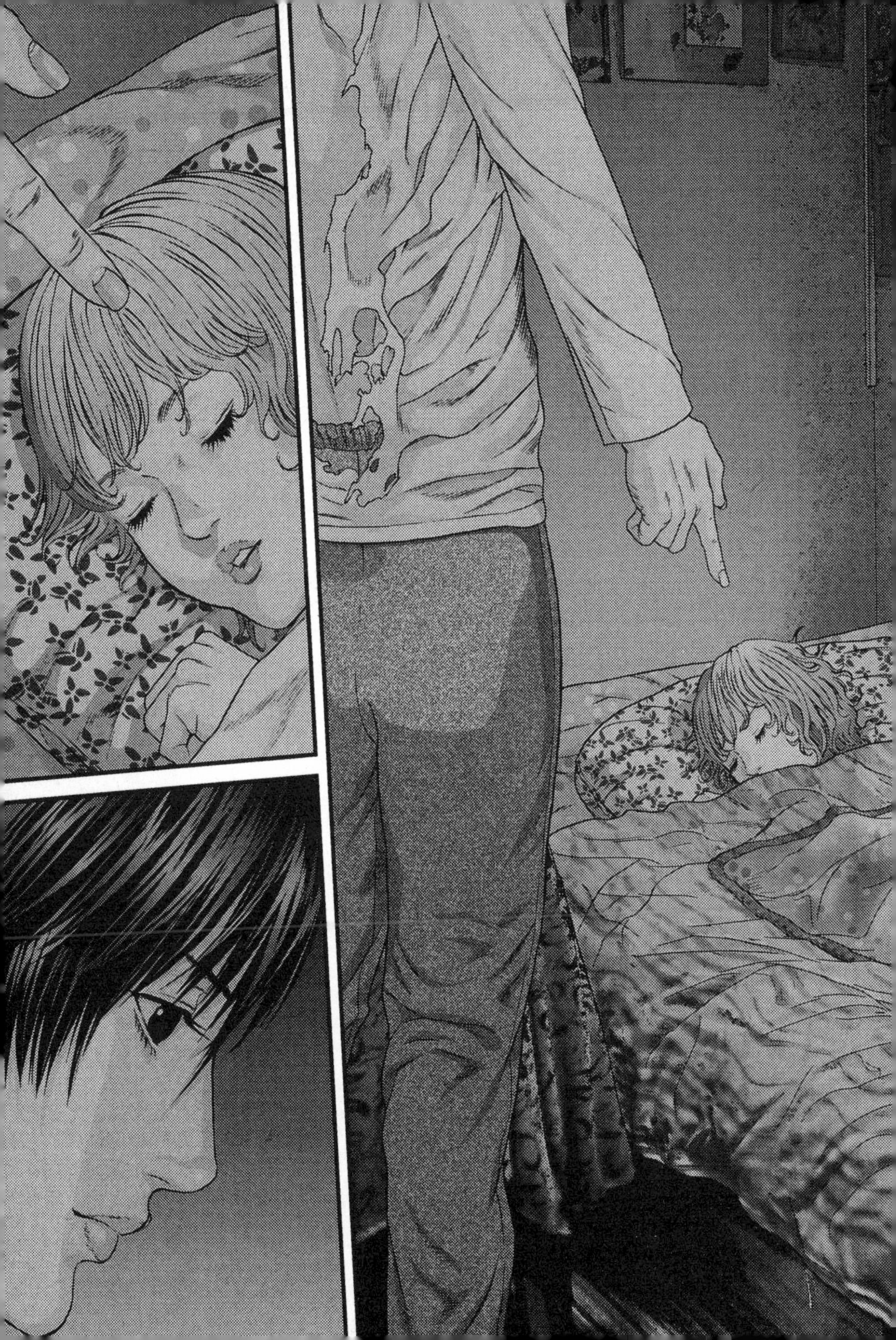

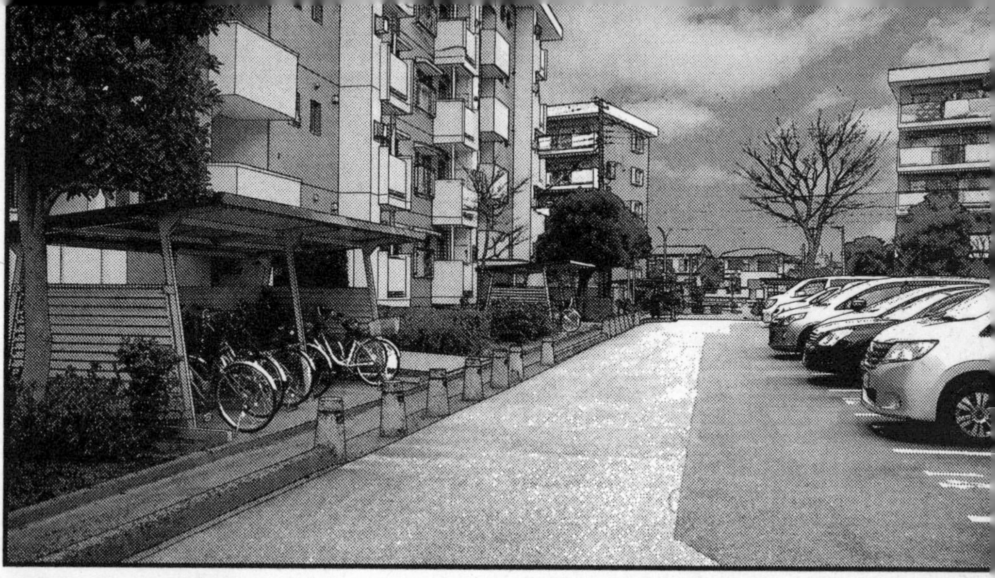
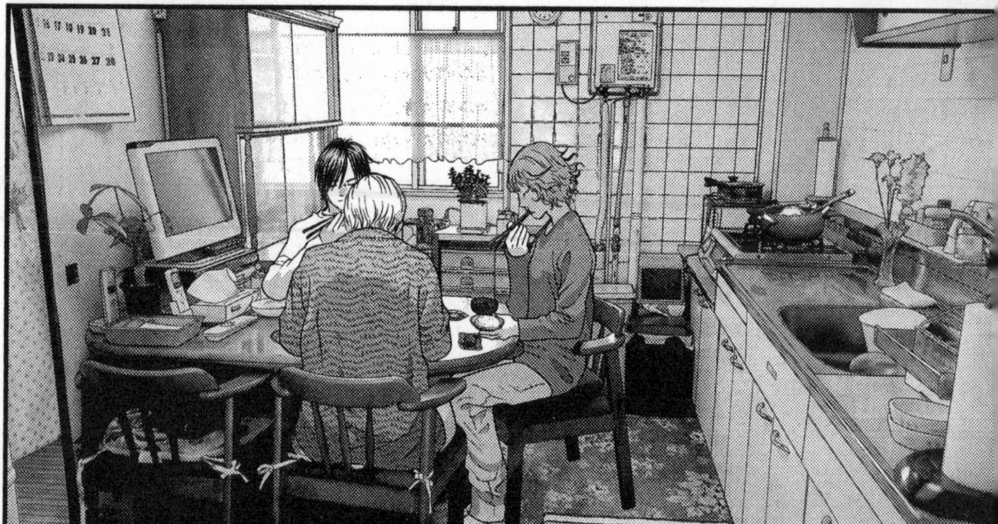
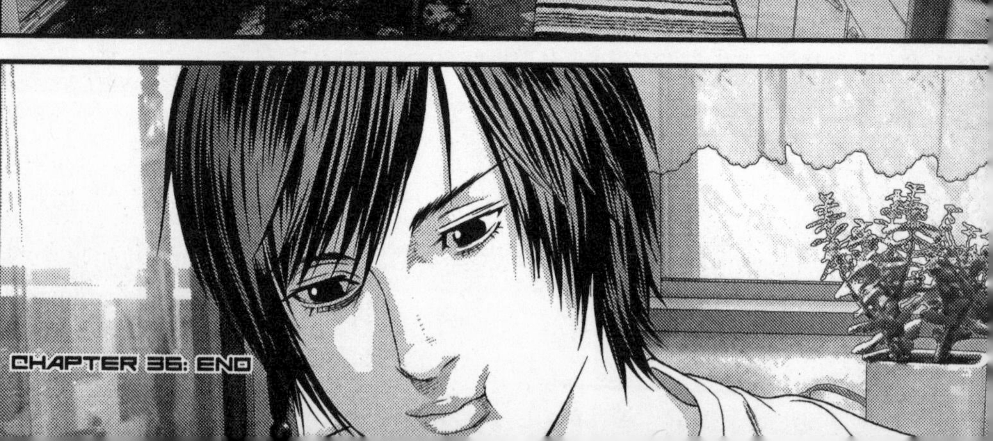
CHAPTER 36: END

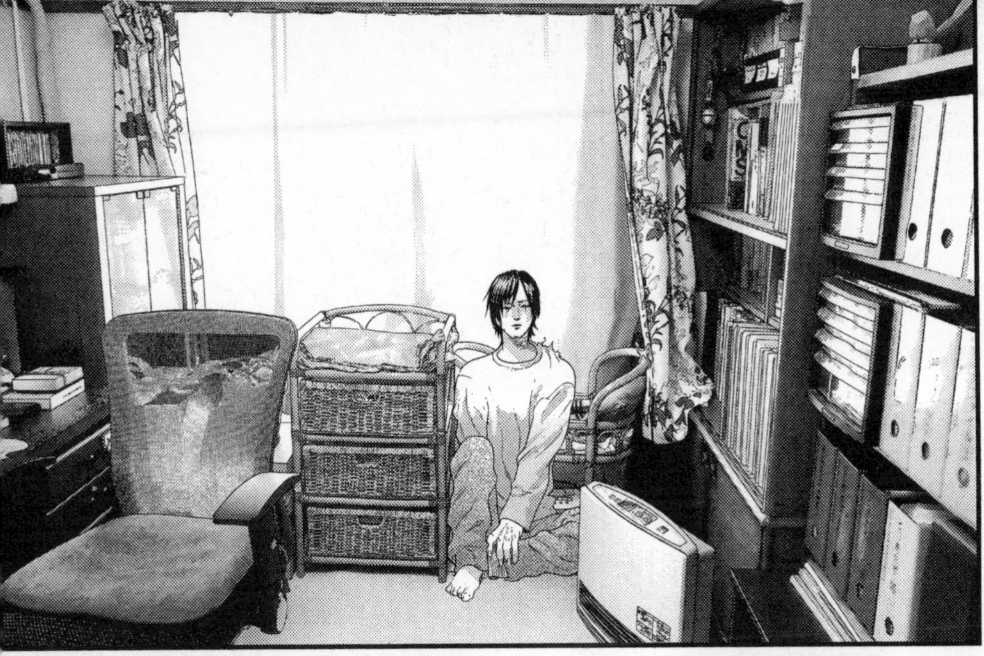
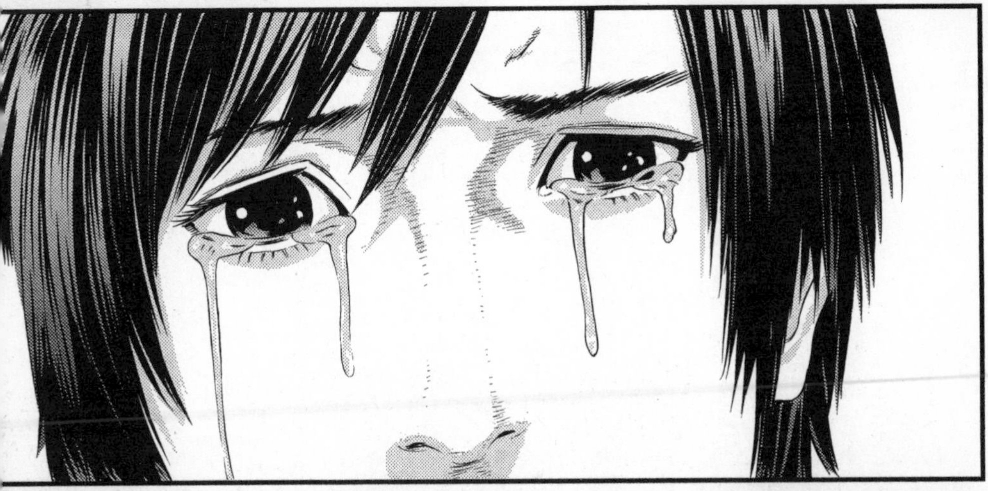
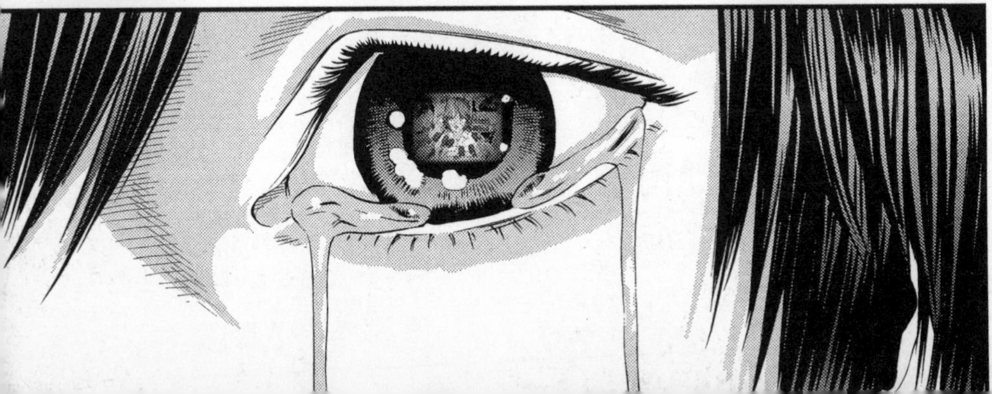

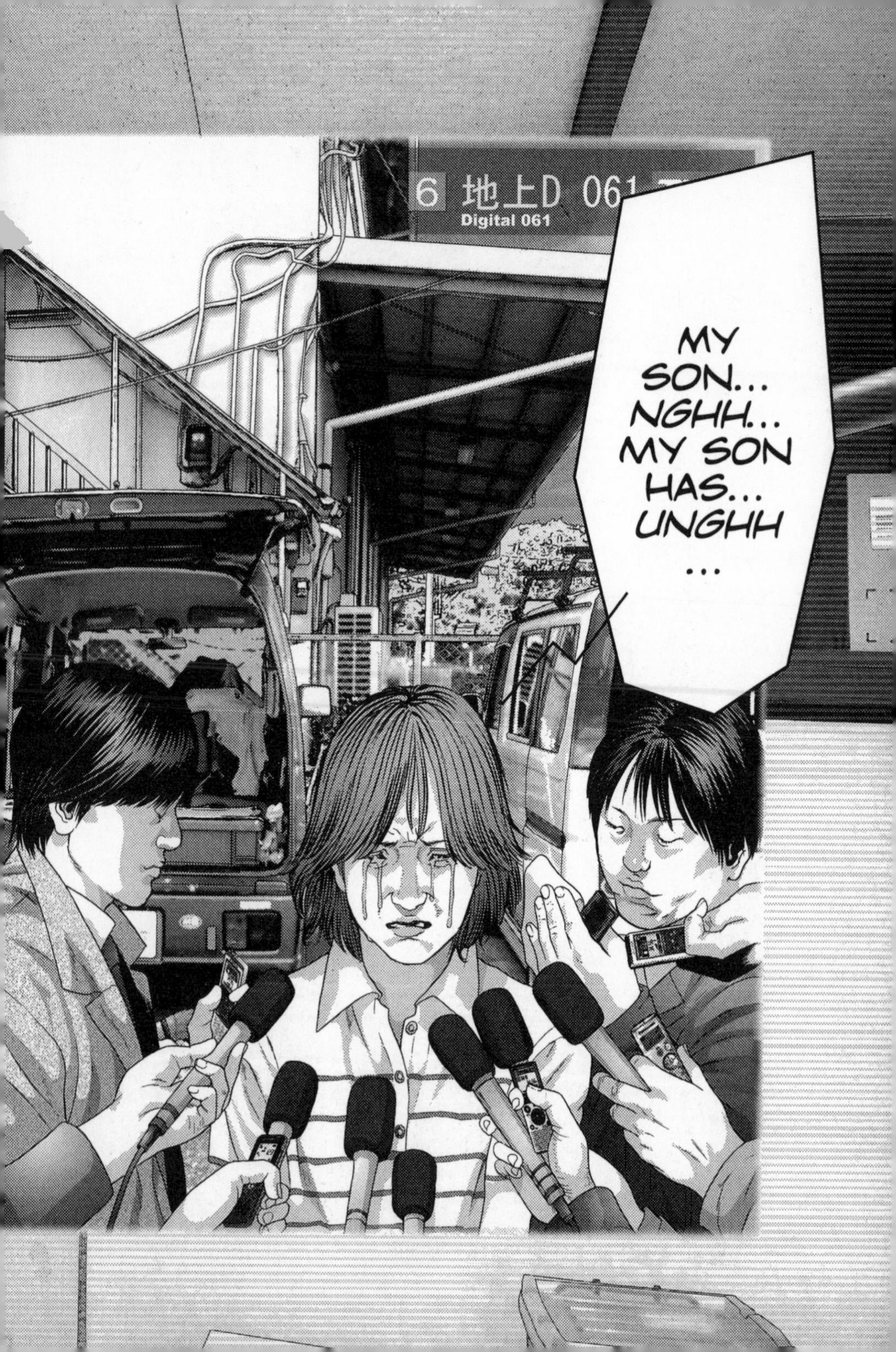
6 地上D 061
Digital 061
MY SON... NGHH... MY SON HAS... UNGHH ...

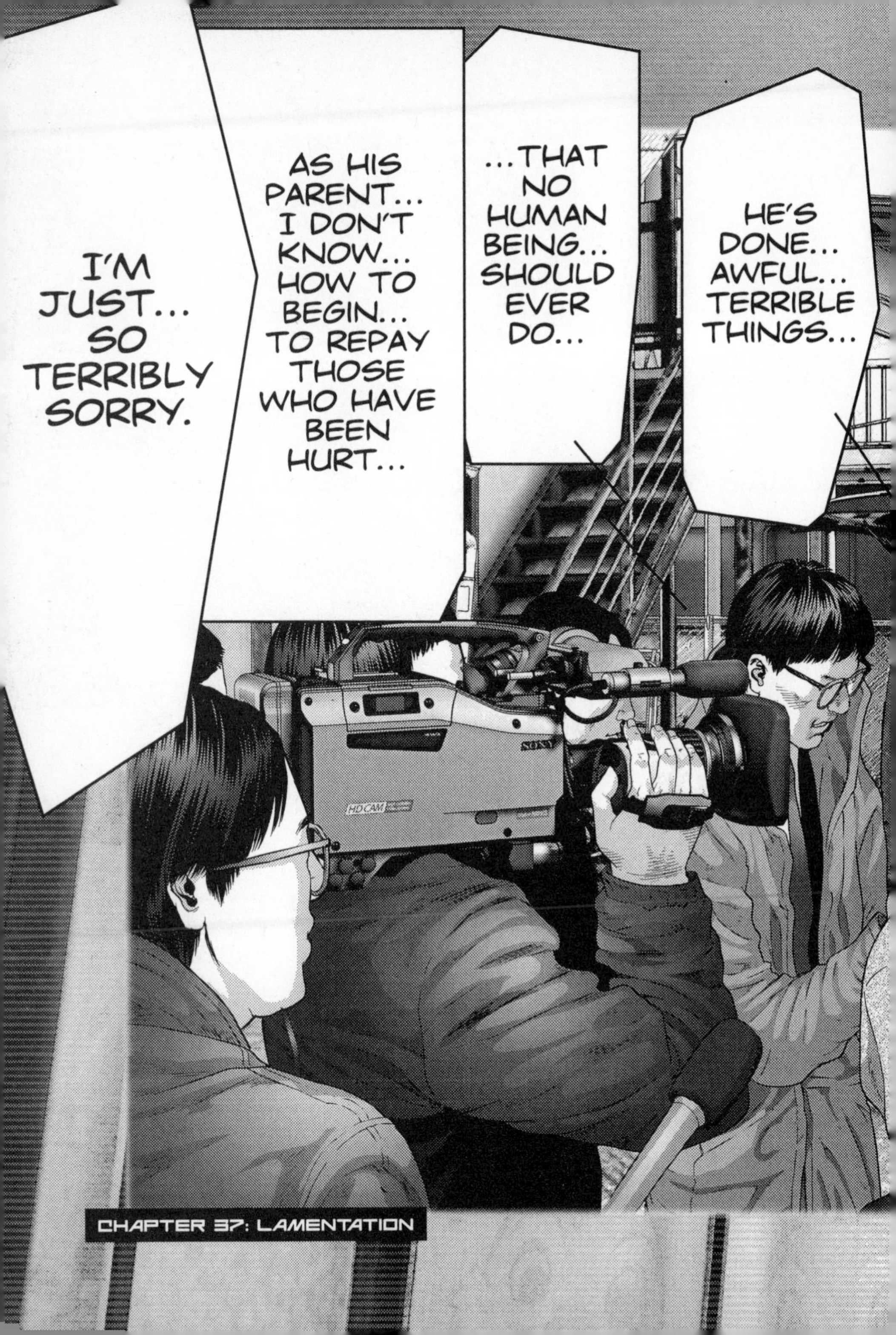
HE'S DONE... AWFUL... TERRIBLE THINGS...
...THAT NO HUMAN BEING... SHOULD EVER DO...
AS HIS PARENT... I DON'T KNOW... HOW TO BEGIN... TO REPAY THOSE WHO HAVE BEEN HURT...
I'M JUST... SO TERRIBLY SORRY.
CHAPTER 37: LAMENTATION

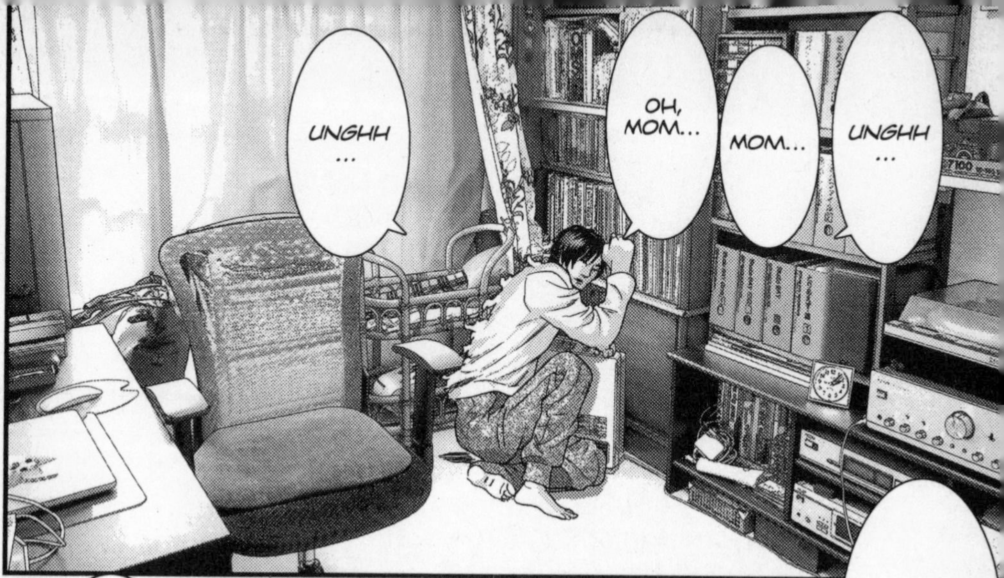
UNGHH ...
MOM...
OH, MOM...
UNGHH ...
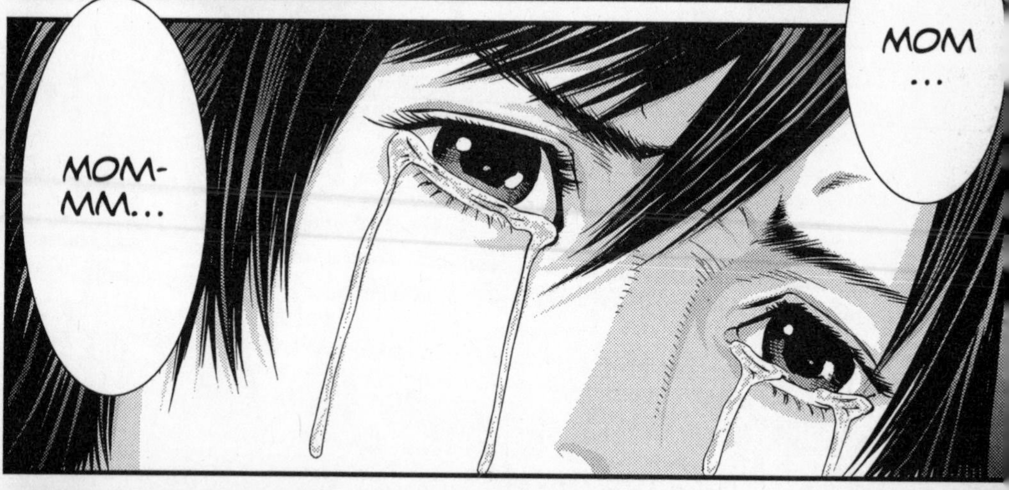
MOM ...
MOM-MM...
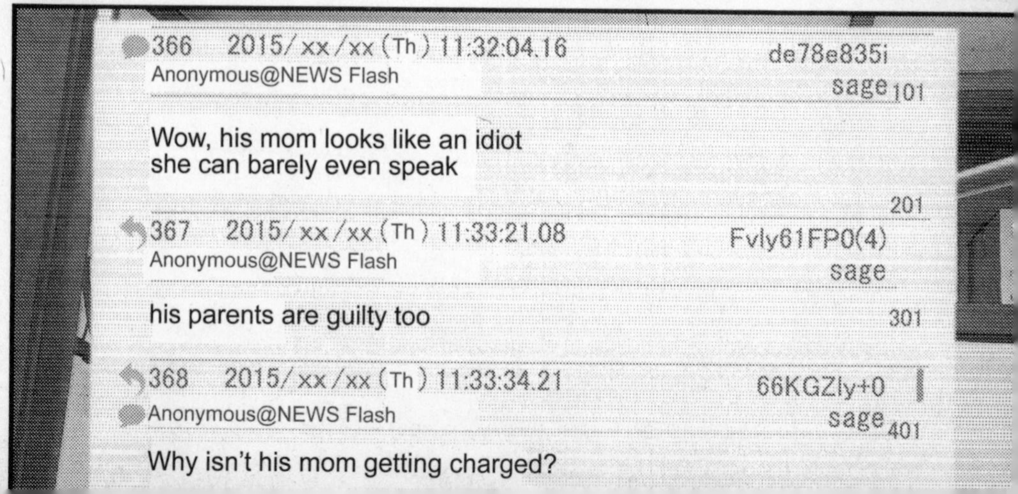
366 2015/xx/xx (Th) 11:32:04.16 de78e835i
Anonymous@NEWS Flash sage 101
Wow, his mom looks like an idiot
she can barely even speak
201
367 2015/xx/xx (Th) 11:33:21.08 Fvly61FP0(4)
Anonymous@NEWS Flash sage
his parents are guilty too
301
368 2015/xx/xx (Th) 11:33:34.21 66KGZly+0
Anonymous@NEWS Flash sage 401
Why isn't his mom getting charged?

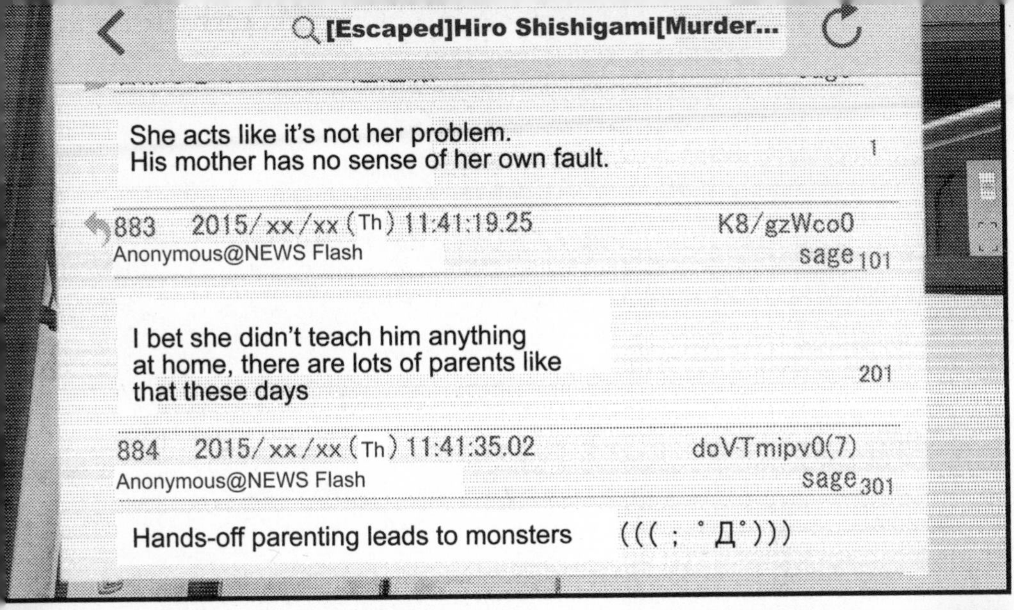
[Escaped]Hiro Shishigami[Murder...
She acts like it's not her problem.
His mother has no sense of her own fault.
1
883 2015/xx/xx (Th) 11:41:19.25 K8/gzWco0
Anonymous@NEWS Flash sage
101
I bet she didn't teach him anything
at home, there are lots of parents like
that these days
201
884 2015/xx/xx (Th) 11:41:35.02 doVTmipv0(7)
Anonymous@NEWS Flash sage
301
Hands-off parenting leads to monsters (((；ﾟДﾟ)))

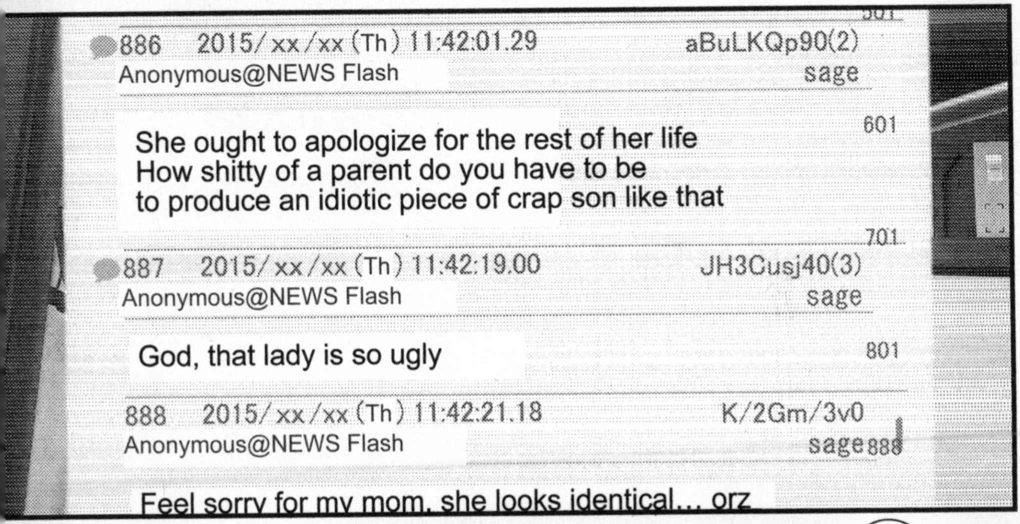
886 2015/xx/xx (Th) 11:42:01.29 aBuLKQp90(2)
Anonymous@NEWS Flash sage
601
She ought to apologize for the rest of her life
How shitty of a parent do you have to be
to produce an idiotic piece of crap son like that
701
887 2015/xx/xx (Th) 11:42:19.00 JH3Cusj40(3)
Anonymous@NEWS Flash sage
God, that lady is so ugly
801
888 2015/xx/xx (Th) 11:42:21.18 K/2Gm/3v0
Anonymous@NEWS Flash sage
888
Feel sorry for my mom, she looks identical... orz

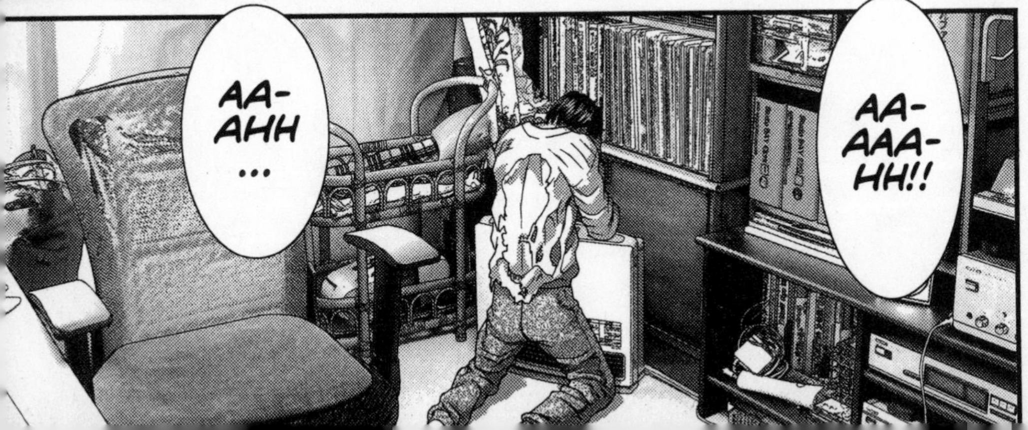
AA-AAA-HH!!
AA-AHH ...

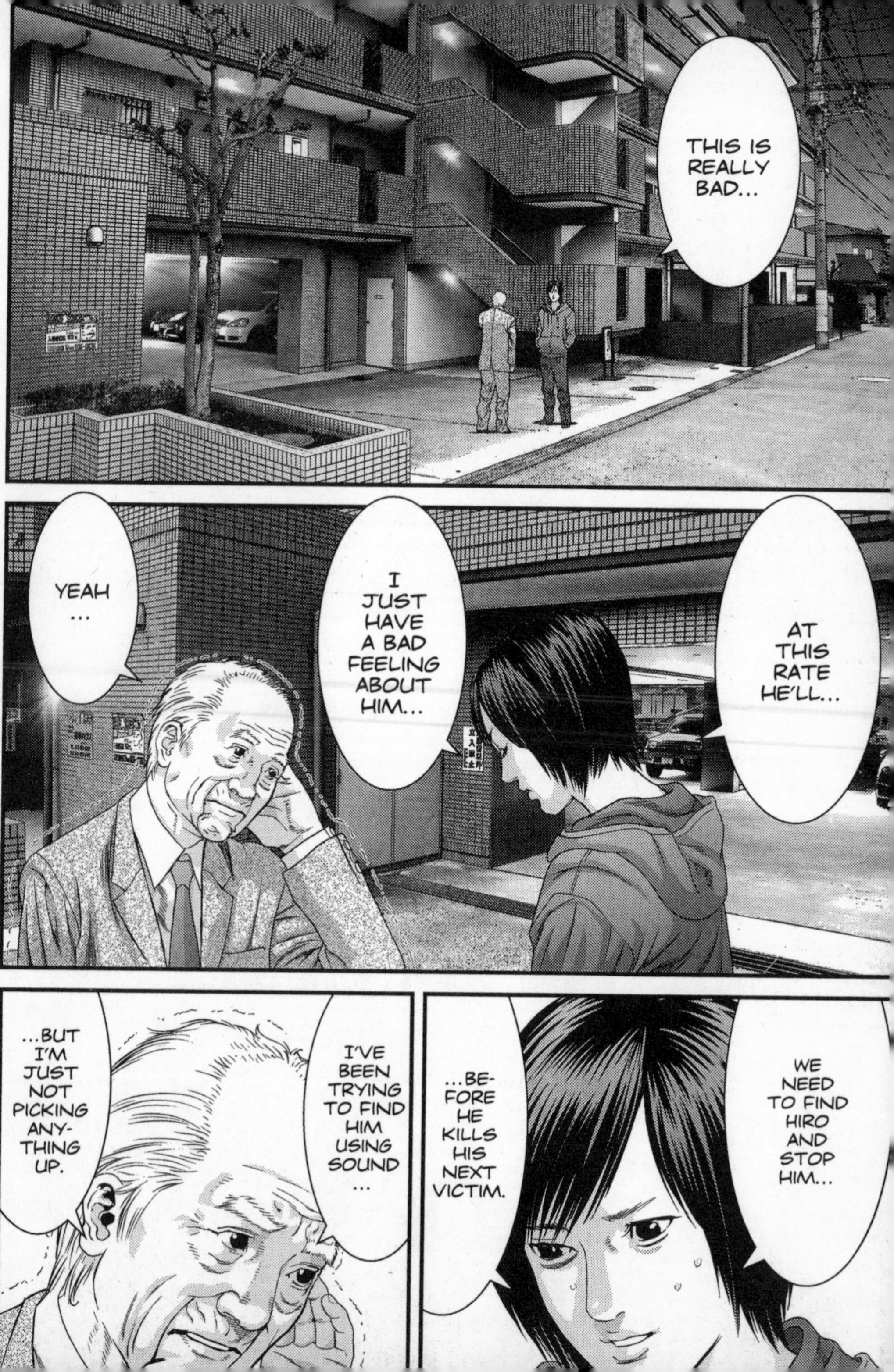
THIS IS REALLY BAD...
AT THIS RATE HE'LL...
I JUST HAVE A BAD FEELING ABOUT HIM...
YEAH ...
WE NEED TO FIND HIRO AND STOP HIM...
...BE-FORE HE KILLS HIS NEXT VICTIM.
I'VE BEEN TRYING TO FIND HIM USING SOUND ...
...BUT I'M JUST NOT PICKING ANY-THING UP.

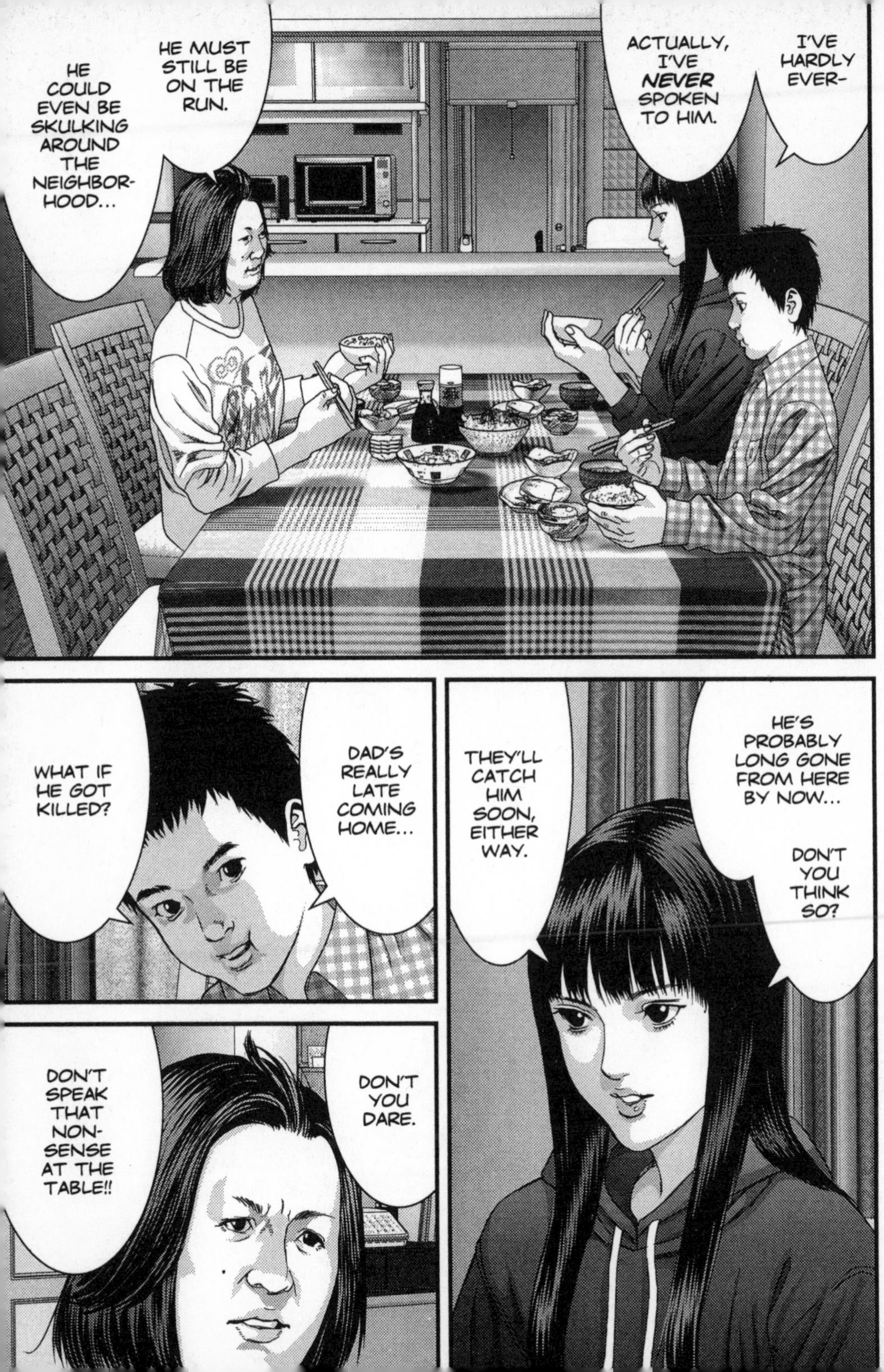
I'VE HARDLY EVER-
ACTUALLY, I'VE **NEVER** SPOKEN TO HIM.
HE MUST STILL BE ON THE RUN.
HE COULD EVEN BE SKULKING AROUND THE NEIGHBOR-HOOD...
HE'S PROBABLY LONG GONE FROM HERE BY NOW...
DON'T YOU THINK SO?
THEY'LL CATCH HIM SOON, EITHER WAY.
DAD'S REALLY LATE COMING HOME...
WHAT IF HE GOT KILLED?
DON'T YOU DARE.
DON'T SPEAK THAT NON-SENSE AT THE TABLE!!

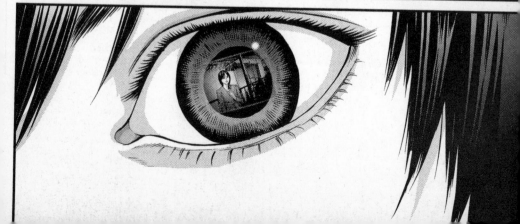

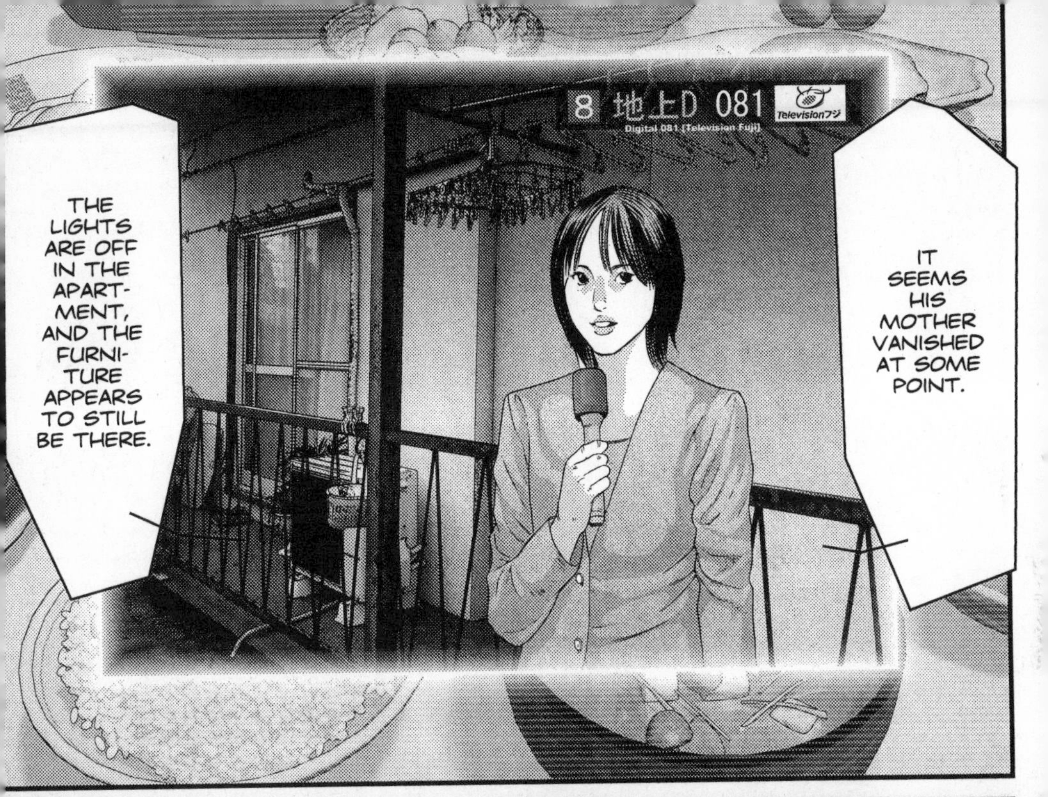
8 地上D 081
Televisionフジ
Digital 081 [Television Fuji]
IT SEEMS HIS MOTHER VANISHED AT SOME POINT.
THE LIGHTS ARE OFF IN THE APART-MENT, AND THE FURNI-TURE APPEARS TO STILL BE THERE.

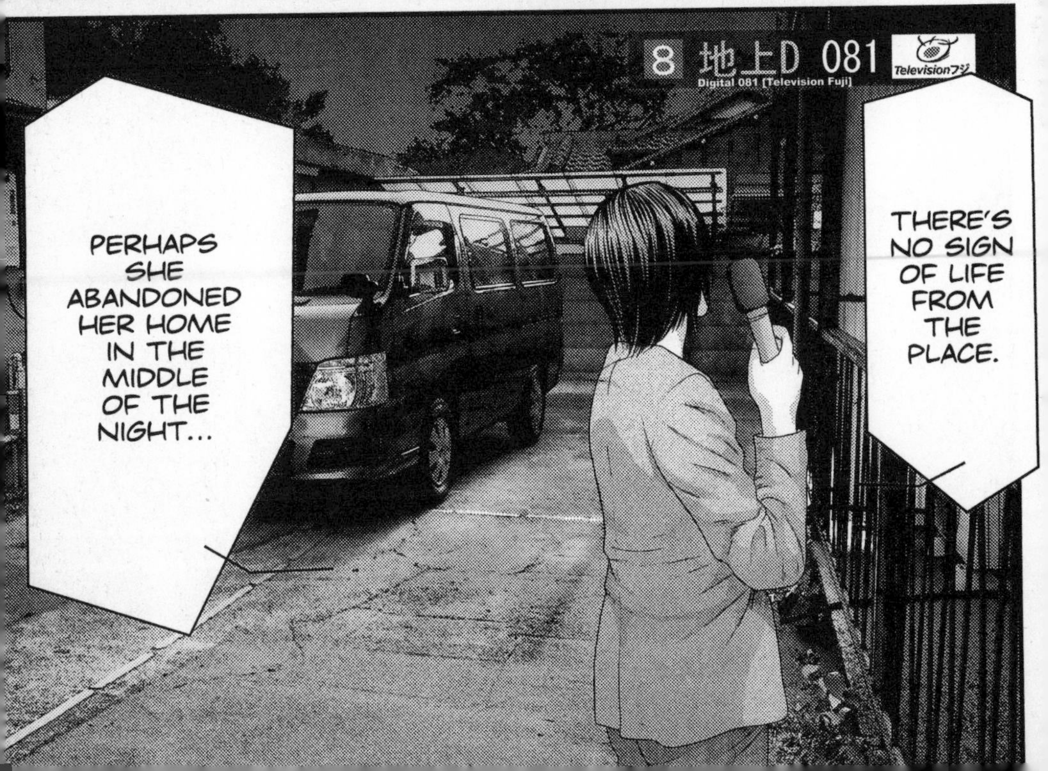
8 地上D 081
Televisionフジ
Digital 081 [Television Fuji]
THERE'S NO SIGN OF LIFE FROM THE PLACE.
PERHAPS SHE ABANDONED HER HOME IN THE MIDDLE OF THE NIGHT...

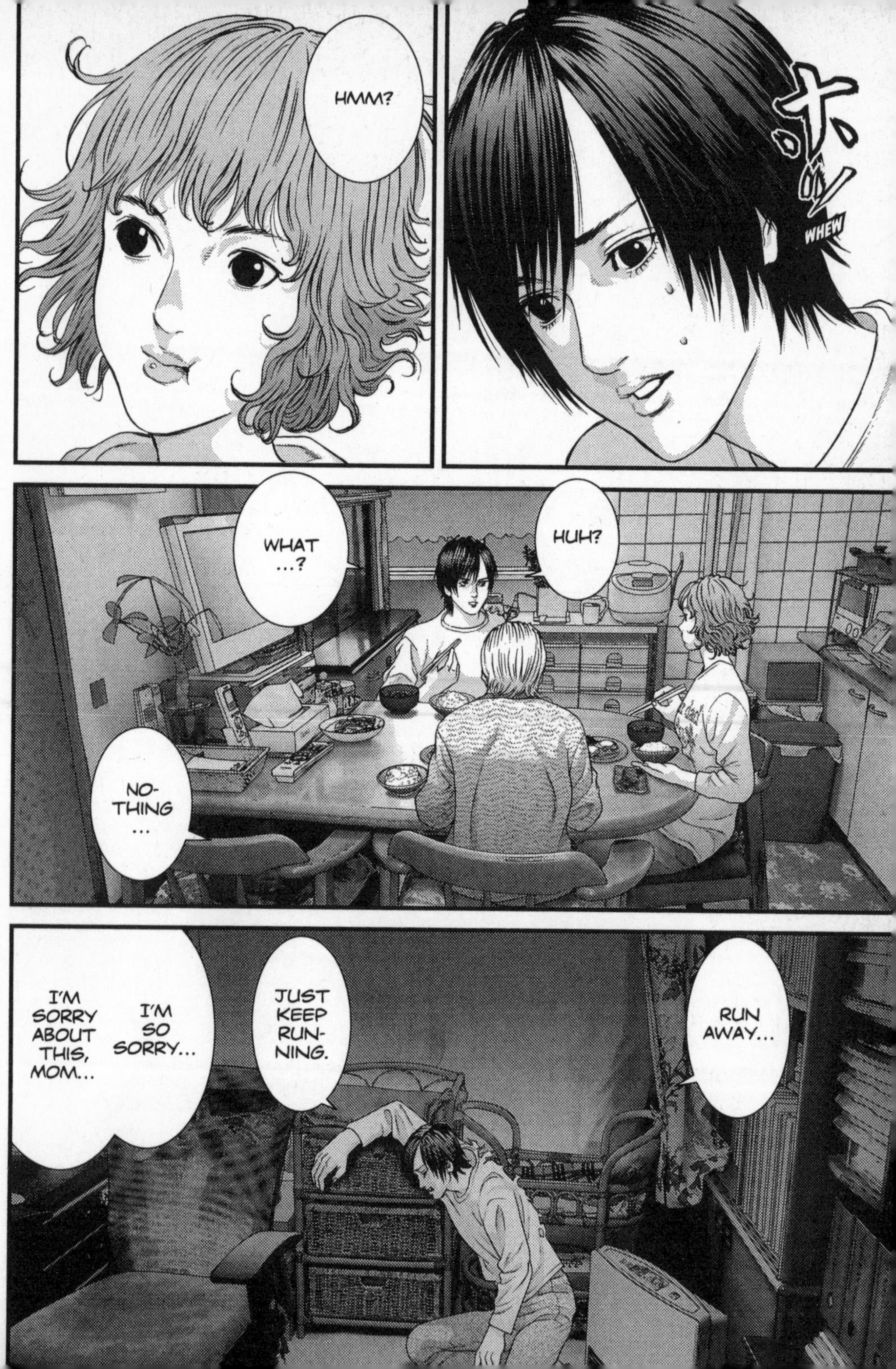
WHEW
HMM?
HUH?
WHAT ...?
NO-THING ...
RUN AWAY...
JUST KEEP RUN-NING.
I'M SO SORRY...
I'M SORRY ABOUT THIS, MOM...

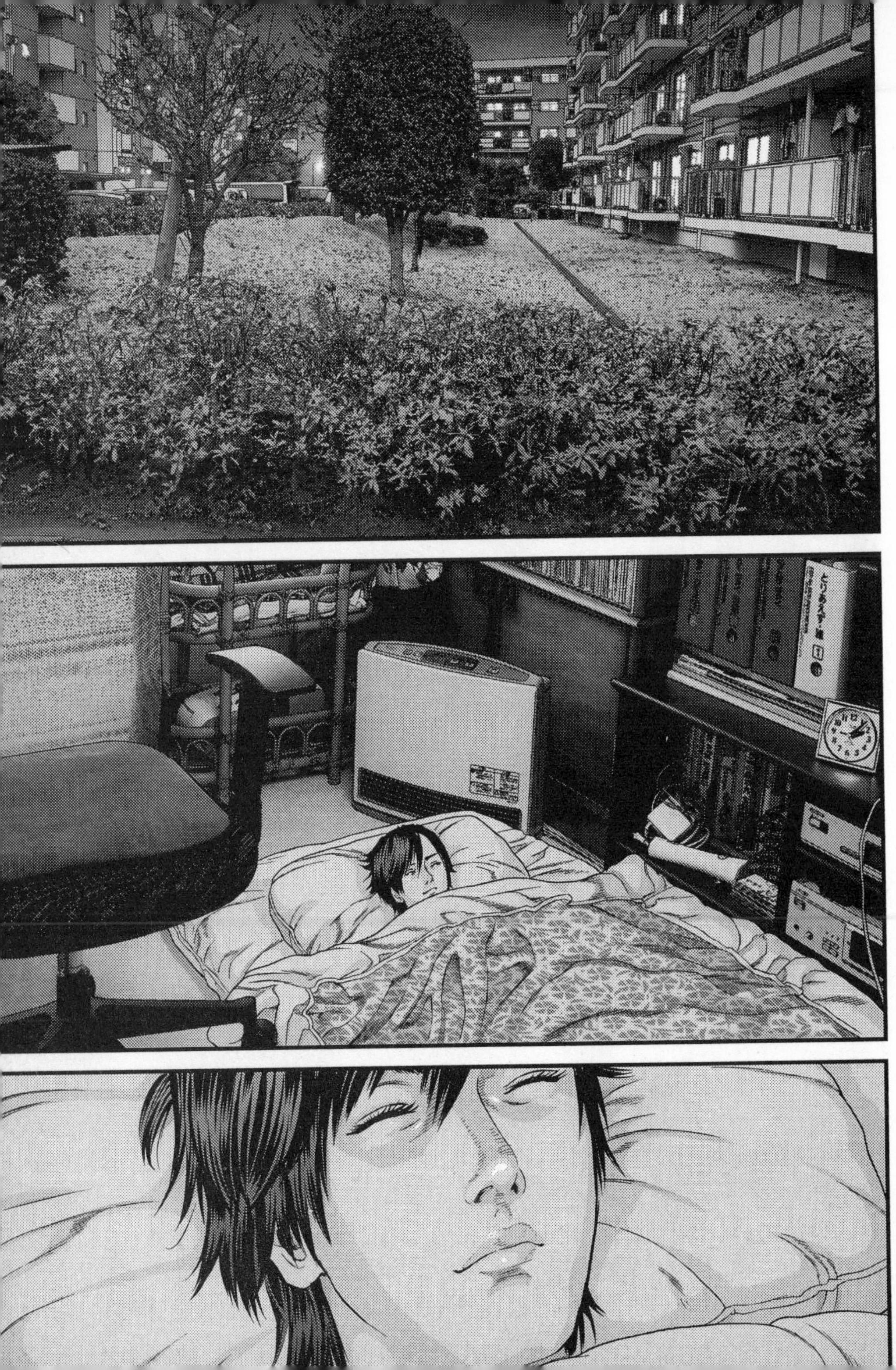

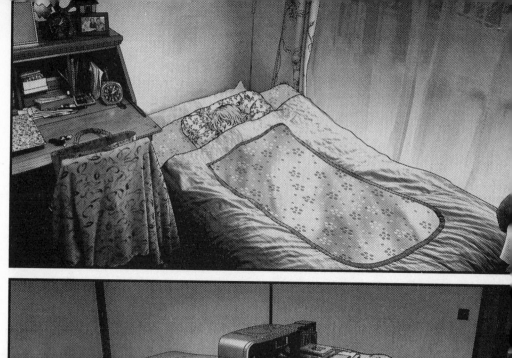

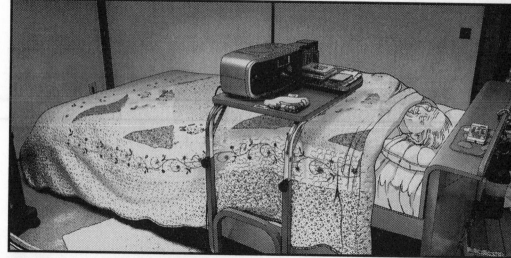

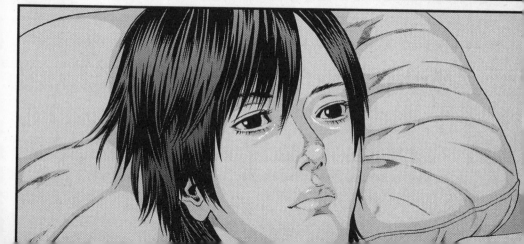

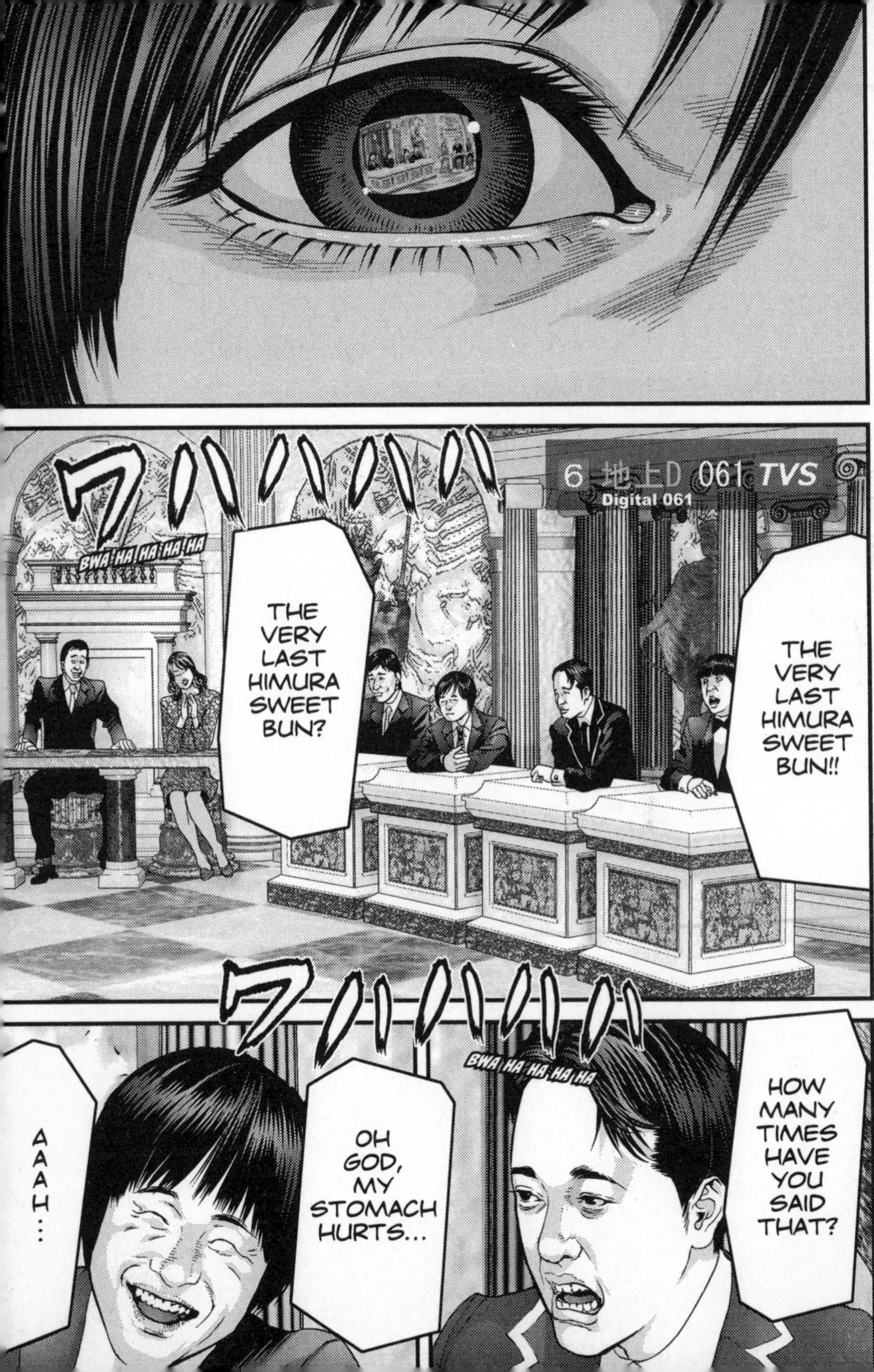
6 地上D 061 TVS
Digital 061
ワハハハハ
BWA HA HA HA HA
THE VERY LAST HIMURA SWEET BUN!!
THE VERY LAST HIMURA SWEET BUN?
ワハハハハ
BWA HA HA HA HA
HOW MANY TIMES HAVE YOU SAID THAT?
OH GOD, MY STOMACH HURTS...
AAAH...

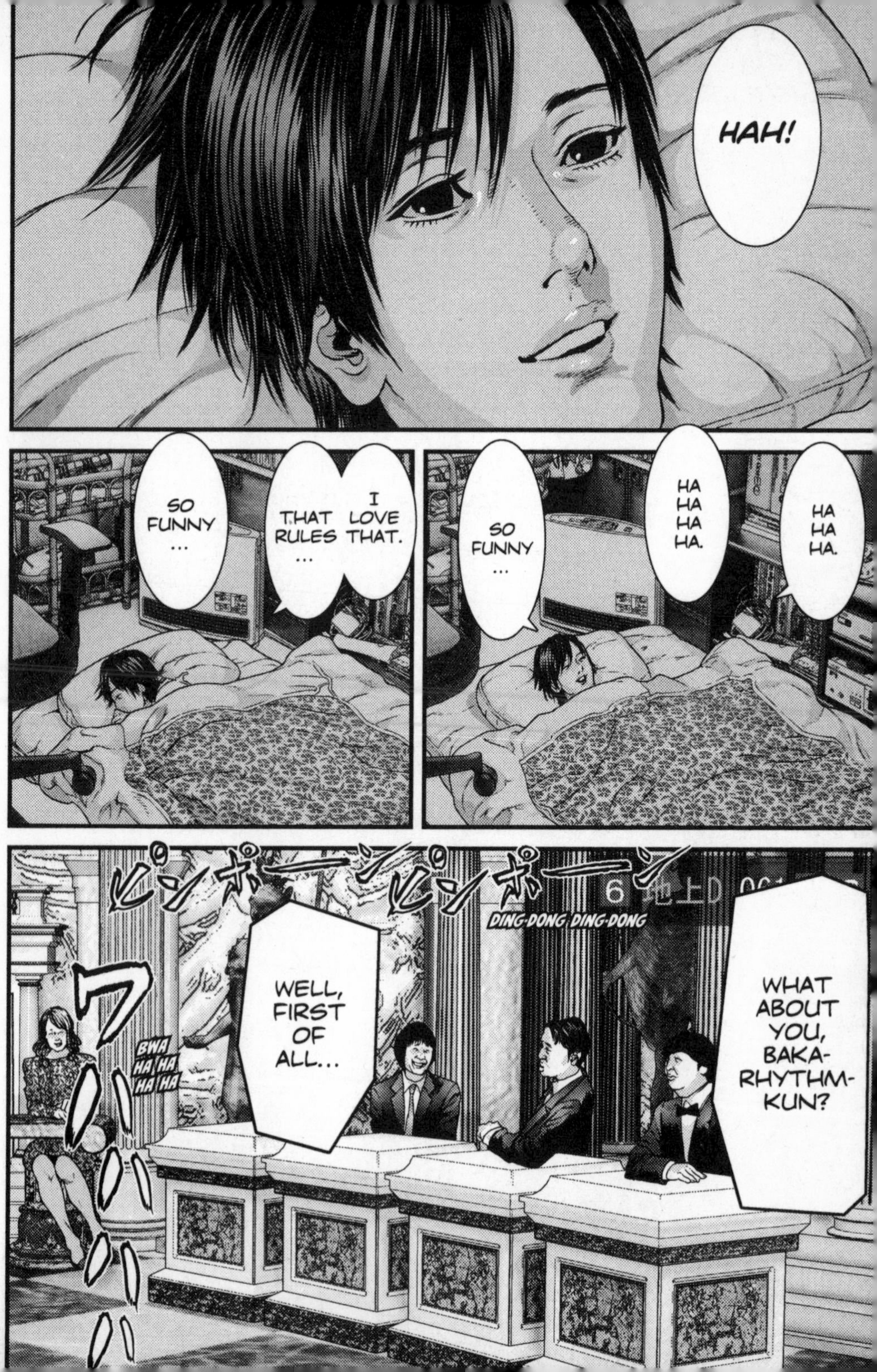
HAH!
HA HA HA.
HA HA HA HA.
SO FUNNY ...
I LOVE THAT.
THAT RULES ...
SO FUNNY ...
ピンポーンピンポーン
DING-DONG DING-DONG
WHAT ABOUT YOU, BAKA-RHYTHM-KUN?
WELL, FIRST OF ALL...
ワ
BWA HA HA HA HA

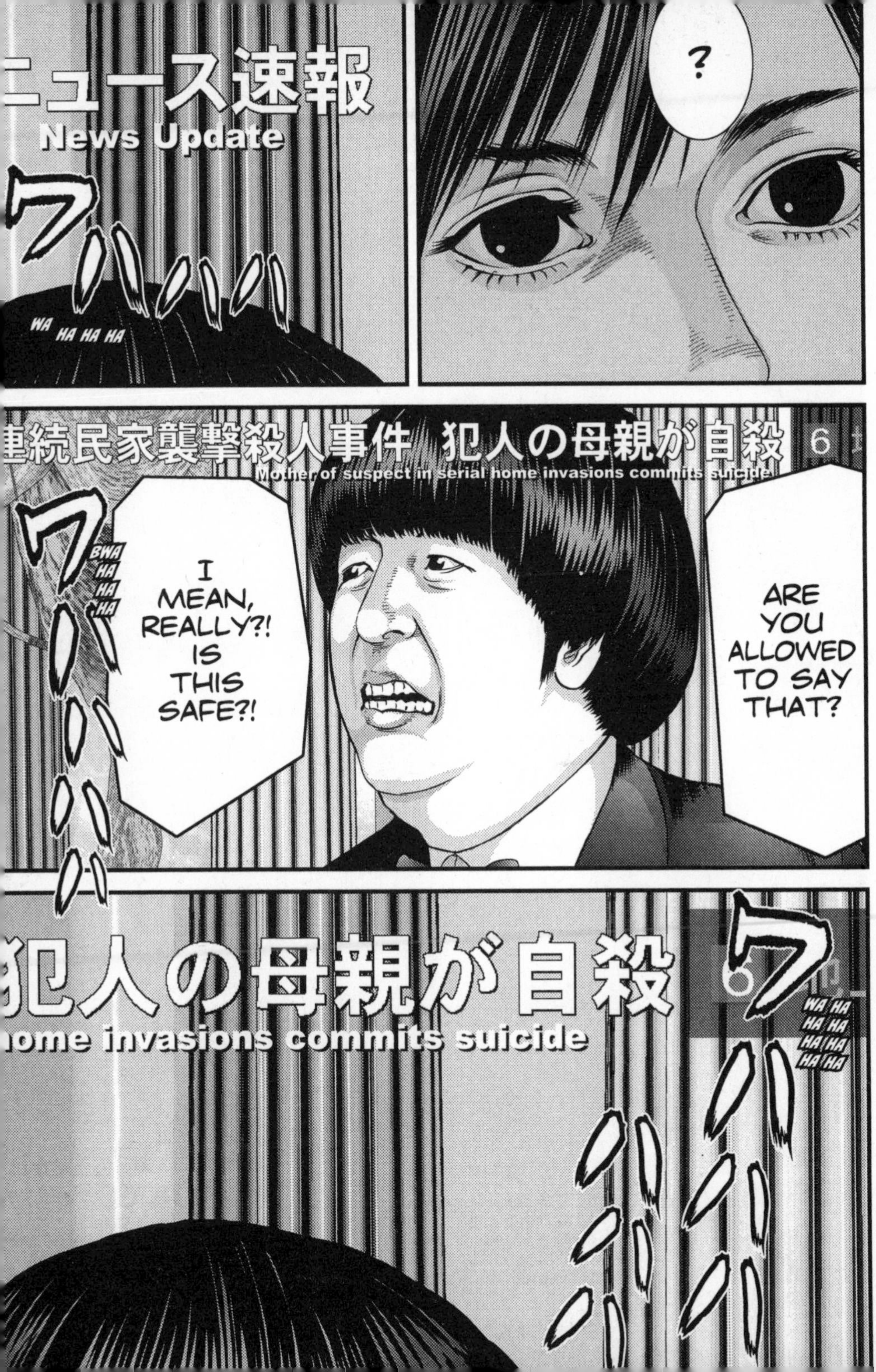
?
ニュース速報
News Update
WA HA HA HA
連続民家襲撃殺人事件 犯人の母親が自殺
Mother of suspect in serial home invasions commits suicide
ARE YOU ALLOWED TO SAY THAT?
I MEAN, REALLY?! IS THIS SAFE?!
BWA HA HA HA
犯人の母親が自殺
ome invasions commits suicide
WA HA HA HA HA HA HA HA

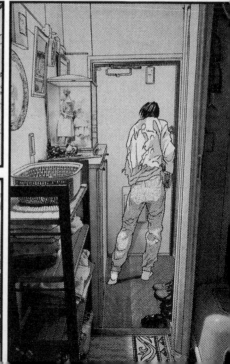

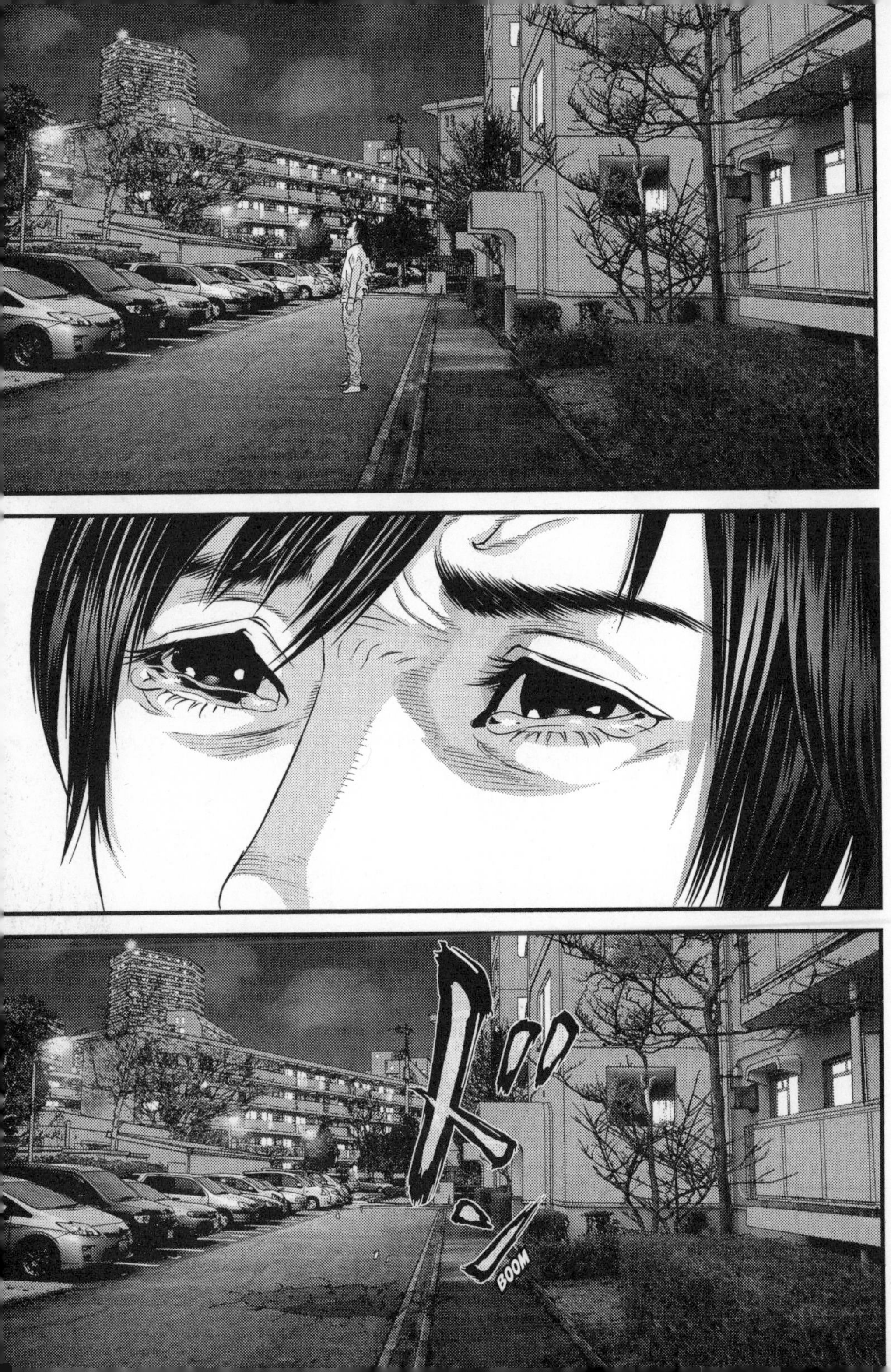
BOOM

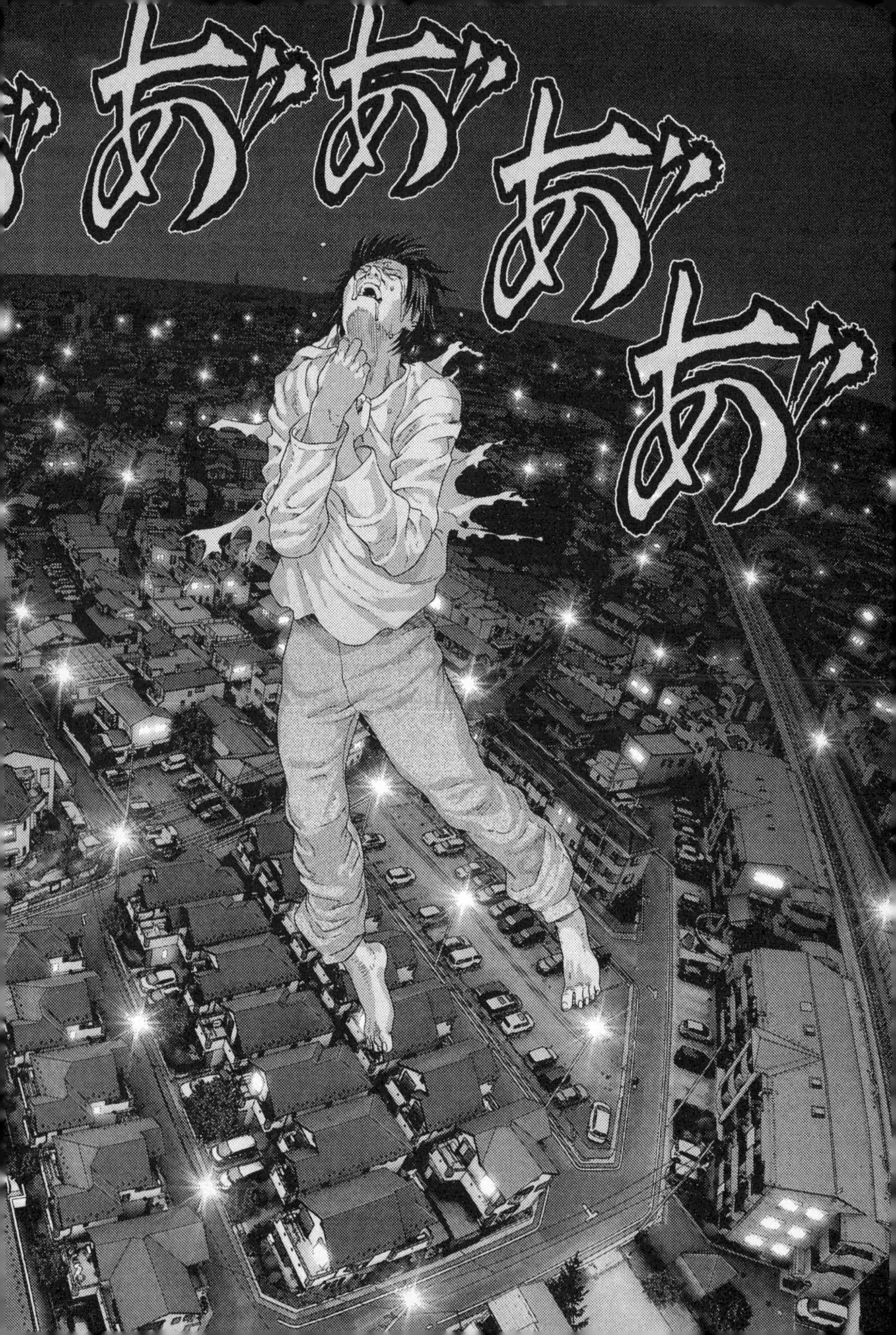
あ゛あ゛あ゛あ゛

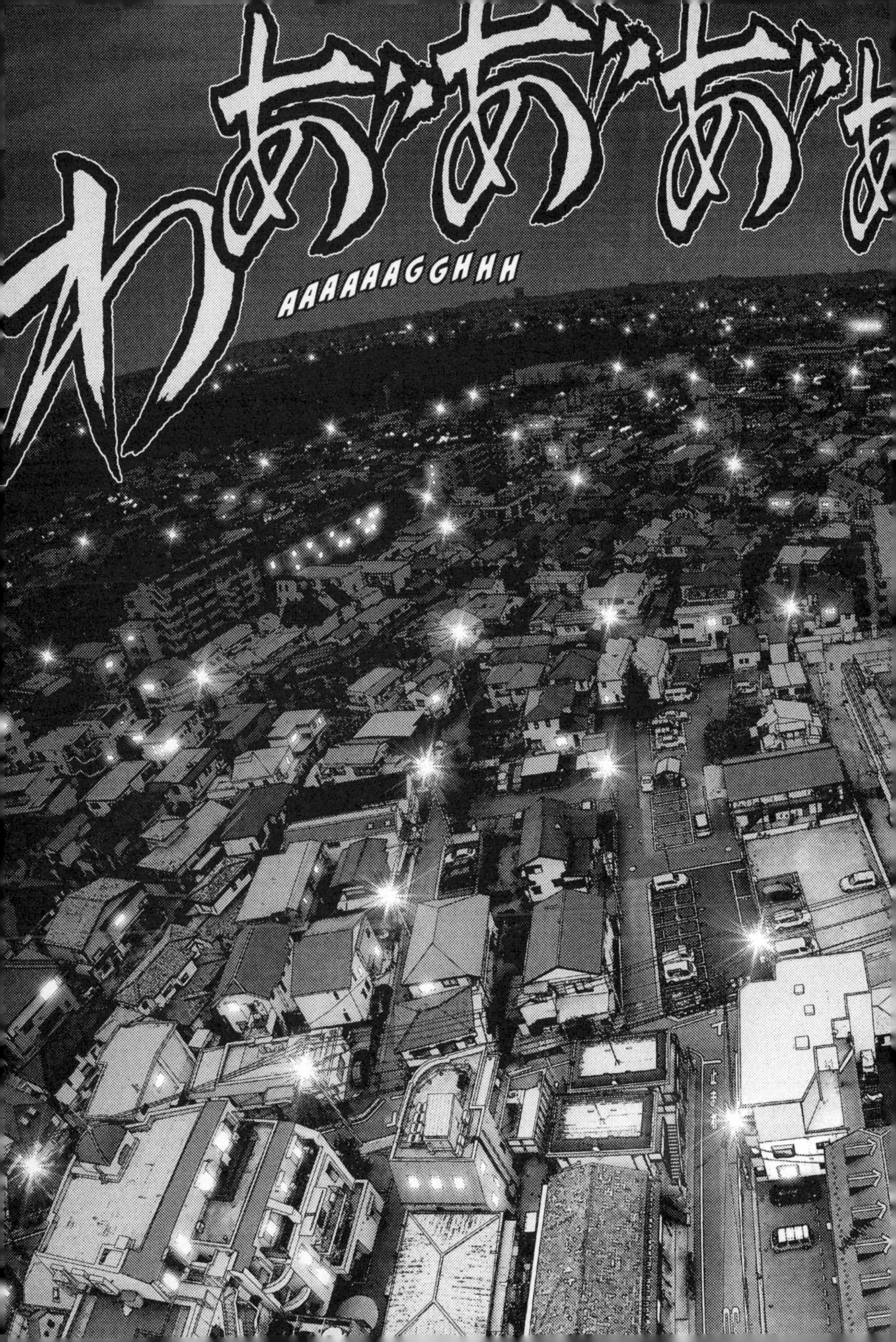
わあ゛あ゛あ゛
AAAAAAGGHHH

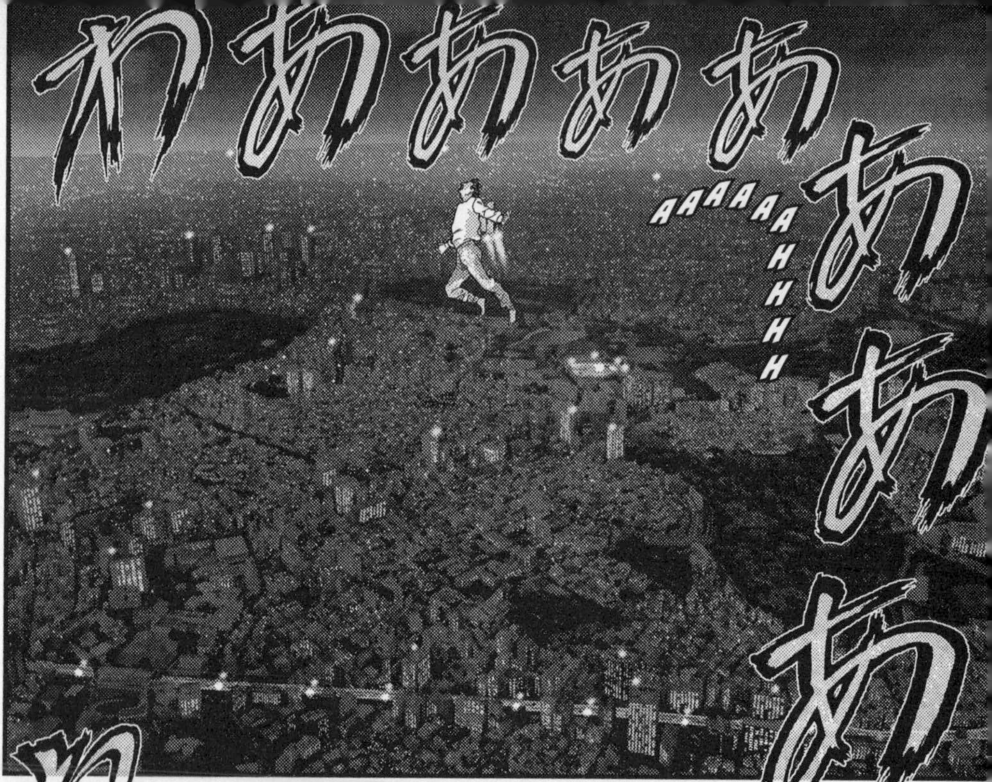
わああああああああああ
AAAAAAHHHH

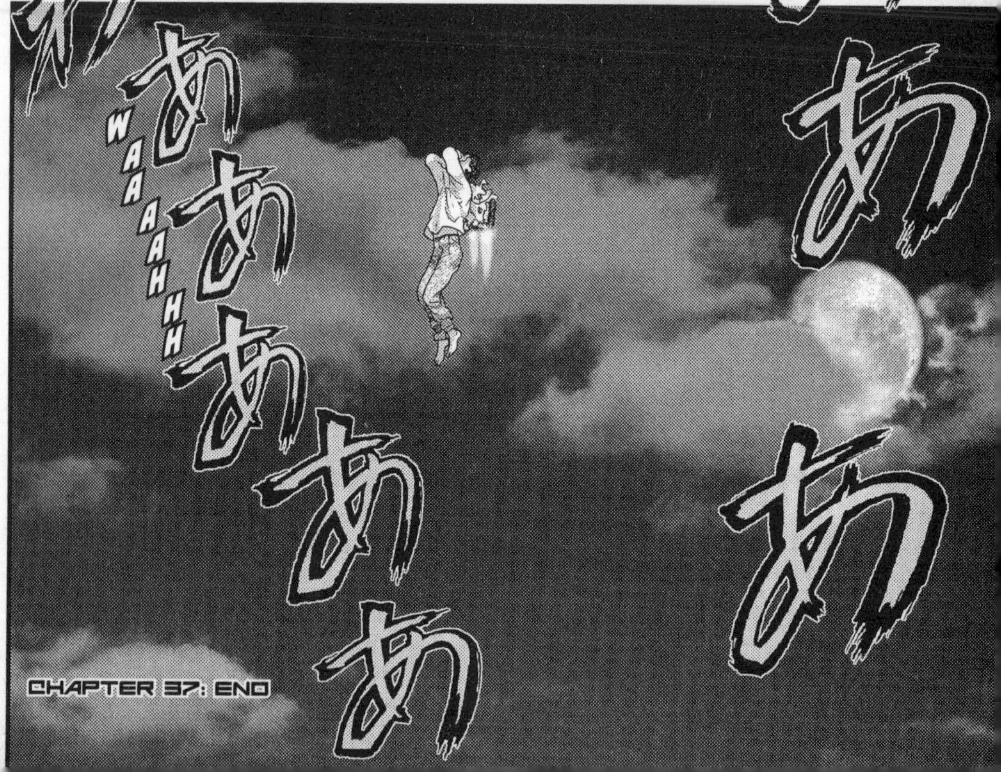
わあああああ
WAAAAHHH
CHAPTER 37: END

INUYASHIKI

INUYASHIKI

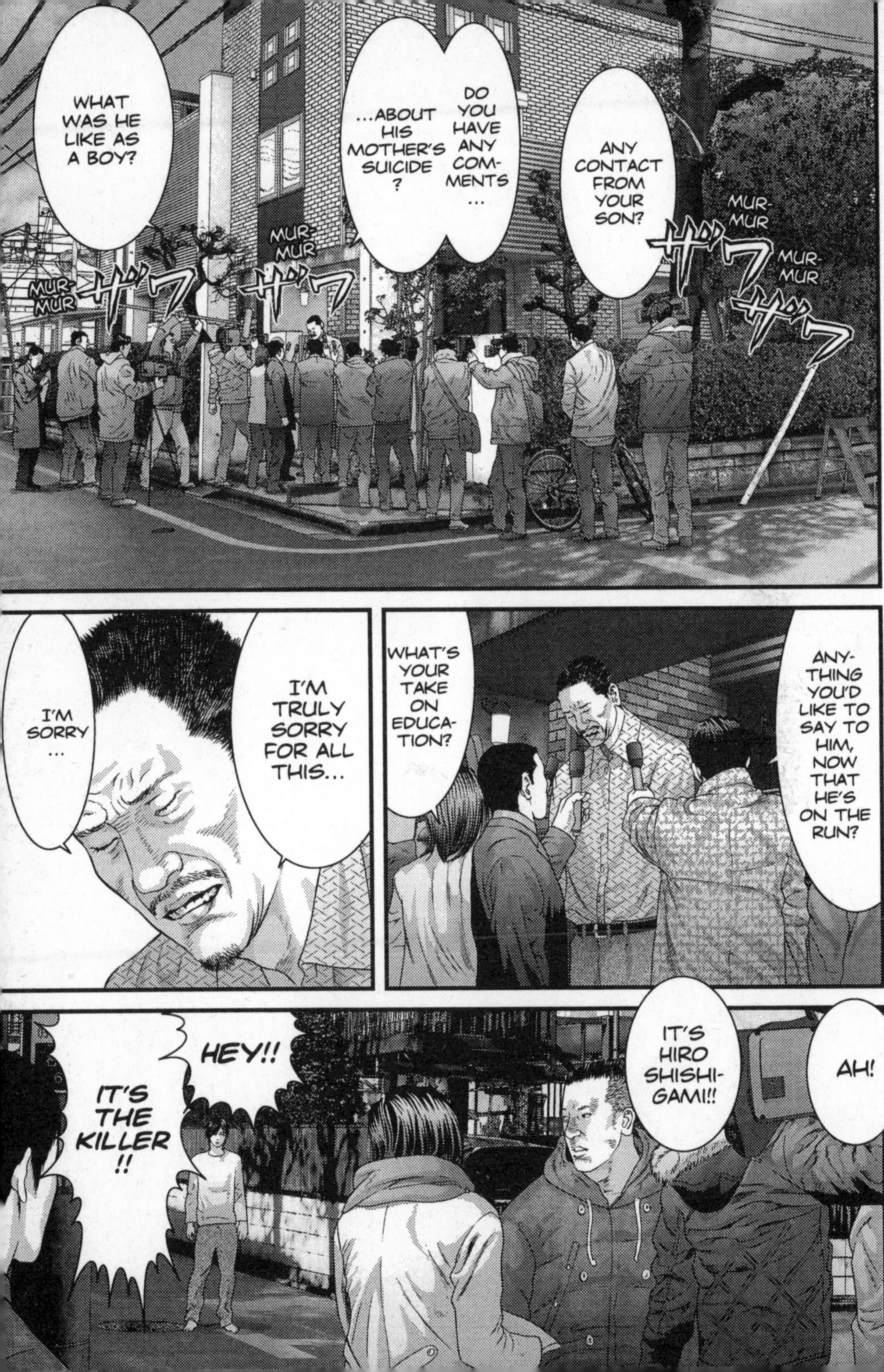
ANY CONTACT FROM YOUR SON?
MUR-MUR
MUR-MUR
DO YOU HAVE ANY COMMENTS...
...ABOUT HIS MOTHER'S SUICIDE?
MUR-MUR
WHAT WAS HE LIKE AS A BOY?
MUR-MUR
ANYTHING YOU'D LIKE TO SAY TO HIM, NOW THAT HE'S ON THE RUN?
WHAT'S YOUR TAKE ON EDUCATION?
I'M TRULY SORRY FOR ALL THIS...
I'M SORRY...
AH!
IT'S HIRO SHISHIGAMI!!
HEY!!
IT'S THE KILLER!!

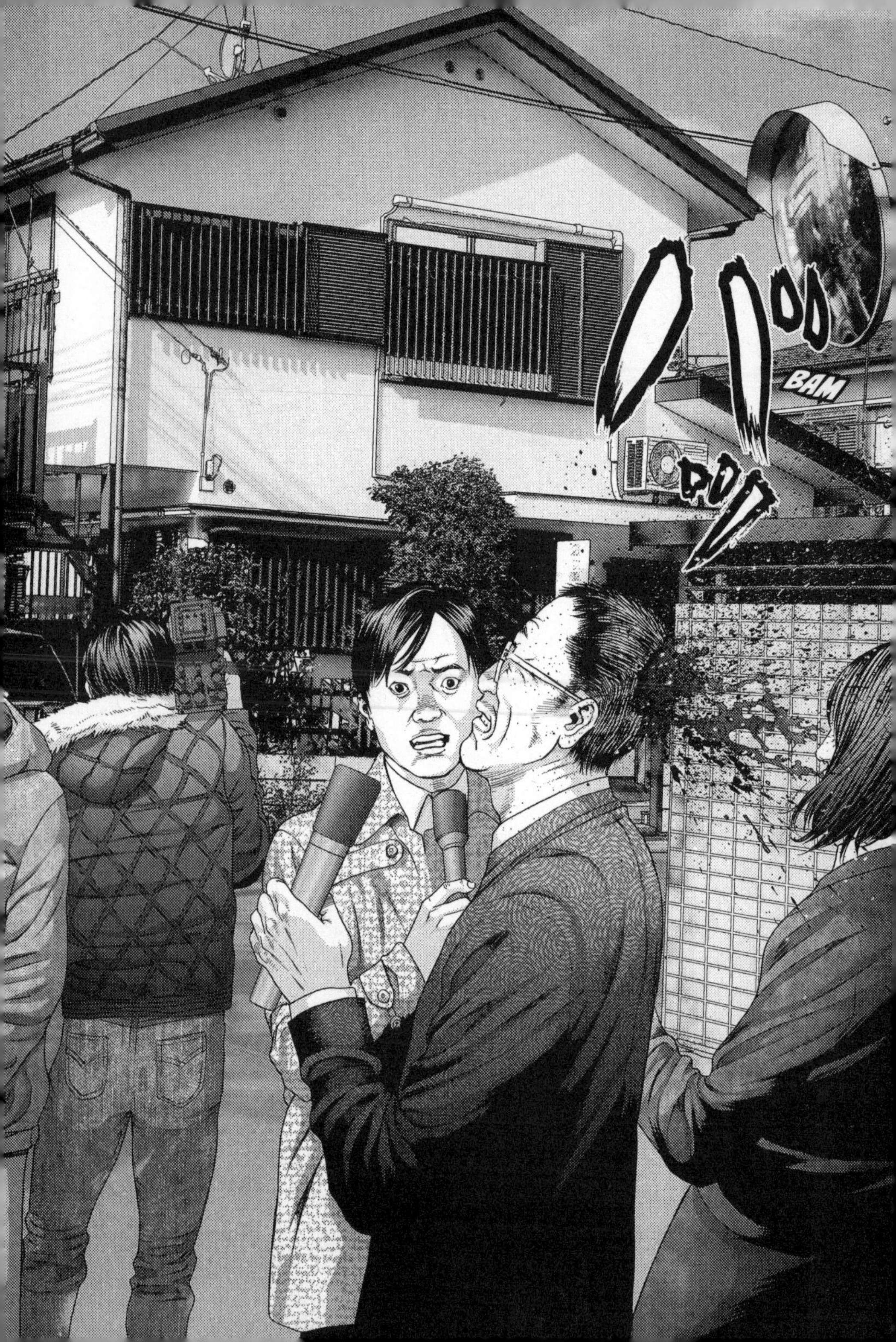
BAM

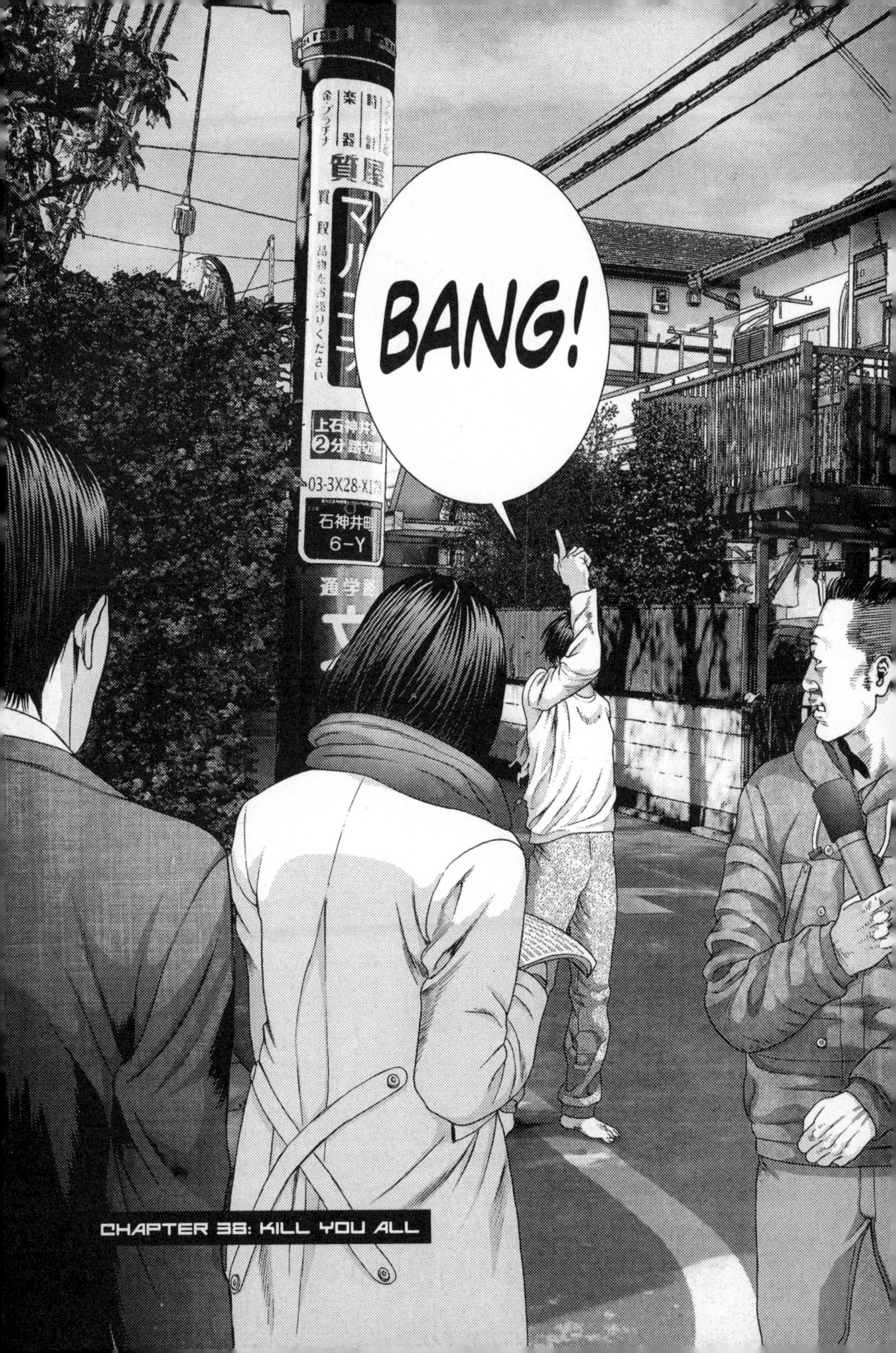
BANG!
CHAPTER 38: KILL YOU ALL

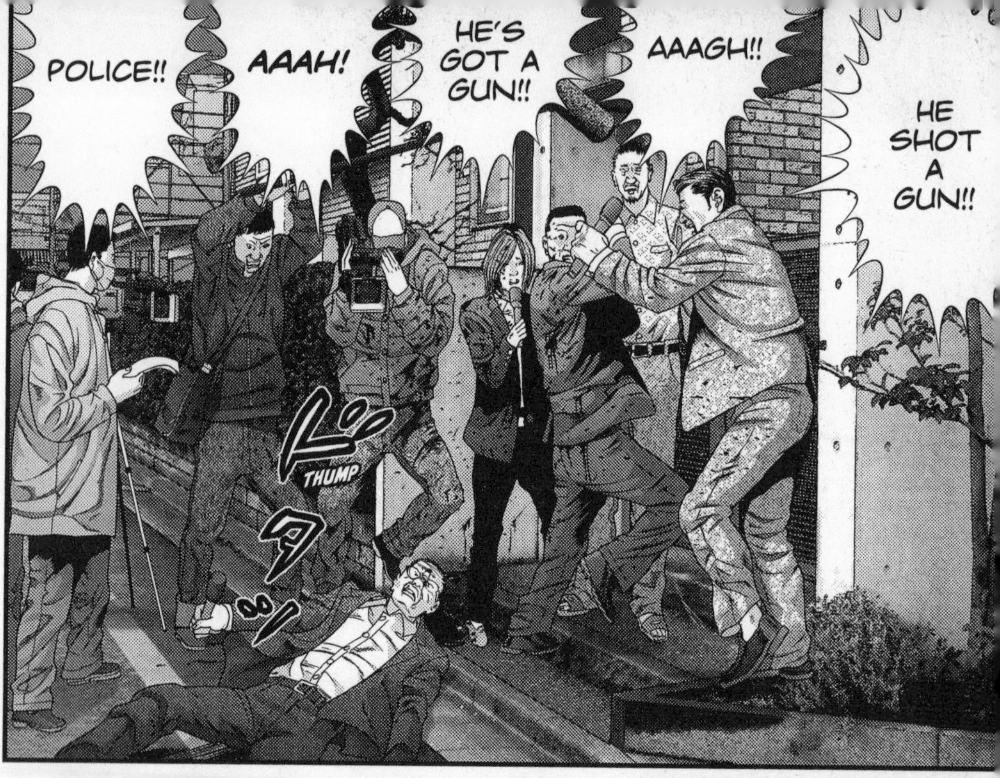
HE SHOT A GUN!!
AAAGH!!
HE'S GOT A GUN!!
AAAH!
POLICE!!
THUMP

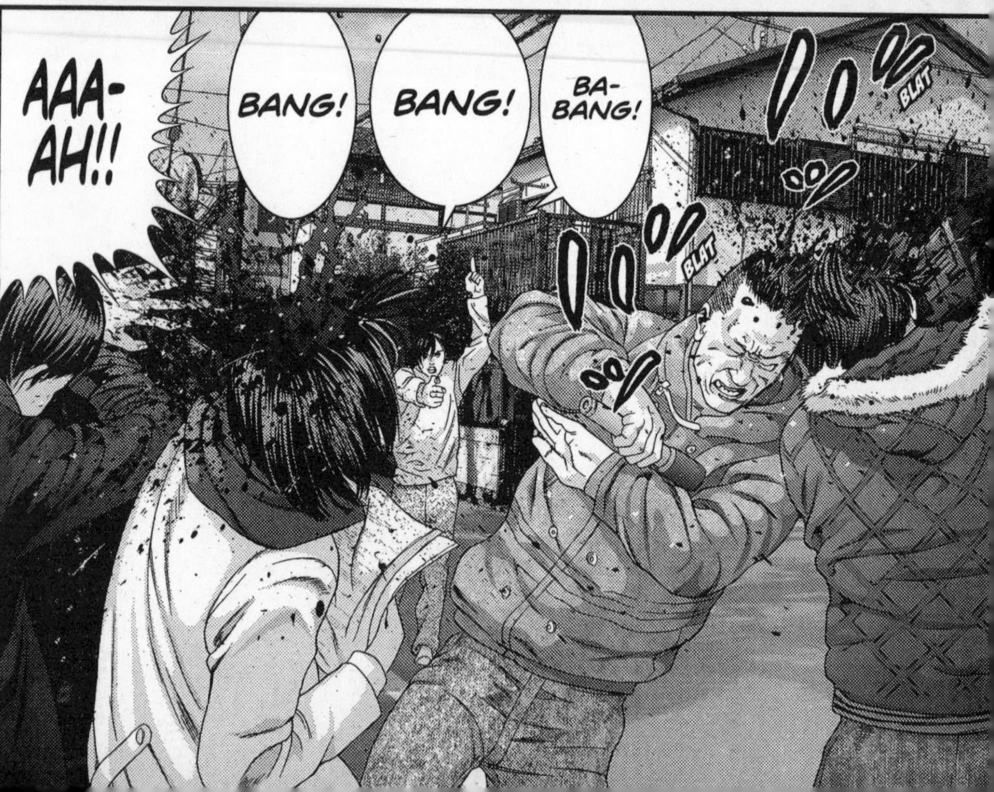
BLAT
BLAT
BA-BANG!
BANG!
BANG!
AAA-AH!!

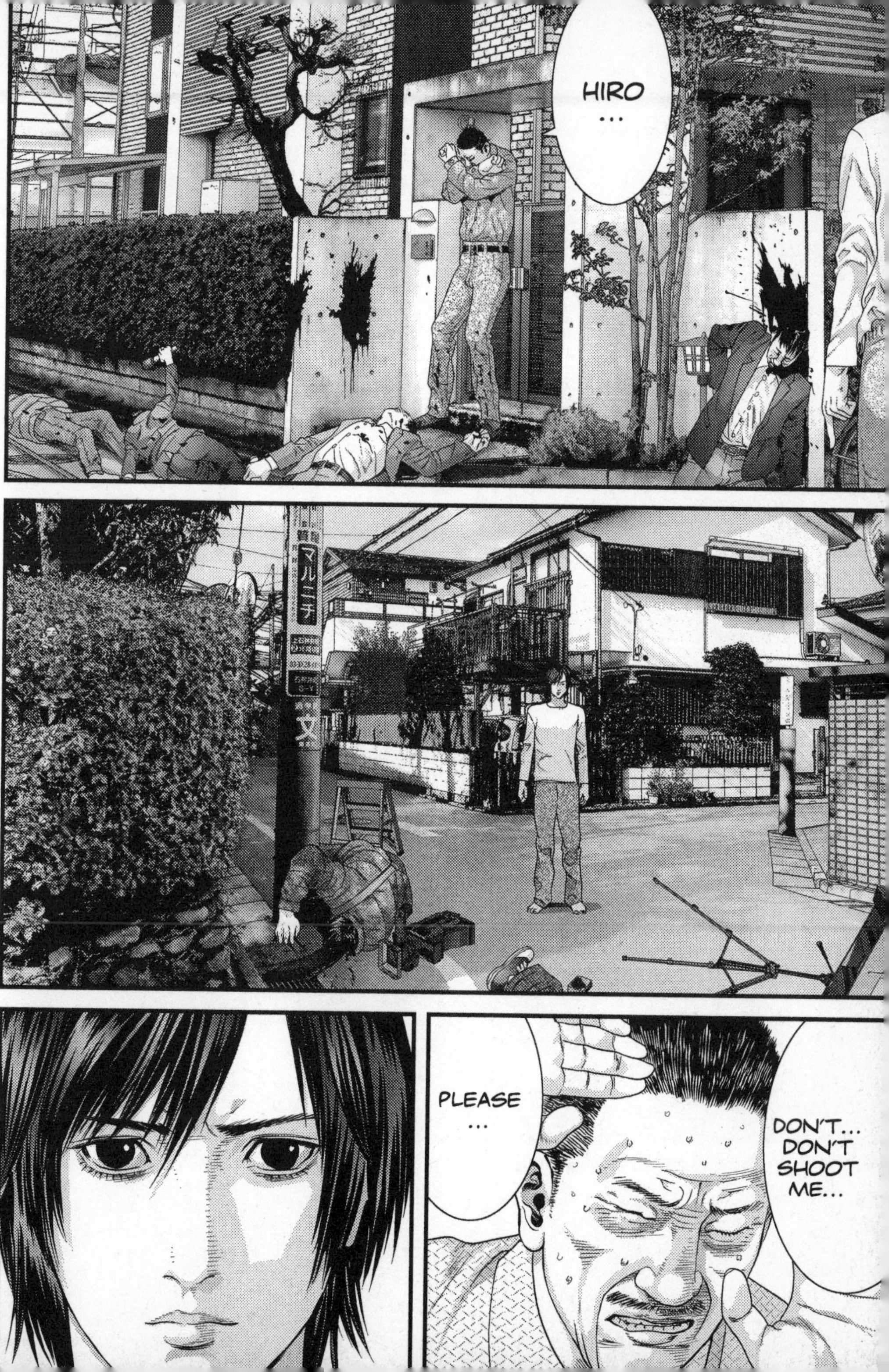
HIRO ...
マルニチ
DON'T... DON'T SHOOT ME...
PLEASE ...

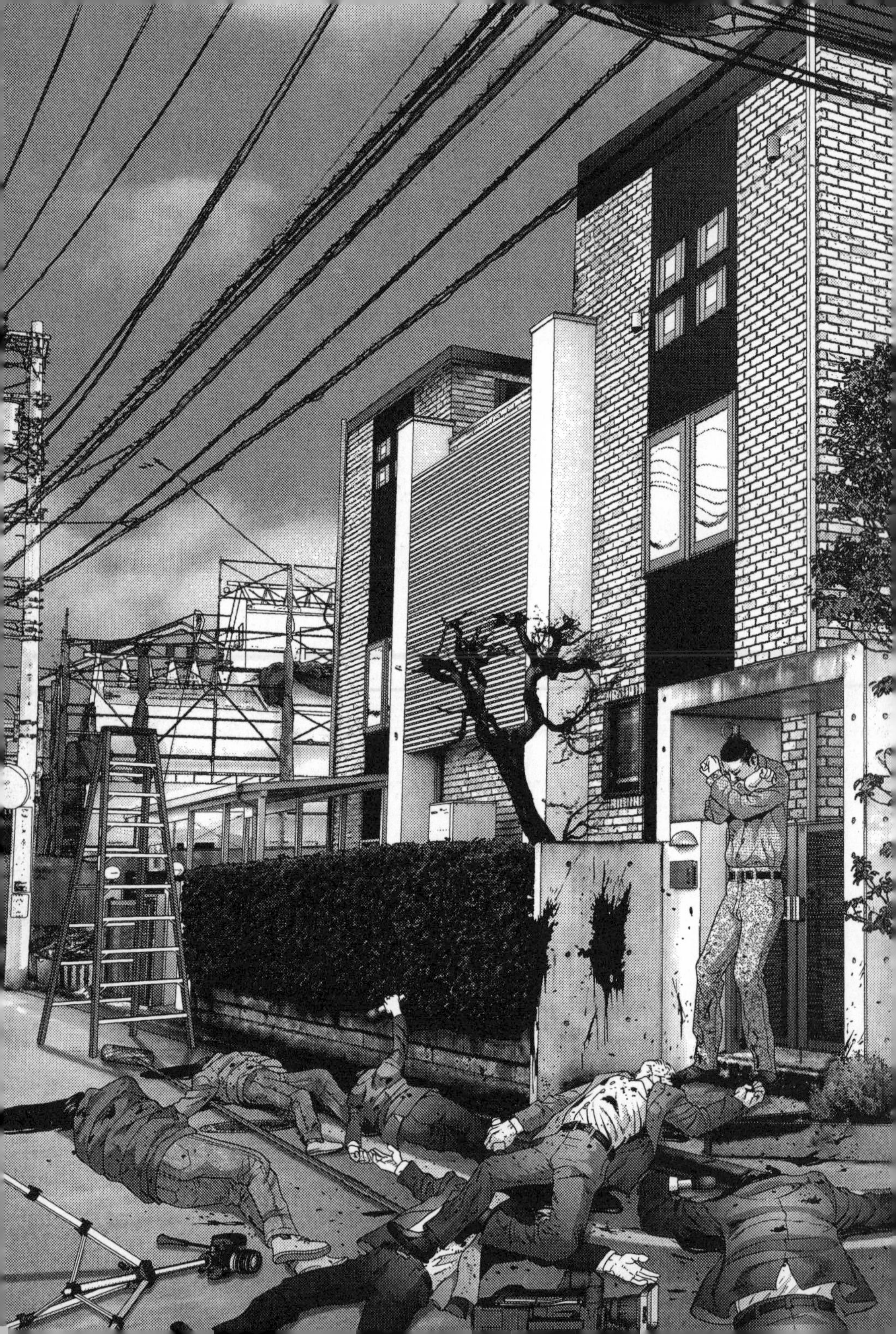

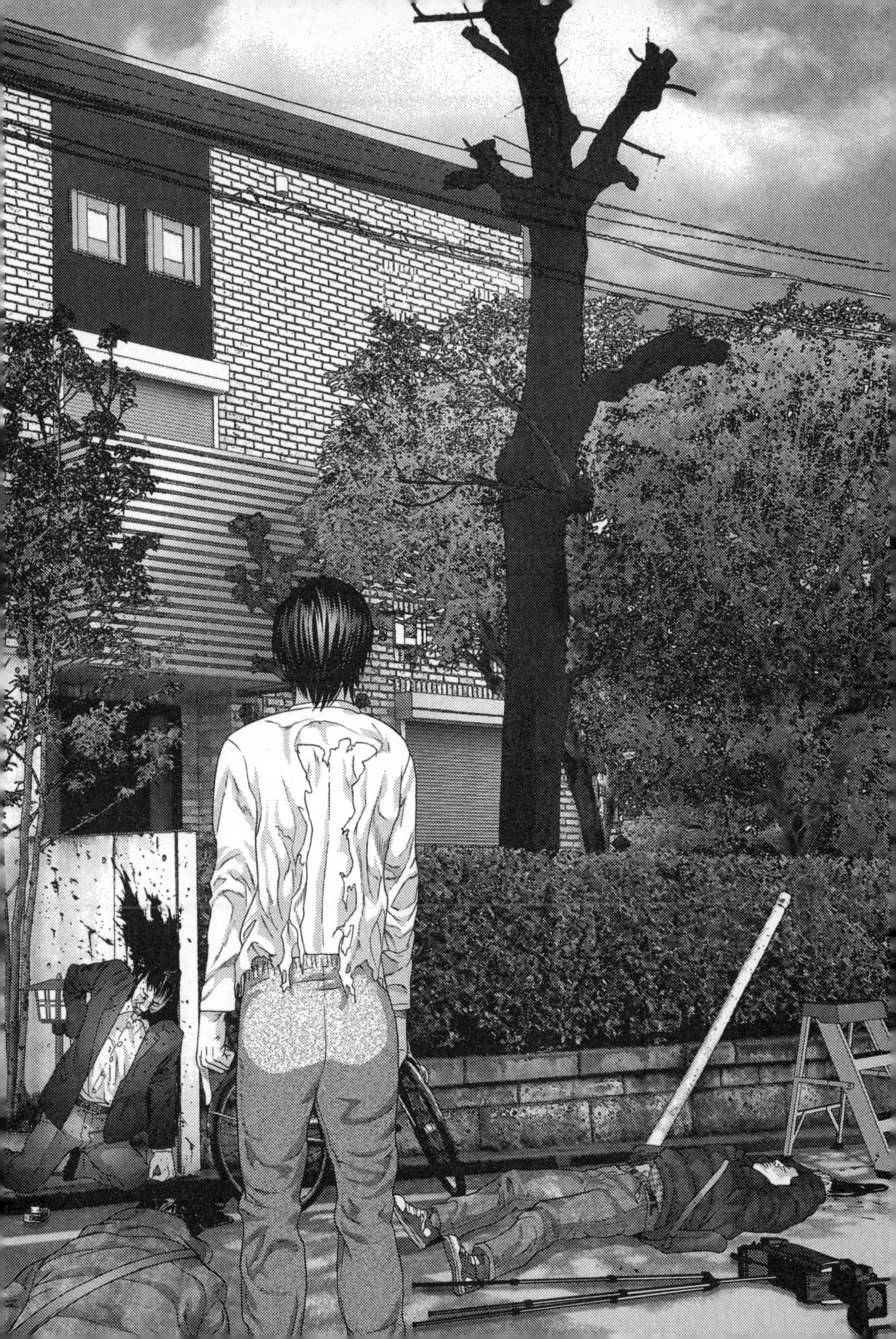

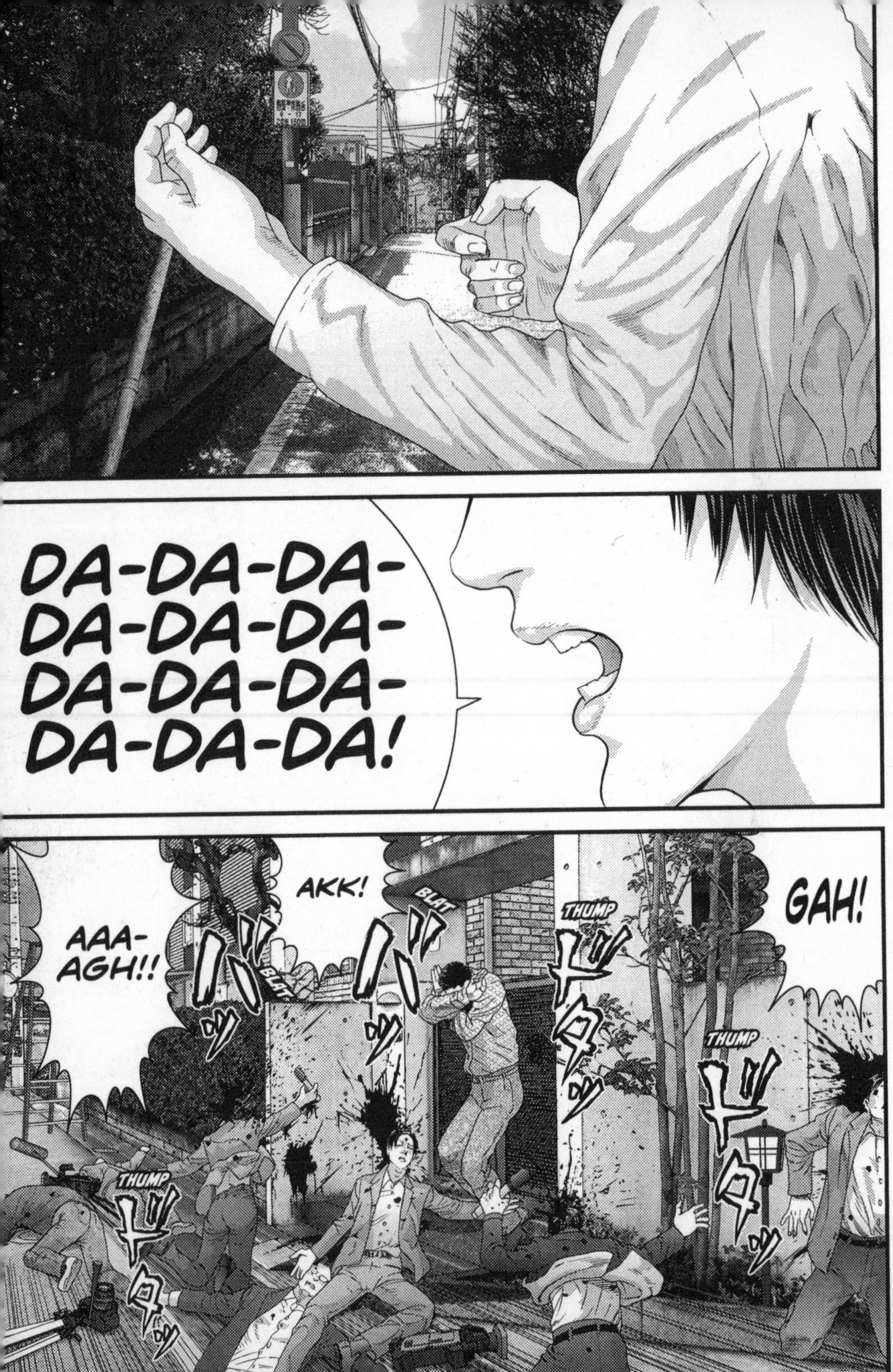
DA-DA-DA-
DA-DA-DA-
DA-DA-DA-
DA-DA-DA!
GAH!
THUMP
THUMP
AKK!
BLAT
BLAT
AAA-
AGH!!
THUMP

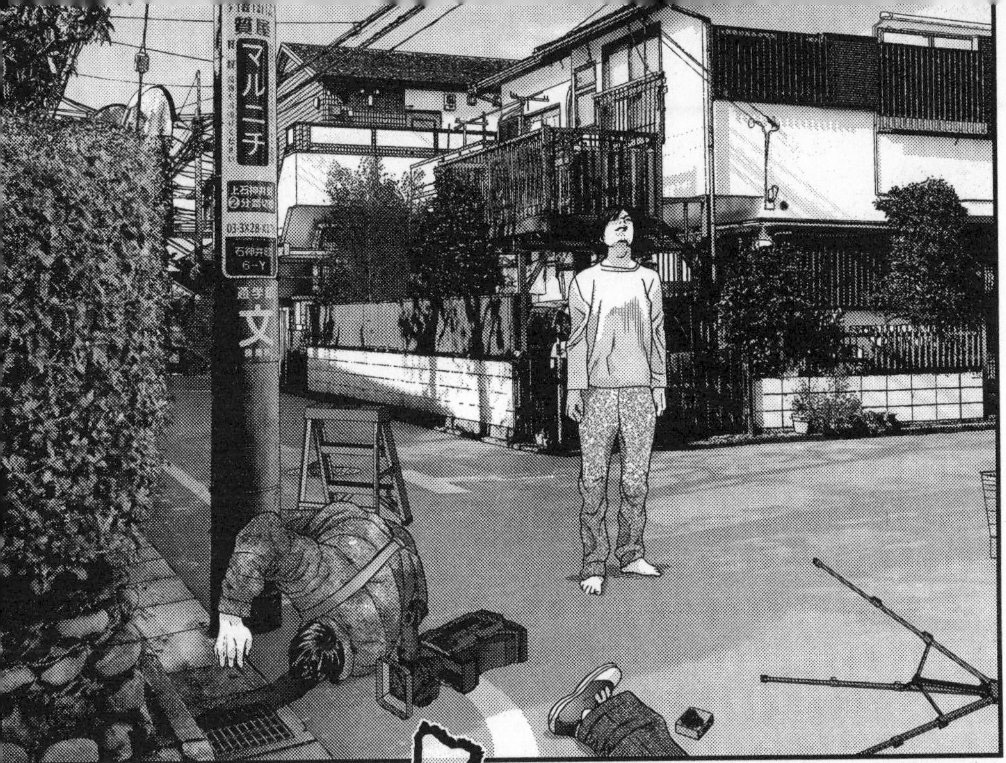
質屋
マルニチ
6-Y
文
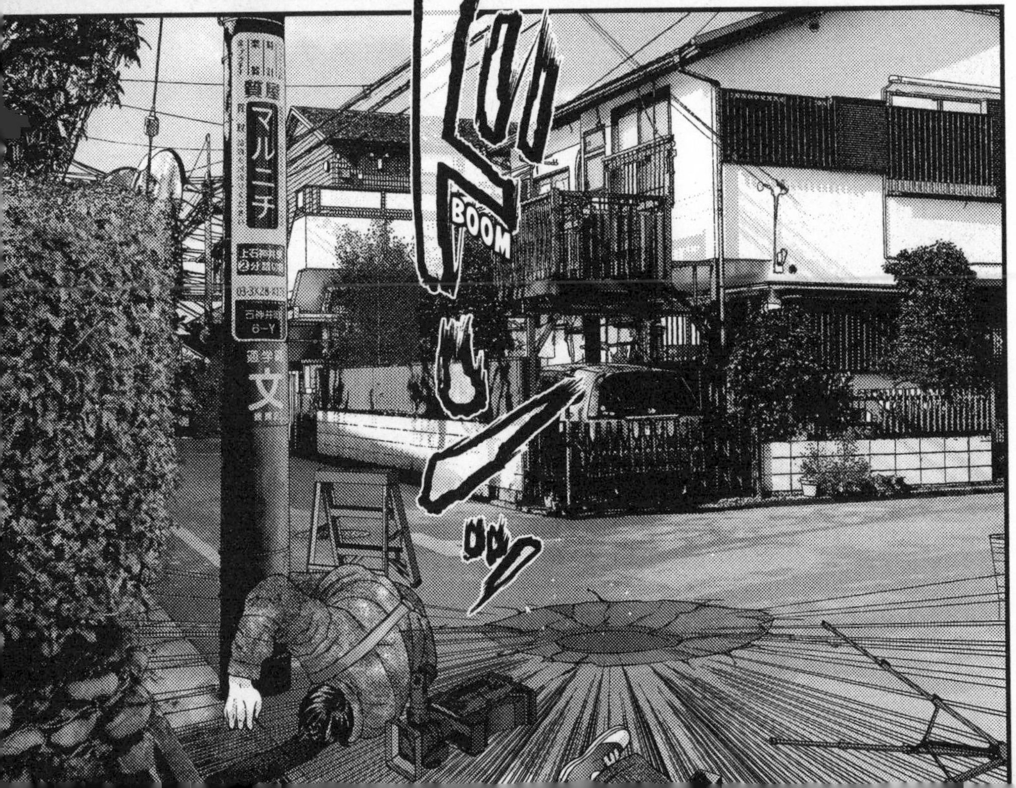
質屋
マルニチ
6-Y
文
BOOM

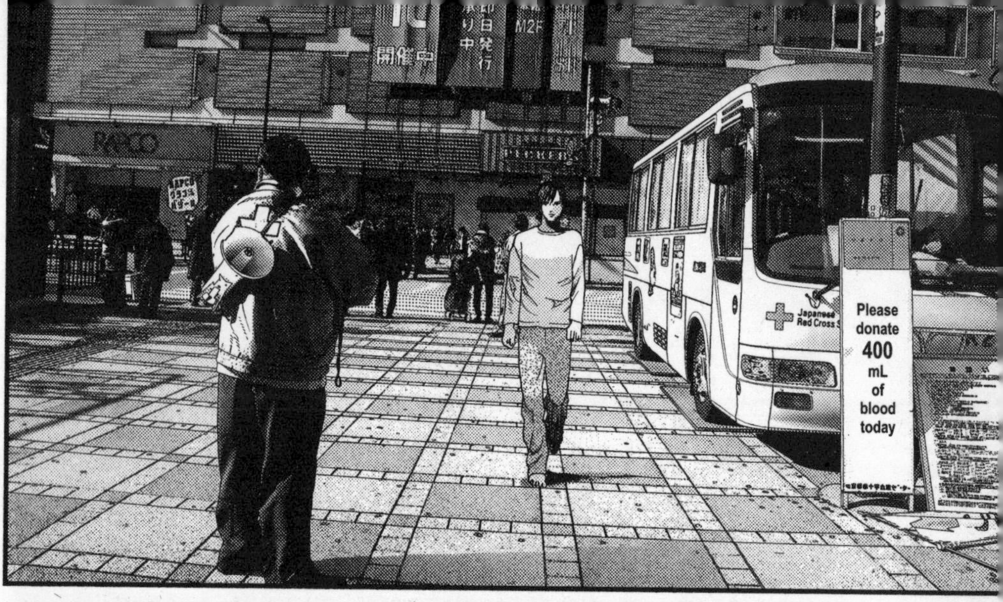
開催中
Japanese
Red Cross
Please
donate
400
mL
of
blood
today
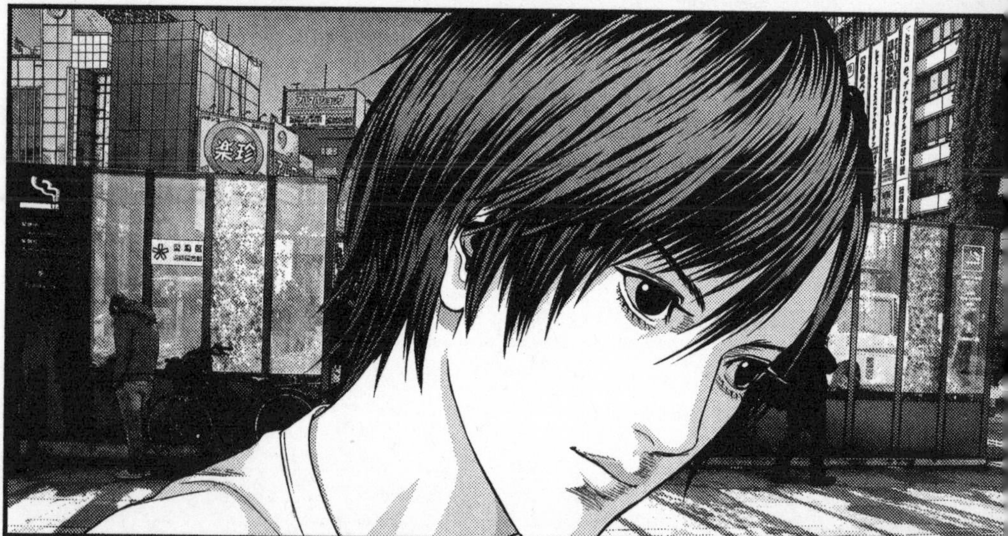
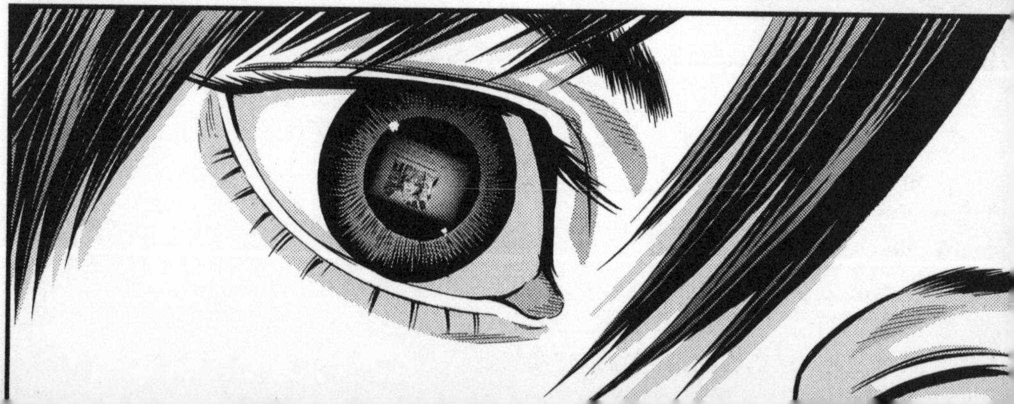

Hiro Shishigami's mom
commited suicide lololololol

2   2015/xx/xx(F)10:35:35.22   dTgynGJp0
VIP speaking for Anonymous   sage

Suckaaa lolll

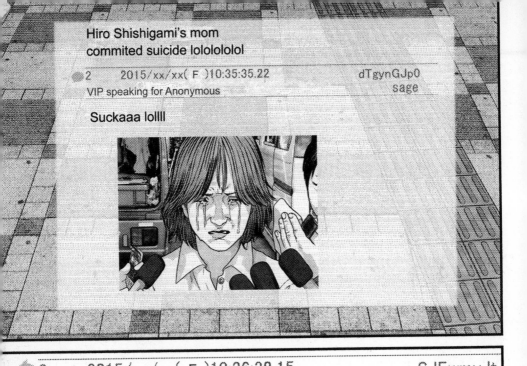

↪3   2015/xx/xx(F)10:36:38.15   SJEwmvJt
VIP speaking for Anonymous   sage

In your face Shishigami!

loooooool

↪4   2015/xx/xx(F)10:36:45.35   +B/INz5C0
VIP speaking for Anonymous   sage

It's perfect

↪17   2015/xx/xx(F)10:37:45.42   dTgynGJp0
VIP speaking for Anonymous   sage

She brought that mass-murderer into the world
so it's a fitting end

↪18   2015/xx/xx(F)10:38:05.17   66KGZIy+0
VIP speaking for Anonymous   sage

His dad should kill himself too

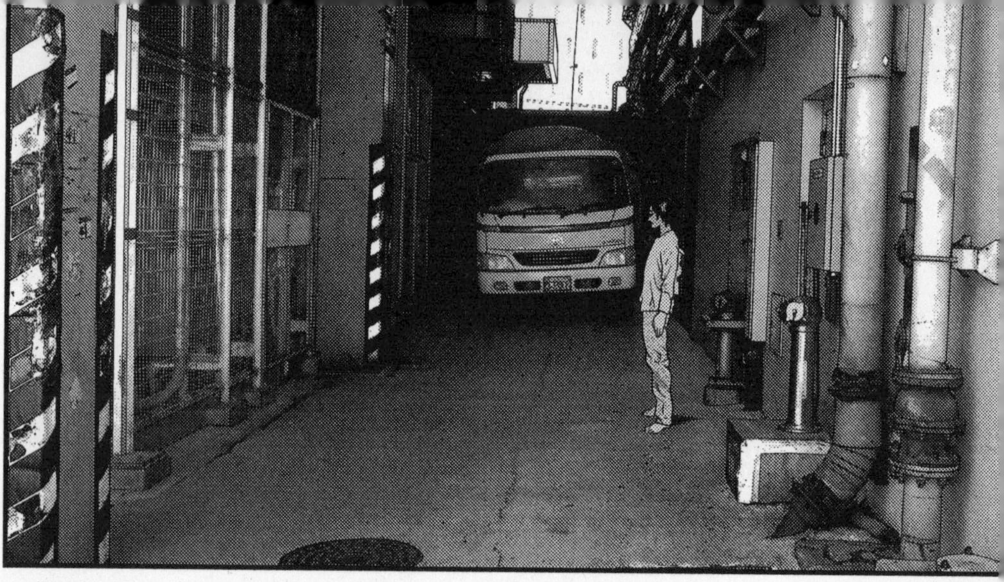

153 2015/xx/xx(F)10:39:24.13
VIP speaking for Anonymous

They live in my neighborhood, so I sent the media all their addresses and pictures of the houses
Way too quick to kill herself before the end of the day tho

154 2015/xx/xx(F)10:39:52.35
VIP speaking for Anonymous

GJ nice work

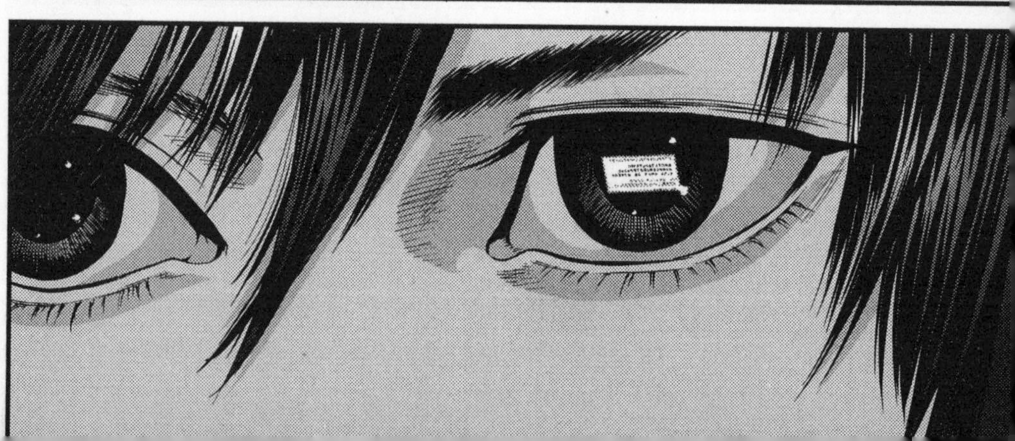

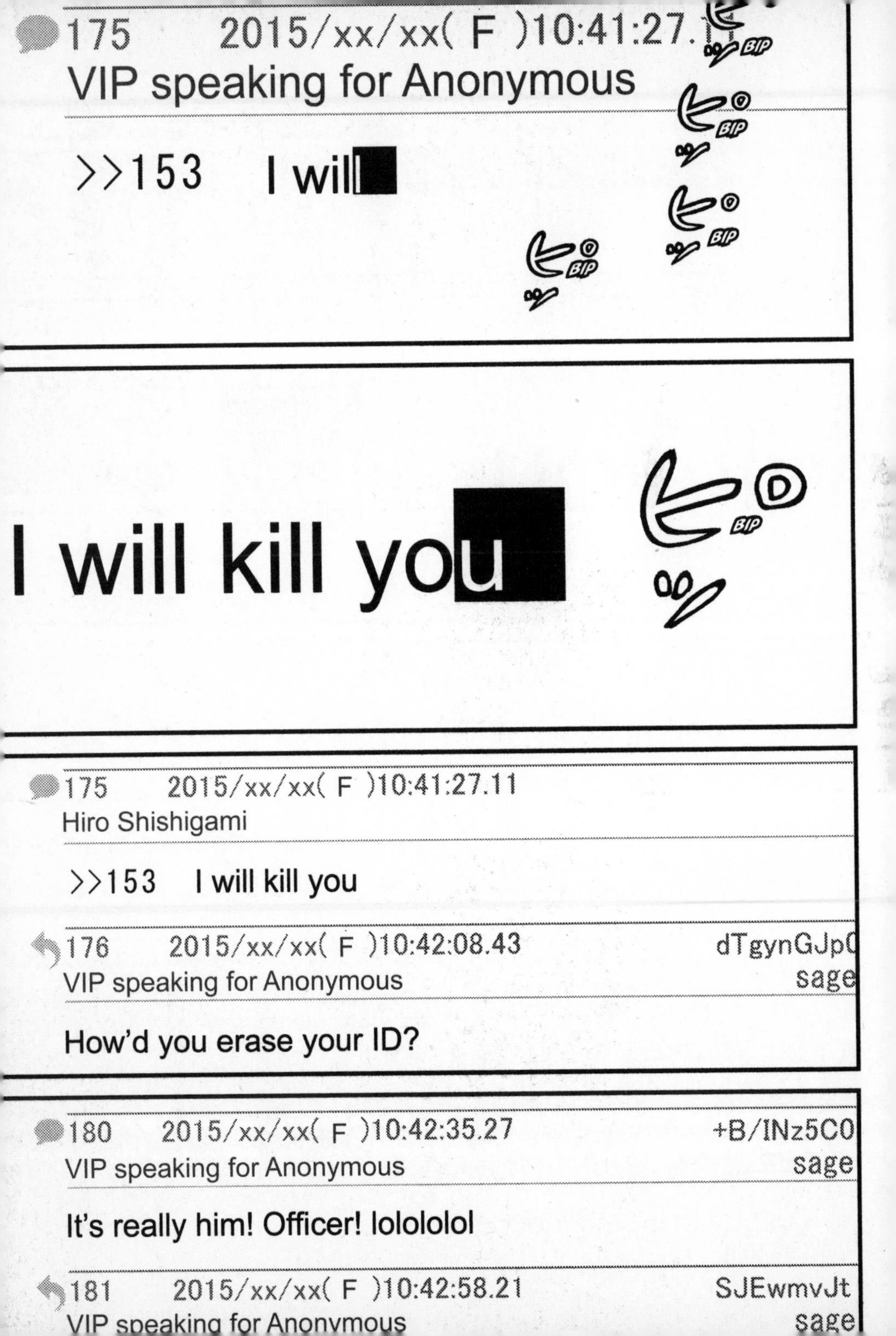

175 2015/xx/xx(F)10:41:27.11
VIP speaking for Anonymous
>>153 I will
BIP
BIP
BIP
BIP
I will kill you
BIP
175 2015/xx/xx(F)10:41:27.11
Hiro Shishigami
>>153 I will kill you
176 2015/xx/xx(F)10:42:08.43 dTgynGJp0
VIP speaking for Anonymous sage
How'd you erase your ID?
180 2015/xx/xx(F)10:42:35.27 +B/INz5C0
VIP speaking for Anonymous sage
It's really him! Officer! lolololol
181 2015/xx/xx(F)10:42:58.21 SJEwmvJt
VIP speaking for Anonymous sage

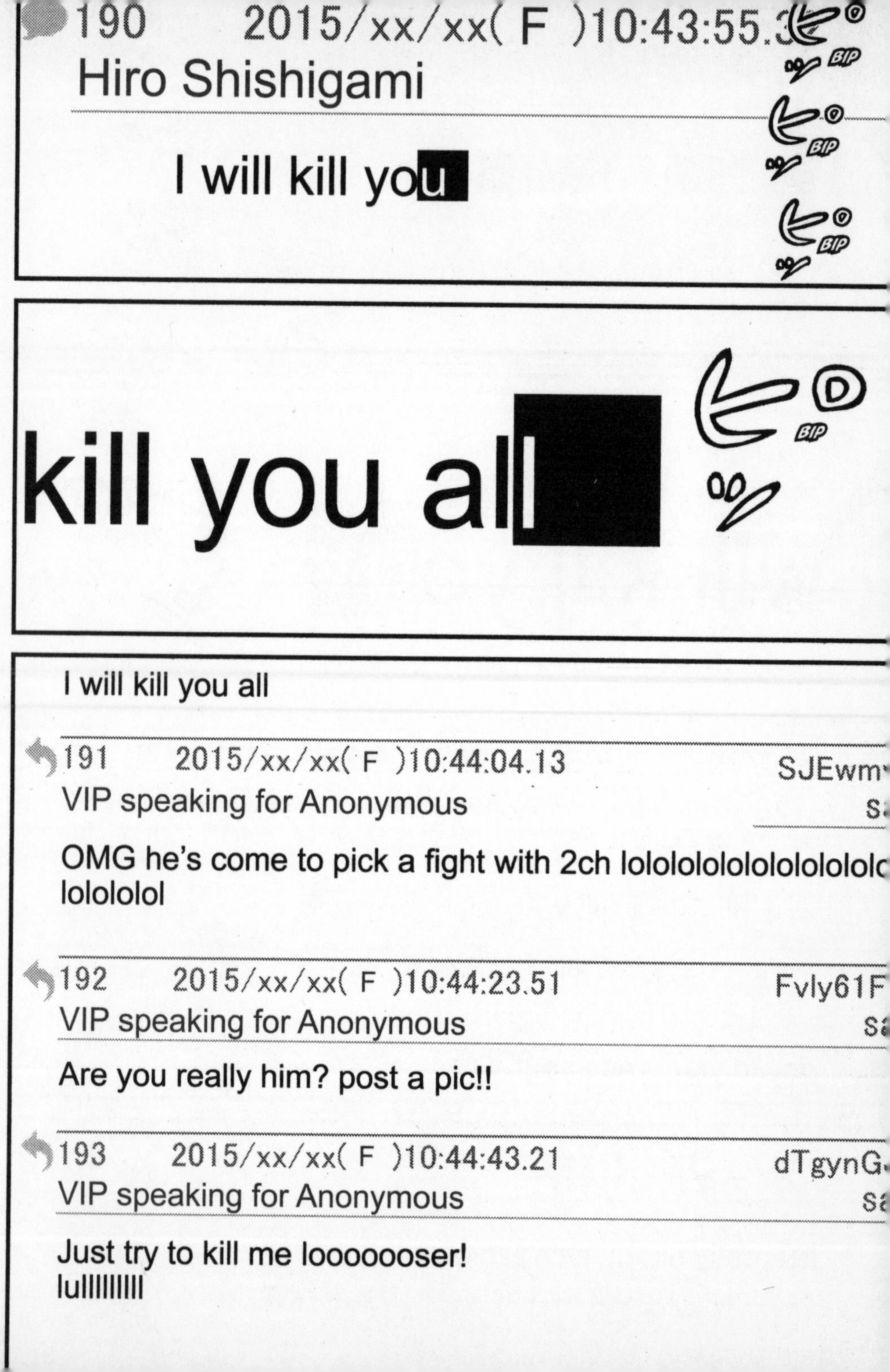
190 2015/xx/xx(F)10:43:55.3
Hiro Shishigami
I will kill you
BIP
BIP
BIP
kill you all
BIP
I will kill you all
191 2015/xx/xx(F)10:44:04.13 SJEwm
VIP speaking for Anonymous
OMG he's come to pick a fight with 2ch lolololololololololol
lolololol
192 2015/xx/xx(F)10:44:23.51 Fvly61F
VIP speaking for Anonymous
Are you really him? post a pic!!
193 2015/xx/xx(F)10:44:43.21 dTgynG
VIP speaking for Anonymous
Just try to kill me loooooooser!
lullllllll

194 2015/xx/xx(F)10:45:05.46   FvIy6TFPU

VIP speaking for Anonymous   sage

Are the police seeing this?

195 2015/xx/xx(F)10:45:34.27   bRzkiyg9Jt

VIP speaking for Anonymous   sage

Hey you murderer, turn yourself in
stupid piece of shit

---

200 2015/xx/xx(F)10:46:08.13   +B/INz5CC

VIP speaking for Anonymous   sage

And that was the end of 2ch lol

201 2015/xx/xx(F)10:46:32.31   SJEwmvJt

VIP speaking for Anonymous   sage

I for one think Shishigami-kun is very handsome lol

---

325 2015/xx/xx(F)10:49:48.28

VIP speaking for Anonymous

>>175   Come and kill me, I'll give you
what's coming to you

---

326 2015/xx/xx(F)10:50:15.24

Hiro Shishigami

>>325
Found you… I'm on my way

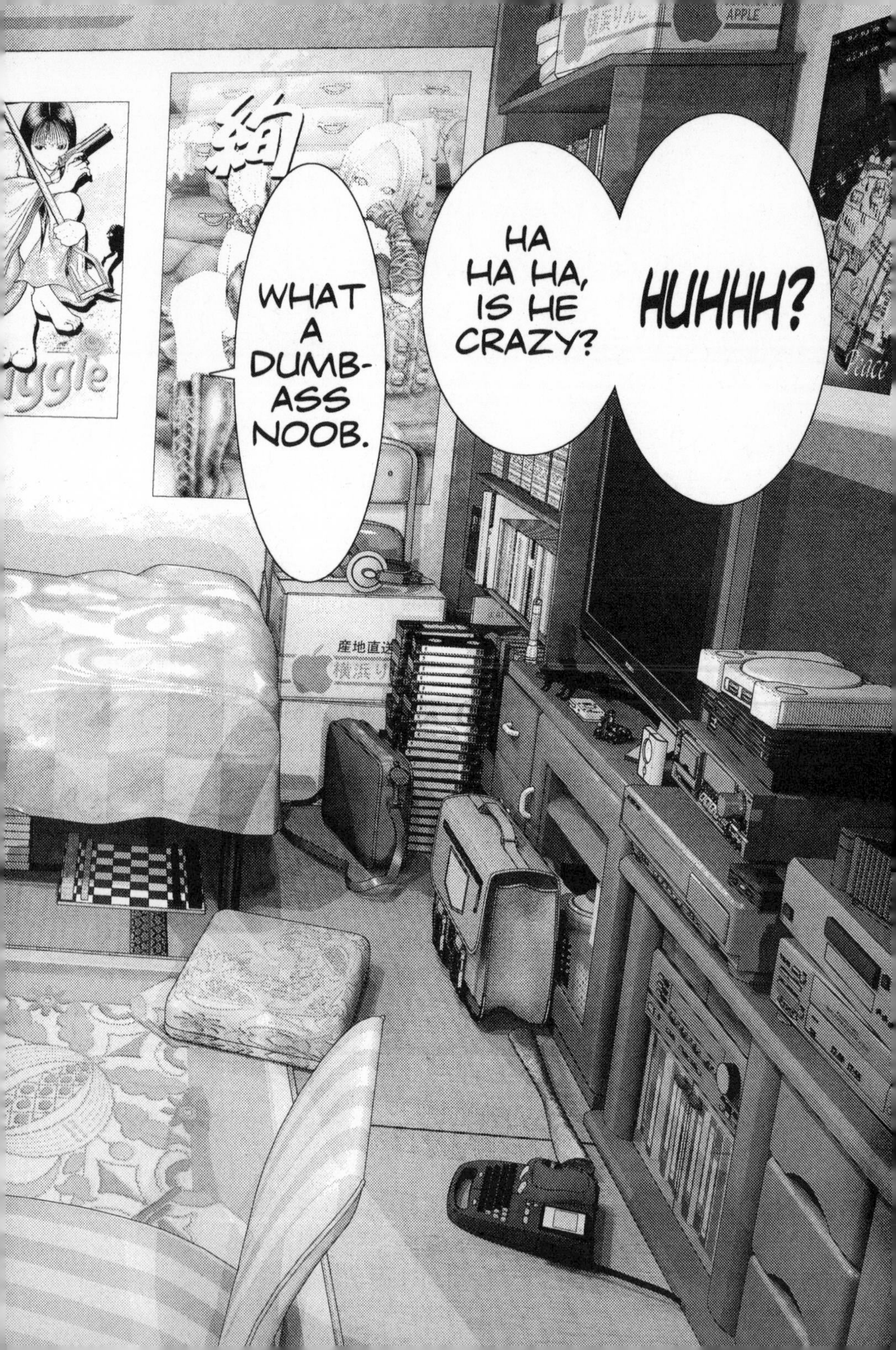
HUHHH?
HA HA HA, IS HE CRAZY?
WHAT A DUMB-ASS NOOB.
APPLE
産地直送

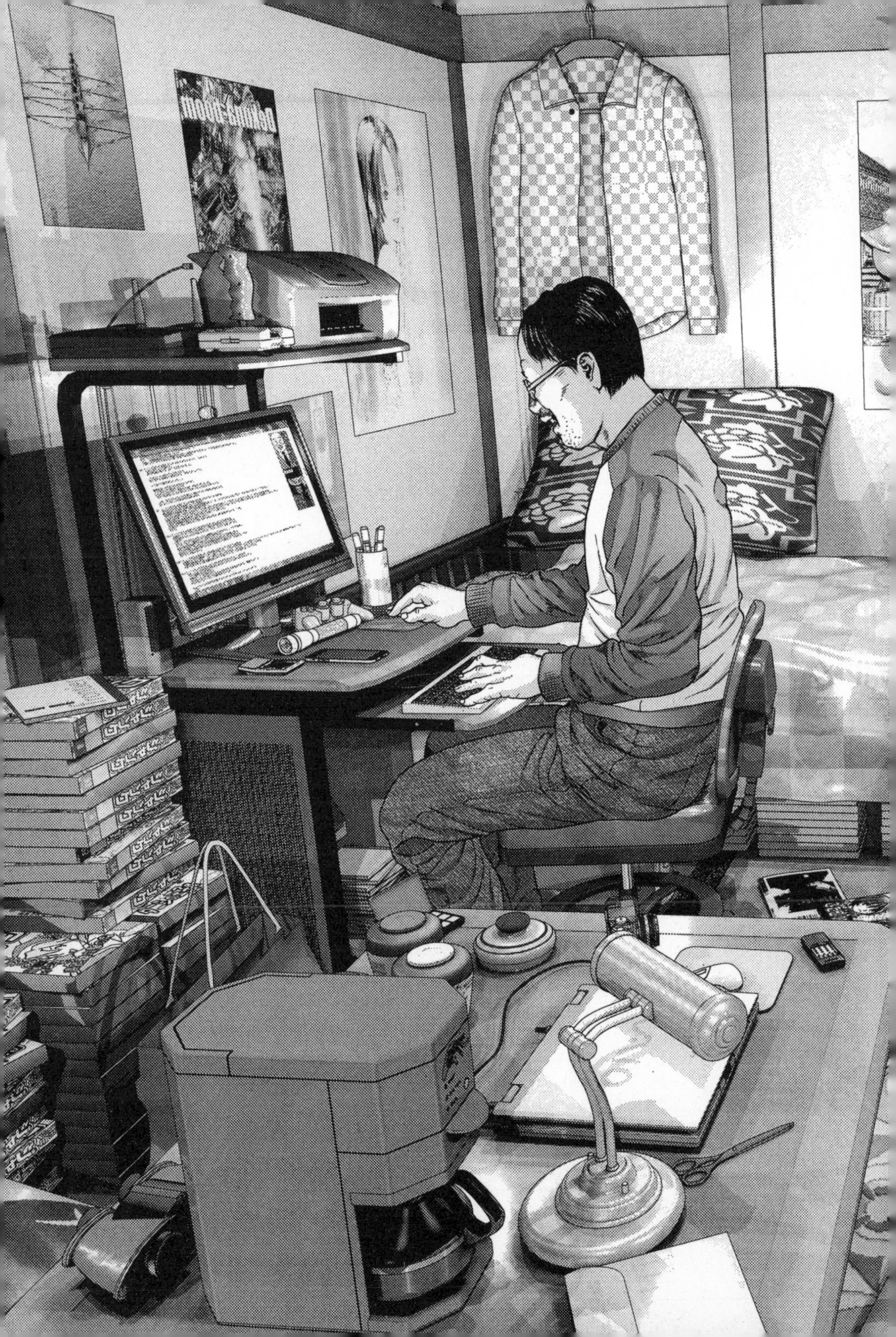

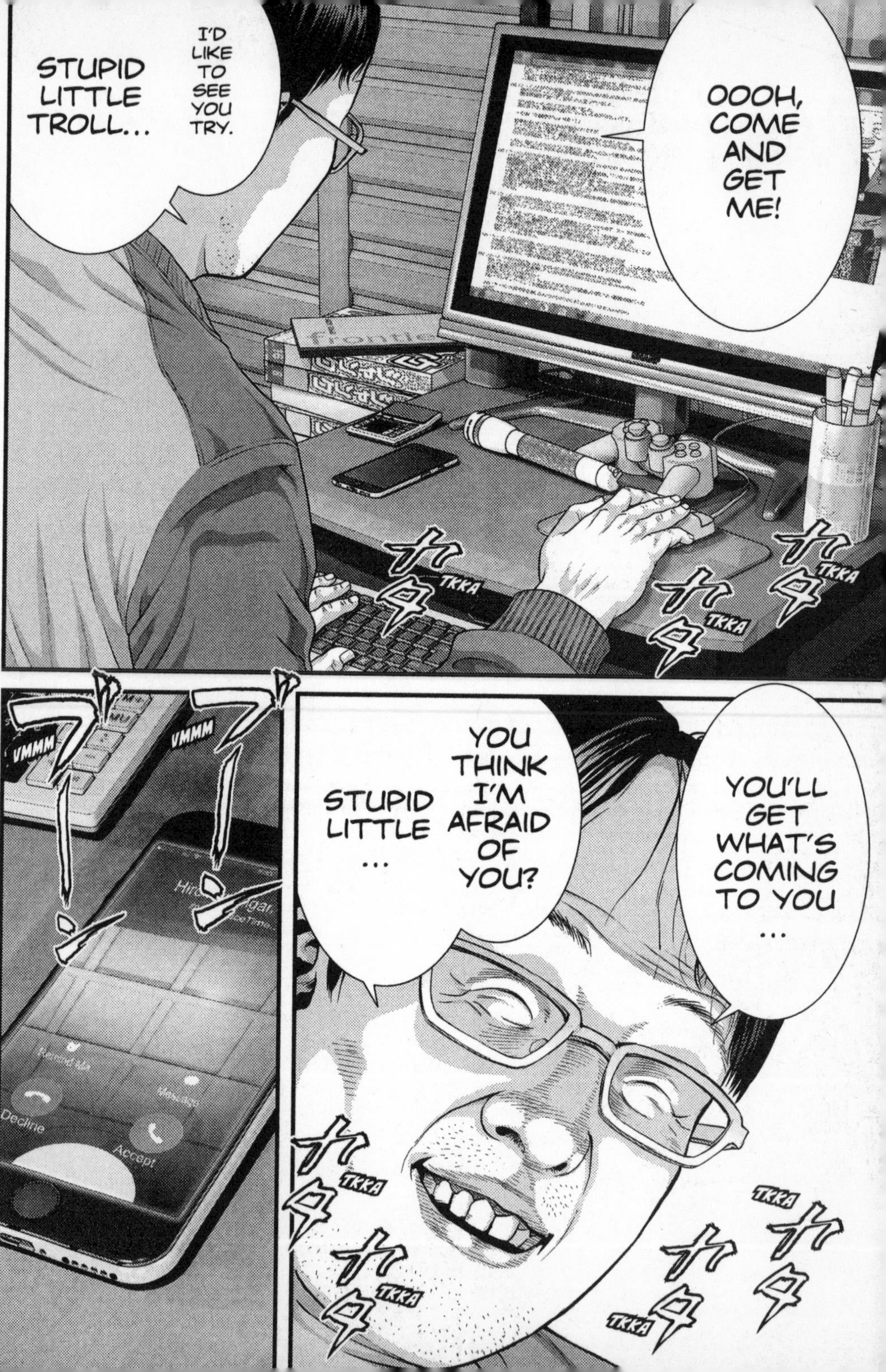
OOOH, COME AND GET ME!
I'D LIKE TO SEE YOU TRY.
STUPID LITTLE TROLL...
TKKA
TKKA
TKKA
YOU'LL GET WHAT'S COMING TO YOU ...
YOU THINK I'M AFRAID OF YOU?
STUPID LITTLE ...
TKKA
TKKA
TKKA
TKKA
VMMM
VMMM
Decline
Accept

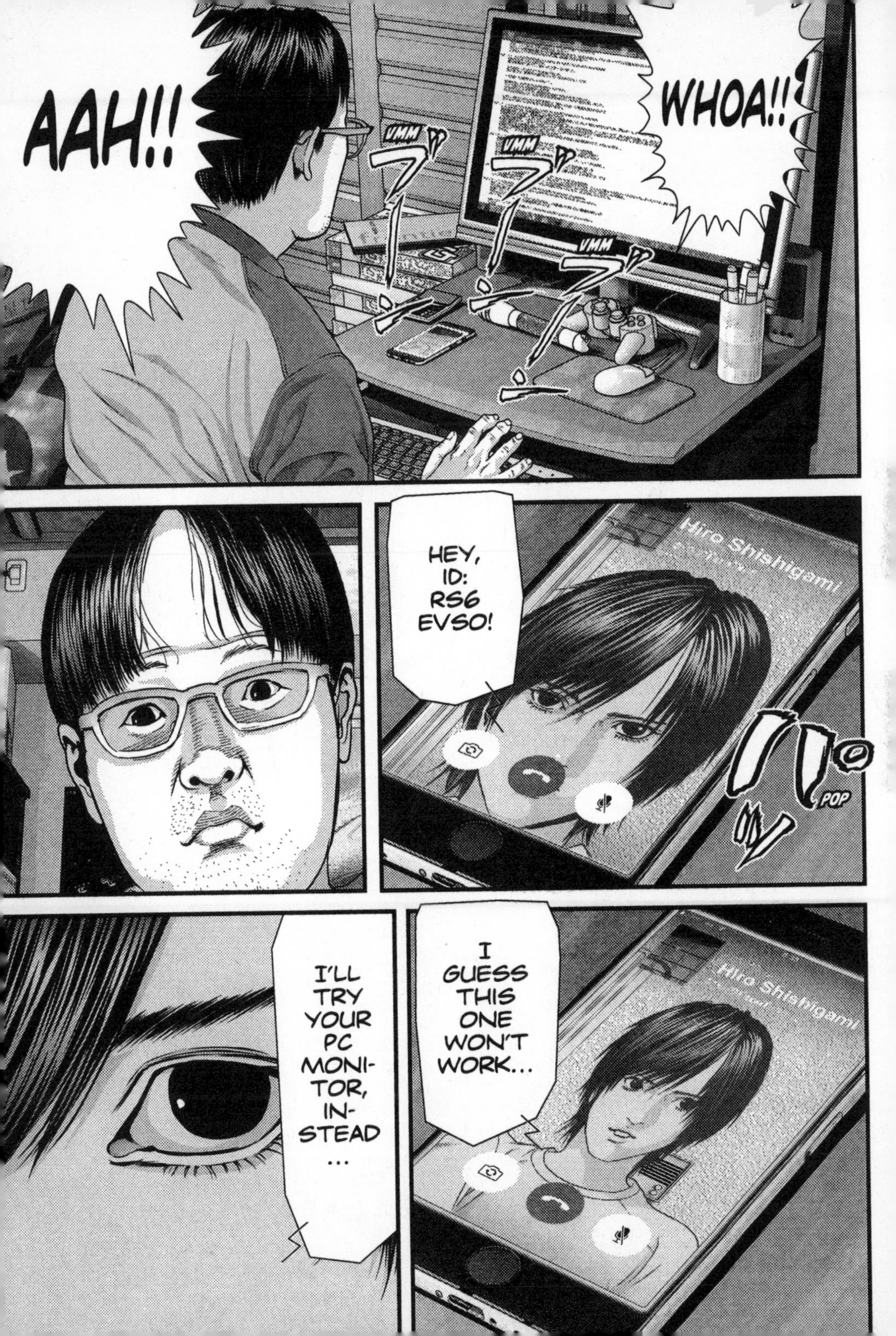
WHOA!!
VMM
VMM
VMM
AAH!!
Hiro Shishigami
HEY, ID: RS6 EVSO!
POP
Hiro Shishigami
I GUESS THIS ONE WON'T WORK...
I'LL TRY YOUR PC MONI-TOR, IN-STEAD...

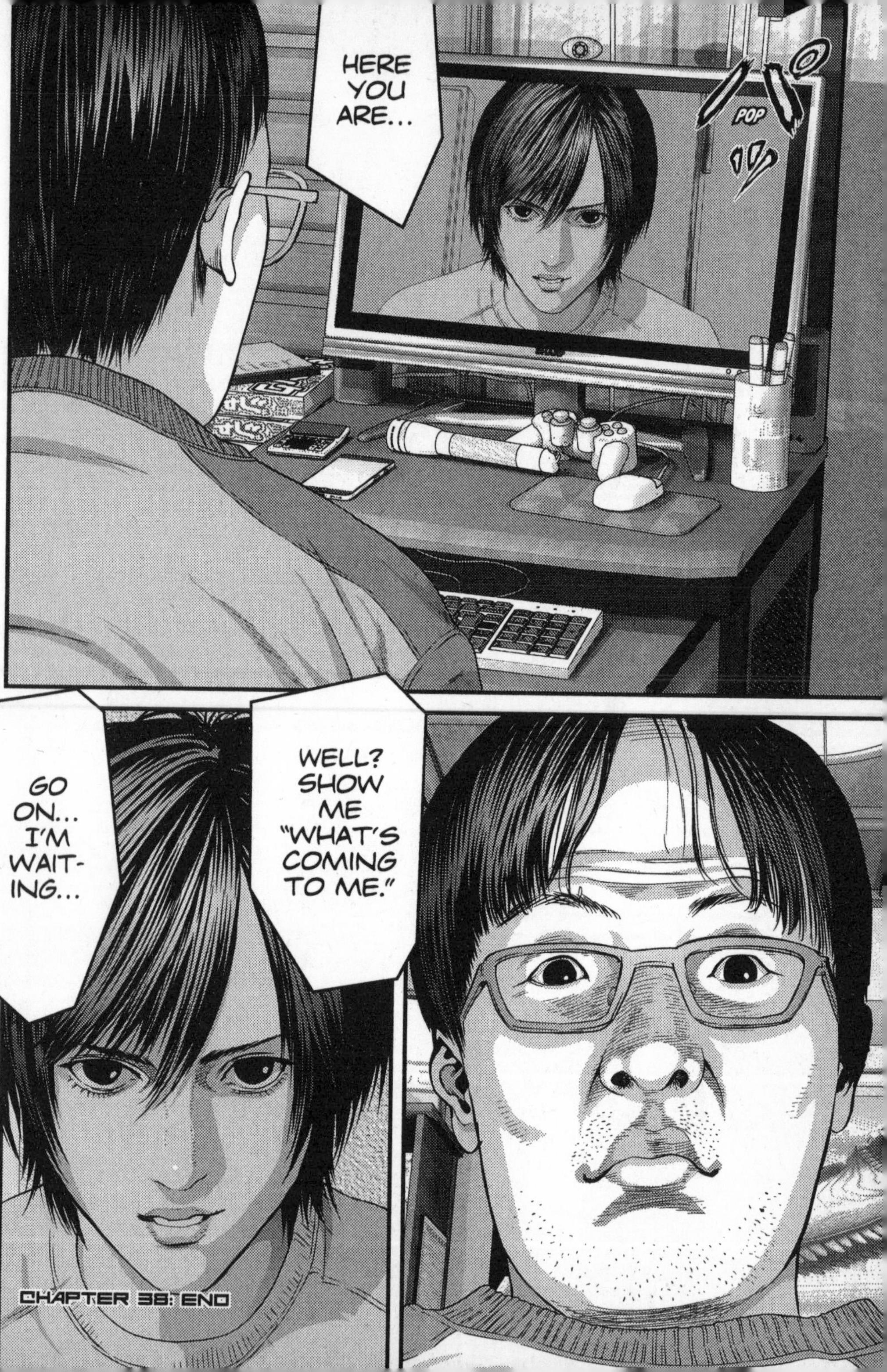
HERE YOU ARE...
POP
WELL? SHOW ME "WHAT'S COMING TO ME."
GO ON... I'M WAITING...
CHAPTER 38: END

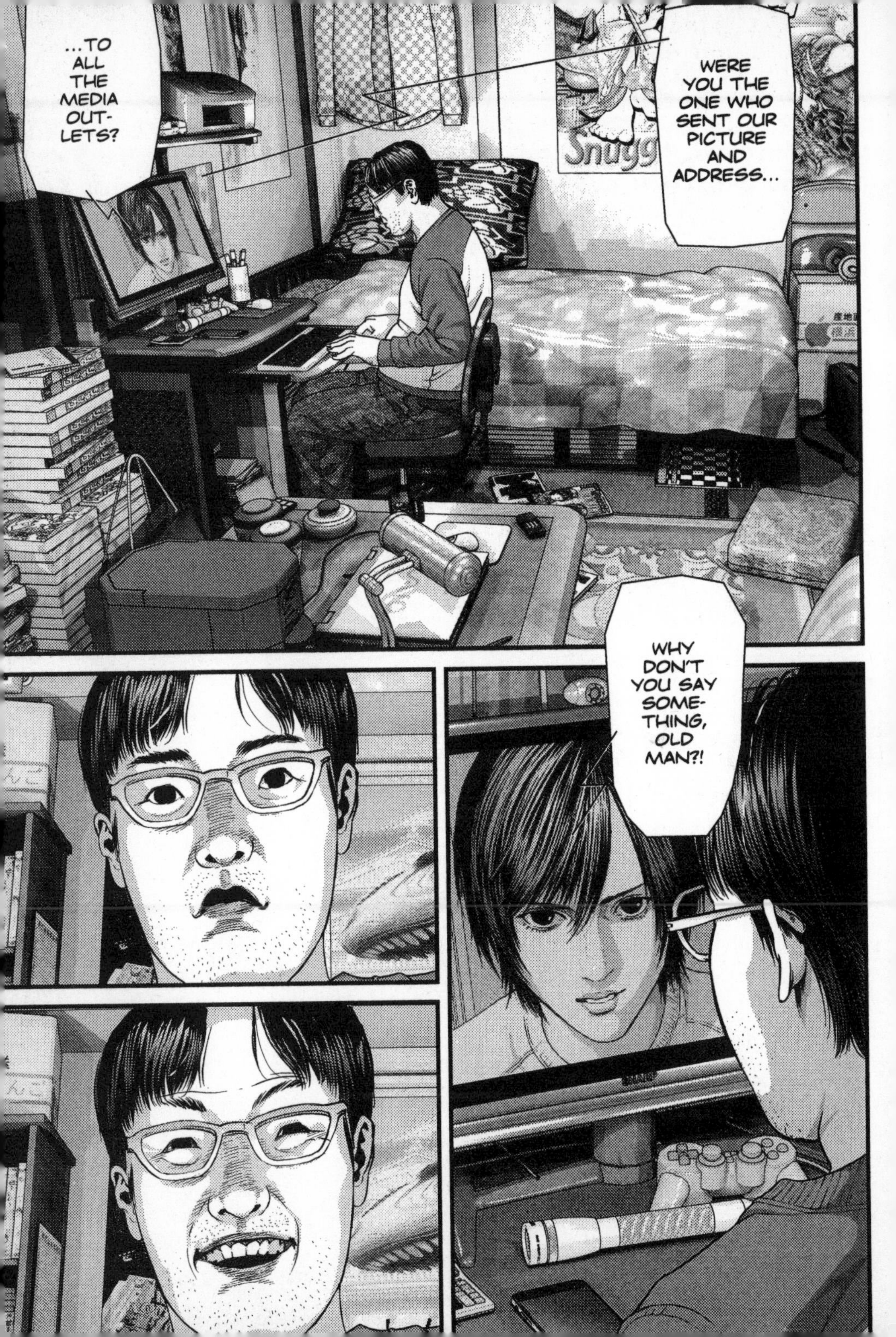
WERE YOU THE ONE WHO SENT OUR PICTURE AND ADDRESS...
...TO ALL THE MEDIA OUT-LETS?
WHY DON'T YOU SAY SOME-THING, OLD MAN?!

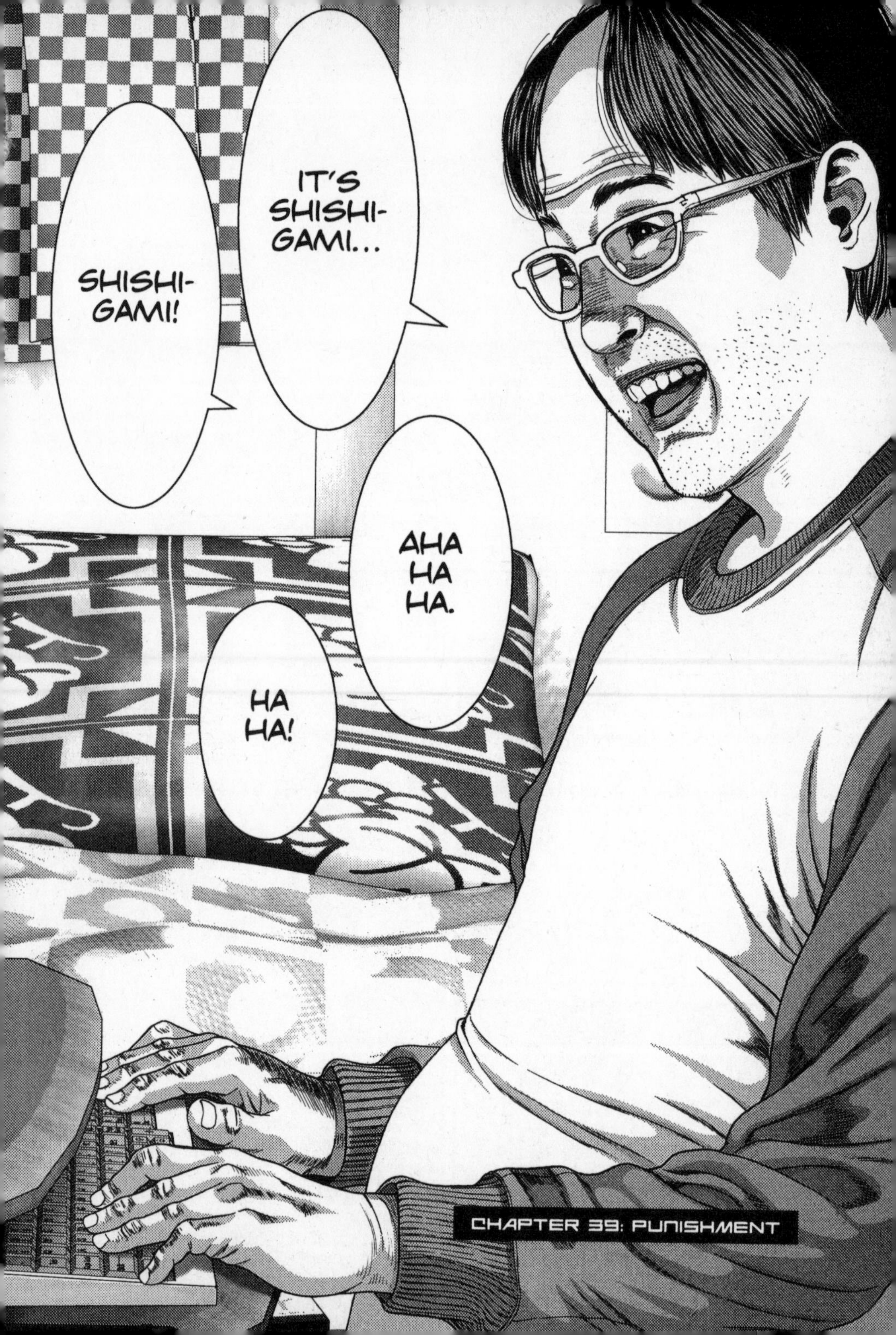
IT'S SHISHI-GAMI...
SHISHI-GAMI!
AHA HA HA.
HA HA!
CHAPTER 39: PUNISHMENT

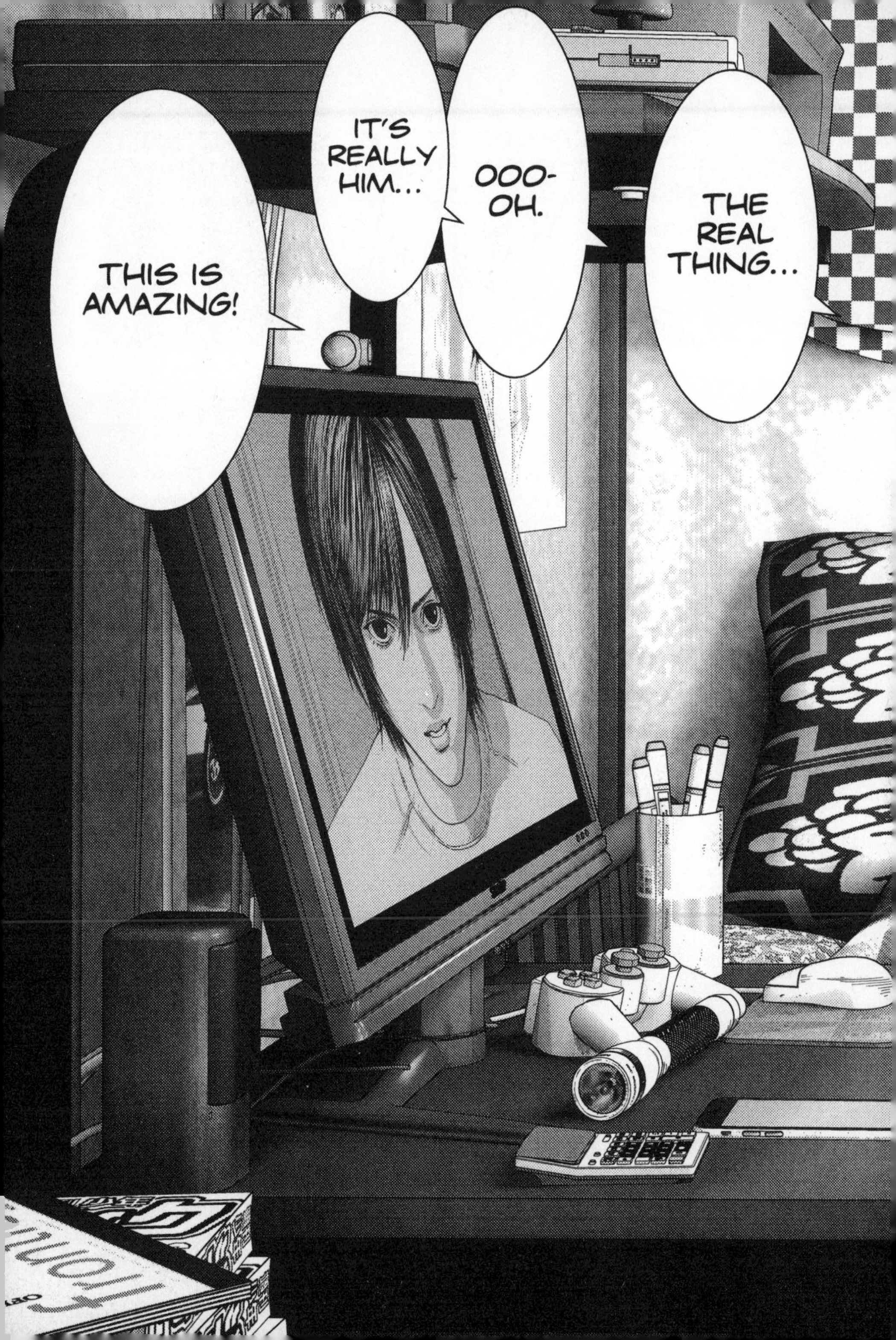
THE REAL THING...
OOO-OH.
IT'S REALLY HIM...
THIS IS AMAZING!

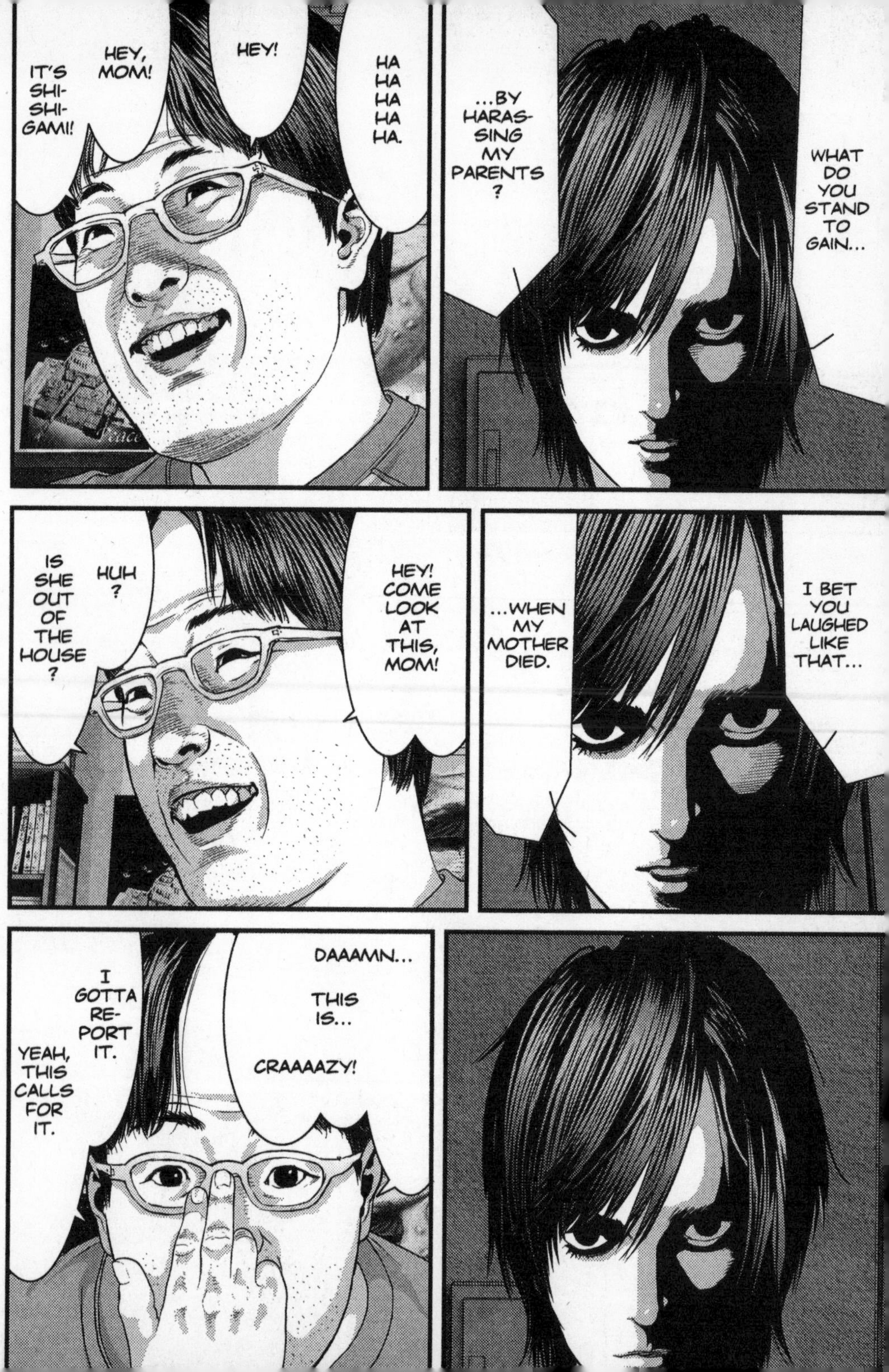
WHAT DO YOU STAND TO GAIN...
...BY HARAS-SING MY PARENTS?
HA HA HA HA HA HA.
HEY!
HEY, MOM!
IT'S SHI-SHI-GAMI!
I BET YOU LAUGHED LIKE THAT...
...WHEN MY MOTHER DIED.
HEY! COME LOOK AT THIS, MOM!
HUH?
IS SHE OUT OF THE HOUSE?
DAAAMN...
THIS IS...
CRAAAAZY!
I GOTTA RE-PORT IT.
YEAH, THIS CALLS FOR IT.

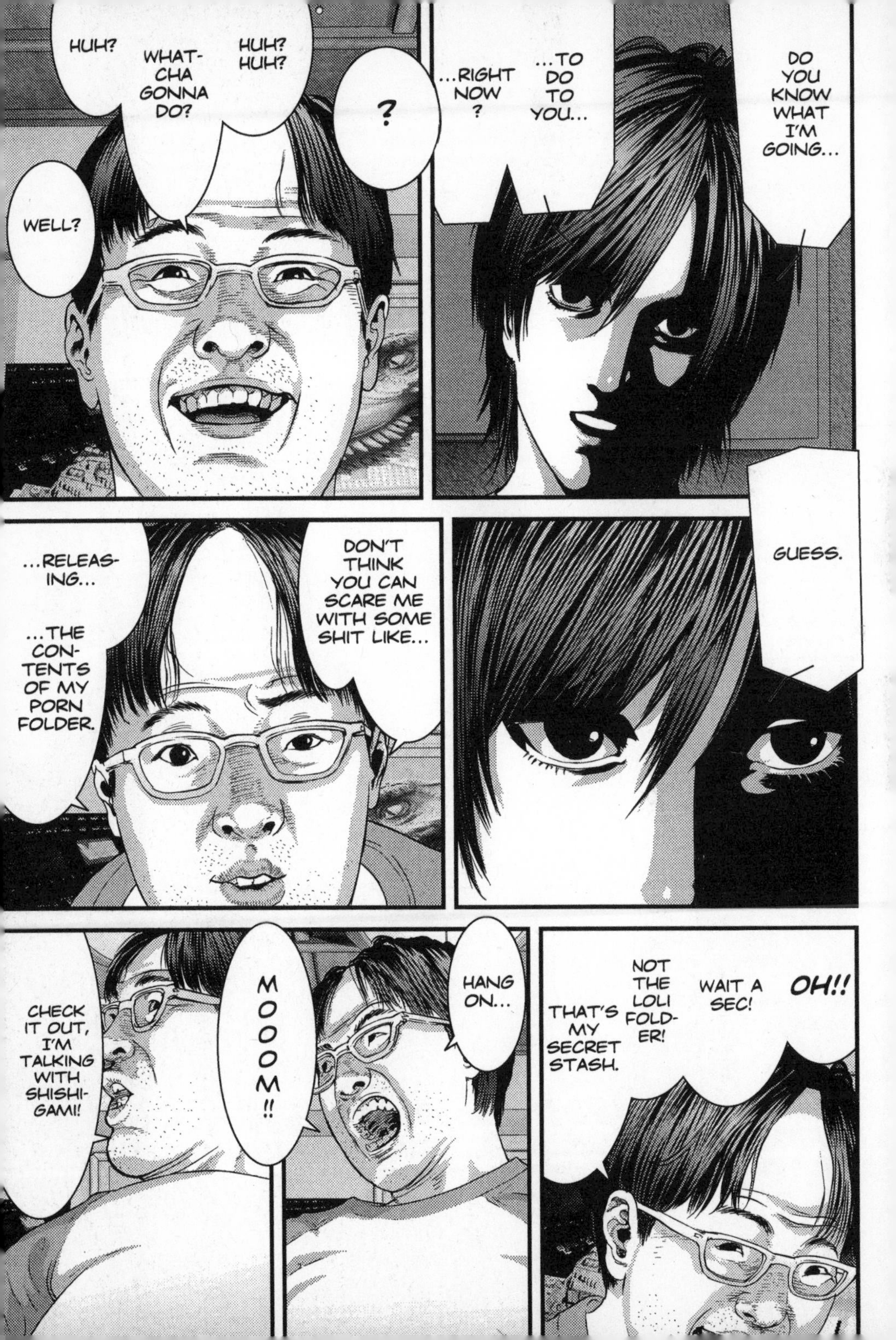
DO YOU KNOW WHAT I'M GOING...
...TO DO TO YOU...
...RIGHT NOW?
?
HUH? HUH?
WHAT-CHA GONNA DO?
HUH?
WELL?
GUESS.
DON'T THINK YOU CAN SCARE ME WITH SOME SHIT LIKE...
...RELEAS-ING...
...THE CON-TENTS OF MY PORN FOLDER.
OH!!
WAIT A SEC!
NOT THE LOLI FOLD-ER!
THAT'S MY SECRET STASH.
HANG ON...
MOOOOM!!
CHECK IT OUT, I'M TALKING WITH SHISHI-GAMI!

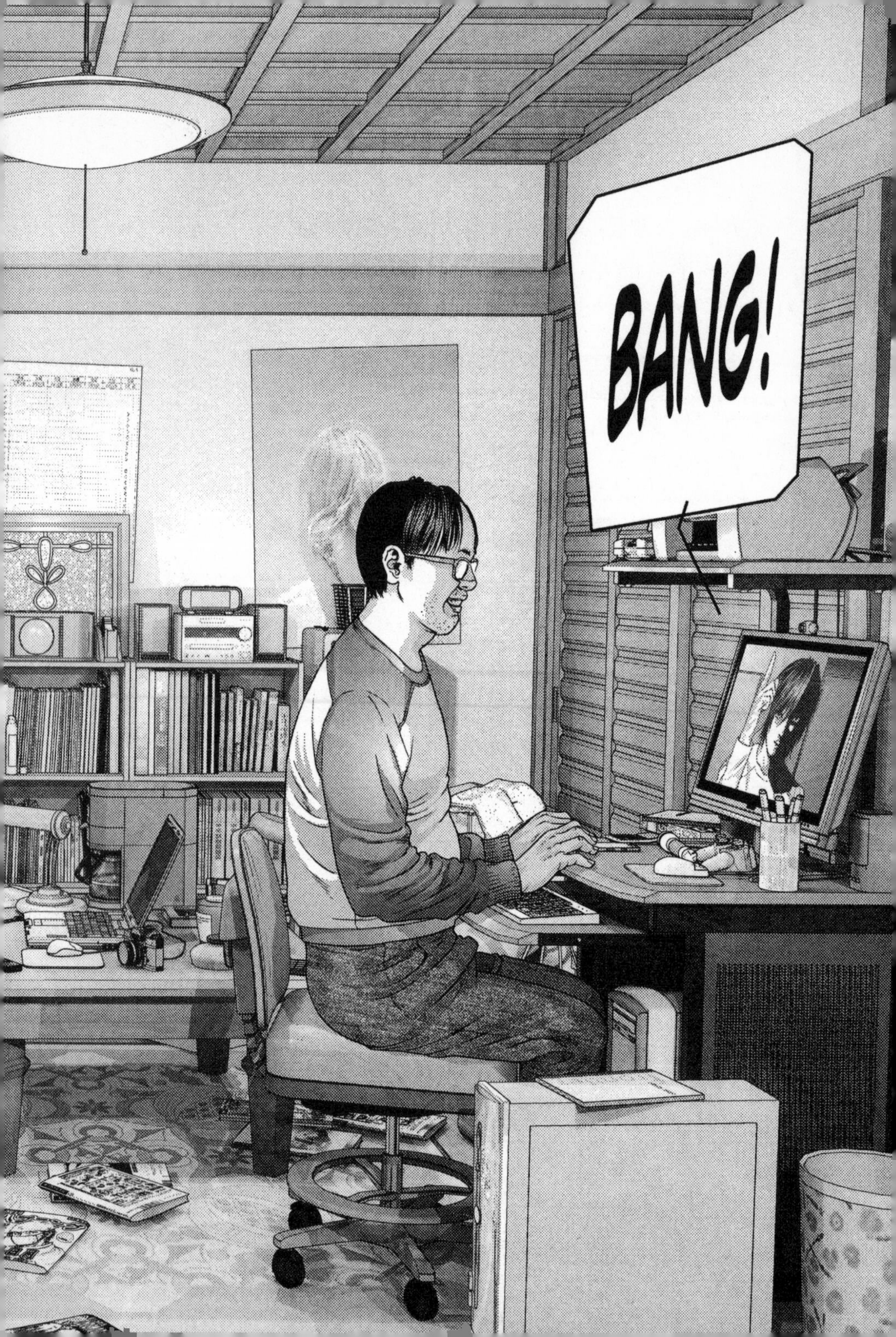
BANG!

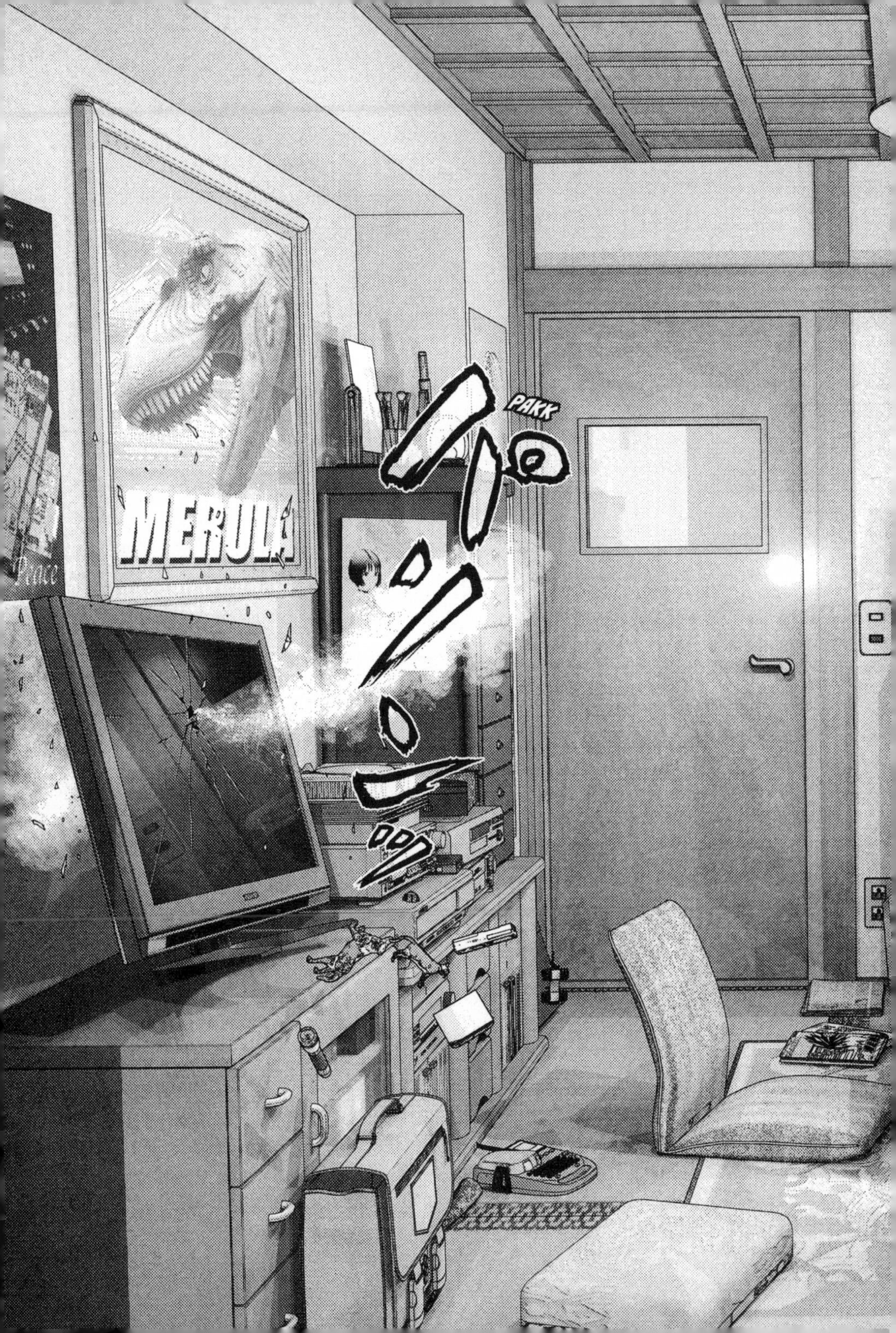
MERULA
Peace
PAKK

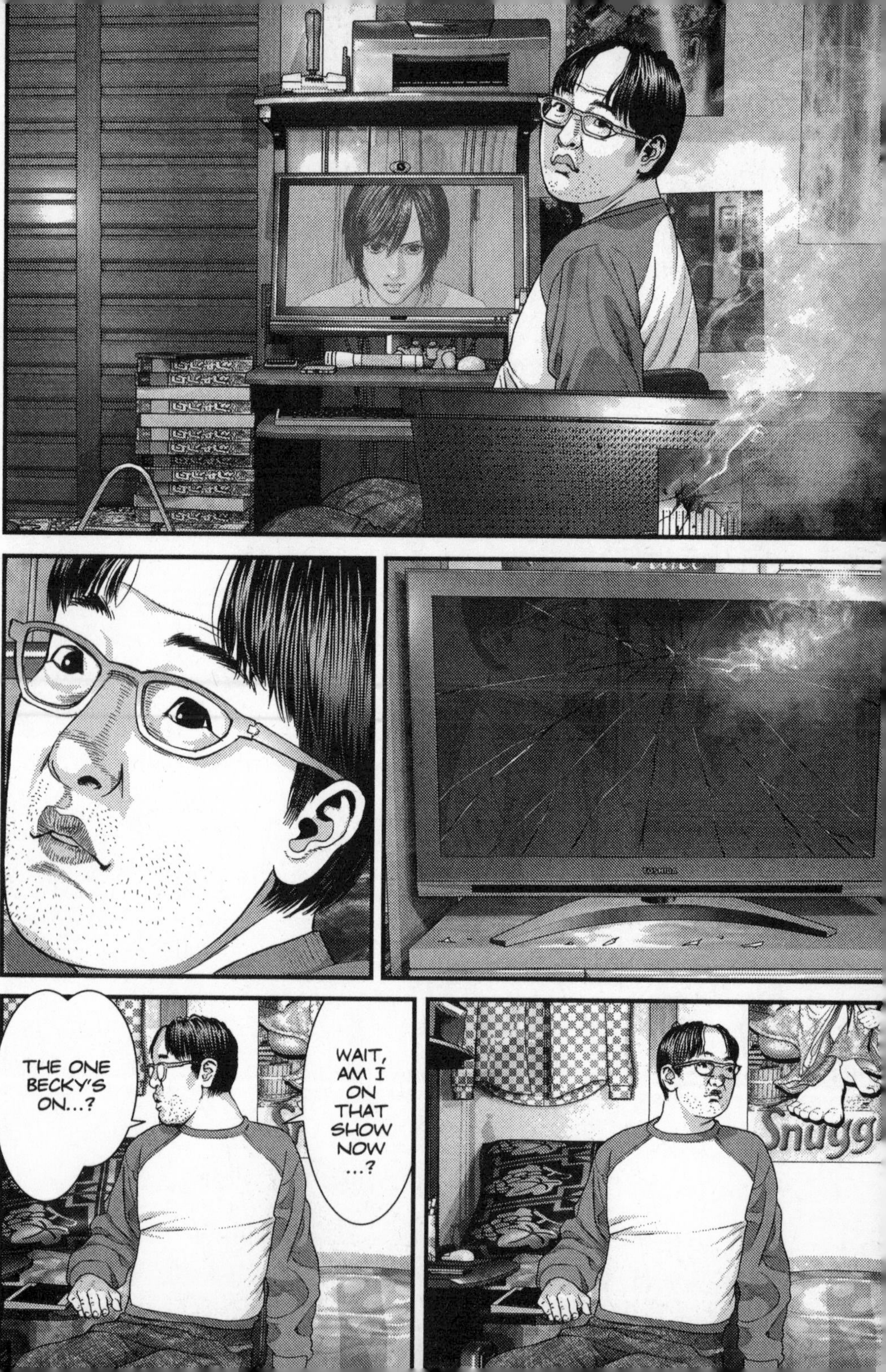
WAIT, AM I ON THAT SHOW NOW ...?
THE ONE BECKY'S ON...?

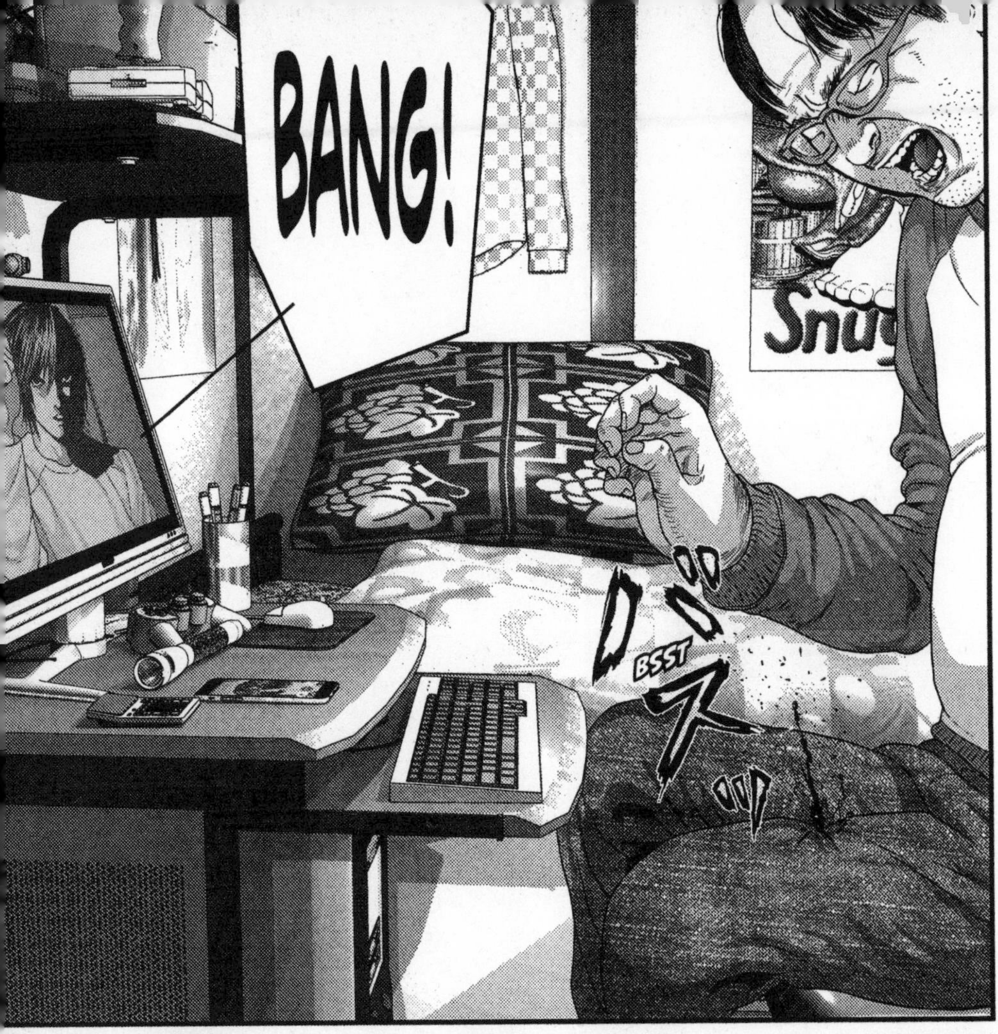
BANG!
Snug
BSST
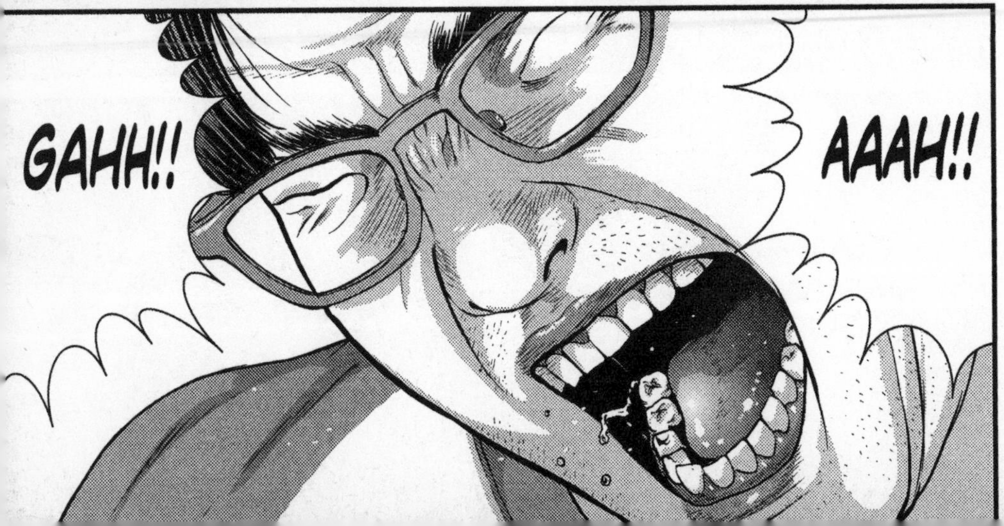
AAAH!!
GAHH!!

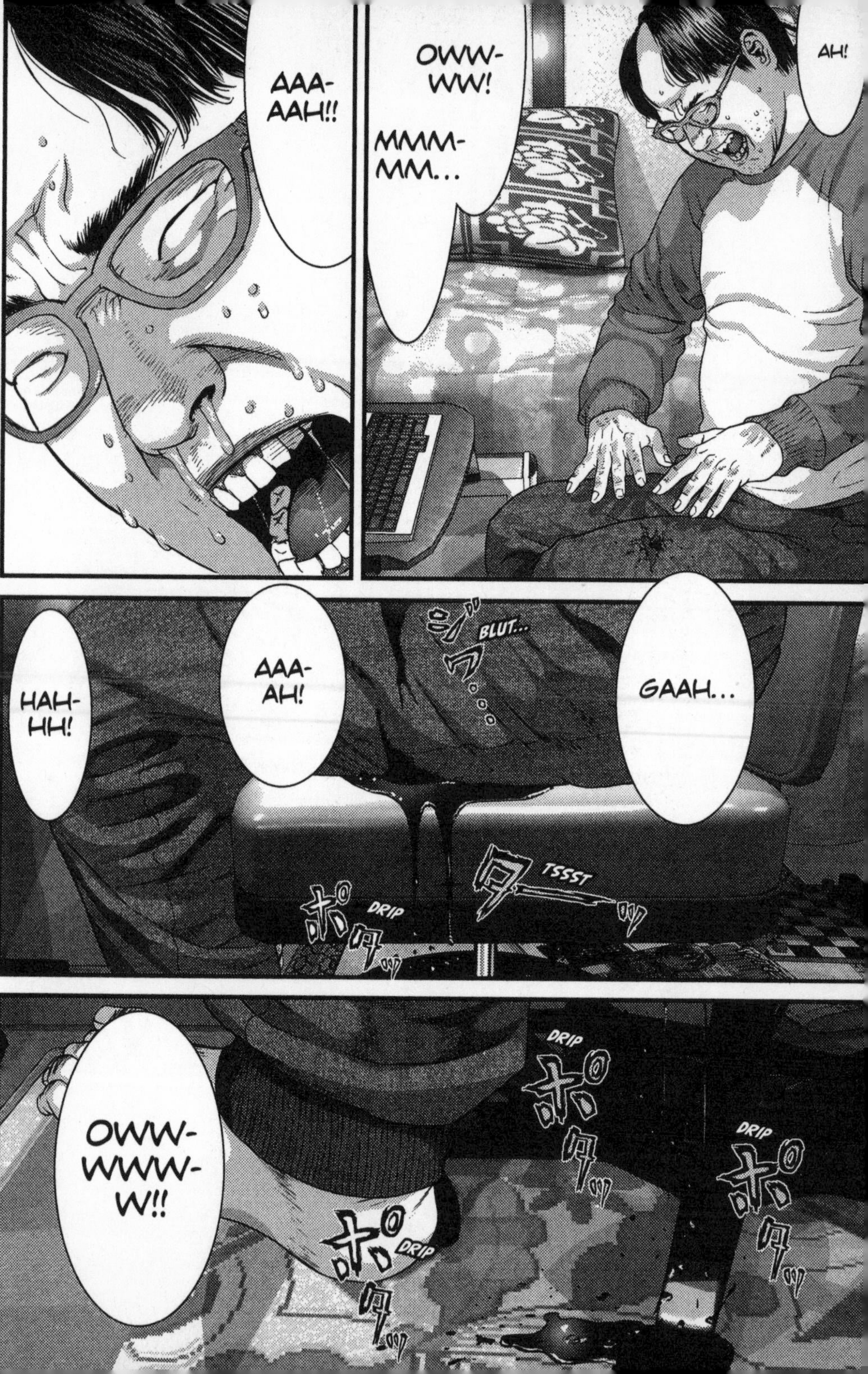
AH!
OWW-WW!
MMM-MM...
AAA-AAH!!
GAAH...
BLUT...
TSSST
AAA-AH!
HAH-HH!
DRIP
DRIP
DRIP
DRIP
OWW-WWW-W!!

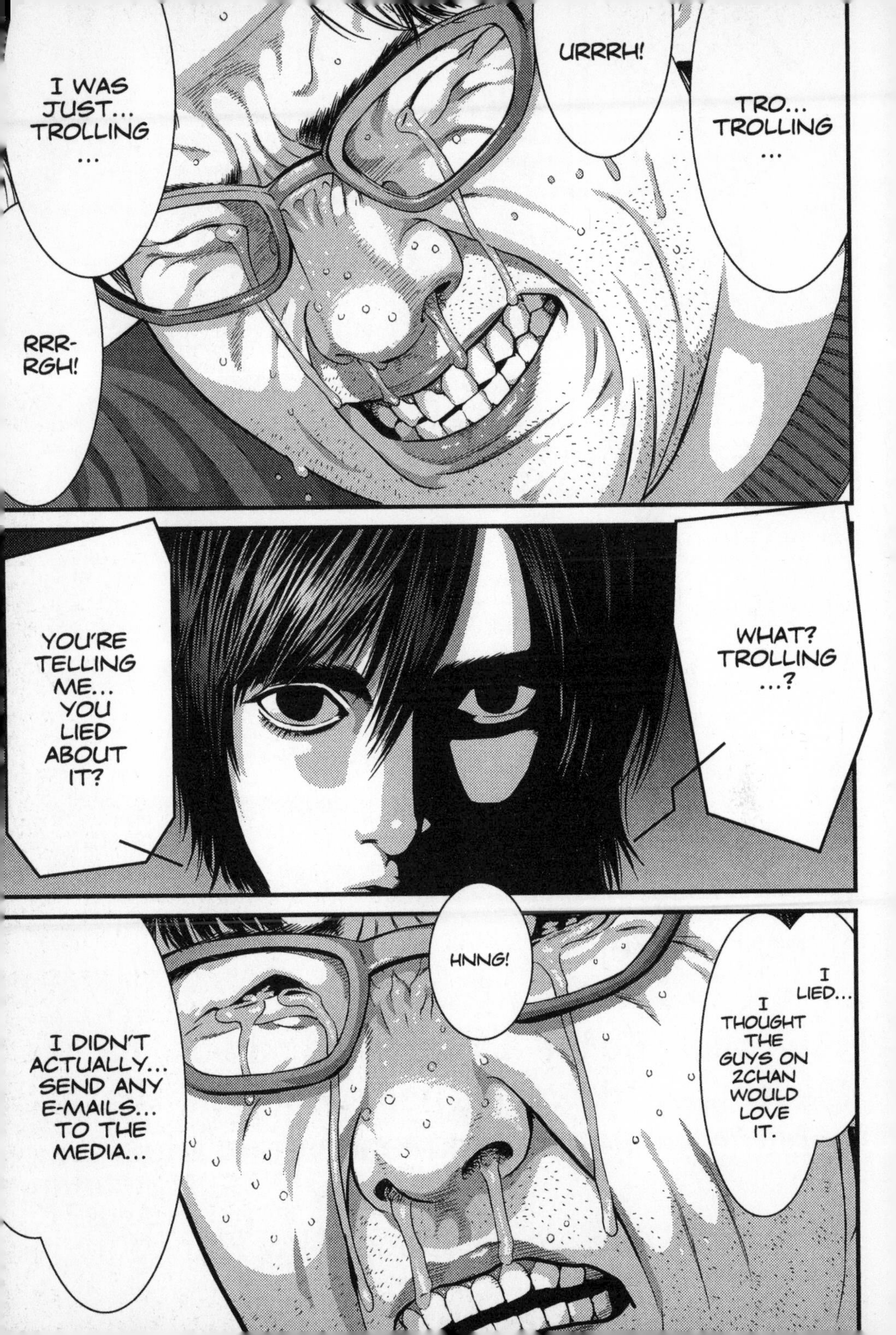
TRO... TROLLING ...
URRRH!
I WAS JUST... TROLLING ...
RRR-RGH!
WHAT? TROLLING ...?
YOU'RE TELLING ME... YOU LIED ABOUT IT?
I LIED... I THOUGHT THE GUYS ON 2CHAN WOULD LOVE IT.
HNNG!
I DIDN'T ACTUALLY... SEND ANY E-MAILS... TO THE MEDIA...

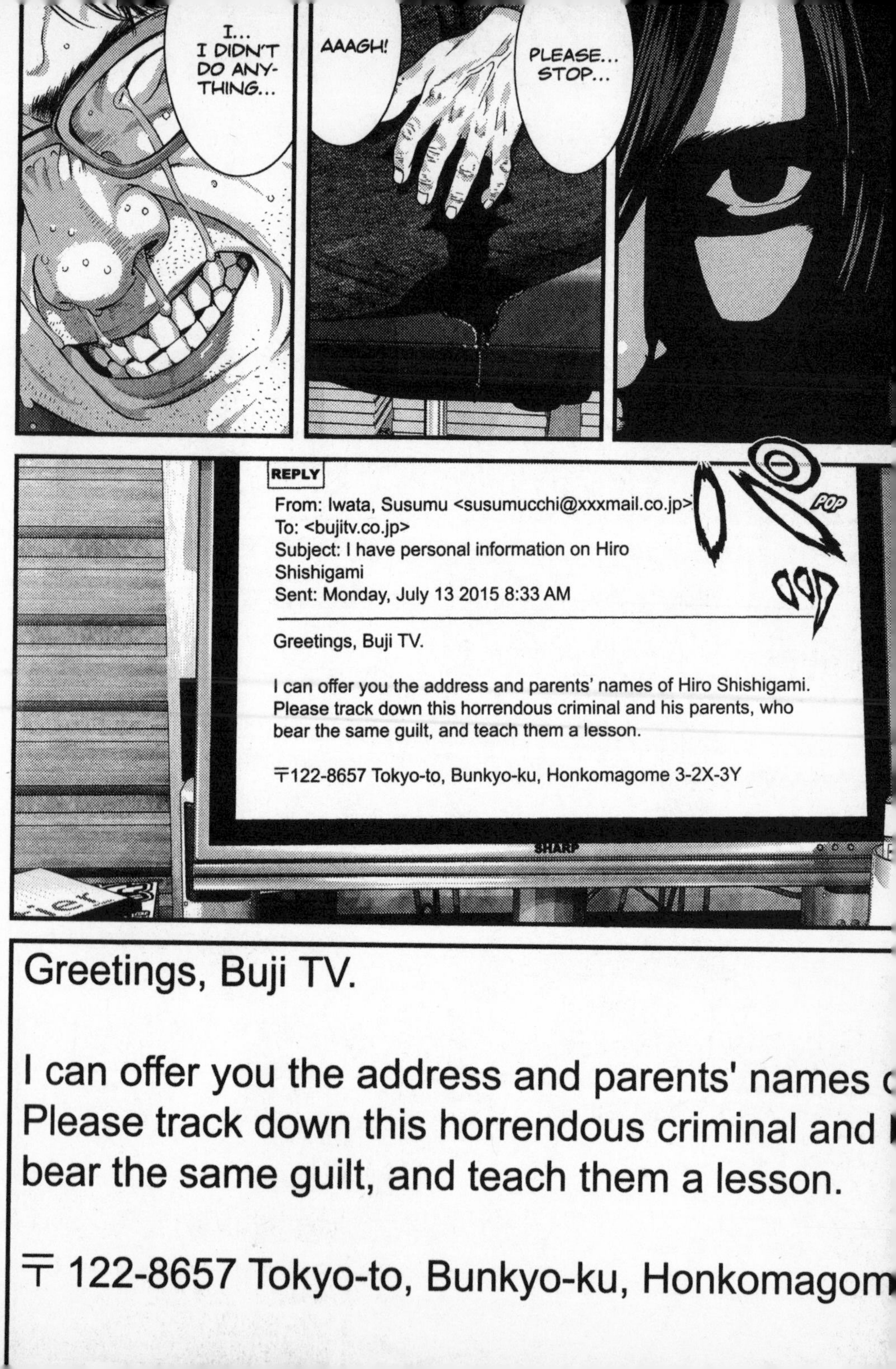
PLEASE... STOP...
AAAGH!
I... I DIDN'T DO ANYTHING...
REPLY
From: Iwata, Susumu <susumucchi@xxxmail.co.jp>
To: <bujitv.co.jp>
Subject: I have personal information on Hiro Shishigami
Sent: Monday, July 13 2015 8:33 AM
Greetings, Buji TV.
I can offer you the address and parents' names of Hiro Shishigami. Please track down this horrendous criminal and his parents, who bear the same guilt, and teach them a lesson.
〒122-8657 Tokyo-to, Bunkyo-ku, Honkomagome 3-2X-3Y
POP
SHARP
Greetings, Buji TV.
I can offer you the address and parents' names
Please track down this horrendous criminal and
bear the same guilt, and teach them a lesson.
〒 122-8657 Tokyo-to, Bunkyo-ku, Honkomagom

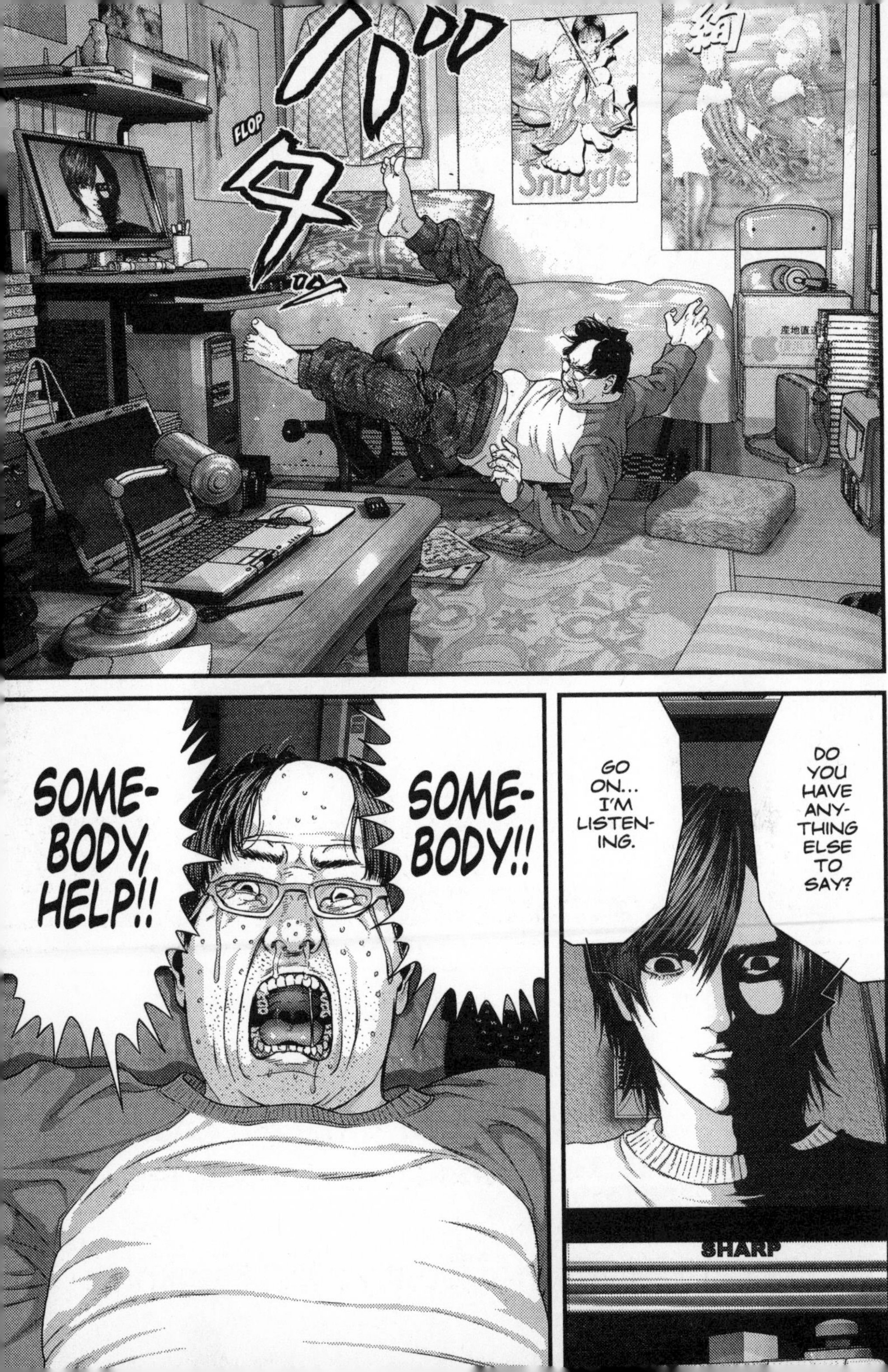
FLOP
Snuggle
DO YOU HAVE ANYTHING ELSE TO SAY?
GO ON... I'M LISTENING.
SHARP
SOME-BODY!!
SOME-BODY, HELP!!

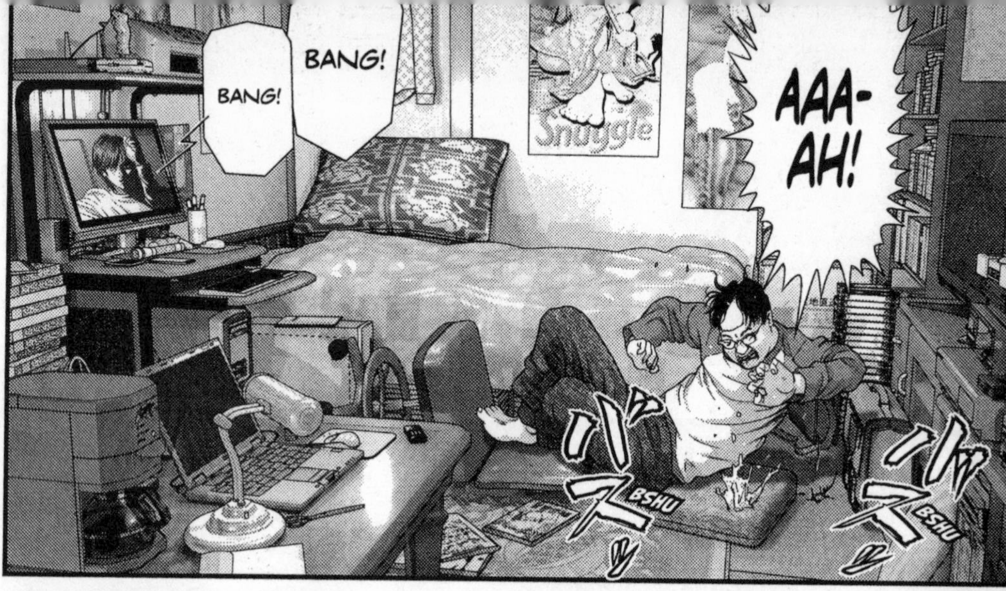
AAA-
AH!
BSHU
BSHU
Snuggle
BANG!
BANG!
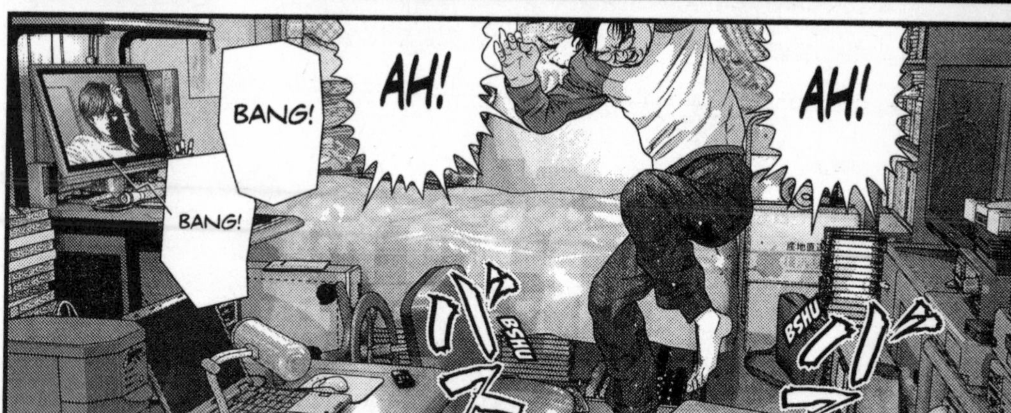
AH!
BSHU
AH!
BSHU
BANG!
BANG!
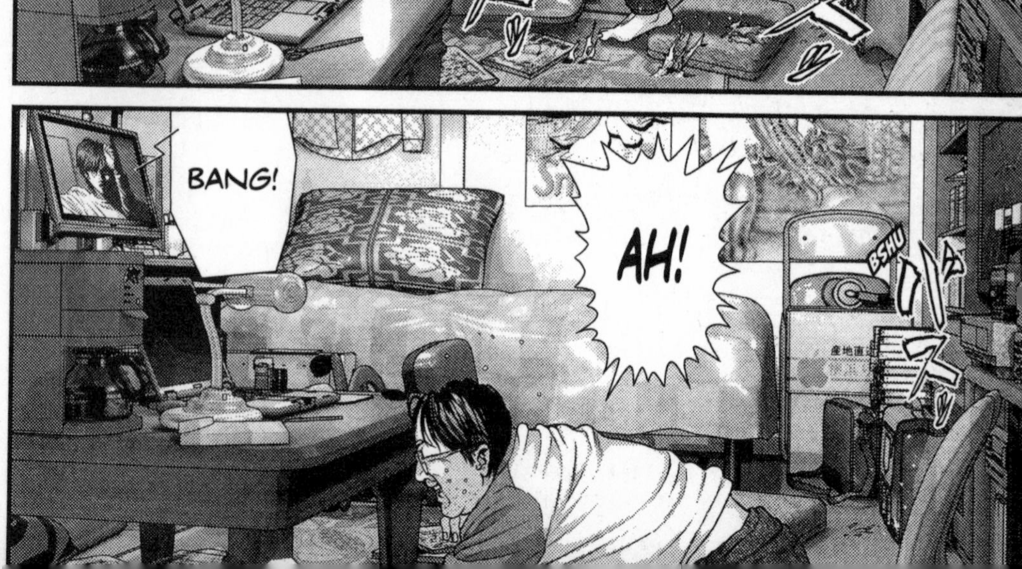
BSHU
AH!
BANG!

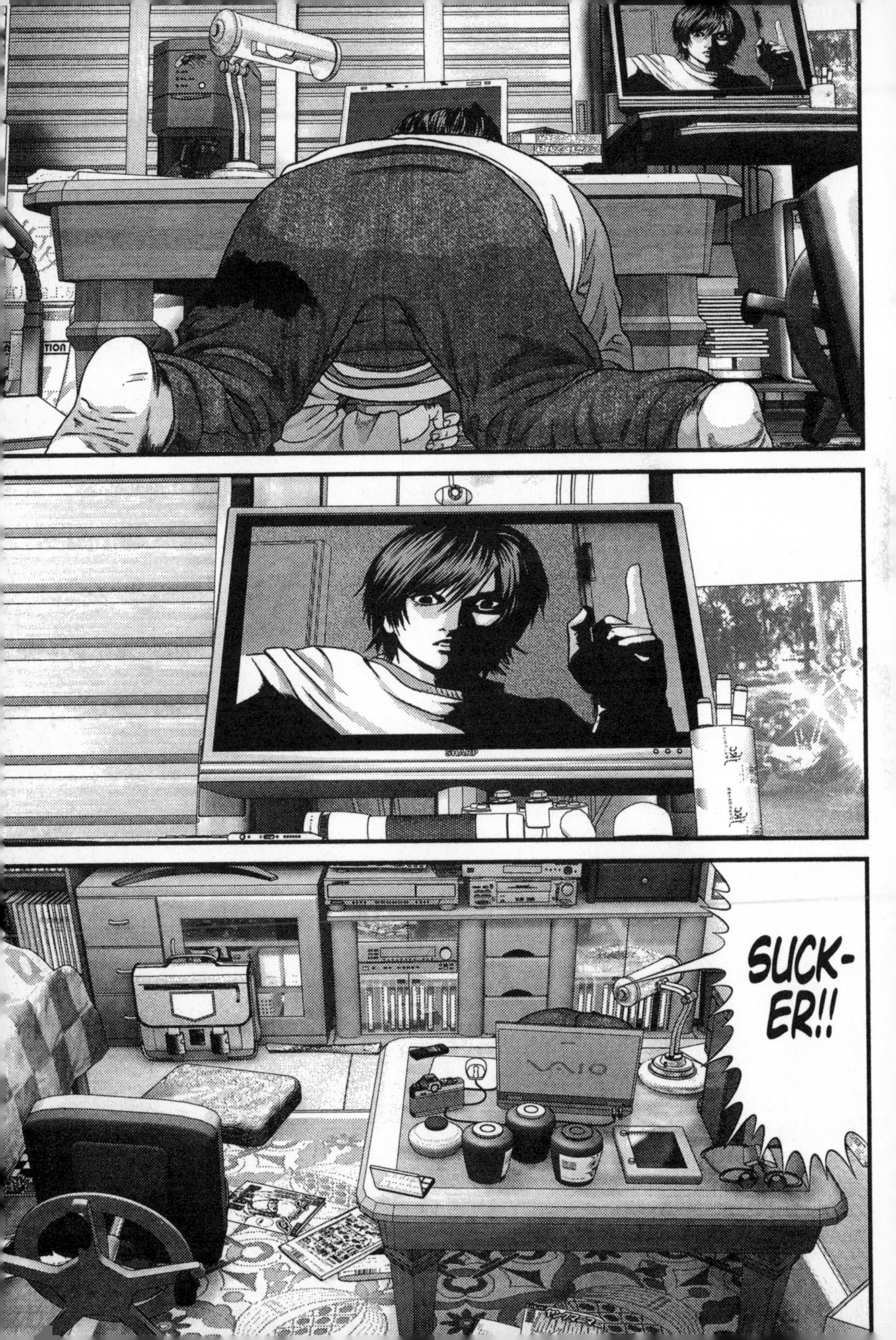
SUCK-
ER!!

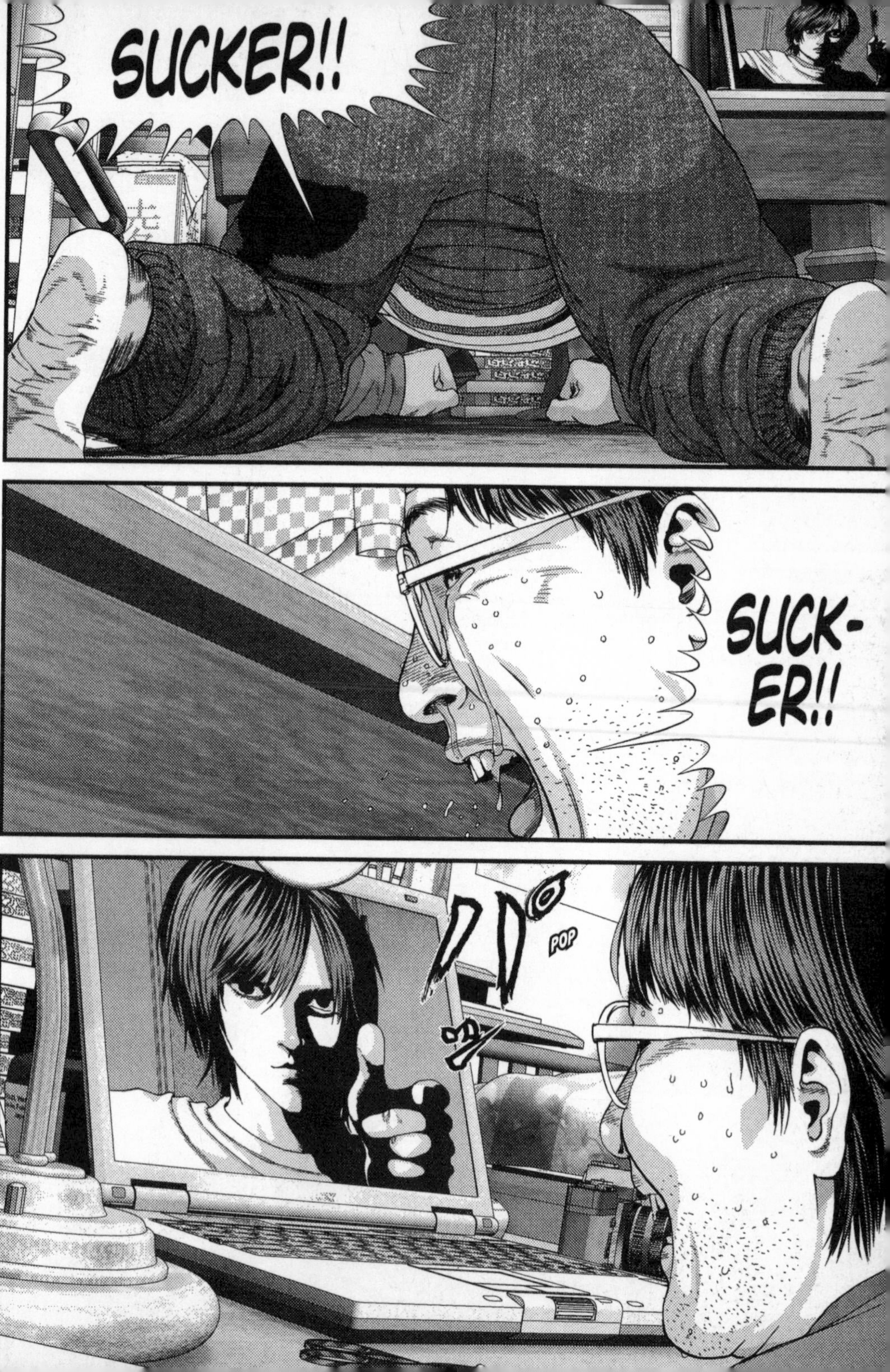
SUCKER!!
SUCK-ER!!
POP

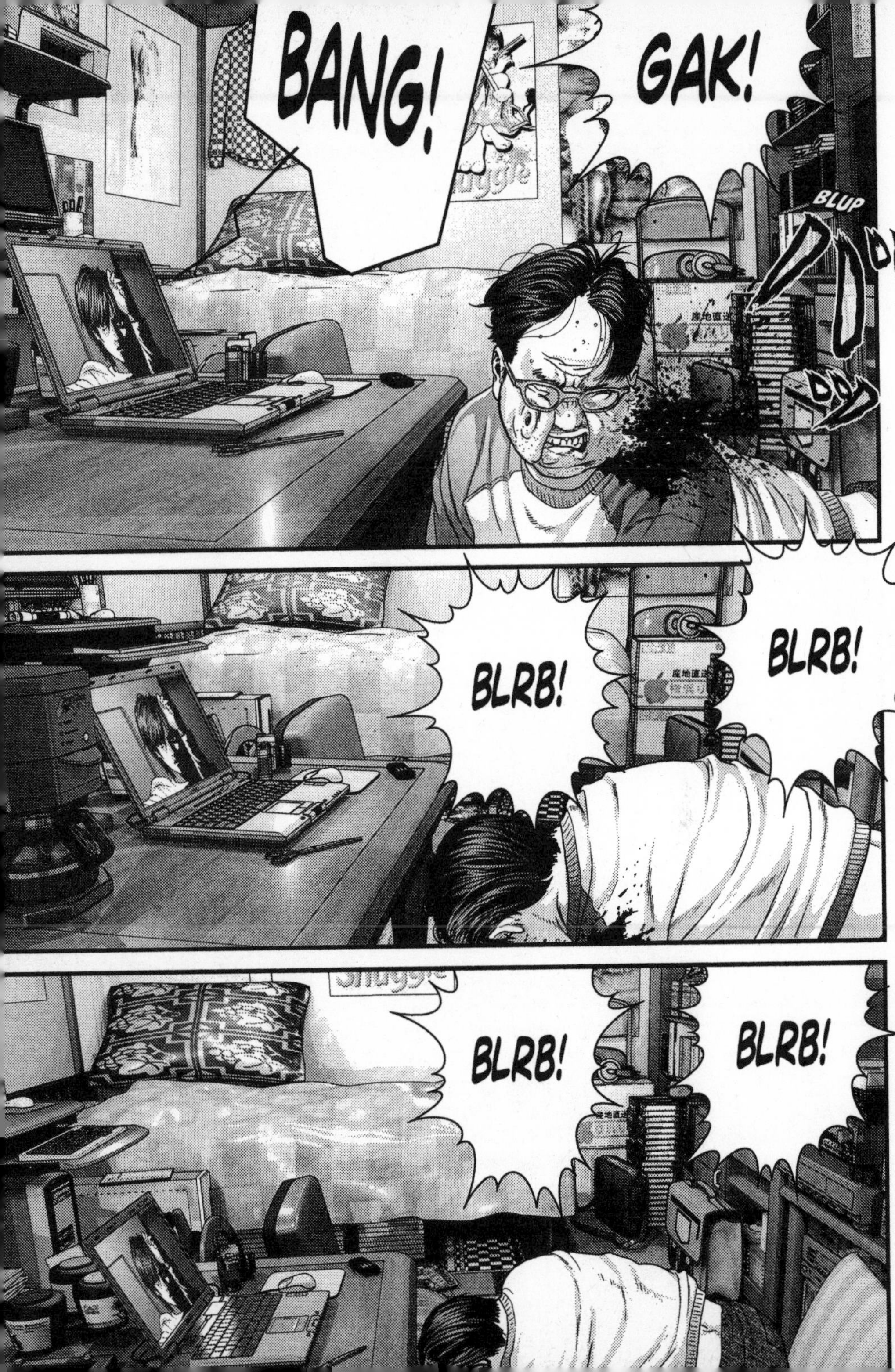
GAK!
BANG!
BLUP
BLRB!
BLRB!
BLRB!
BLRB!

475 2015/xx/xx(F)11:02:01.13 Dtawn5Gtk
VIP speaking for Anonymous sage

Where'd that guy go who said he would do us all?

476 2015/xx/xx(F)11:02:16.10 N7ghetkoQ
VIP speaking for Anonymous sage

Just some dumb-ass kid trolling

477 2015/xx/xx(F)11:02:35.04 Zik8Y7wpla
VIP speaking for Anonymous sage

Damn, just when I finally got excited about this
What a letdown

478 2015/xx/xx(F)11:03:23.07
Hiro Shishigami

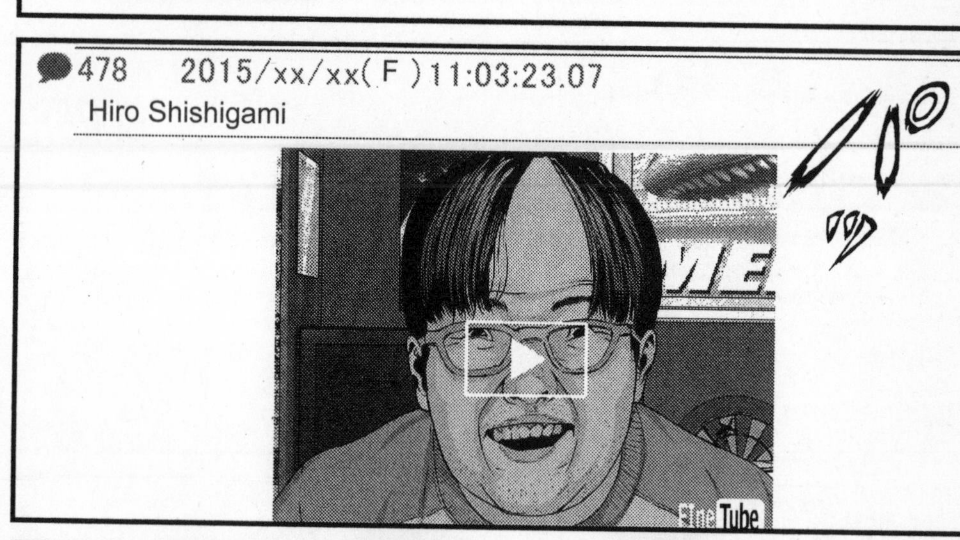
FineTube

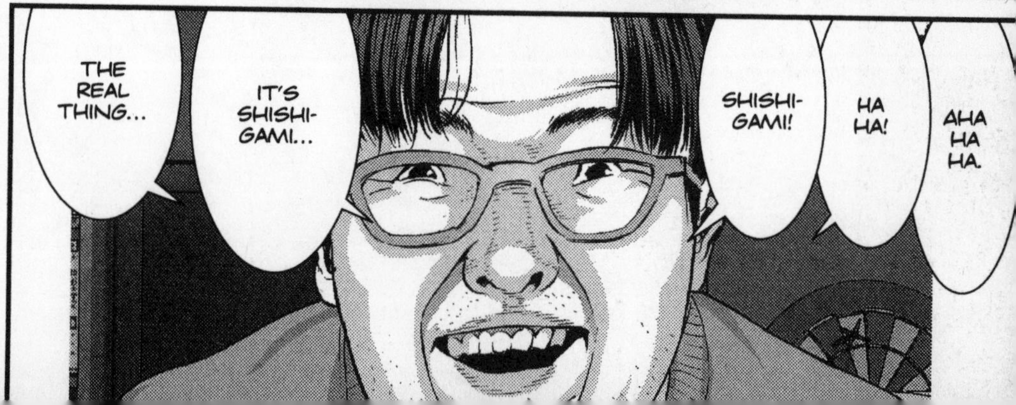
AHA HA HA.
HA HA!
SHISHI-GAMI!
IT'S SHISHI-GAMI...
THE REAL THING...

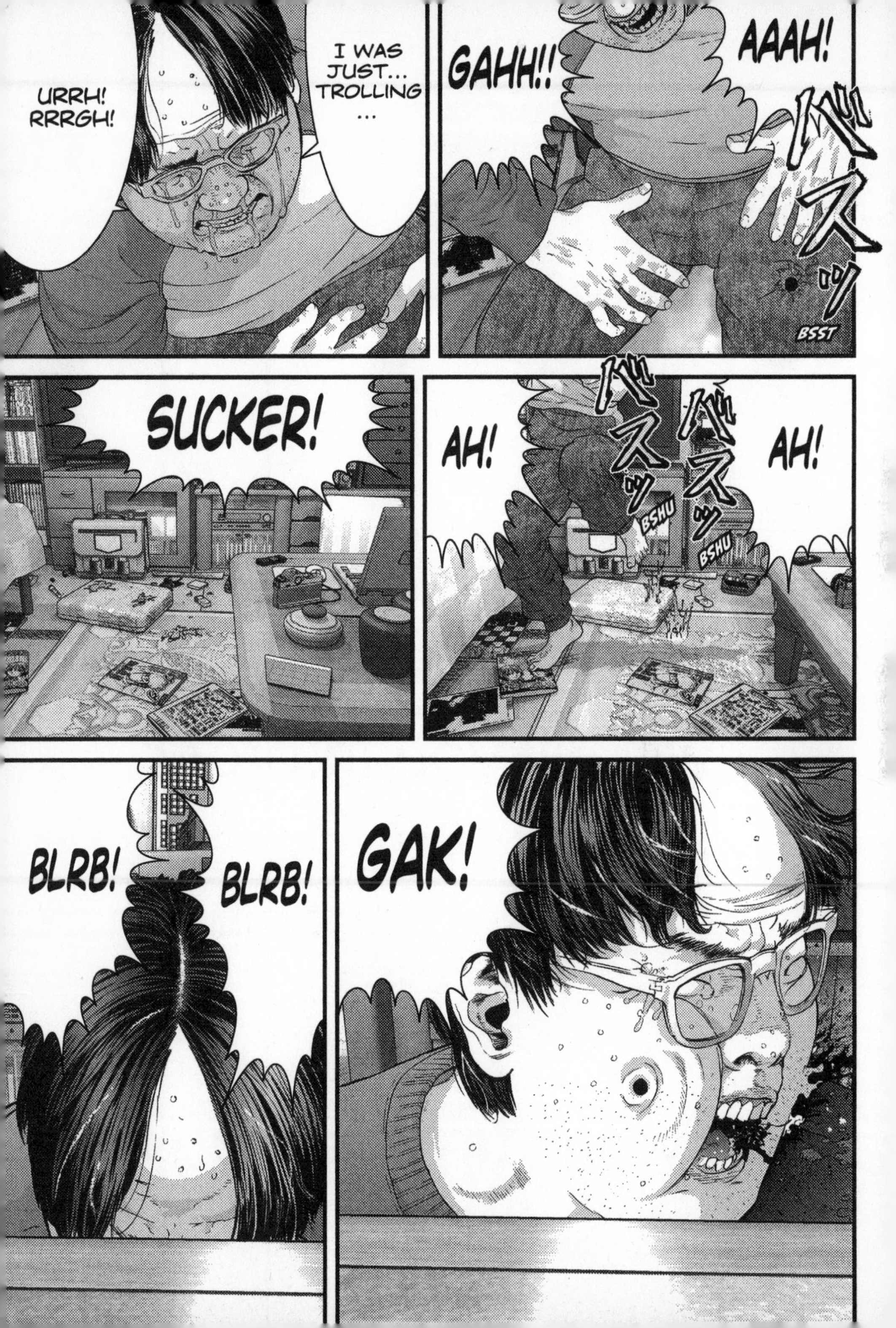
AAAH!
GAHH!!
バスッ
BSST
I WAS JUST... TROLLING ...
URRH! RRRGH!
AH!
バスッ
BSHU
バスッ
BSHU
AH!
SUCKER!
GAK!
BLRB!
BLRB!

💬479   2015/xx/xx(F)11:04:02.16   Y5ertAgfw
VIP speaking for Anonymous   sage

Damn, that scared me...
Got a chill down my back

↰480   2015/xx/xx(F)11:04:12.21   Aerio5Wpw
VIP speaking for Anonymous   sage

That's a weak shoop, I can tell from the pixels

💬481   2015/xx/xx(F)11:04:35.02   Zer8Ygwpa
VIP speaking for Anonymous   sage

Hmm. that was crazy

↰482   2015/xx/xx(F)11:04:52.03   SewrQ4nlm

💬483   2015/xx/xx(F)11:05:0
Hiro Shishigami

I will kill you in order,
starting from 2

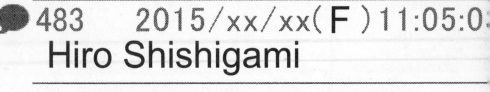

Wait your turns, all of you

CHAPTER 39: END

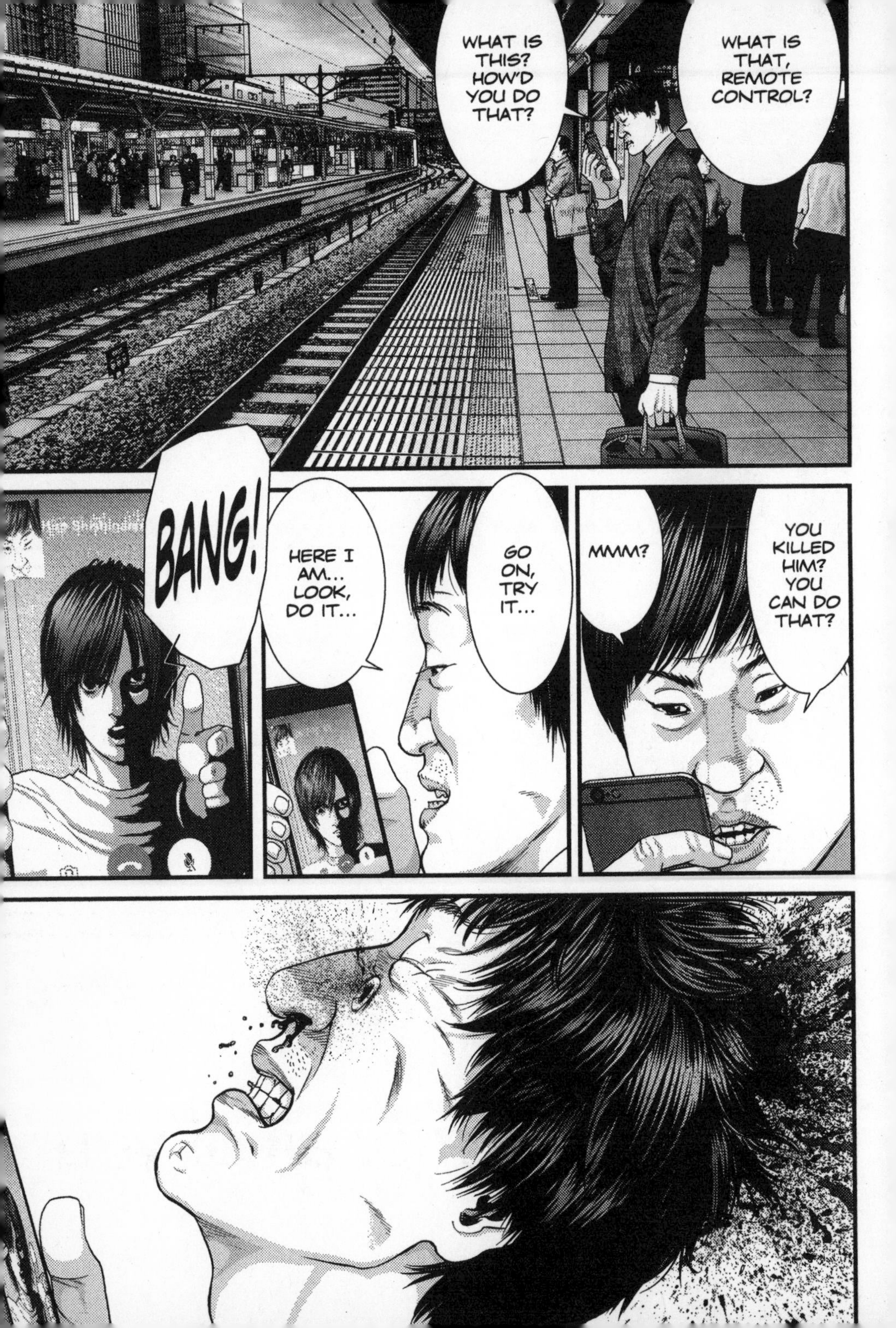
WHAT IS THAT, REMOTE CONTROL?
WHAT IS THIS? HOW'D YOU DO THAT?
YOU KILLED HIM? YOU CAN DO THAT?
MMM?
GO ON, TRY IT...
HERE I AM... LOOK, DO IT...
BANG!

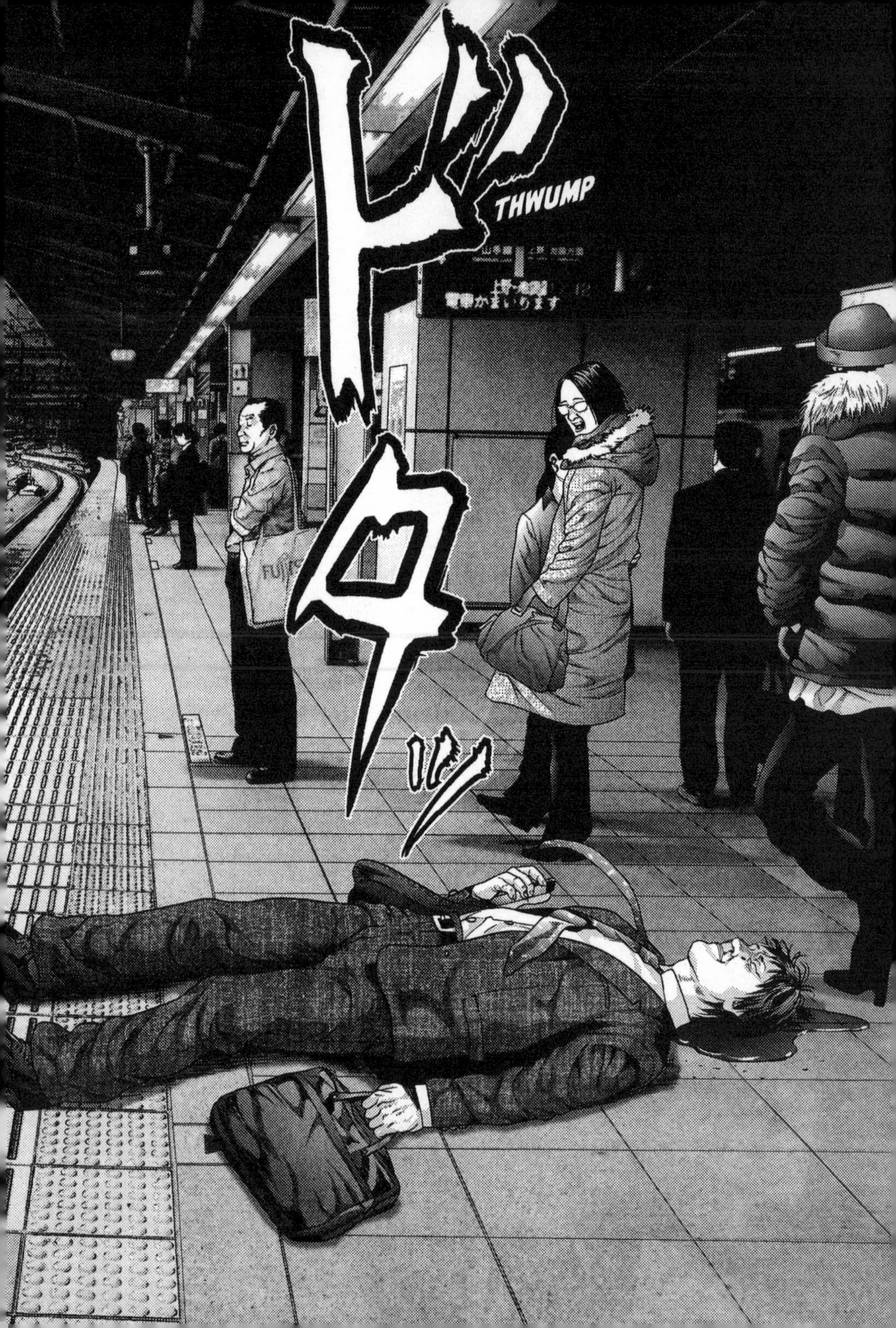
ドタッ
THWUMP

CHAPTER 40: IS 3 ALIVE?

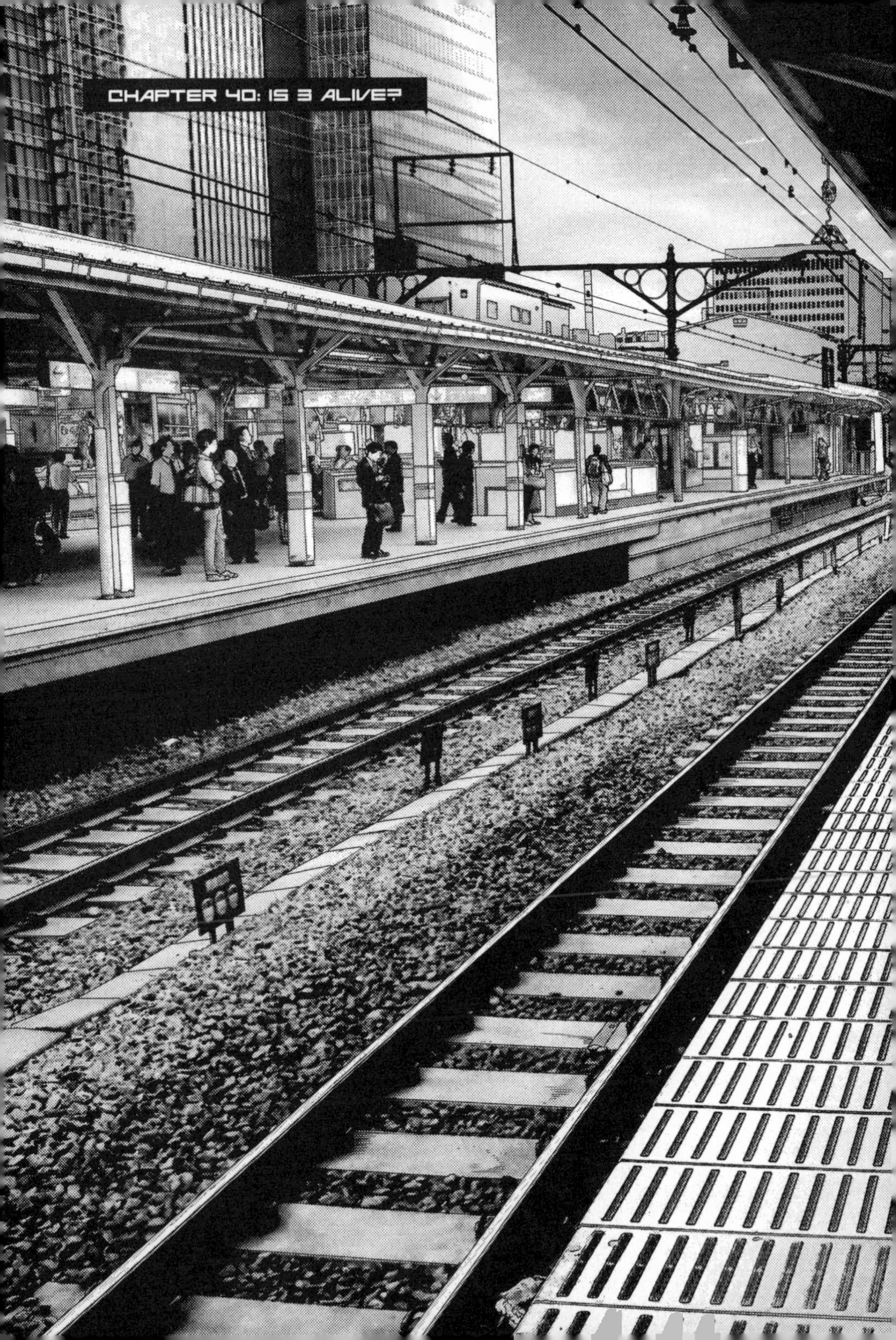

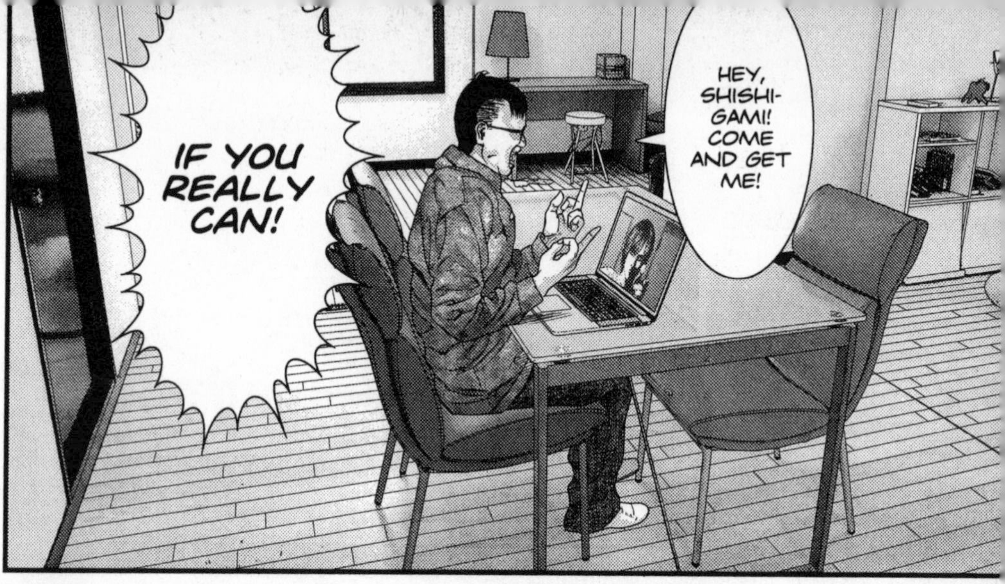
HEY, SHISHI-GAMI! COME AND GET ME!
IF YOU REALLY CAN!
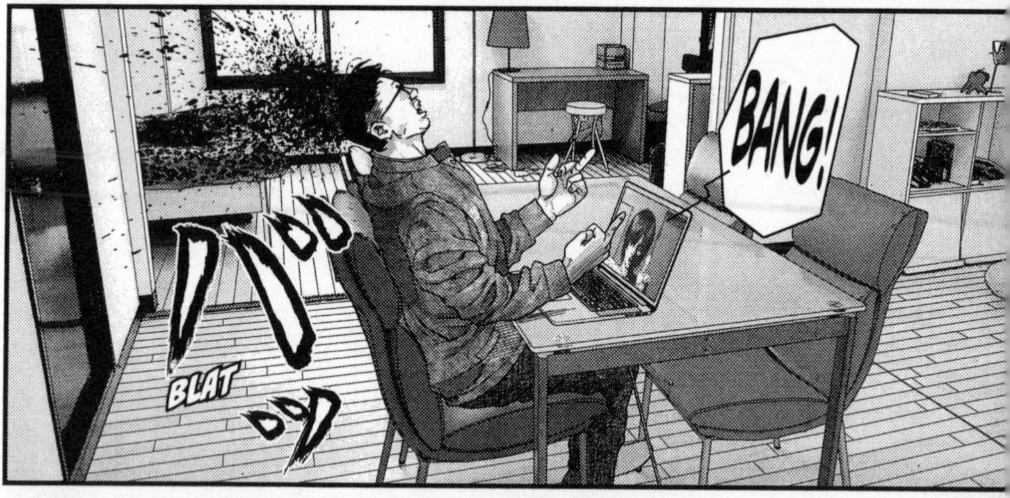
BANG!
BLAT
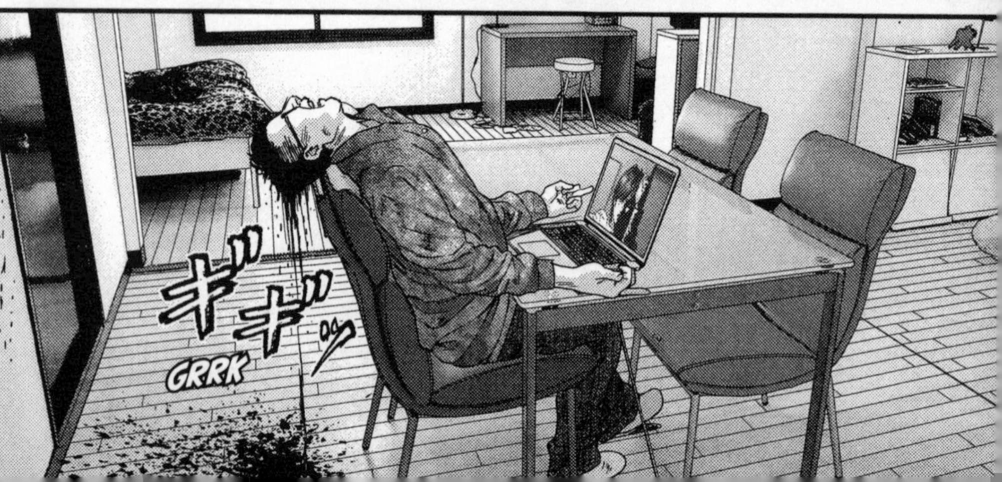
GRRK

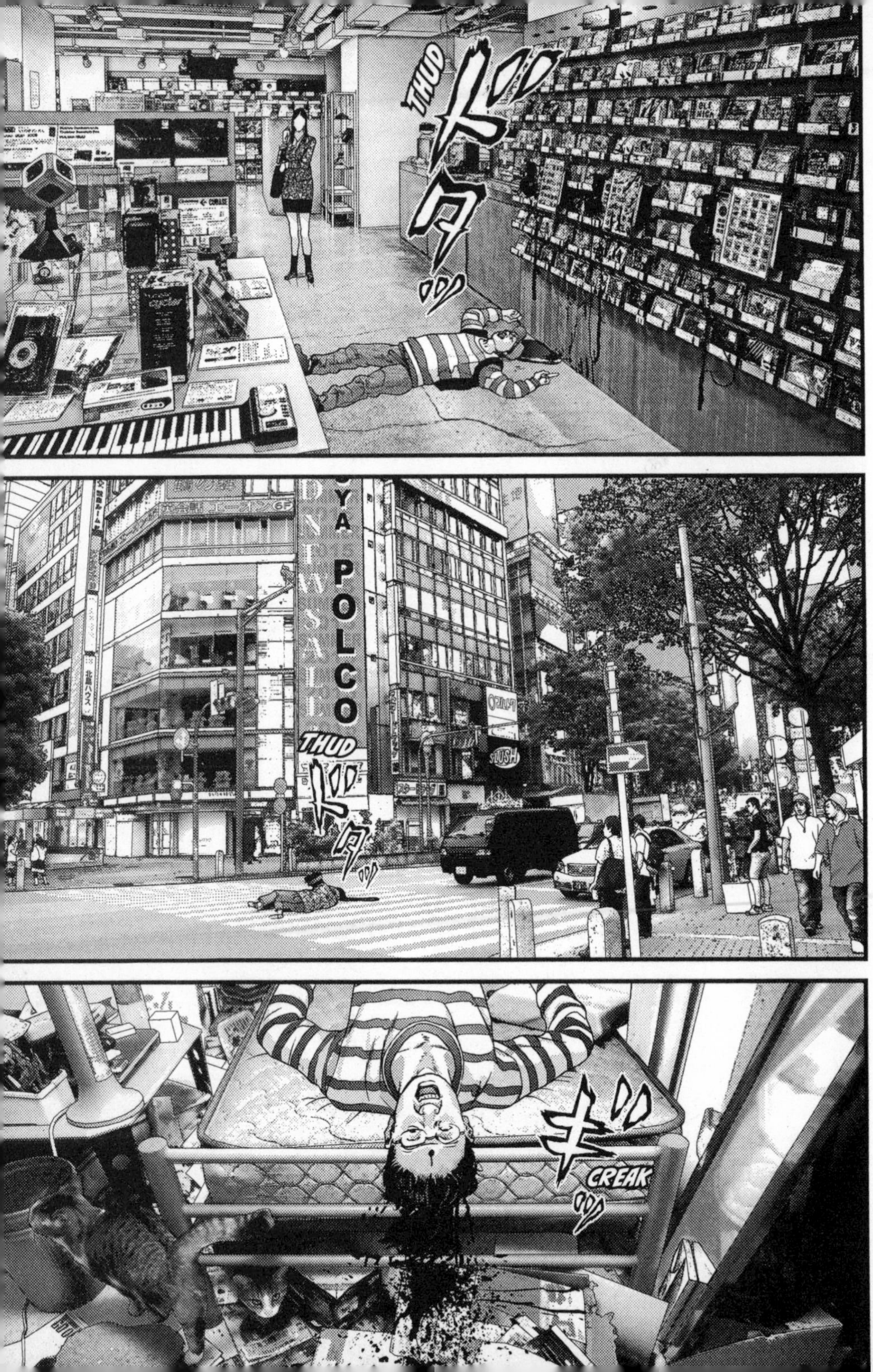
THUD
THUD
CREAK

495   2015/xx/xx(F)11:07:12.24   Y5ertAgfw
   VIP speaking for Anonymous   sage

>>2 you dead?

496   2015/xx/xx(F)11:08:20.53   Aerio5Wpw
   VIP speaking for Anonymous   sage

He can't answer you if he's dead lol

497   2015/xx/xx(F)11:09:25.28   Zer8Ygwpa
   VIP speaking for Anonymous   sage

Hey, 2!
Honest…I'm freakin out over here, lolol

498   2015/xx/xx(F)11:011:18.33   Y5ertAgfw

AAAAH!
AAAAH!
I'M
SORRY!
I'M
SORRY!

498   2015/xx/xx(F)11:011:

VIP speaking for Anonymous

And 3? Is 3 alive?

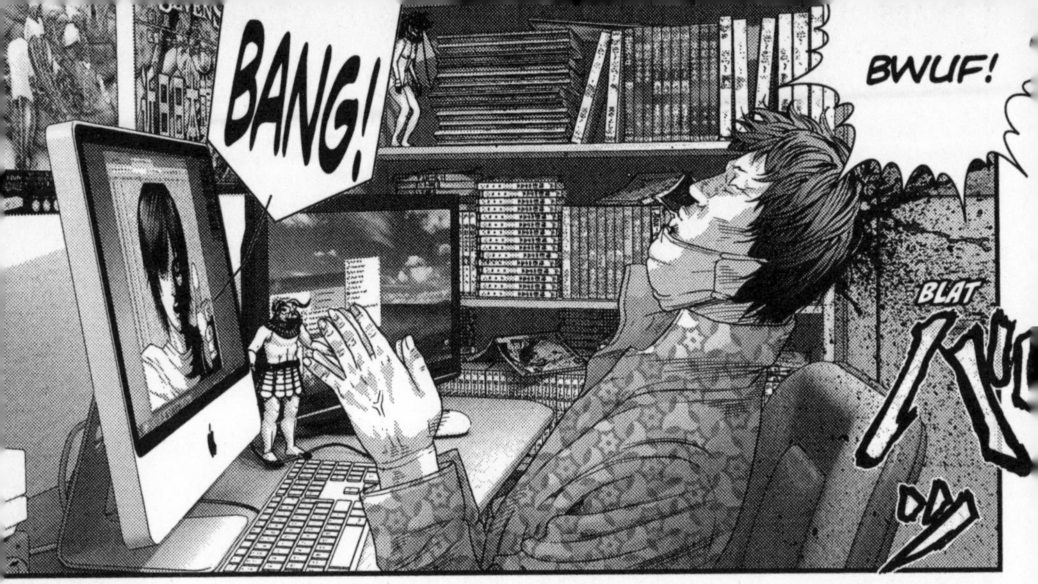
BWUF!
BANG!
BLAT

501 2015/xx/xx(F)11:12:40.58

VIP speaking for Anonymous

Yaaaaaaaaah!
Come at me Shishigami
I'm a 3rd degree karate master gonna whup that ass

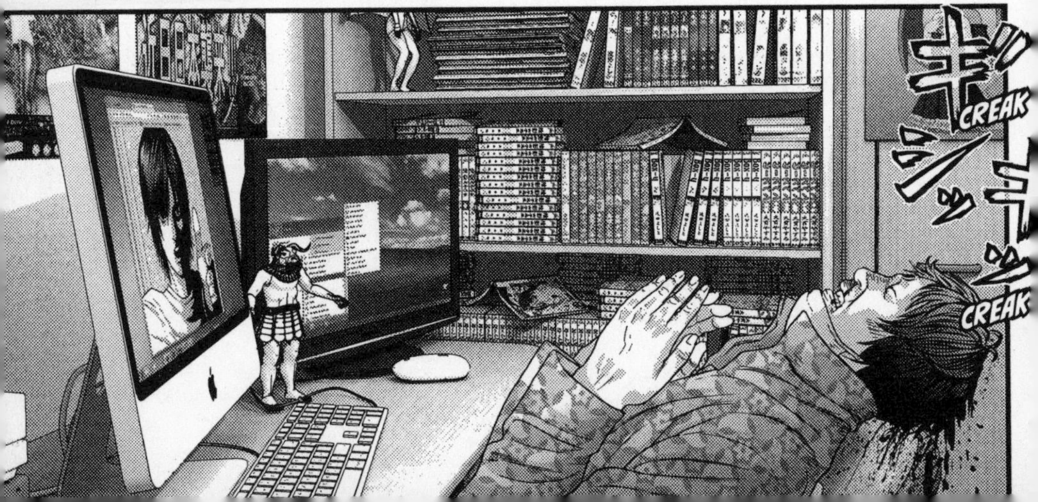
CREAK
CREAK

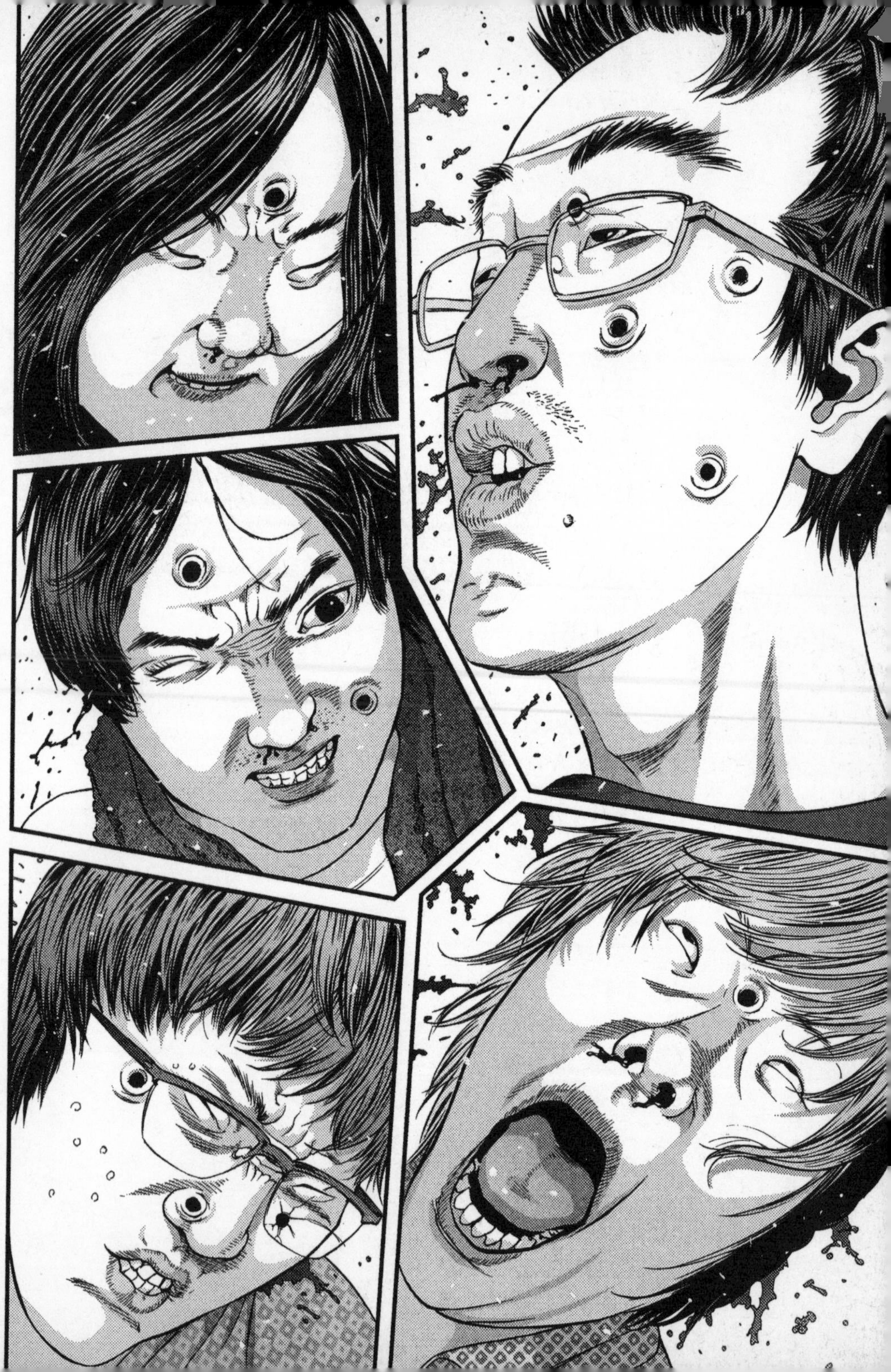

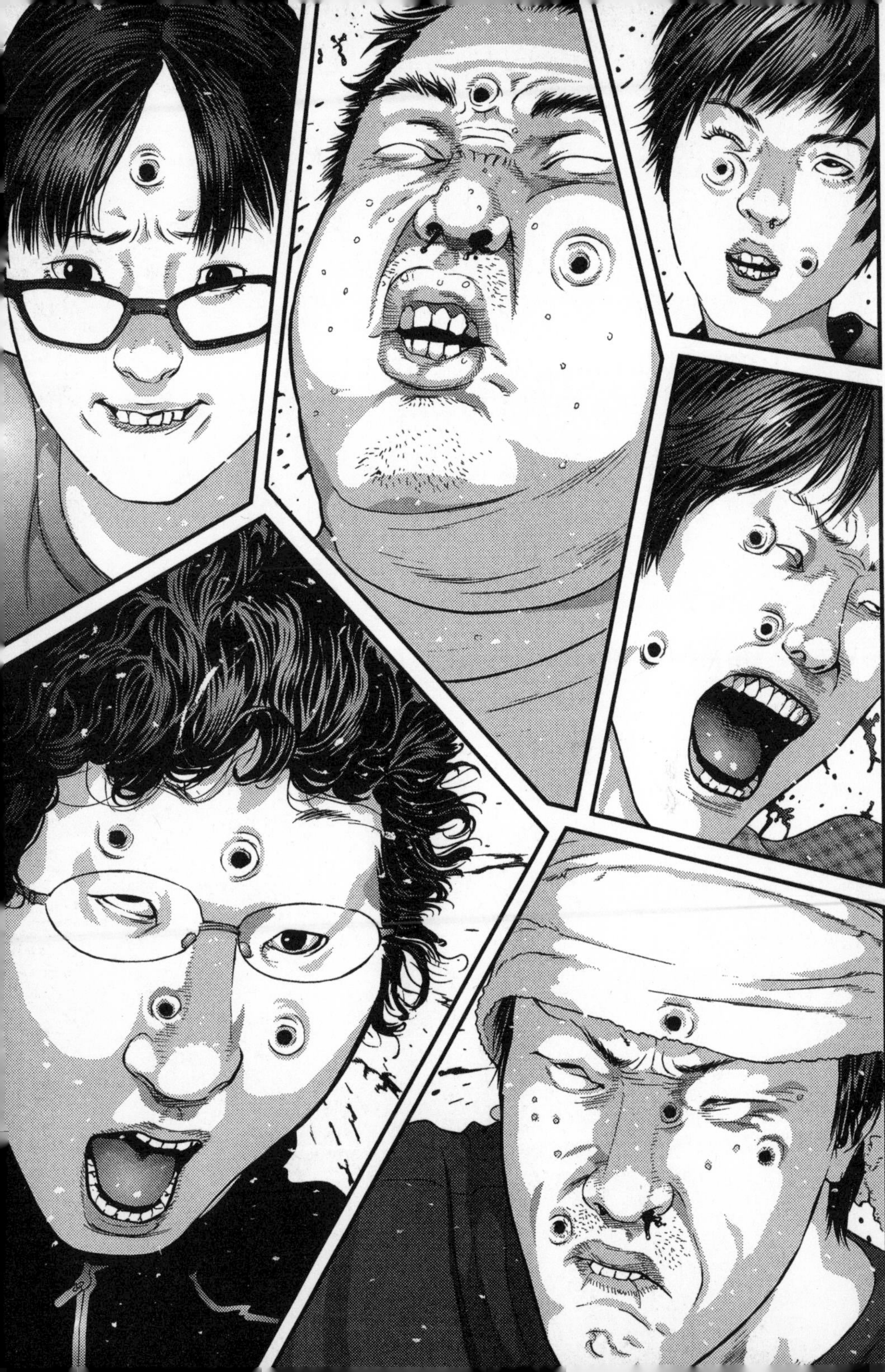

521   2015/xx/xx(F)11:14:25.17
VIP speaking for Anonymous

…What's going on?
Is this real… What? What? lol

522   2015/xx/xx(F)11:15:42.08
VIP speaking for Anonymous

fnkqwttttttttttttttttttttttttttttttttttttttttttttttttttttttttttttttttttttttttttttttttt
tttttttttttttttttttttttttttttttttttttttttttttttttttttttttttttttttttttttttttttttttttttttt

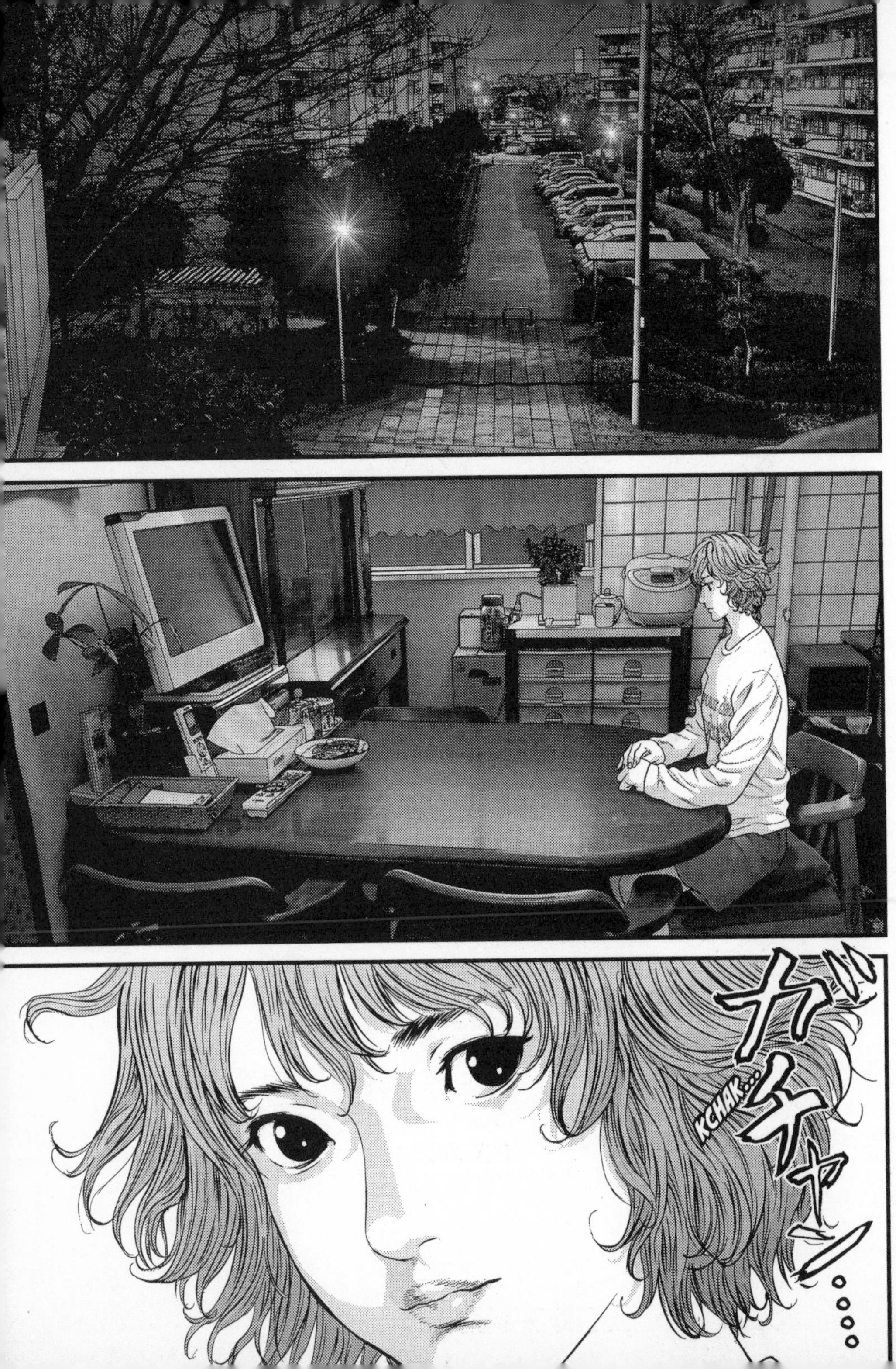
KCHAK...

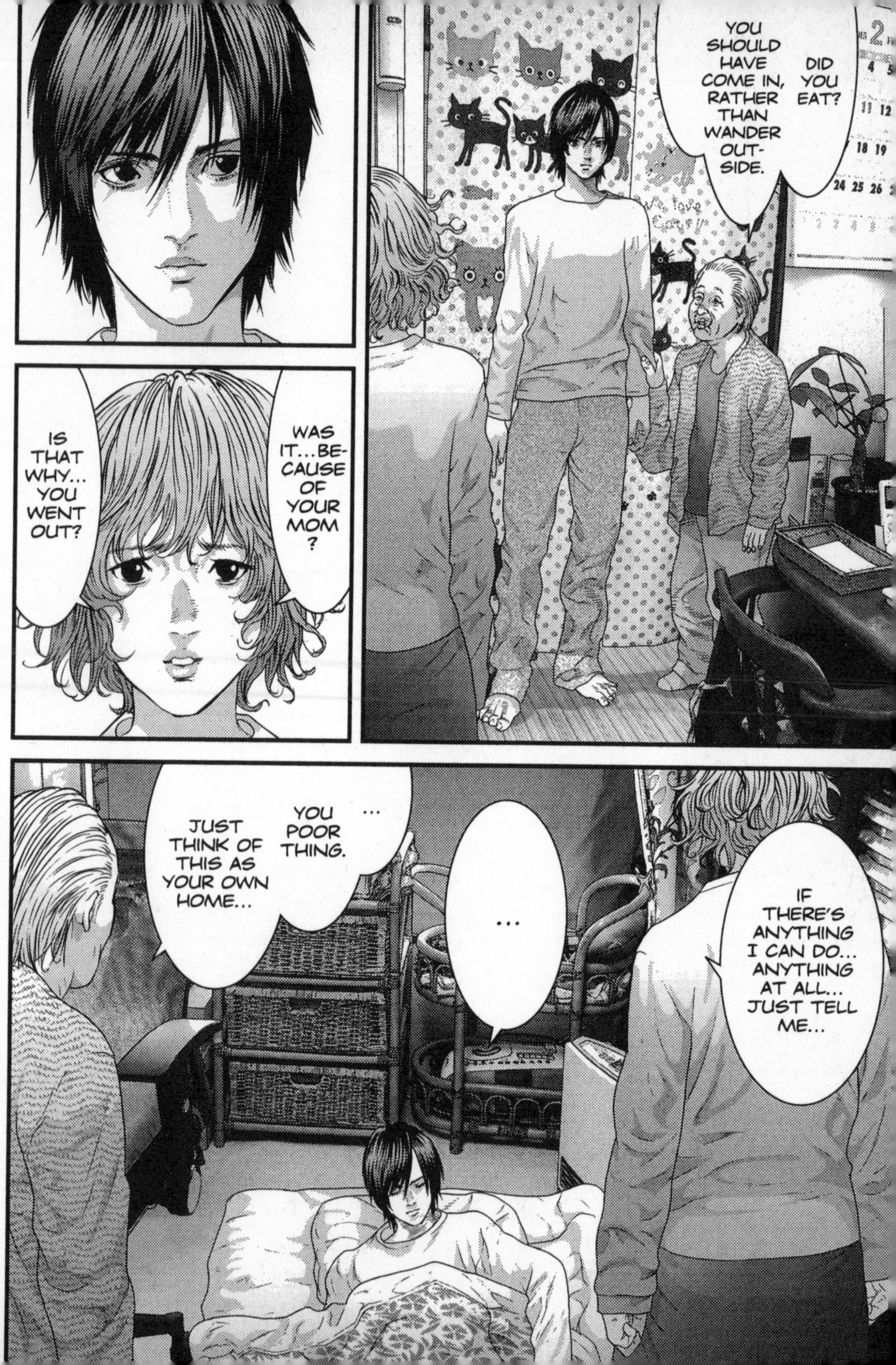
DID YOU EAT?
YOU SHOULD HAVE COME IN, RATHER THAN WANDER OUT-SIDE.
WAS IT...BE-CAUSE OF YOUR MOM?
IS THAT WHY... YOU WENT OUT?
IF THERE'S ANYTHING I CAN DO... ANYTHING AT ALL... JUST TELL ME...
...
...
YOU POOR THING.
JUST THINK OF THIS AS YOUR OWN HOME...

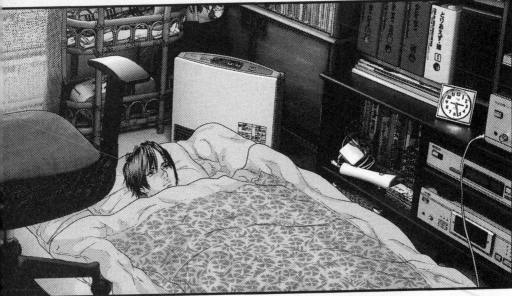

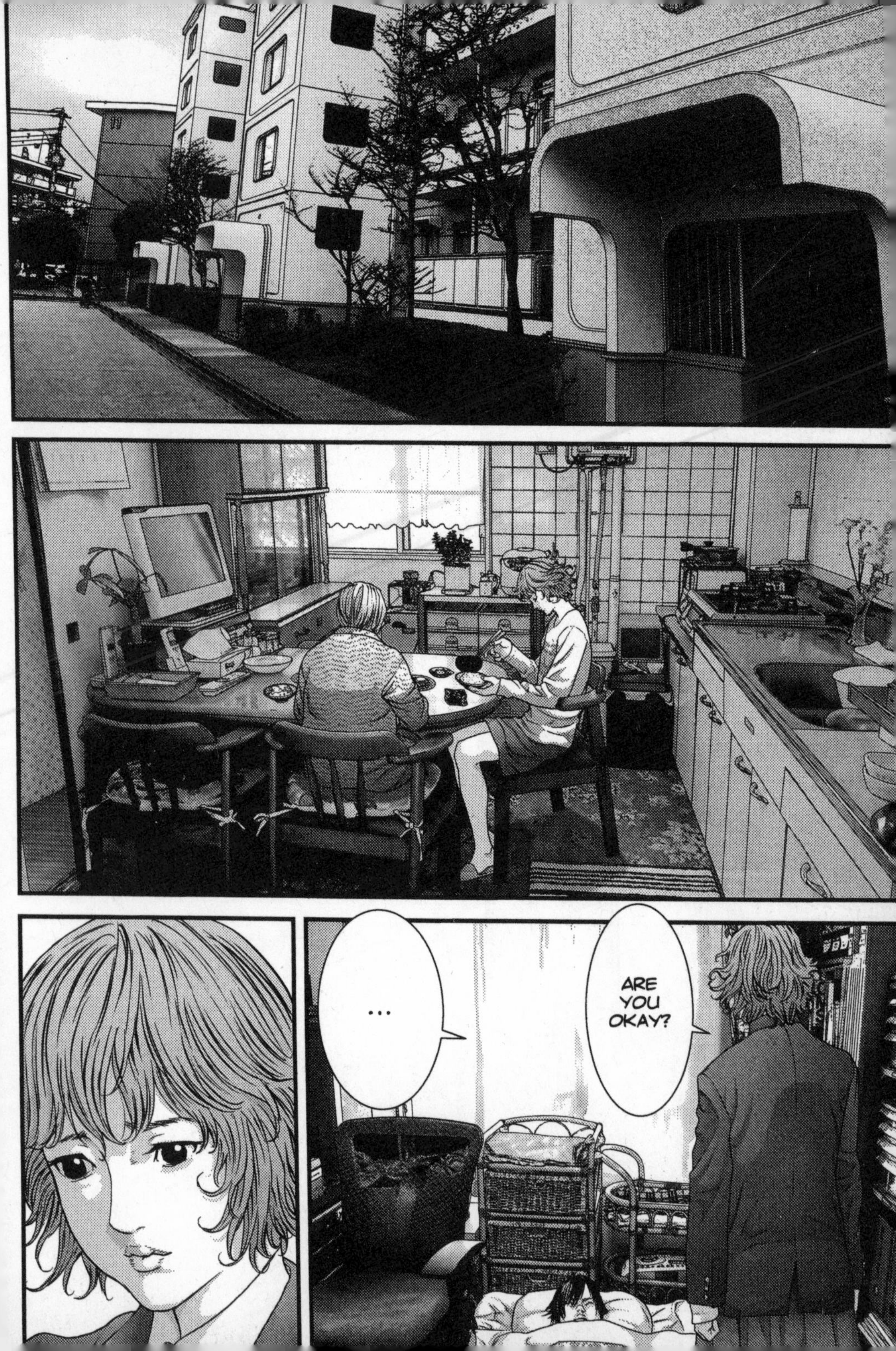
ARE YOU OKAY?
...

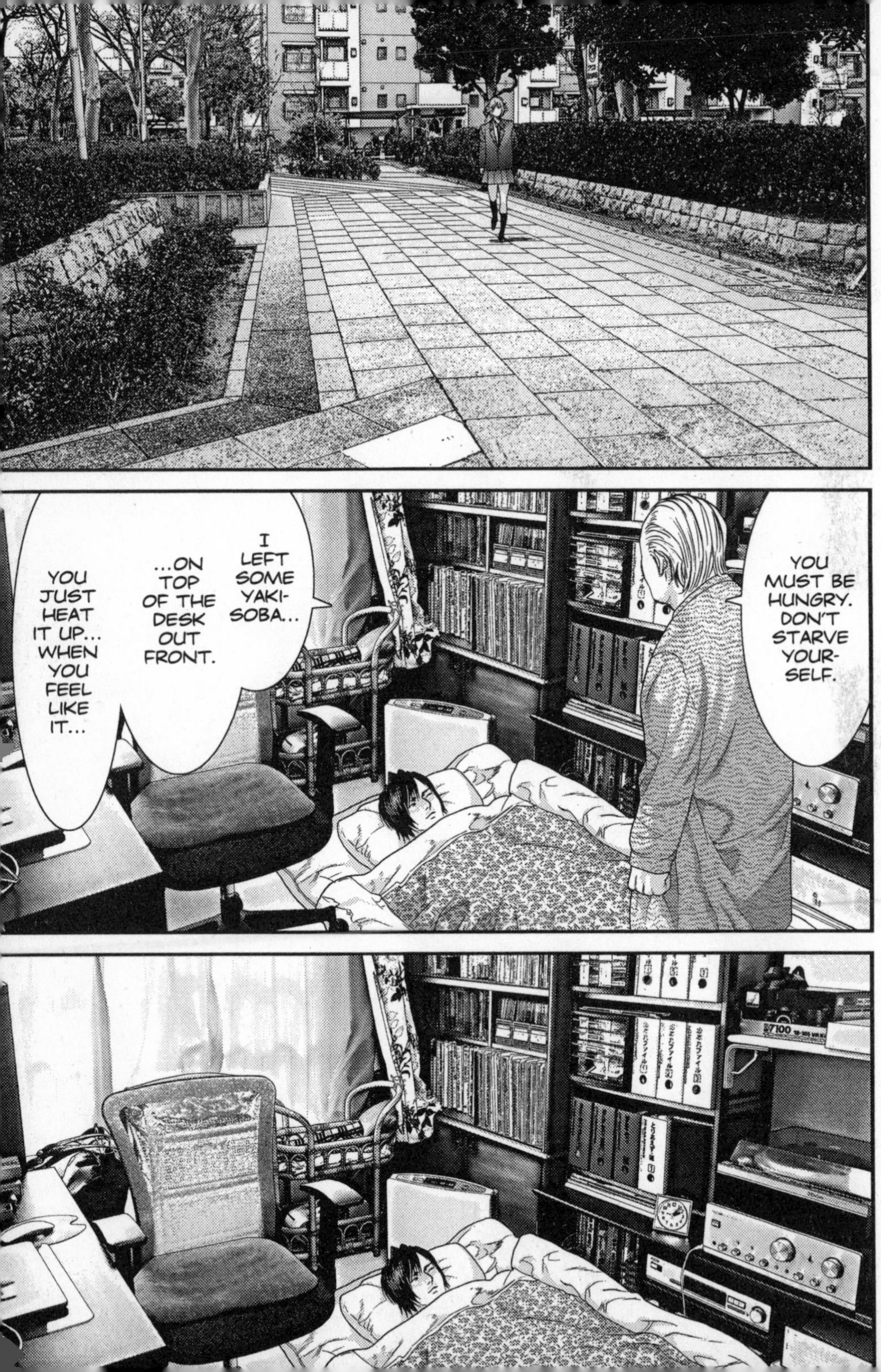
...
YOU MUST BE HUNGRY. DON'T STARVE YOURSELF.
I LEFT SOME YAKI-SOBA...
...ON TOP OF THE DESK OUT FRONT.
YOU JUST HEAT IT UP... WHEN YOU FEEL LIKE IT...

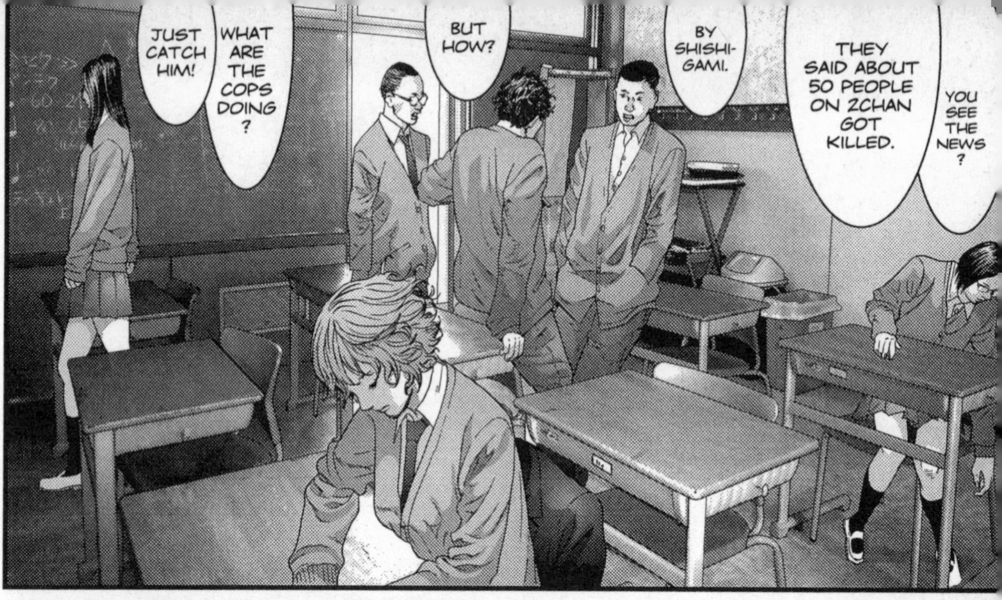
YOU SEE THE NEWS?
THEY SAID ABOUT 50 PEOPLE ON 2CHAN GOT KILLED.
BY SHISHI-GAMI.
BUT HOW?
WHAT ARE THE COPS DOING?
JUST CATCH HIM!

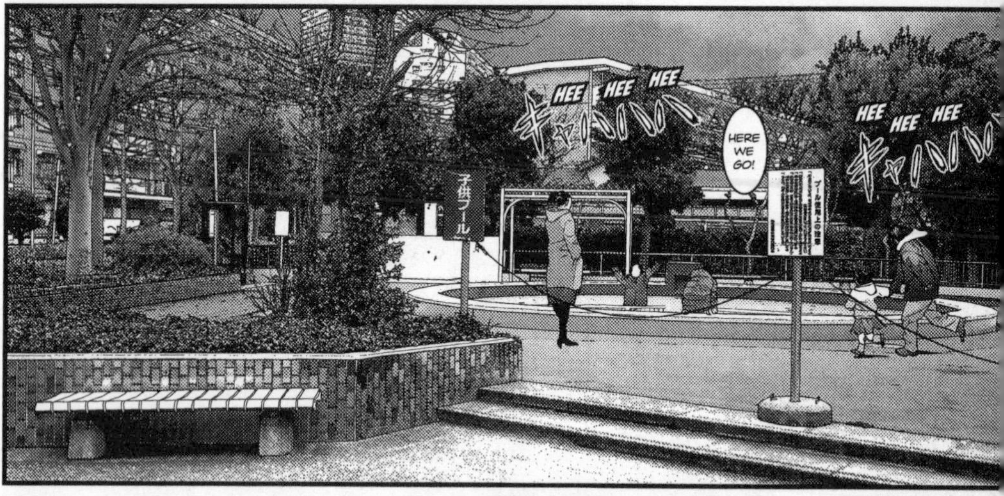
HEE HEE HEE
HERE WE GO!
HEE HEE HEE
子供プール

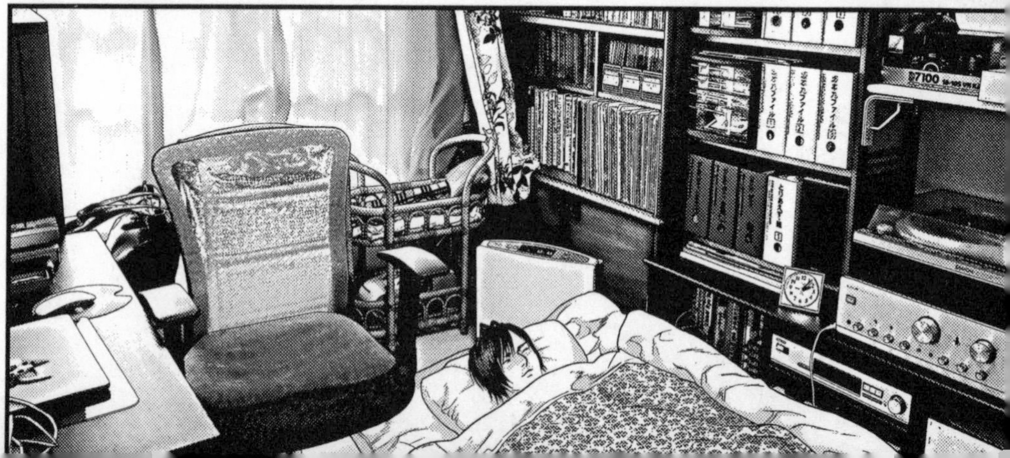

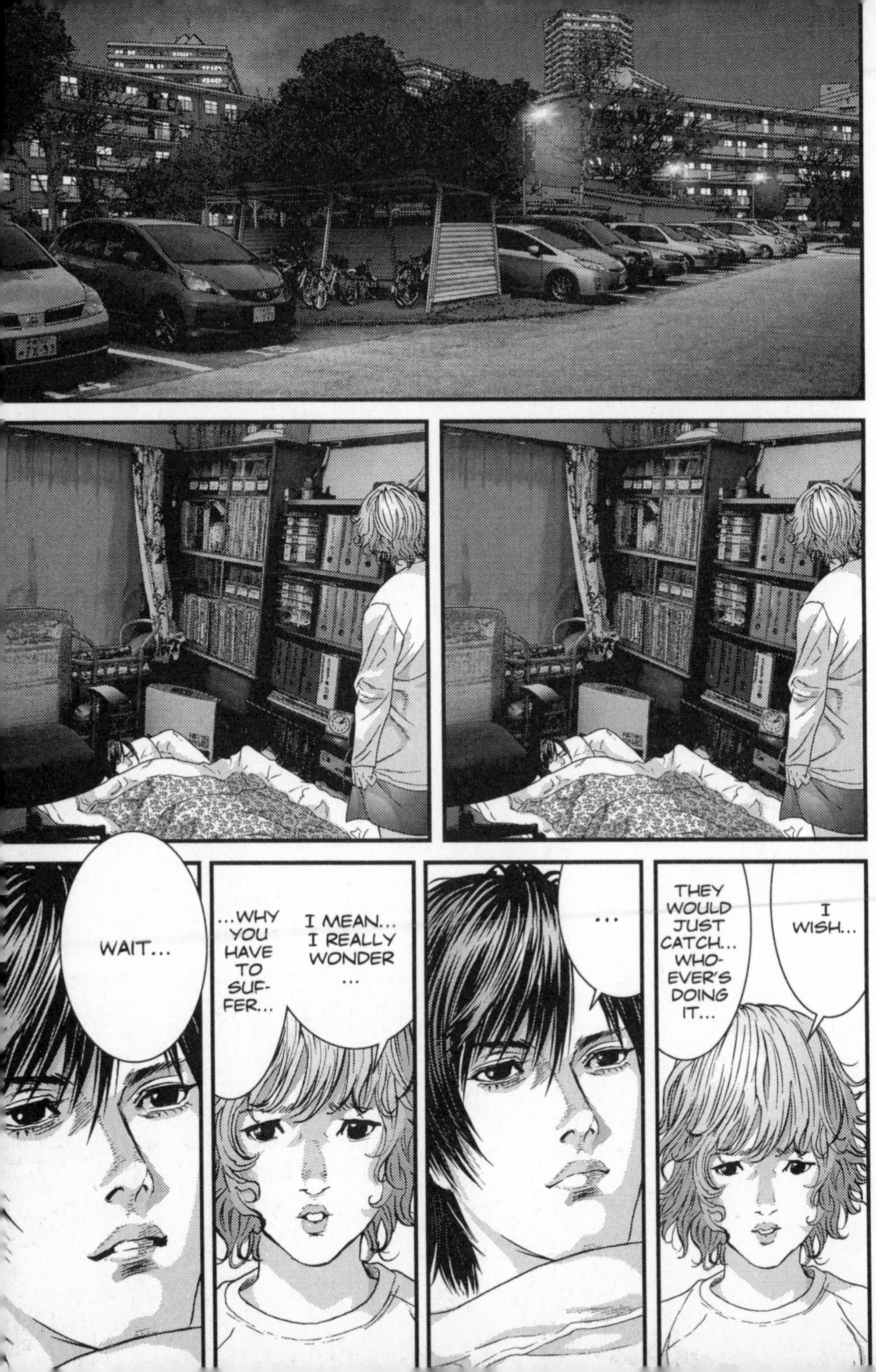
I WISH...
THEY WOULD JUST CATCH... WHO-EVER'S DOING IT...
...
I MEAN... I REALLY WONDER...
...WHY YOU HAVE TO SUF-FER...
WAIT...

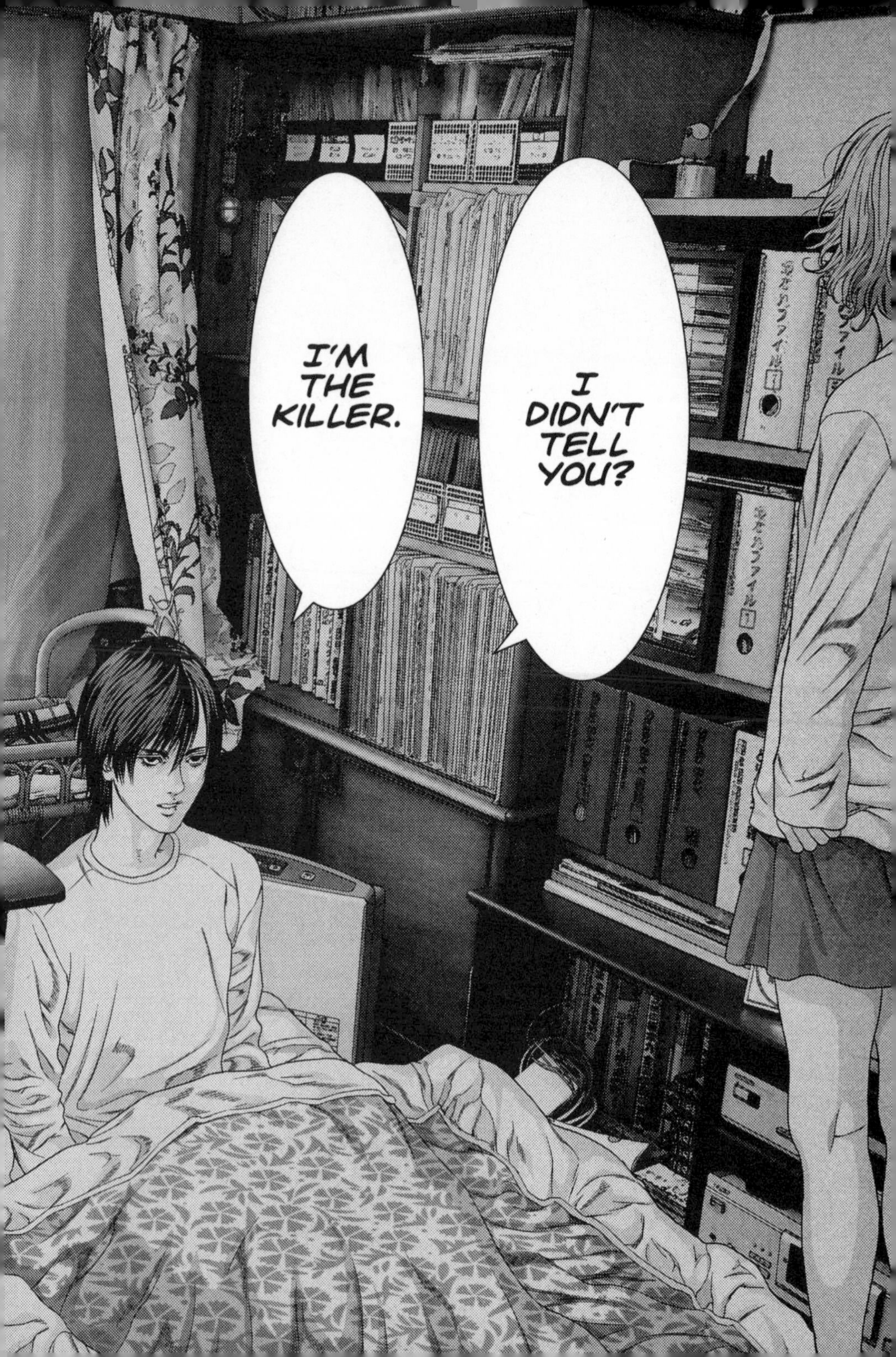
I DIDN'T TELL YOU?
I'M THE KILLER.

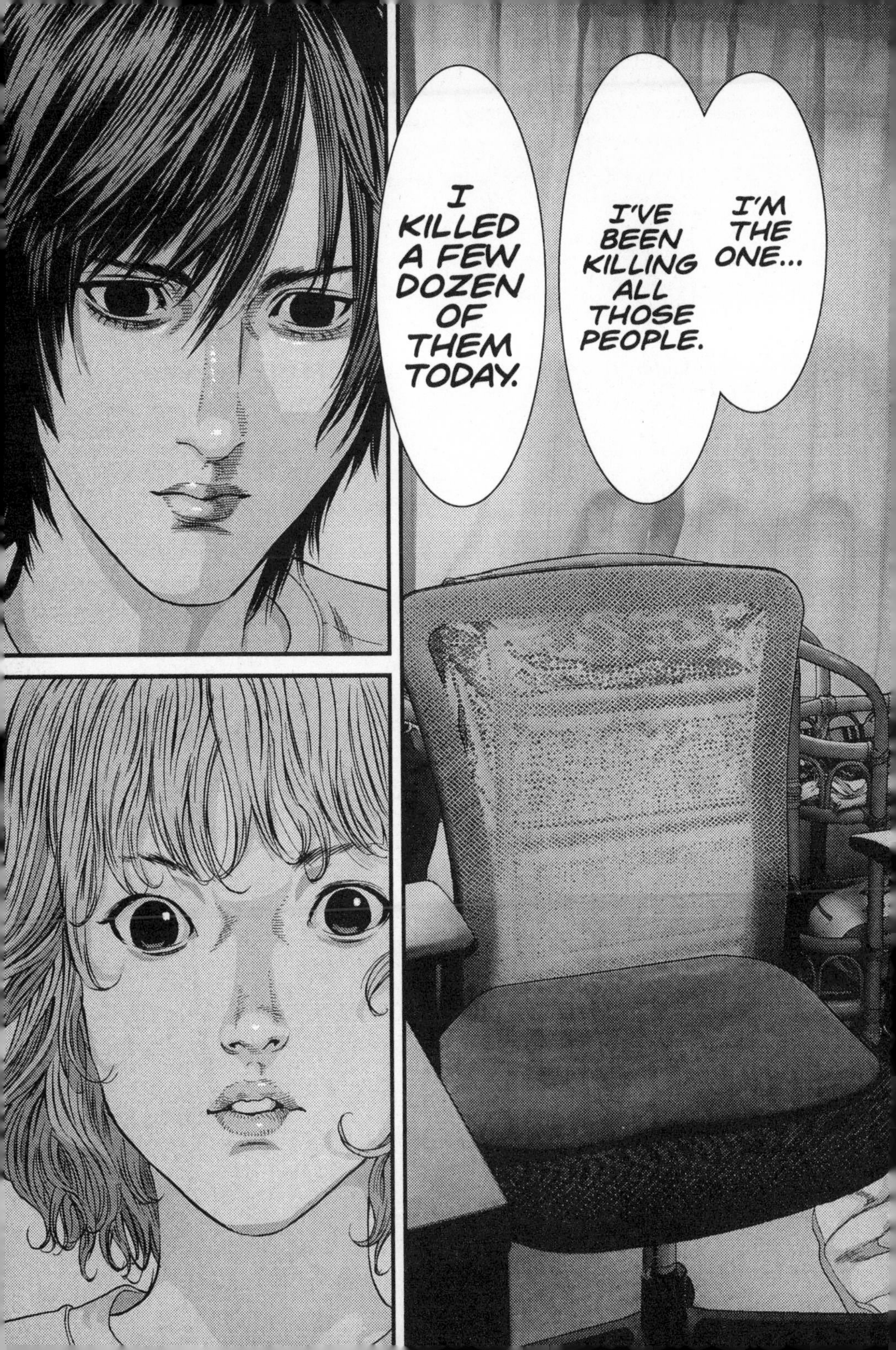
I'M THE ONE...
I'VE BEEN KILLING ALL THOSE PEOPLE.
I KILLED A FEW DOZEN OF THEM TODAY.

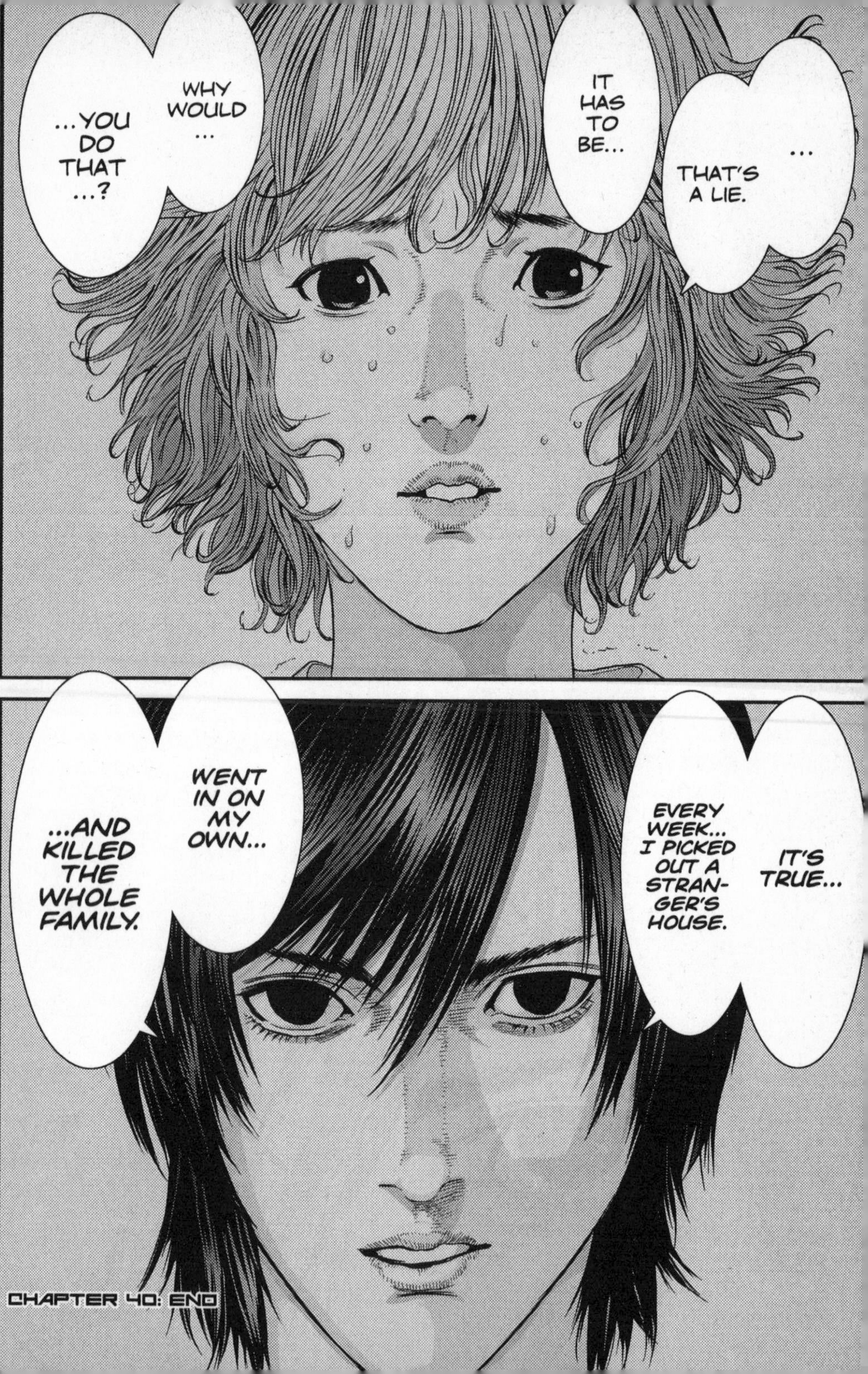
... THAT'S A LIE.
IT HAS TO BE...
WHY WOULD ...
...YOU DO THAT ...?
IT'S TRUE...
EVERY WEEK... I PICKED OUT A STRANGER'S HOUSE.
WENT IN ON MY OWN...
...AND KILLED THE WHOLE FAMILY.
CHAPTER 40: END

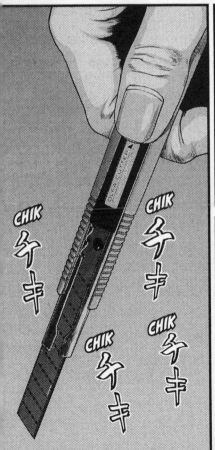

CHIK CHIK CHIK

チキ チキ チキ

チキ

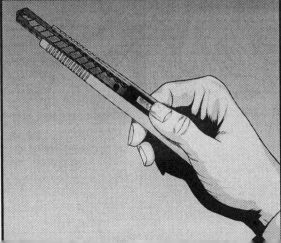

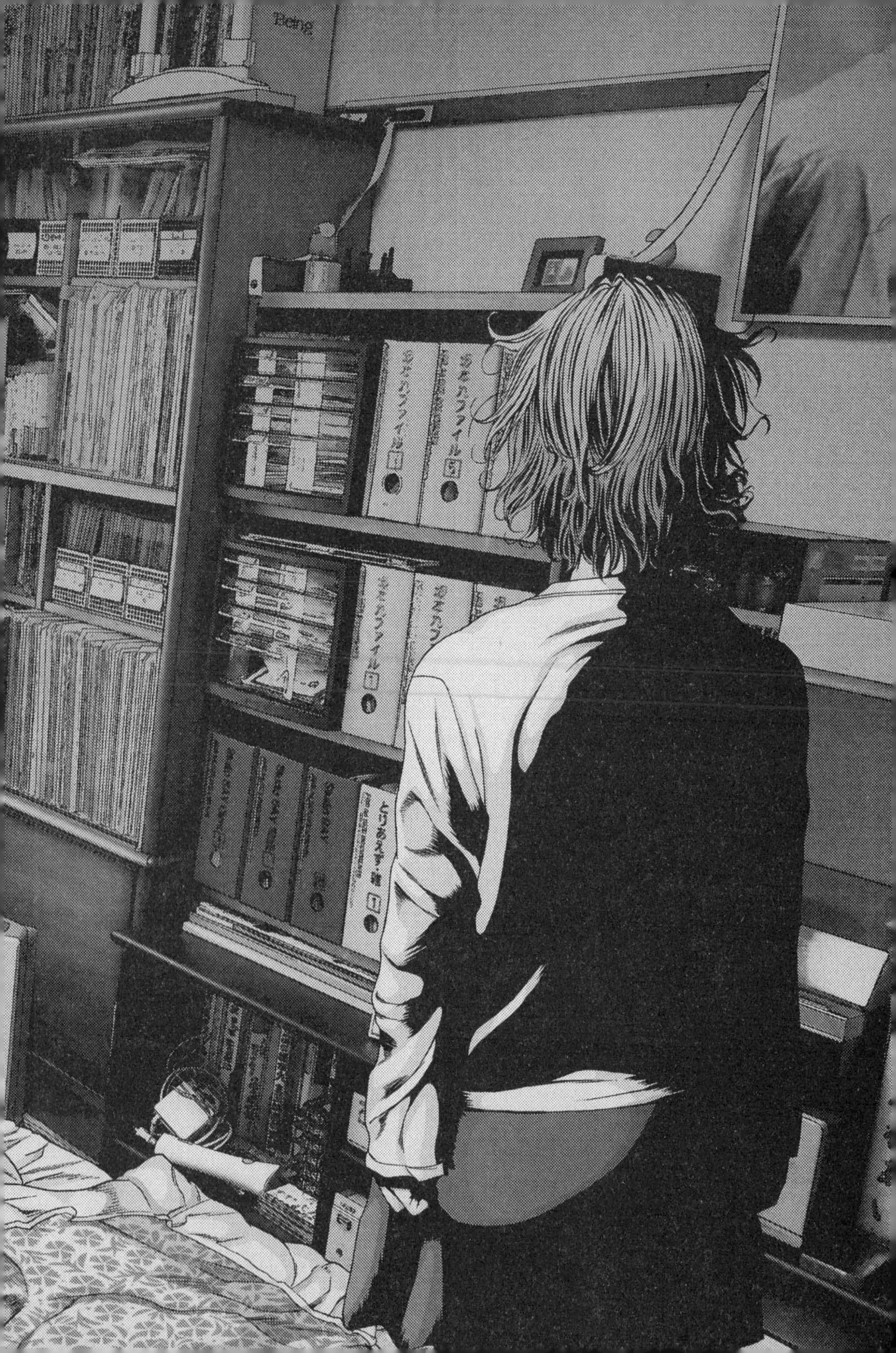
Being
とりあえず・雑

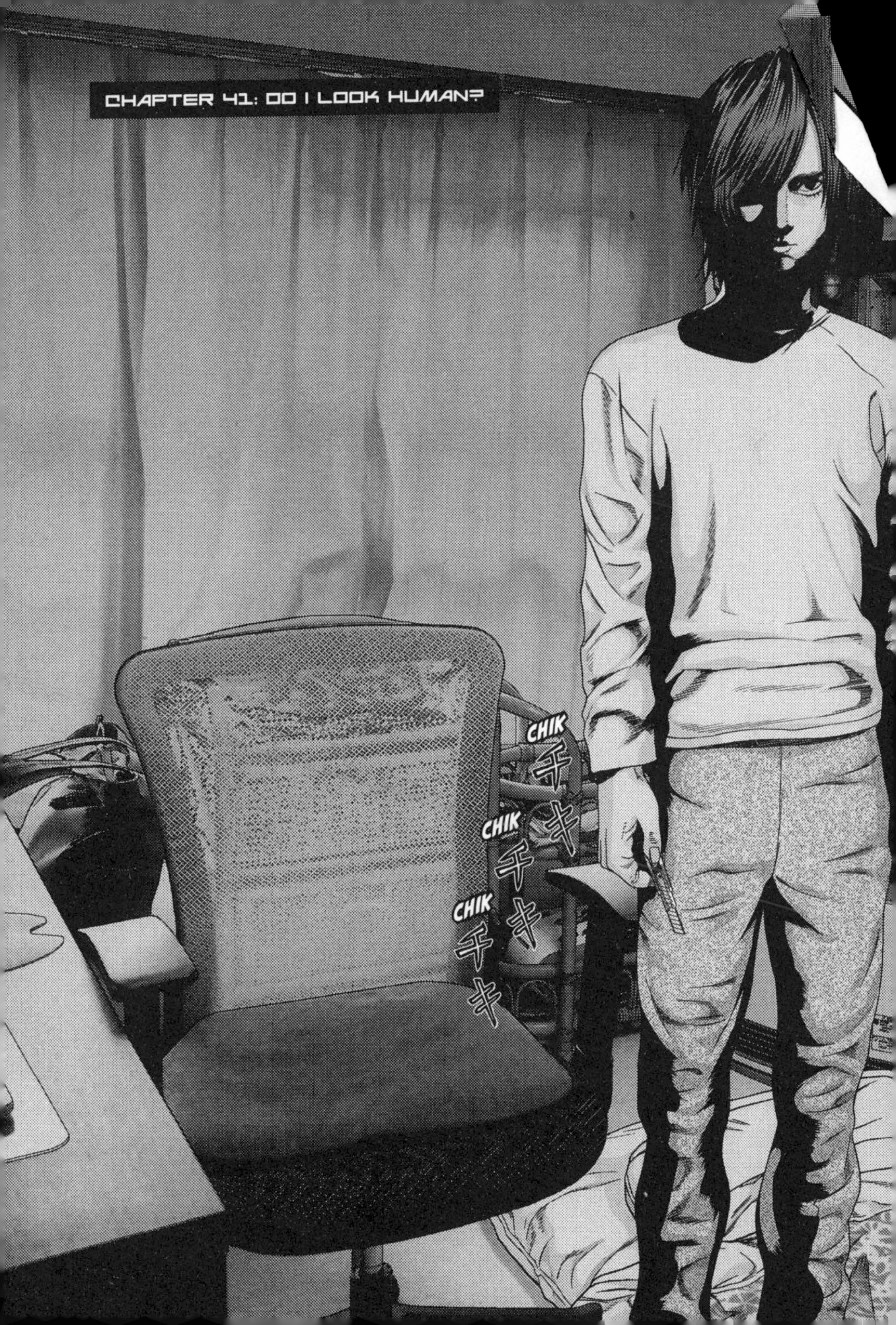
CHAPTER 41: DO I LOOK HUMAN?
CHIK
チキ
CHIK
チキ
CHIK
チキ

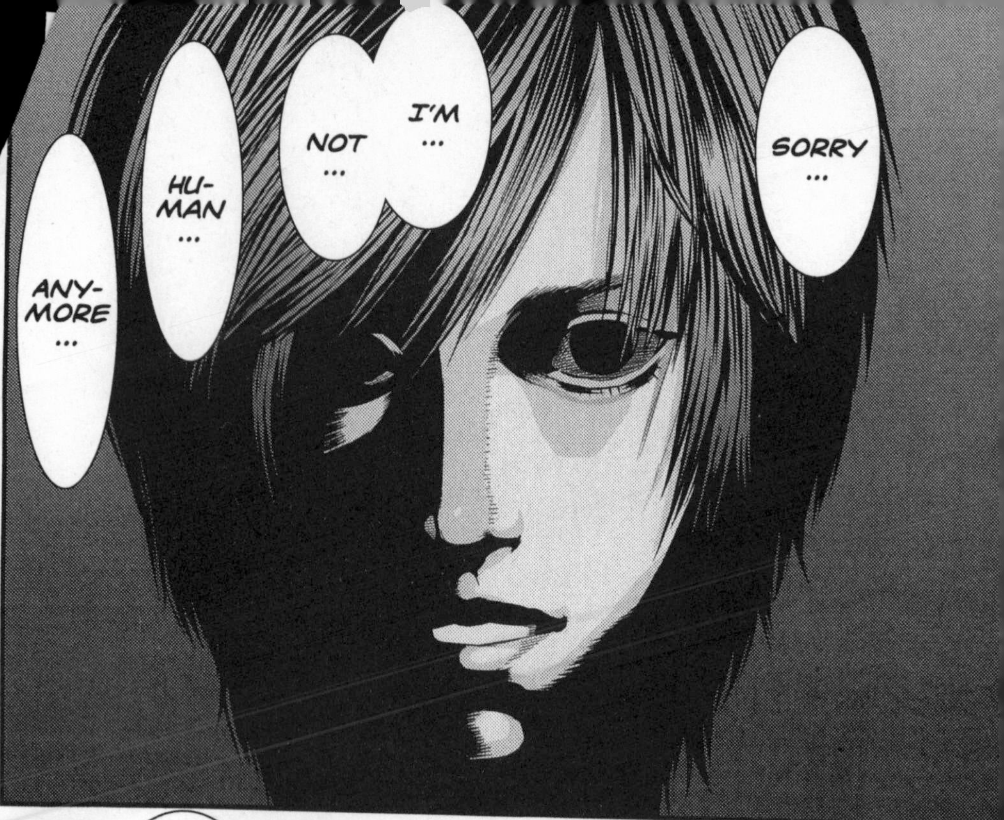
SORRY ...
I'M ...
NOT ...
HU-MAN ...
ANY-MORE ...

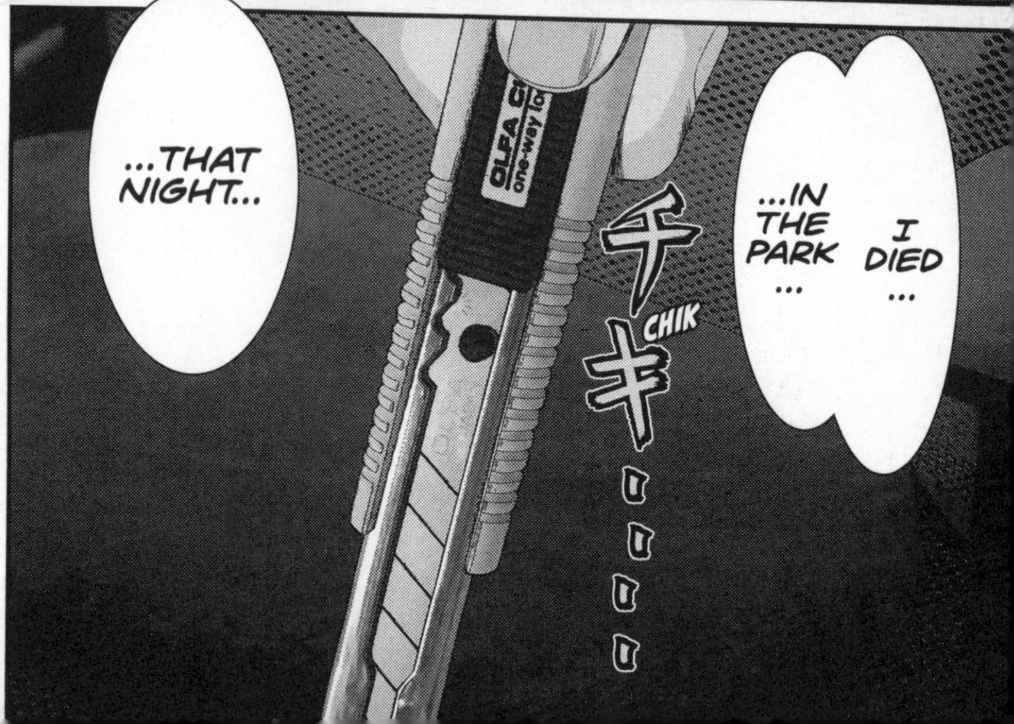
I DIED ...
...IN THE PARK ...
チキロロロロロ
CHIK
...THAT NIGHT...
OLFA
one-way

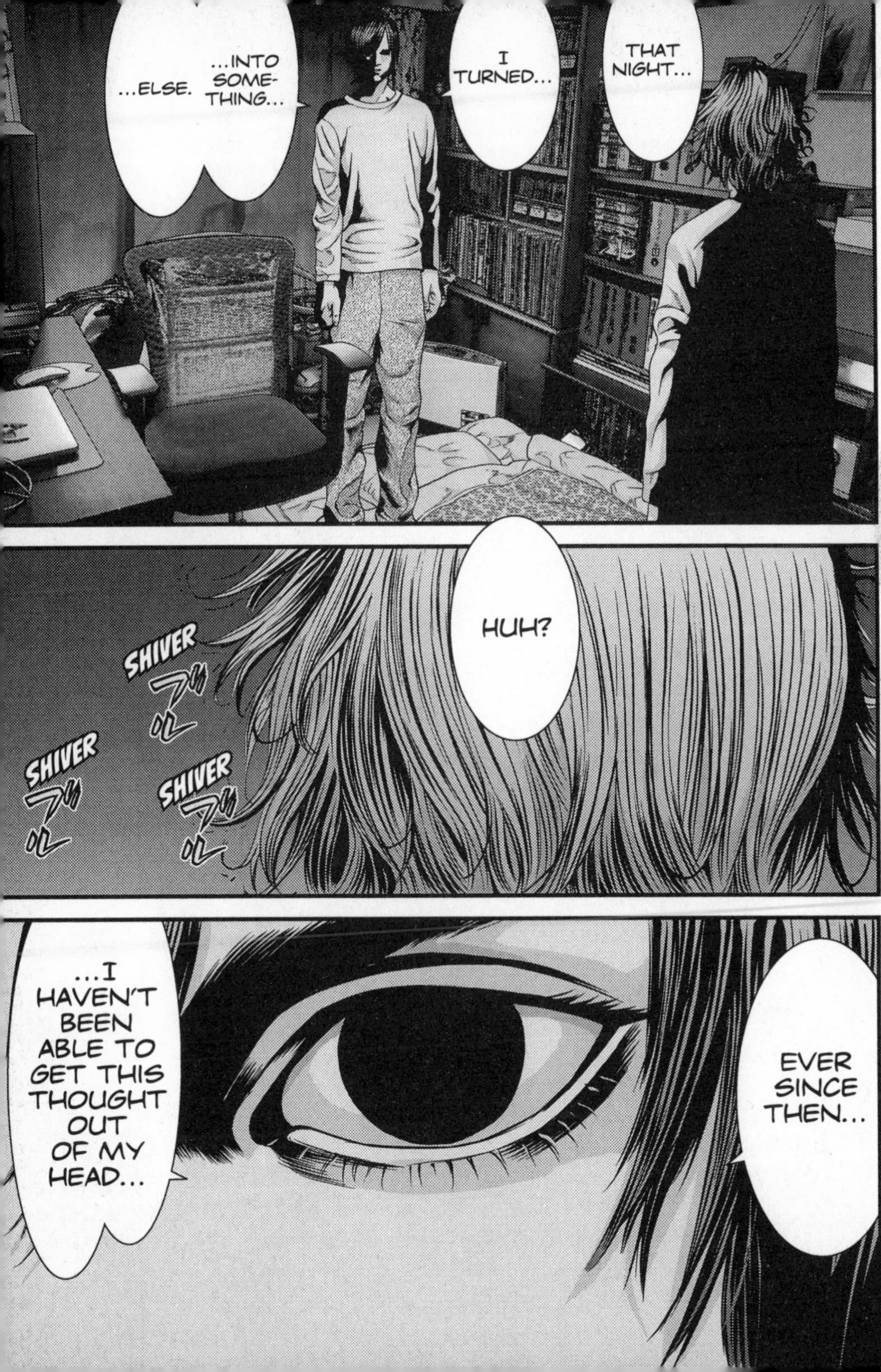
THAT NIGHT...
I TURNED...
...INTO SOMETHING...
...ELSE.
HUH?
SHIVER
SHIVER
SHIVER
EVER SINCE THEN...
...I HAVEN'T BEEN ABLE TO GET THIS THOUGHT OUT OF MY HEAD...

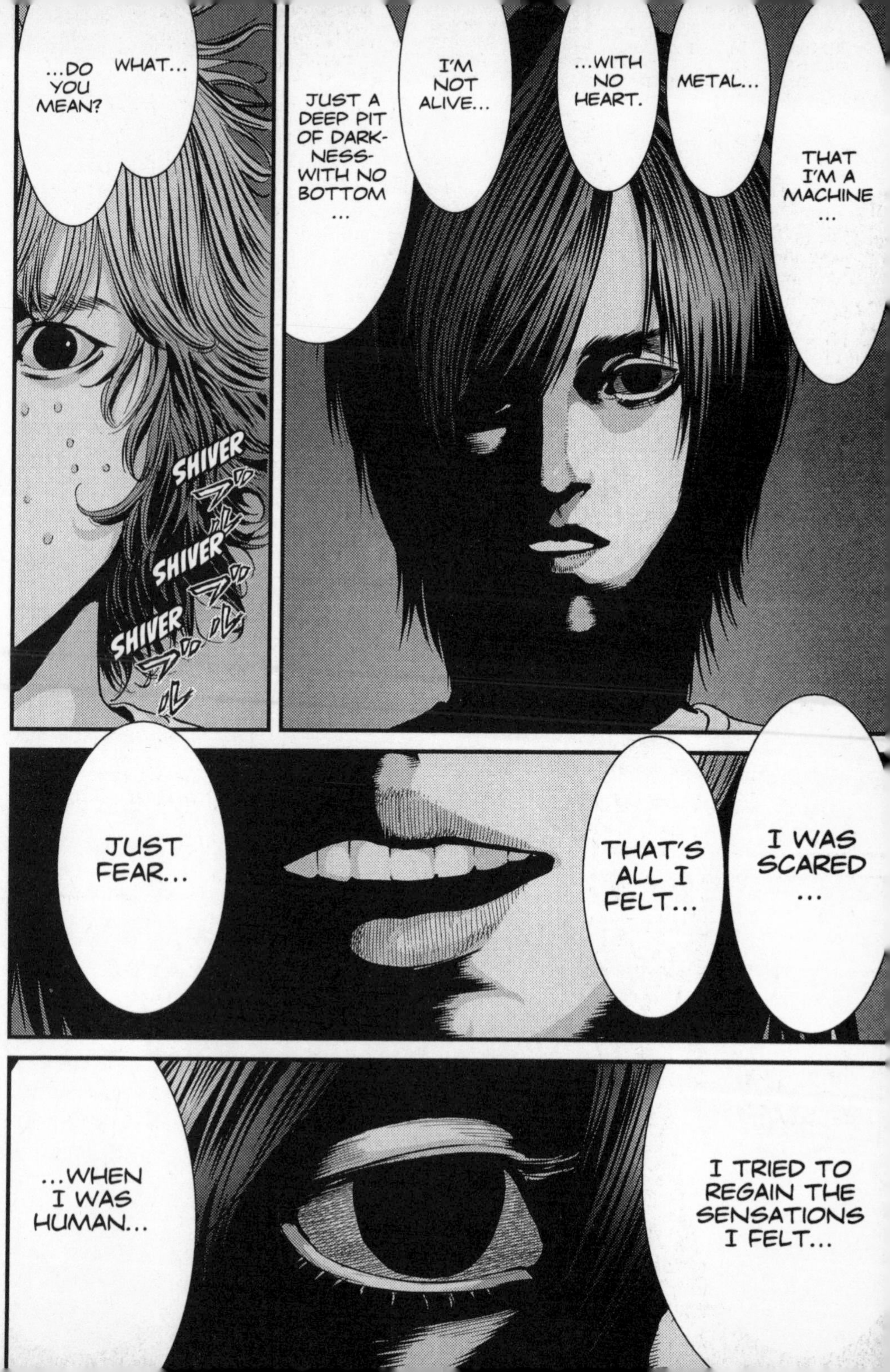
THAT I'M A MACHINE ...
METAL...
...WITH NO HEART.
I'M NOT ALIVE...
JUST A DEEP PIT OF DARK-NESS- WITH NO BOTTOM ...
WHAT...
...DO YOU MEAN?
SHIVER
SHIVER
SHIVER
I WAS SCARED ...
THAT'S ALL I FELT...
JUST FEAR...
I TRIED TO REGAIN THE SENSATIONS I FELT...
...WHEN I WAS HUMAN...

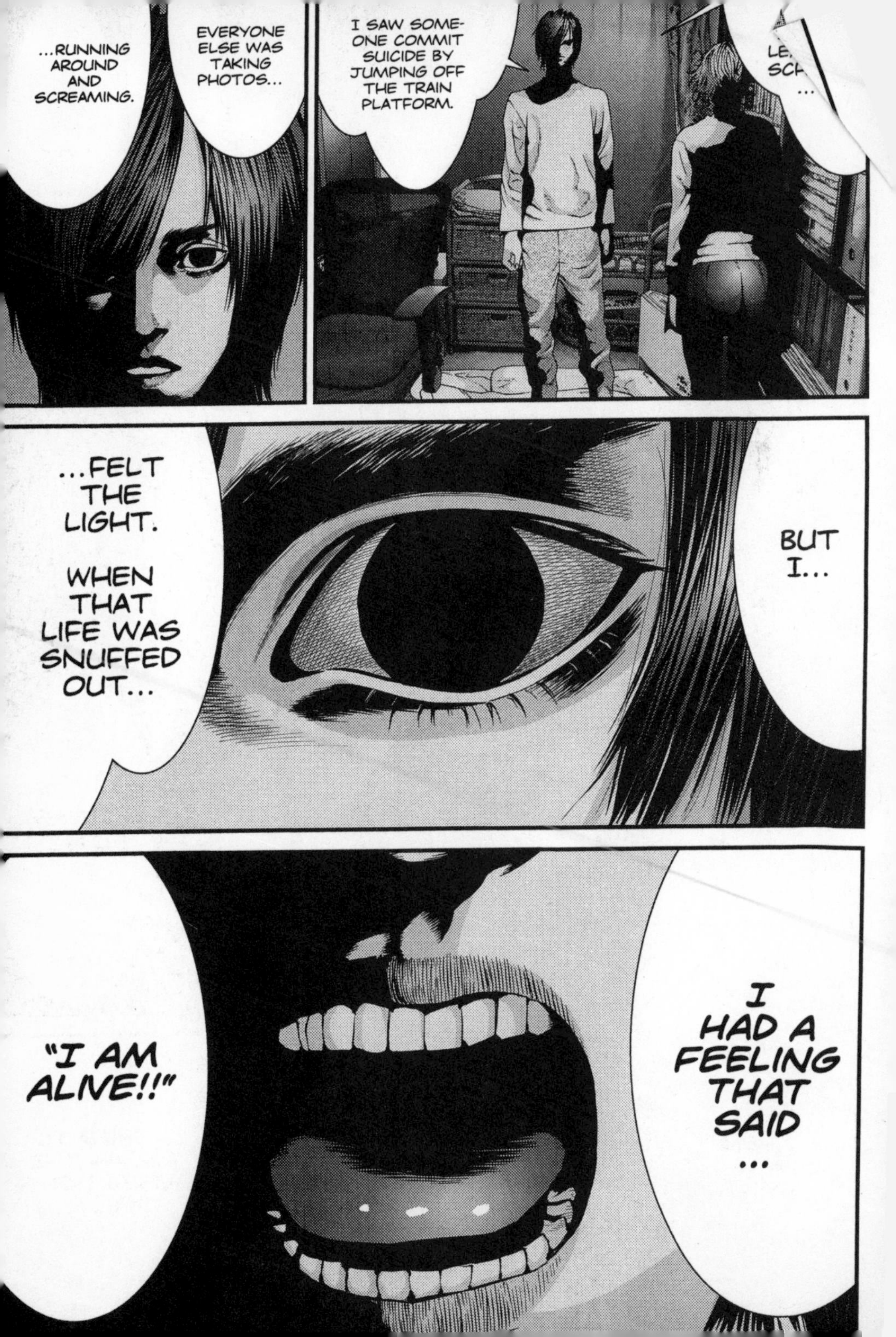
I SAW SOME-ONE COMMIT SUICIDE BY JUMPING OFF THE TRAIN PLATFORM.
EVERYONE ELSE WAS TAKING PHOTOS...
...RUNNING AROUND AND SCREAMING.
BUT I...
...FELT THE LIGHT.
WHEN THAT LIFE WAS SNUFFED OUT...
I HAD A FEELING THAT SAID ...
"I AM ALIVE!!"

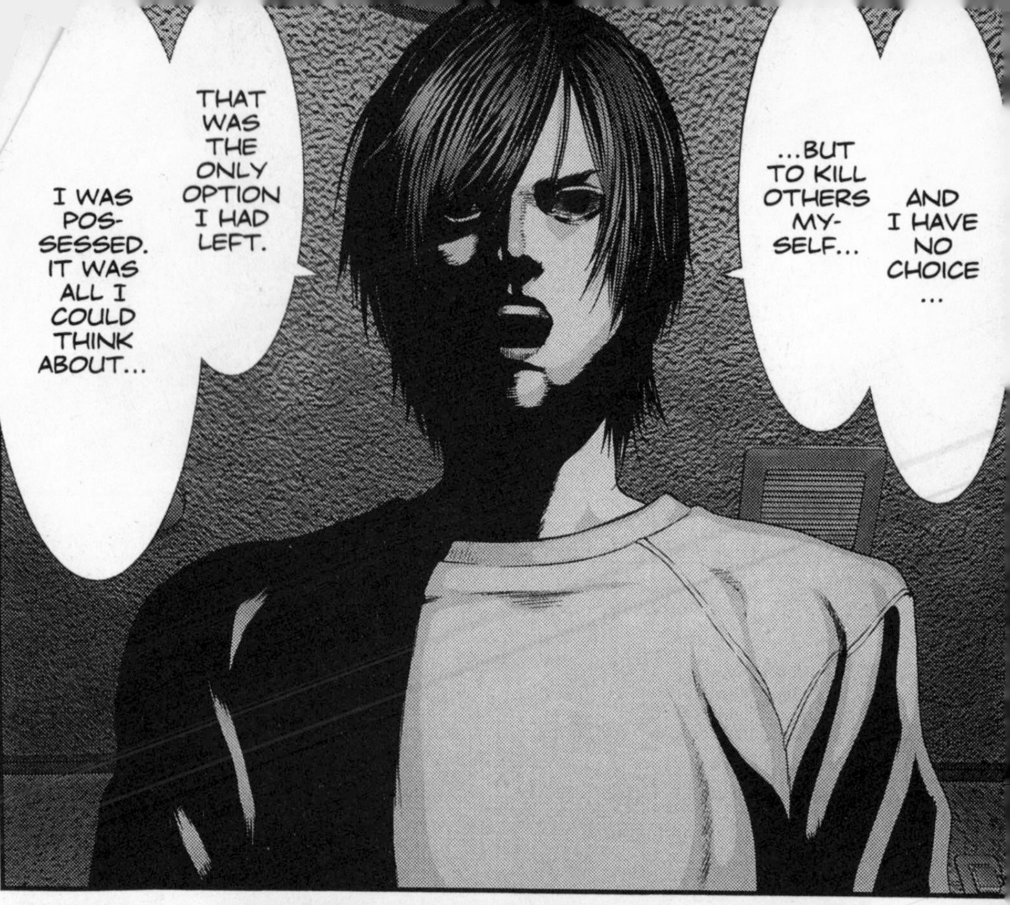
AND I HAVE NO CHOICE ...
...BUT TO KILL OTHERS MYSELF...
THAT WAS THE ONLY OPTION I HAD LEFT.
I WAS POSSESSED. IT WAS ALL I COULD THINK ABOUT...
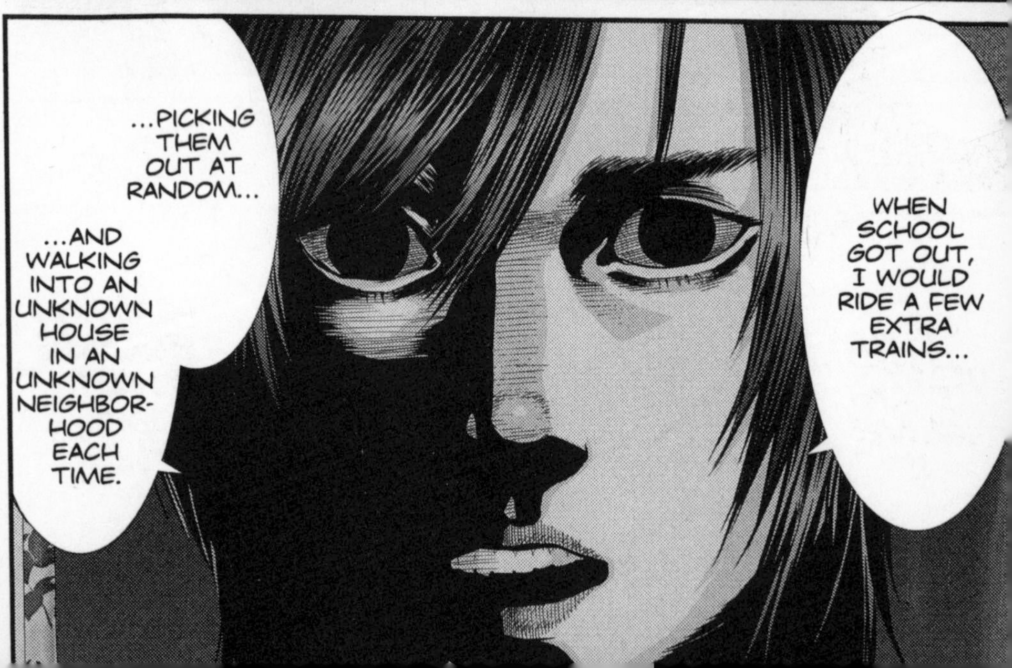
WHEN SCHOOL GOT OUT, I WOULD RIDE A FEW EXTRA TRAINS...
...PICKING THEM OUT AT RANDOM...
...AND WALKING INTO AN UNKNOWN HOUSE IN AN UNKNOWN NEIGHBORHOOD EACH TIME.

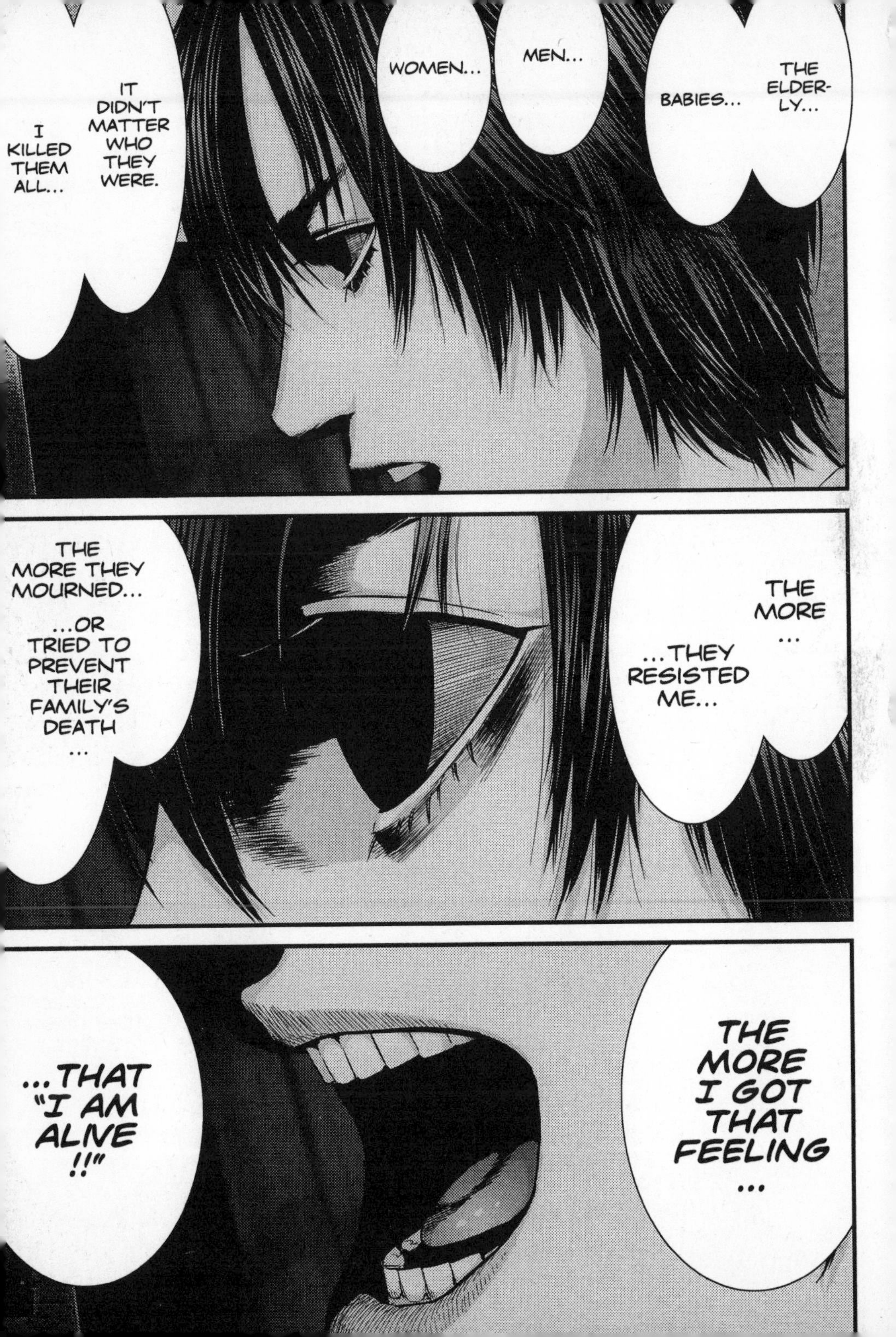
THE ELDERLY...
BABIES...
MEN...
WOMEN...
IT DIDN'T MATTER WHO THEY WERE.
I KILLED THEM ALL...
THE MORE ...
...THEY RESISTED ME...
THE MORE THEY MOURNED...
...OR TRIED TO PREVENT THEIR FAMILY'S DEATH ...
THE MORE I GOT THAT FEELING ...
...THAT "I AM ALIVE !!"

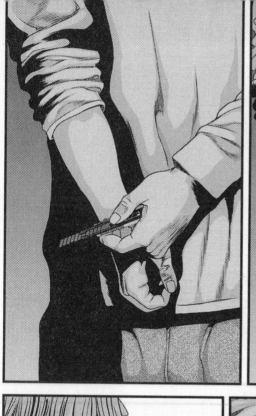

AH!

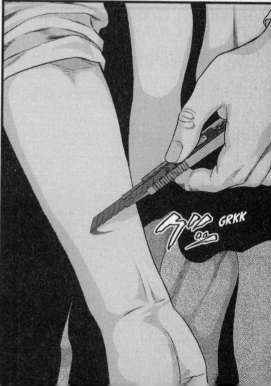

GRKK

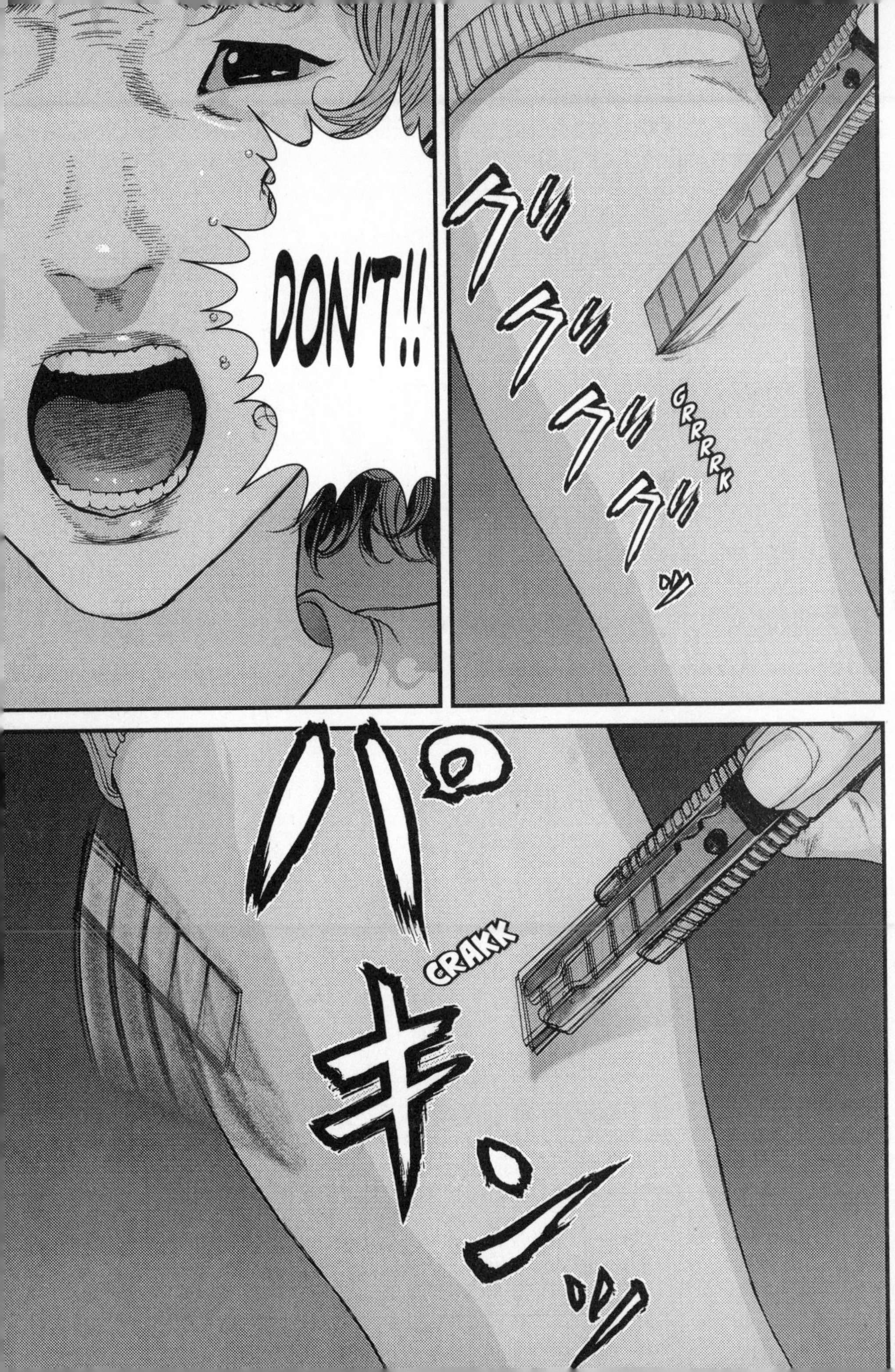
グリグリグリグリッ
GRRRRK
DON'T!!
パキンッ
CRAKK

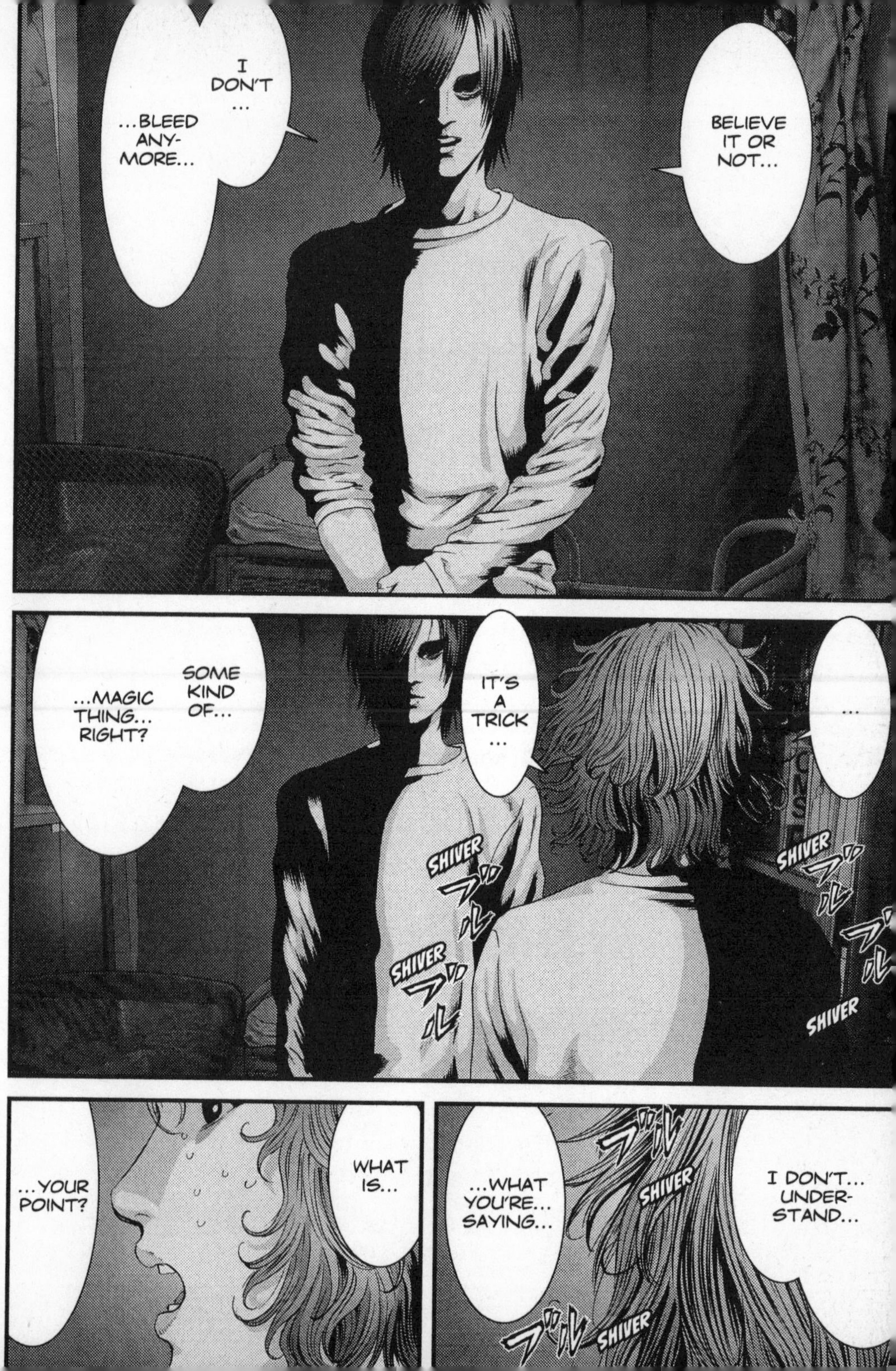
BELIEVE IT OR NOT...
I DON'T ...
...BLEED ANY-MORE...
...
IT'S A TRICK ...
SOME KIND OF...
...MAGIC THING... RIGHT?
SHIVER
SHIVER
SHIVER
SHIVER
I DON'T... UNDER-STAND...
...WHAT YOU'RE... SAYING...
SHIVER
SHIVER
WHAT IS...
...YOUR POINT?

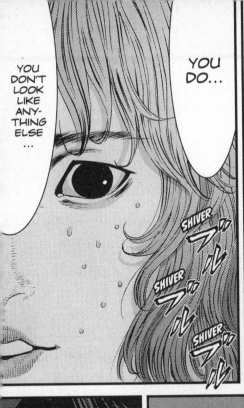

YOU DON'T LOOK LIKE ANYTHING ELSE...

YOU DO...

...HUMAN?

DO I LOOK...

SHIVER

SHIVER

SHIVER

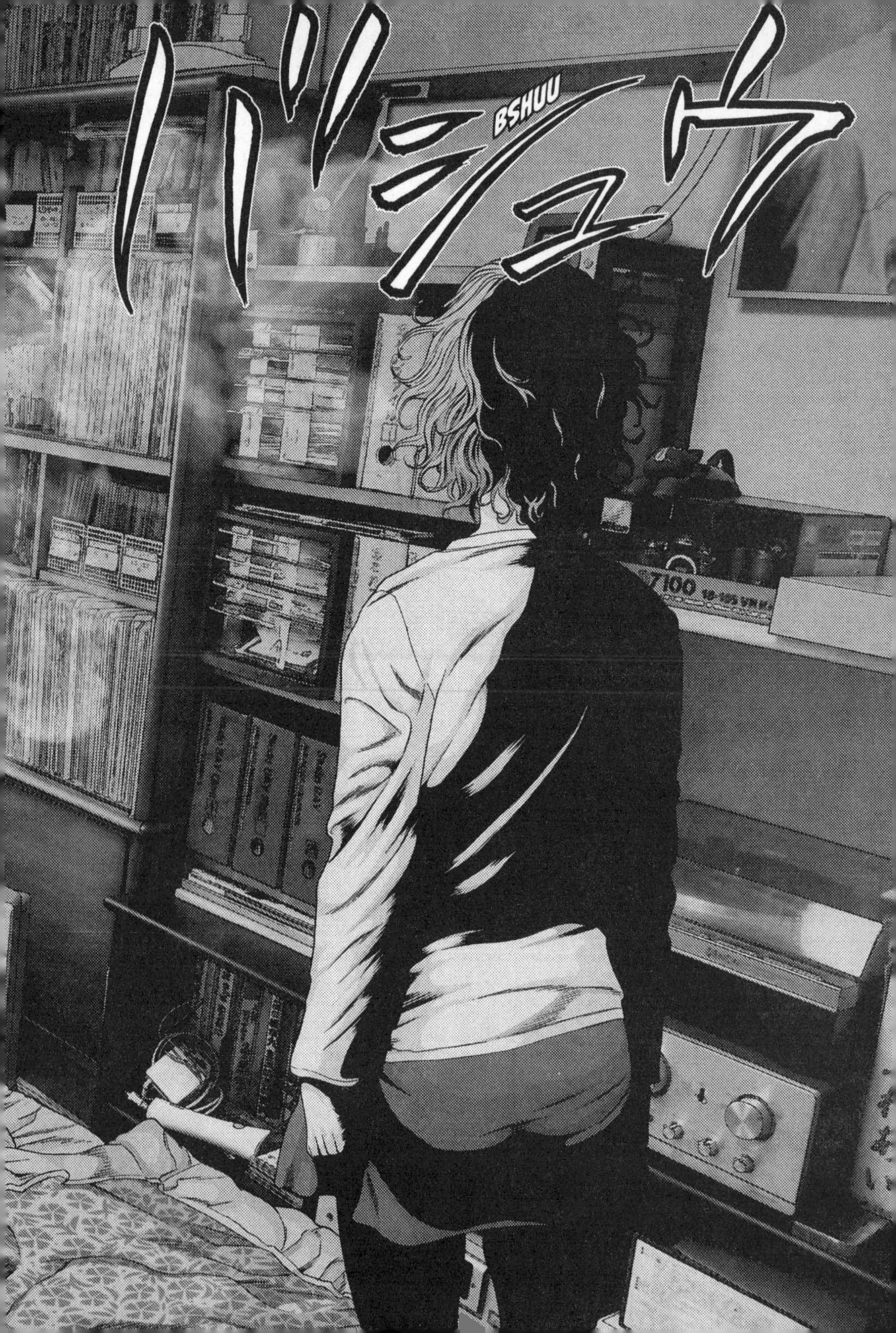
バシュウ
BSHUU
7100

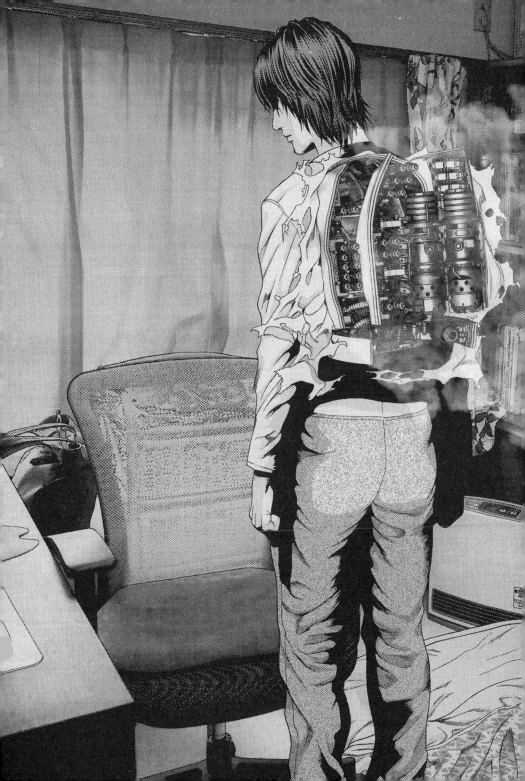

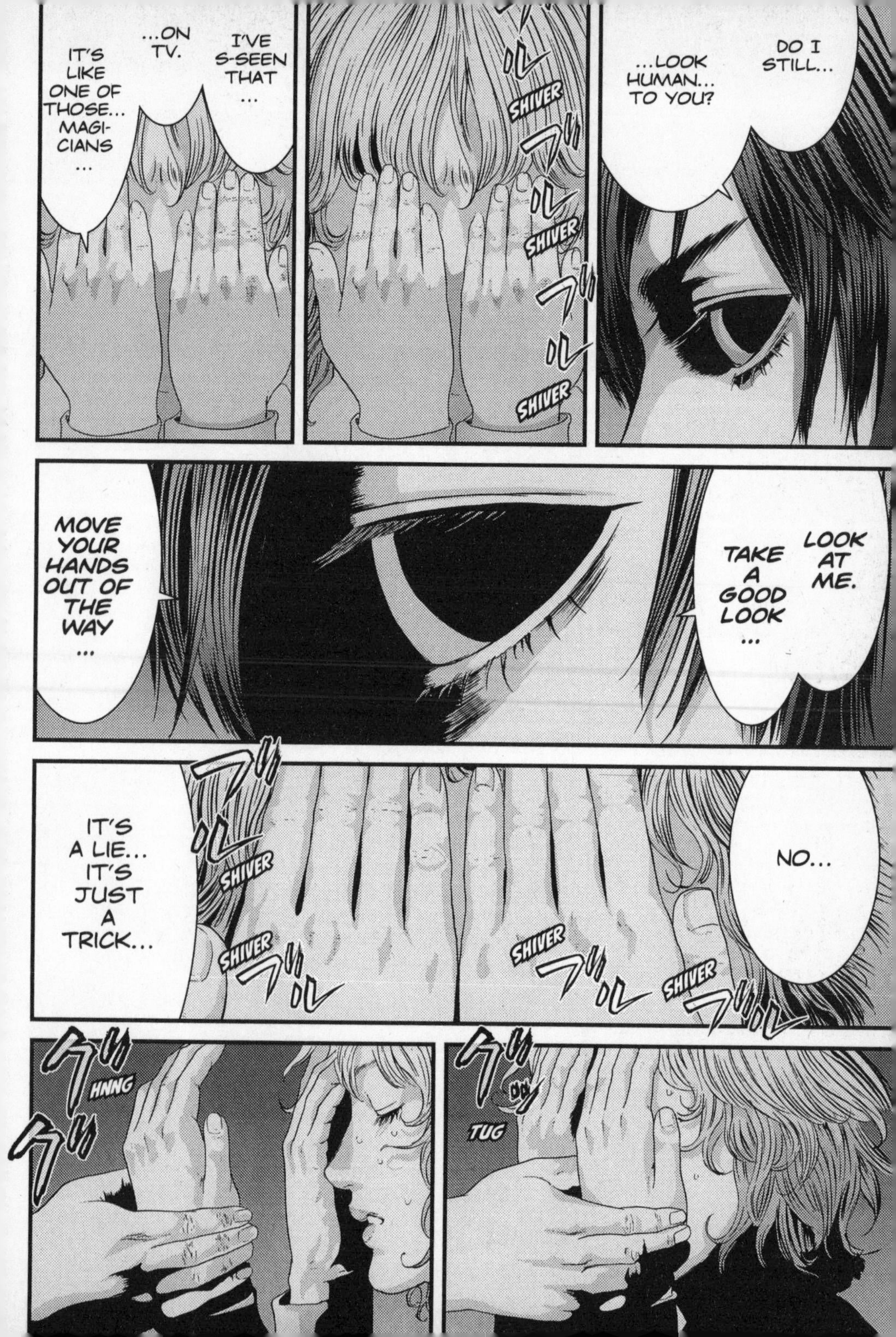
DO I STILL...
...LOOK HUMAN... TO YOU?
SHIVER
SHIVER
SHIVER
I'VE S-SEEN THAT ...
...ON TV.
IT'S LIKE ONE OF THOSE... MAGI-CIANS ...
LOOK AT ME.
TAKE A GOOD LOOK ...
MOVE YOUR HANDS OUT OF THE WAY ...
NO...
SHIVER
SHIVER
IT'S A LIE... IT'S JUST A TRICK...
SHIVER
SHIVER
TUG
HNNG

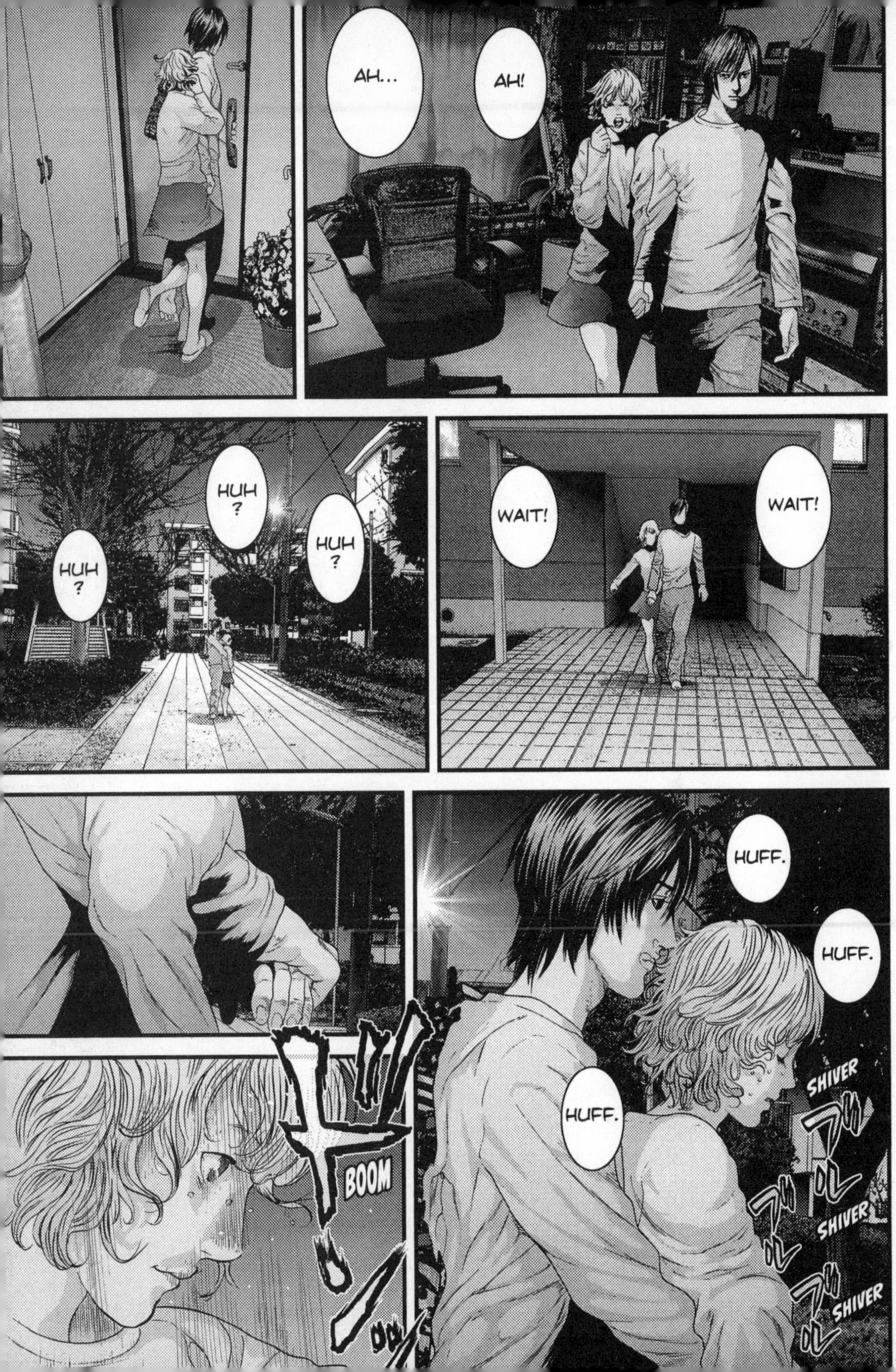

AH!
AH...
WAIT!
WAIT!
HUH ?
HUH ?
HUH ?
HUFF.
HUFF.
HUFF.
SHIVER
SHIVER
SHIVER
BOOM

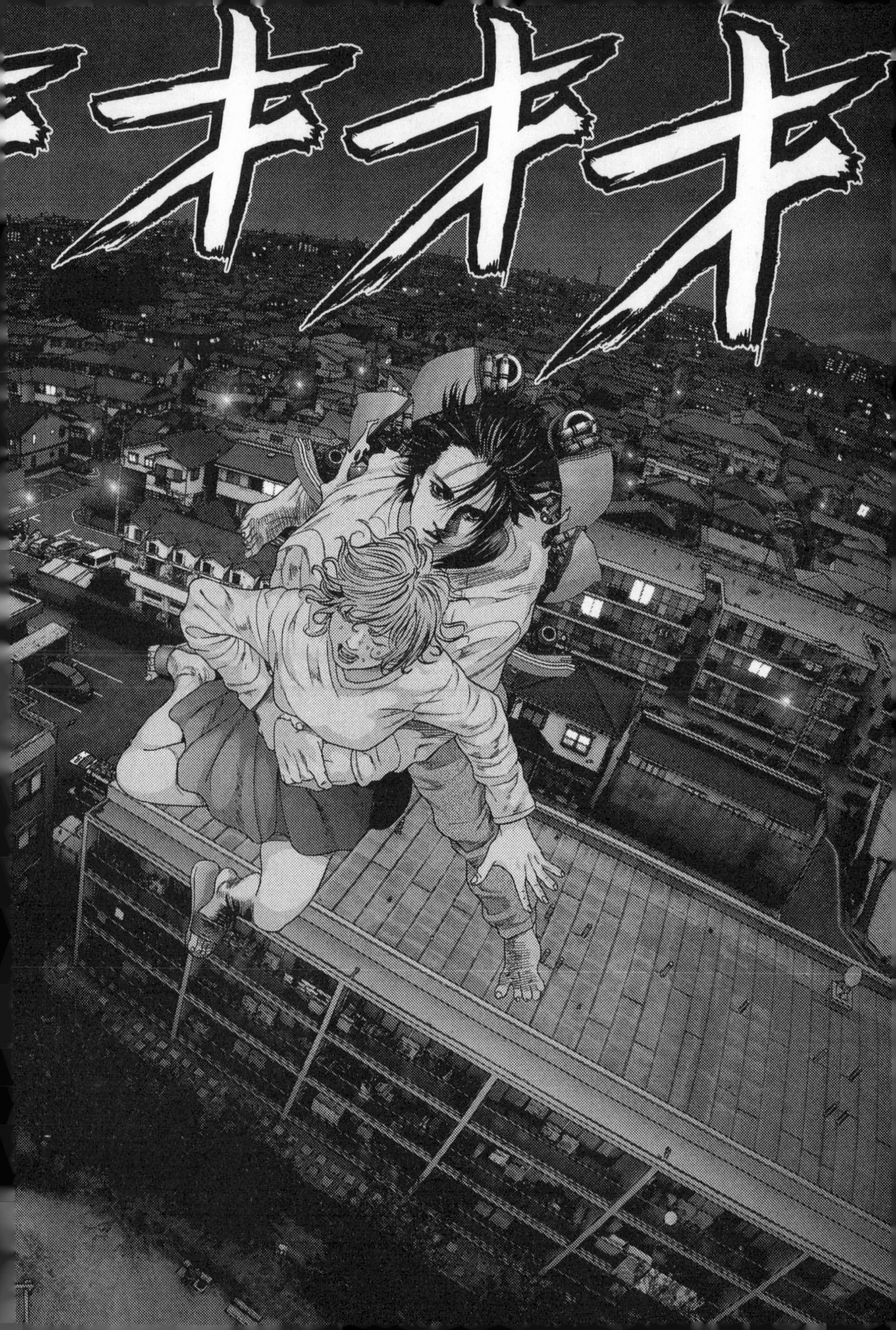
オオオ

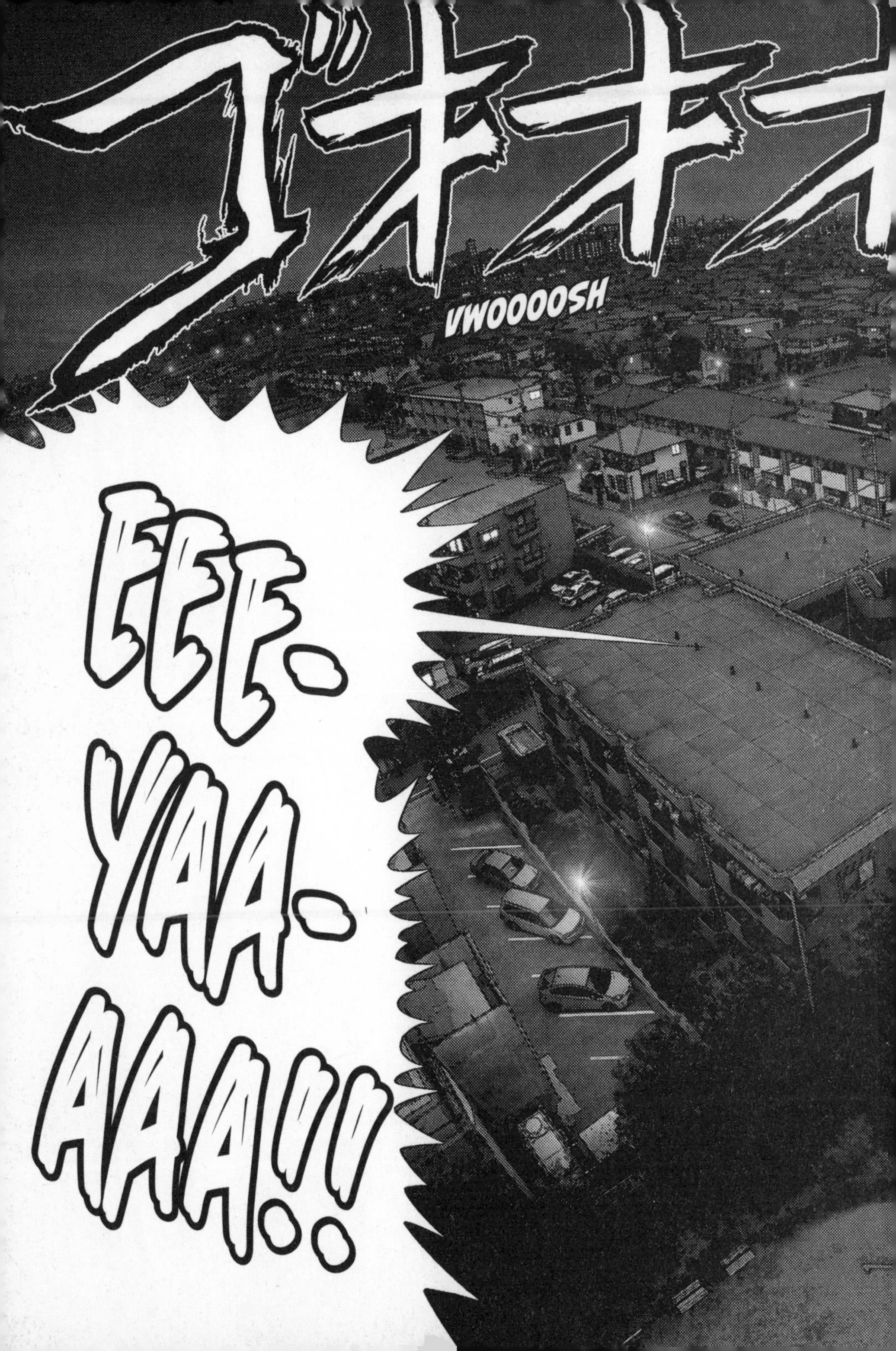
ゴオオオ
VWOOOOSH
EEE-YAA-AAA!!

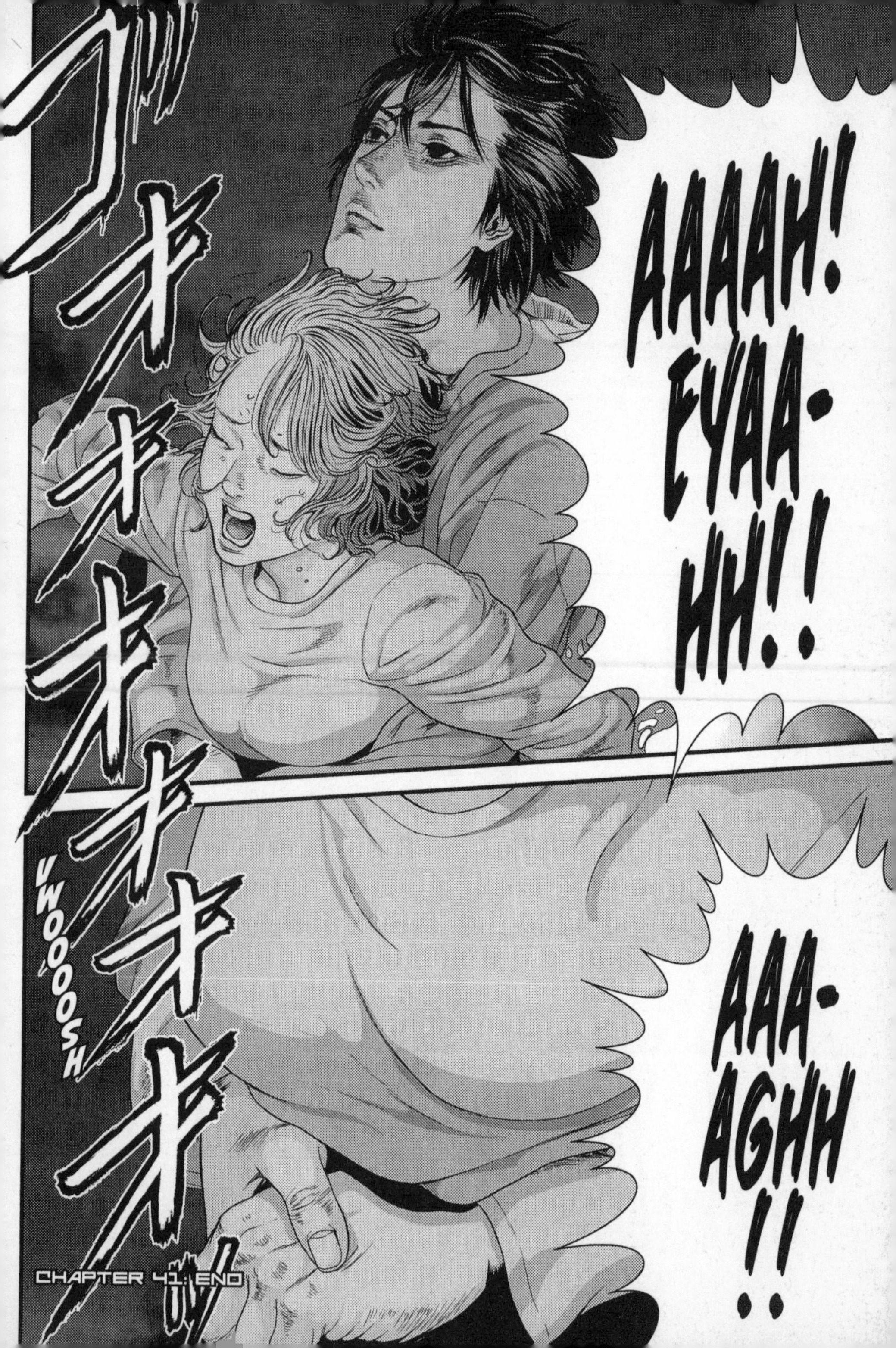
AAAAH! EYAA-HH!!
AAA-AGHH!!
VWOOOOSH
CHAPTER 41: END

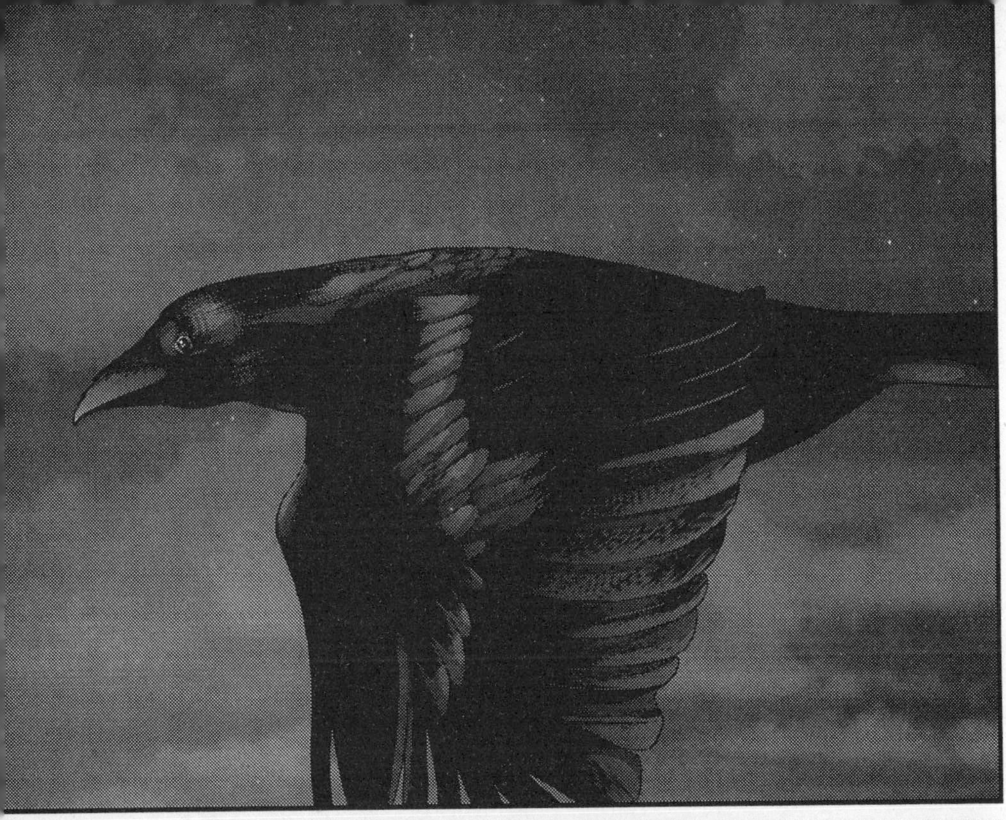
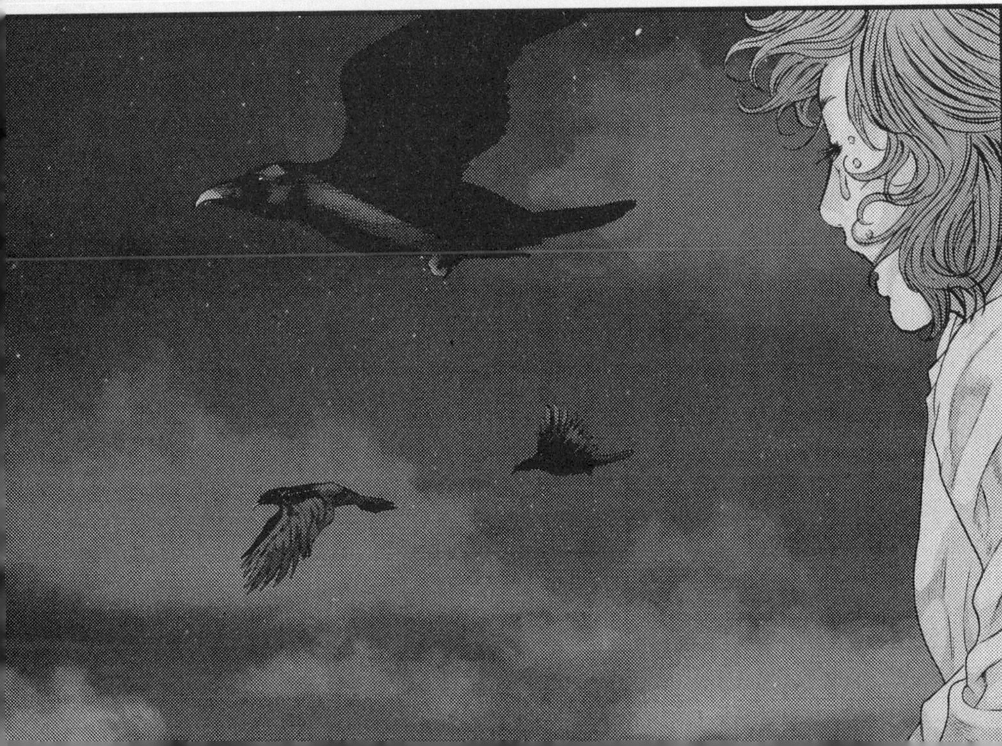

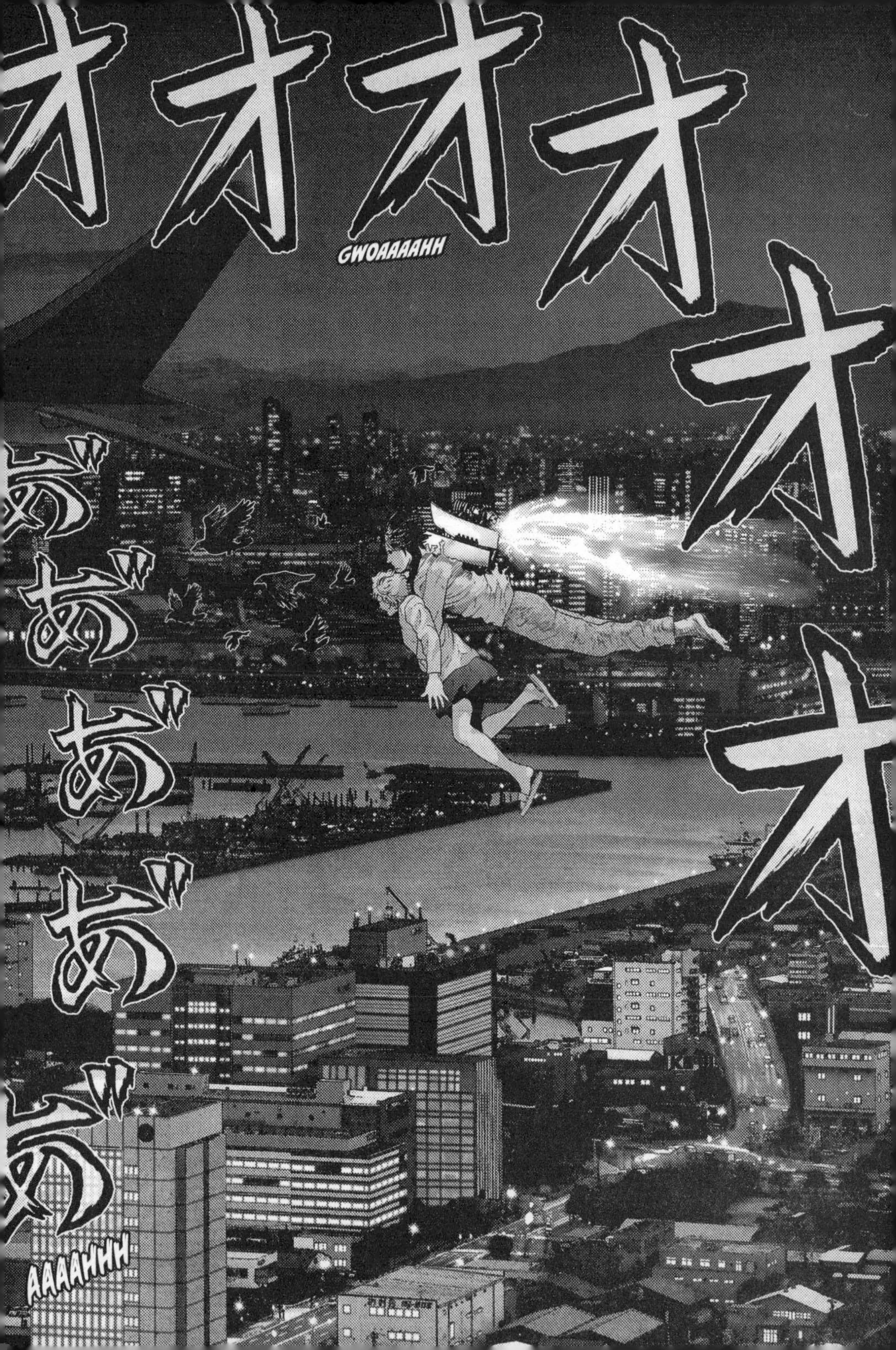
オオオオオオオ
GWOAAAAHH
あ゛あ゛あ゛あ゛あ゛
AAAAHHH

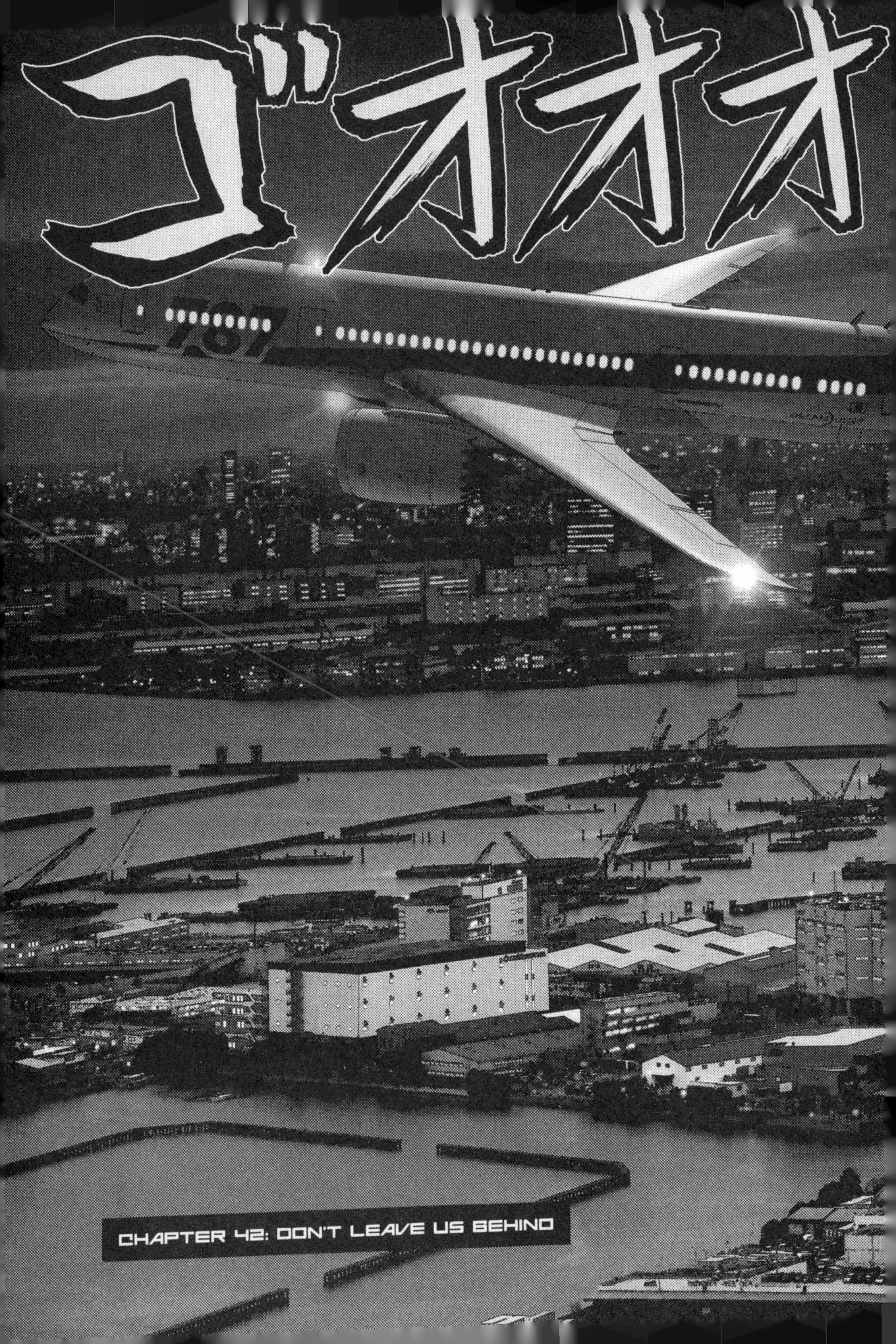
ゴオオオ
787
CHAPTER 42: DON'T LEAVE US BEHIND

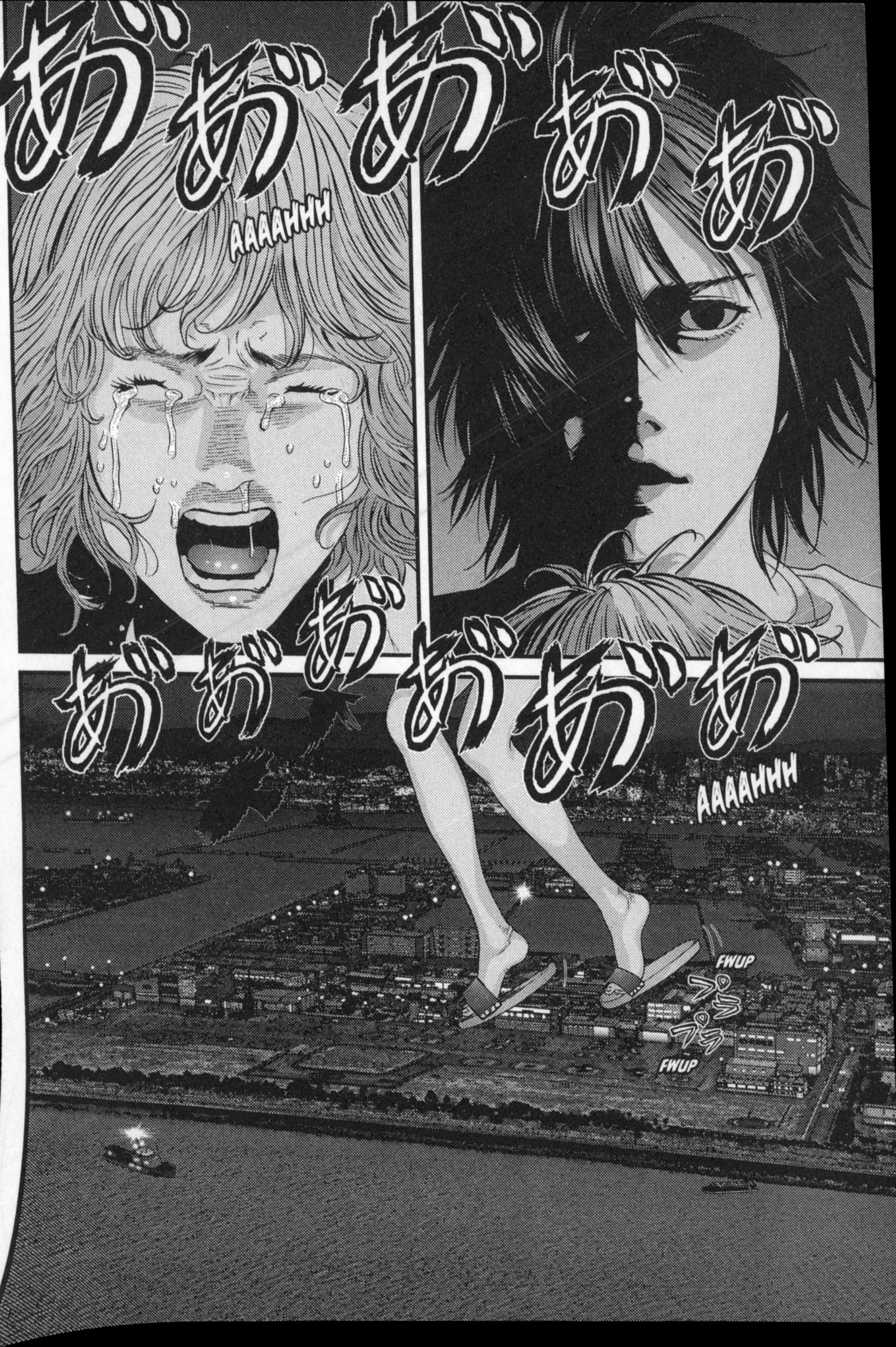
あ゛あ゛あ゛あ゛あ゛
AAAAHHH
あ゛あ゛あ゛あ゛あ゛あ゛
AAAAHHH
FWUP
プラ
プラ
FWUP

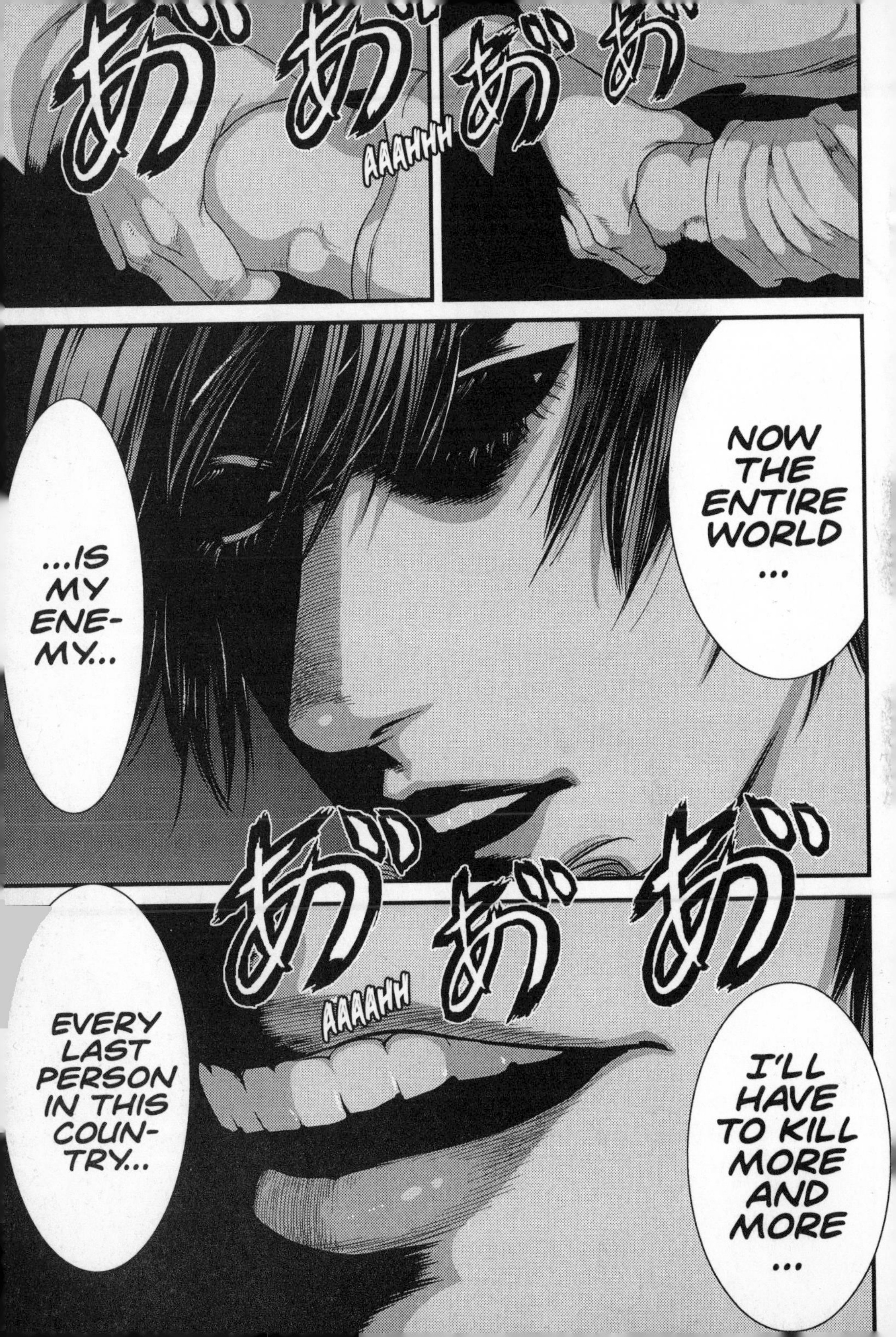

あ゛あ゛あ゛あ゛
AAAHHH
NOW THE ENTIRE WORLD...
...IS MY ENEMY...
あ゛あ゛あ゛
AAAAHH
I'LL HAVE TO KILL MORE AND MORE...
EVERY LAST PERSON IN THIS COUNTRY...

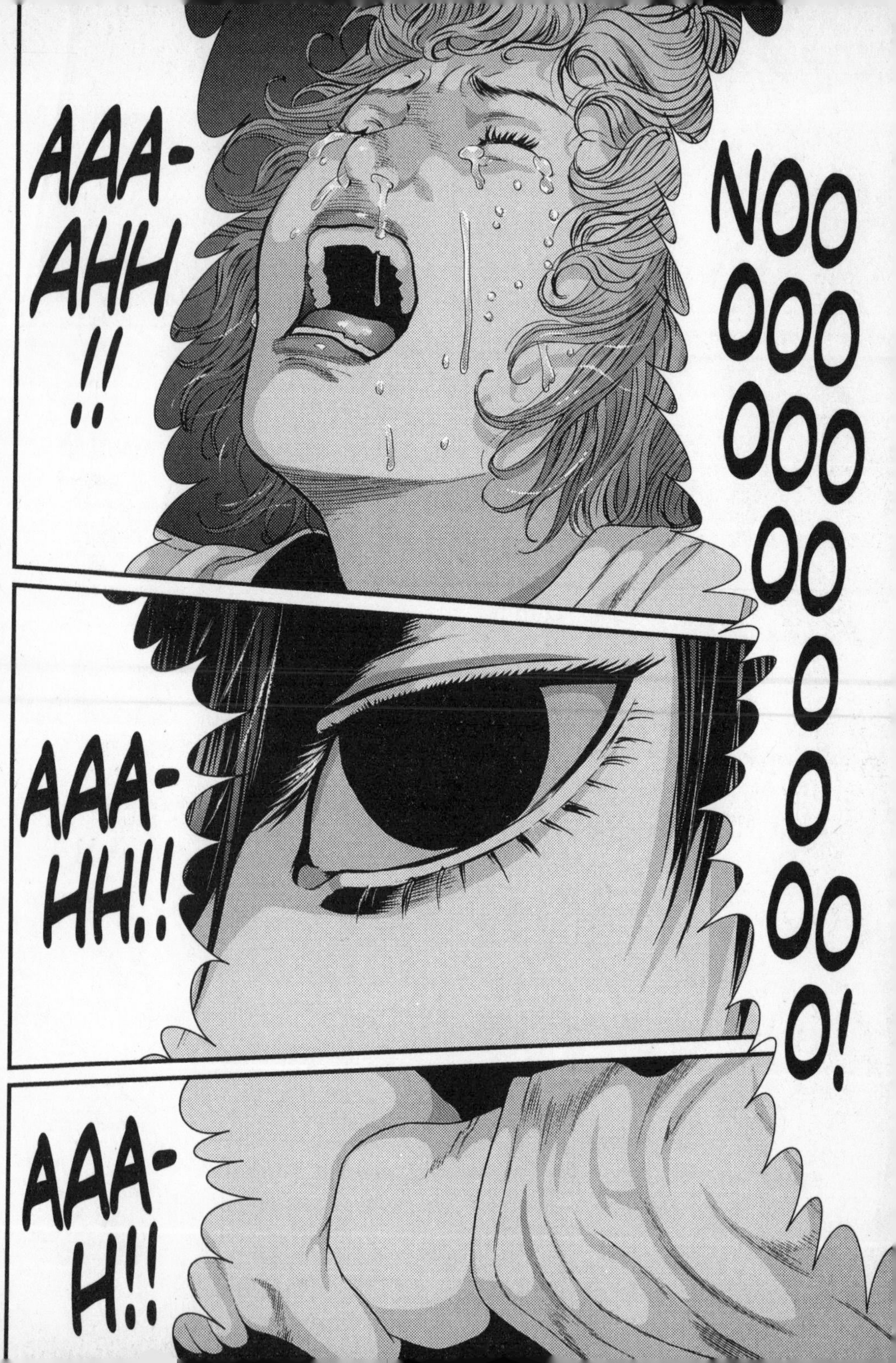
NOOOOOOOOOOOOOOO!
AAA-AHH!!
AAA-HH!!
AAA-H!!

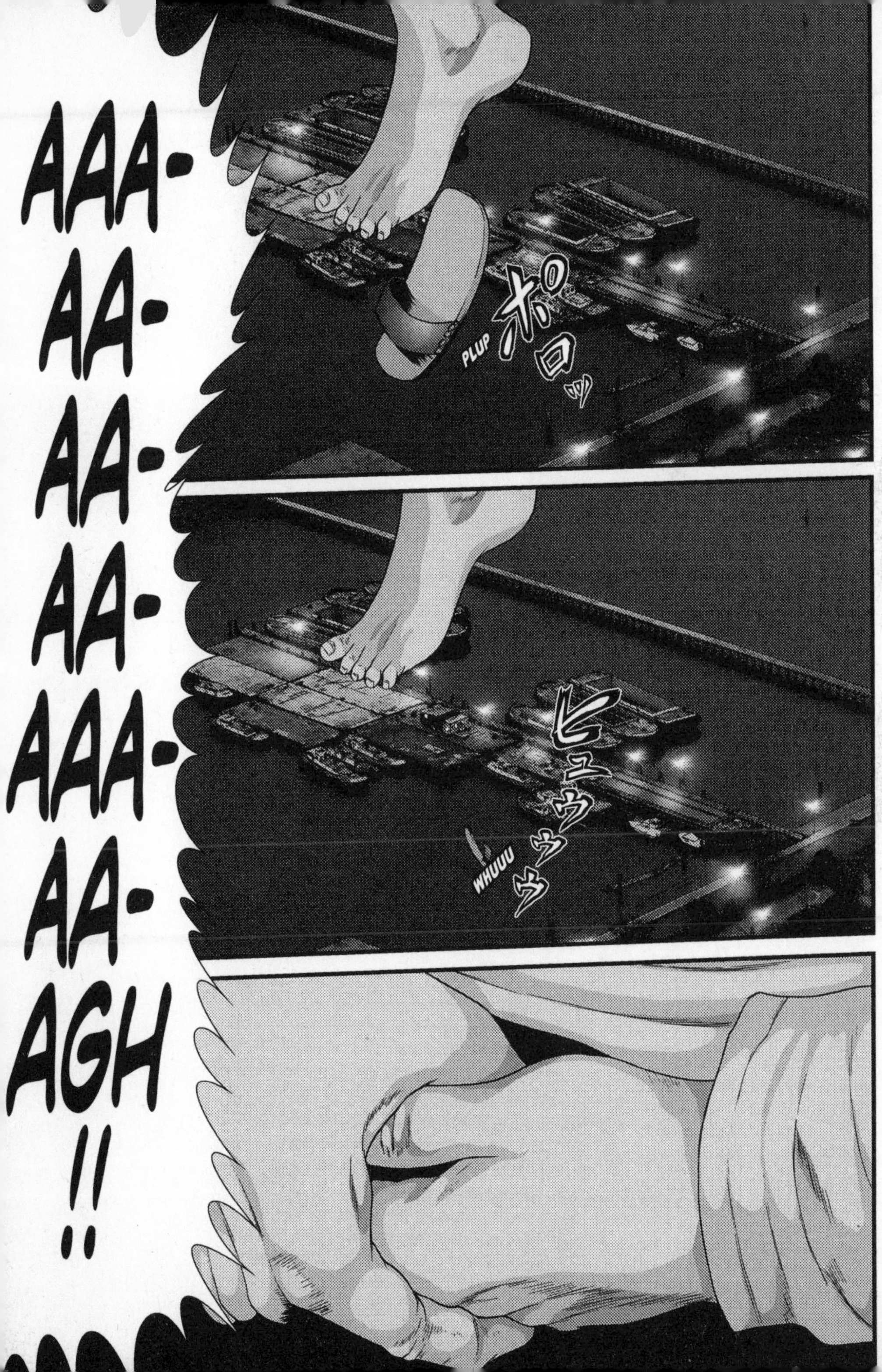
ポロッ
PLUP
ヒュウウウ
WHUUU
AAA-AA-AA-AA-AAA-AA-AGH!!

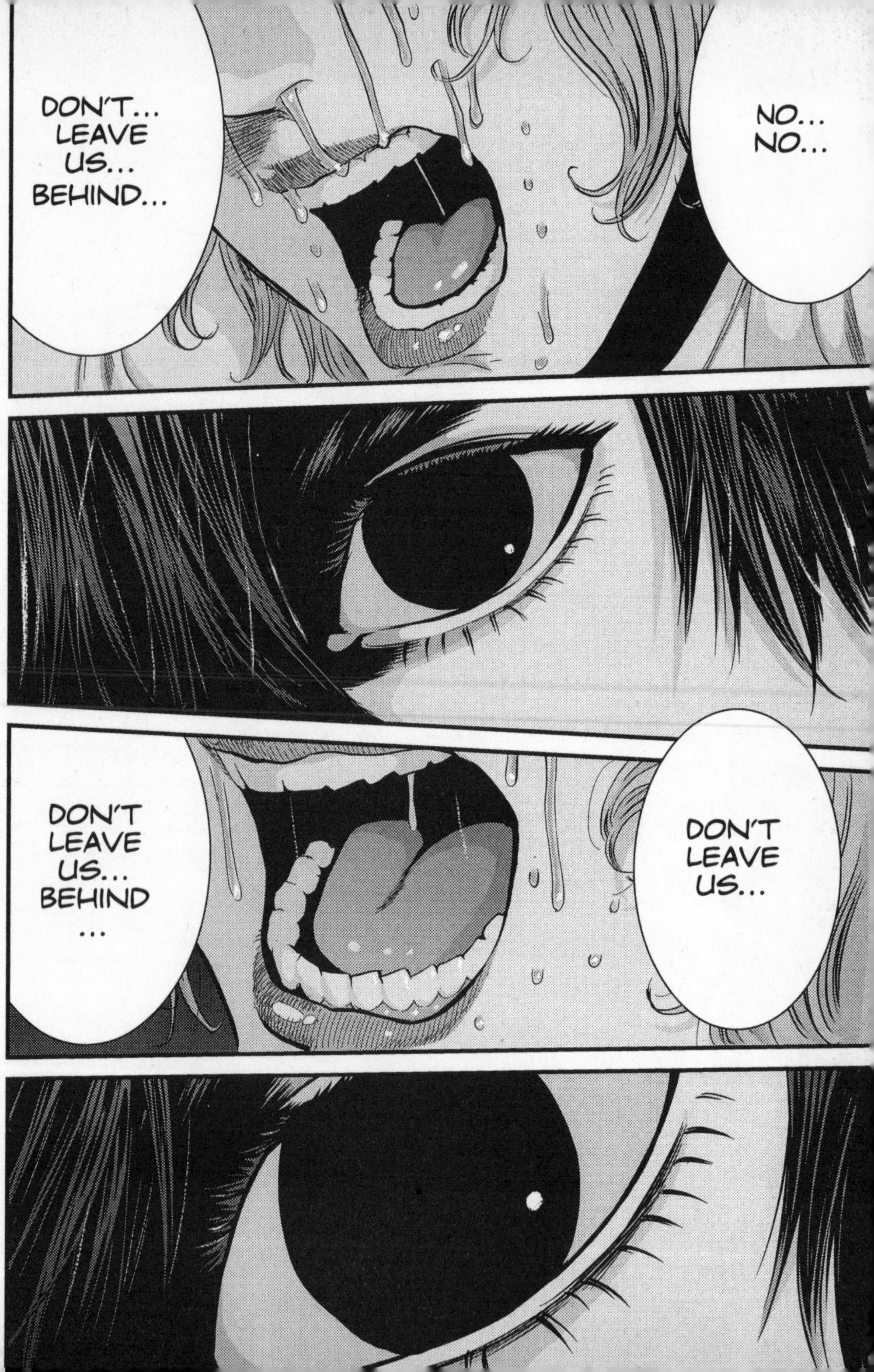
NO... NO...
DON'T... LEAVE US... BEHIND...
DON'T LEAVE US...
DON'T LEAVE US... BEHIND ...

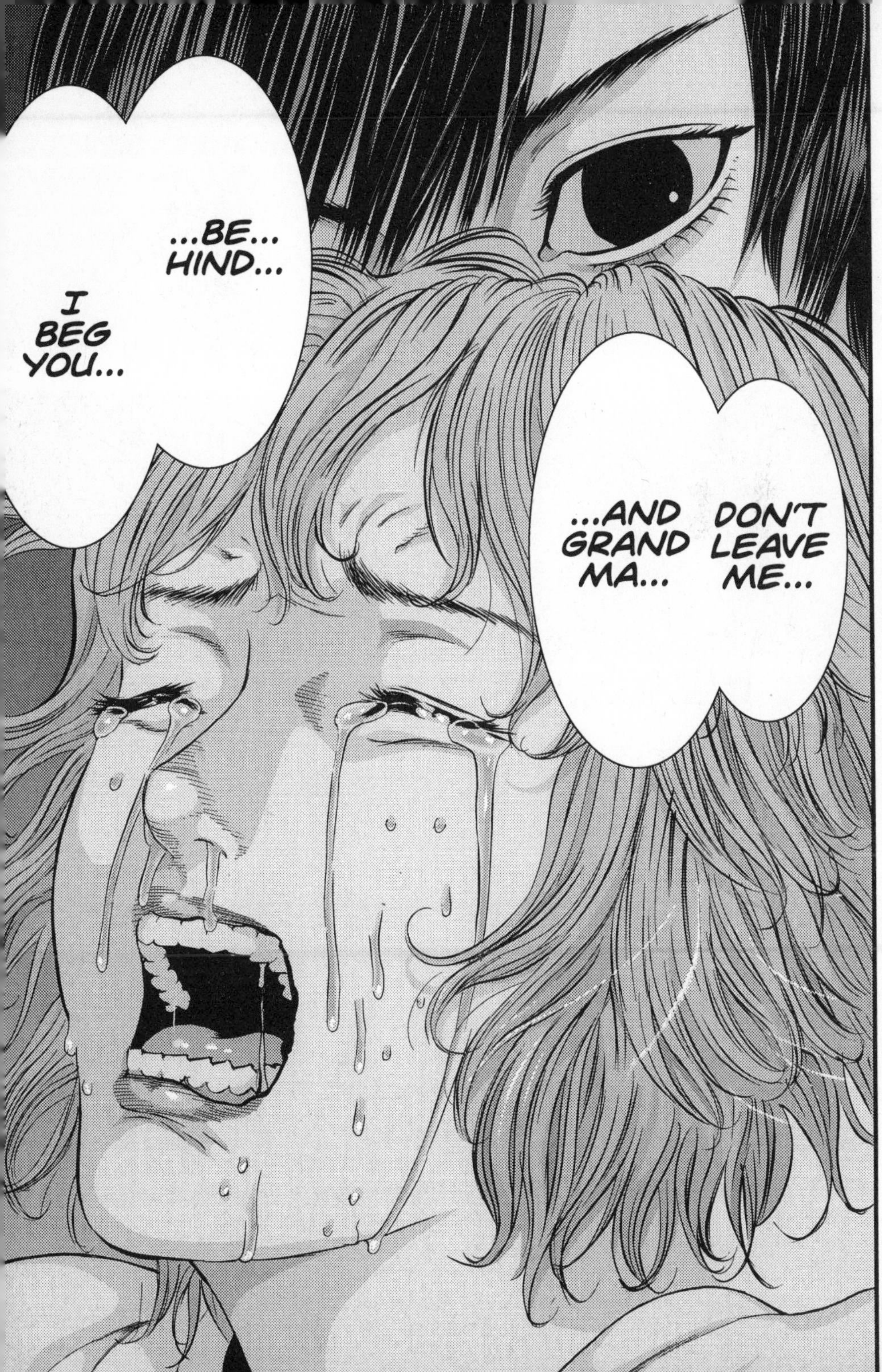
DON'T LEAVE ME... ...AND GRAND MA...
...BE... HIND... I BEG YOU...

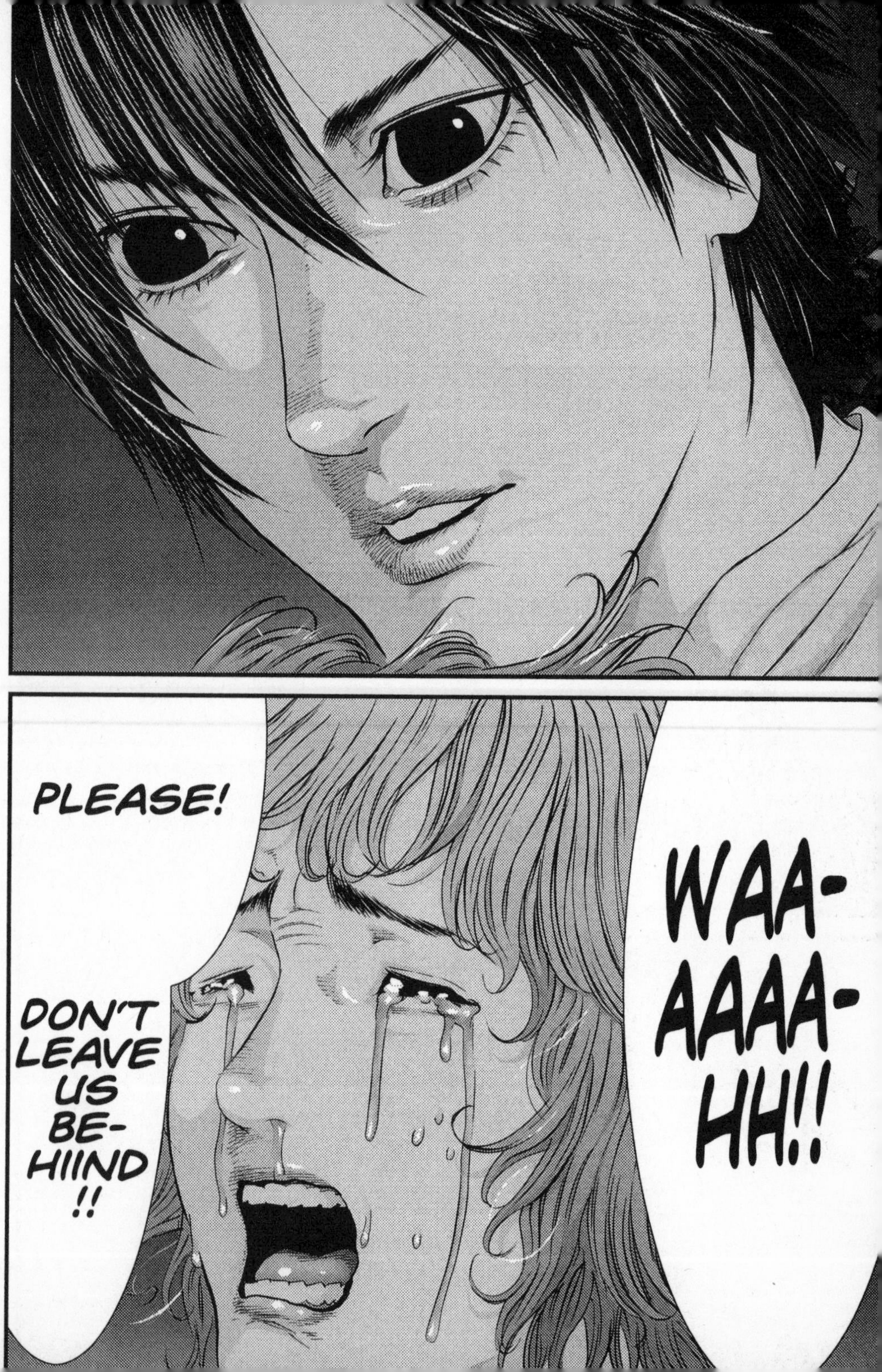
WAA-AAAA-HH!!
PLEASE!
DON'T LEAVE US BE-HIIND !!

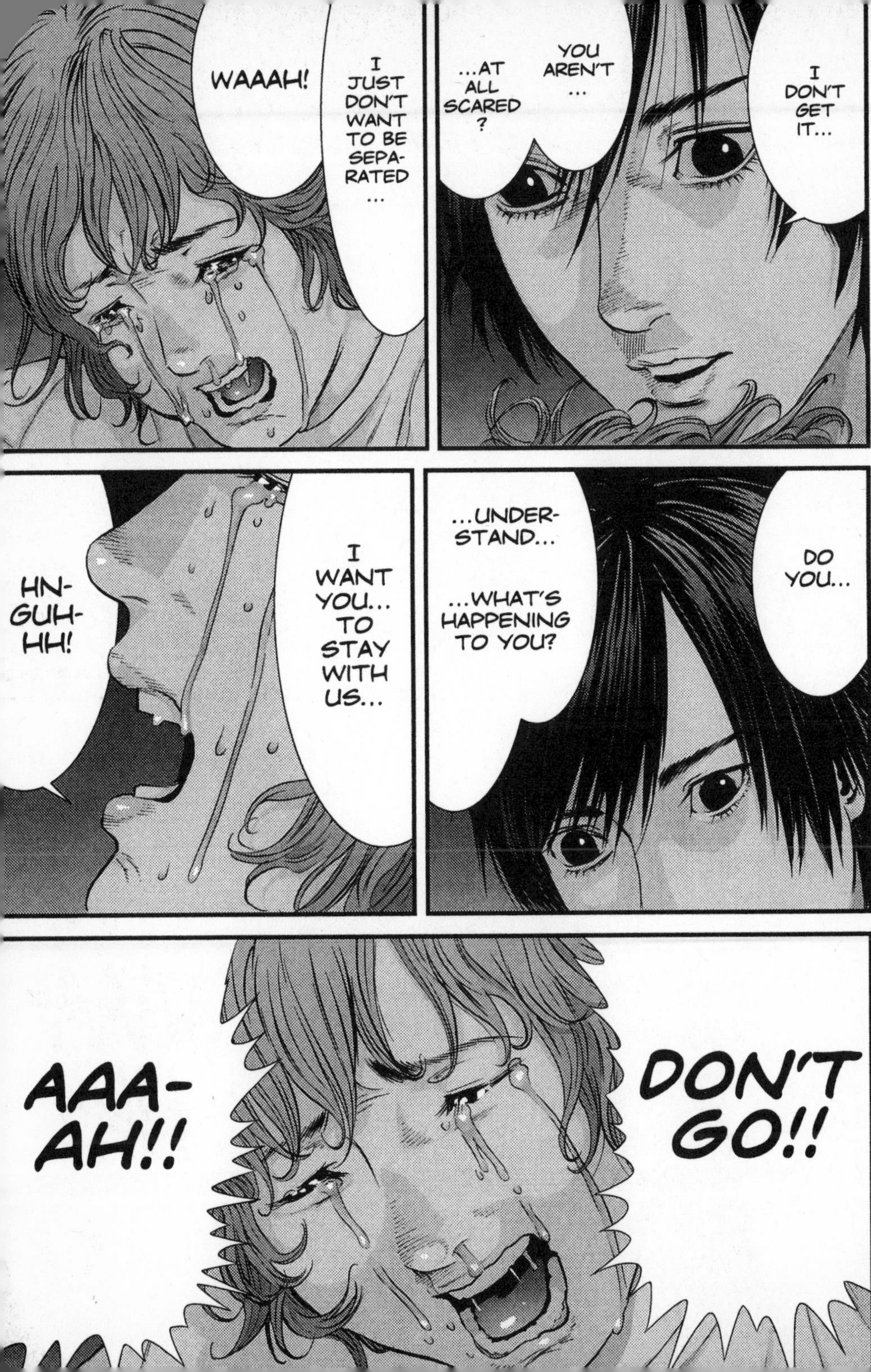
I DON'T GET IT...
YOU AREN'T ...
...AT ALL SCARED ?
I JUST DON'T WANT TO BE SEPA-RATED ...
WAAAH!
DO YOU...
...UNDER-STAND...
...WHAT'S HAPPENING TO YOU?
I WANT YOU... TO STAY WITH US...
HN-GUH-HH!
DON'T GO!!
AAA-AH!!

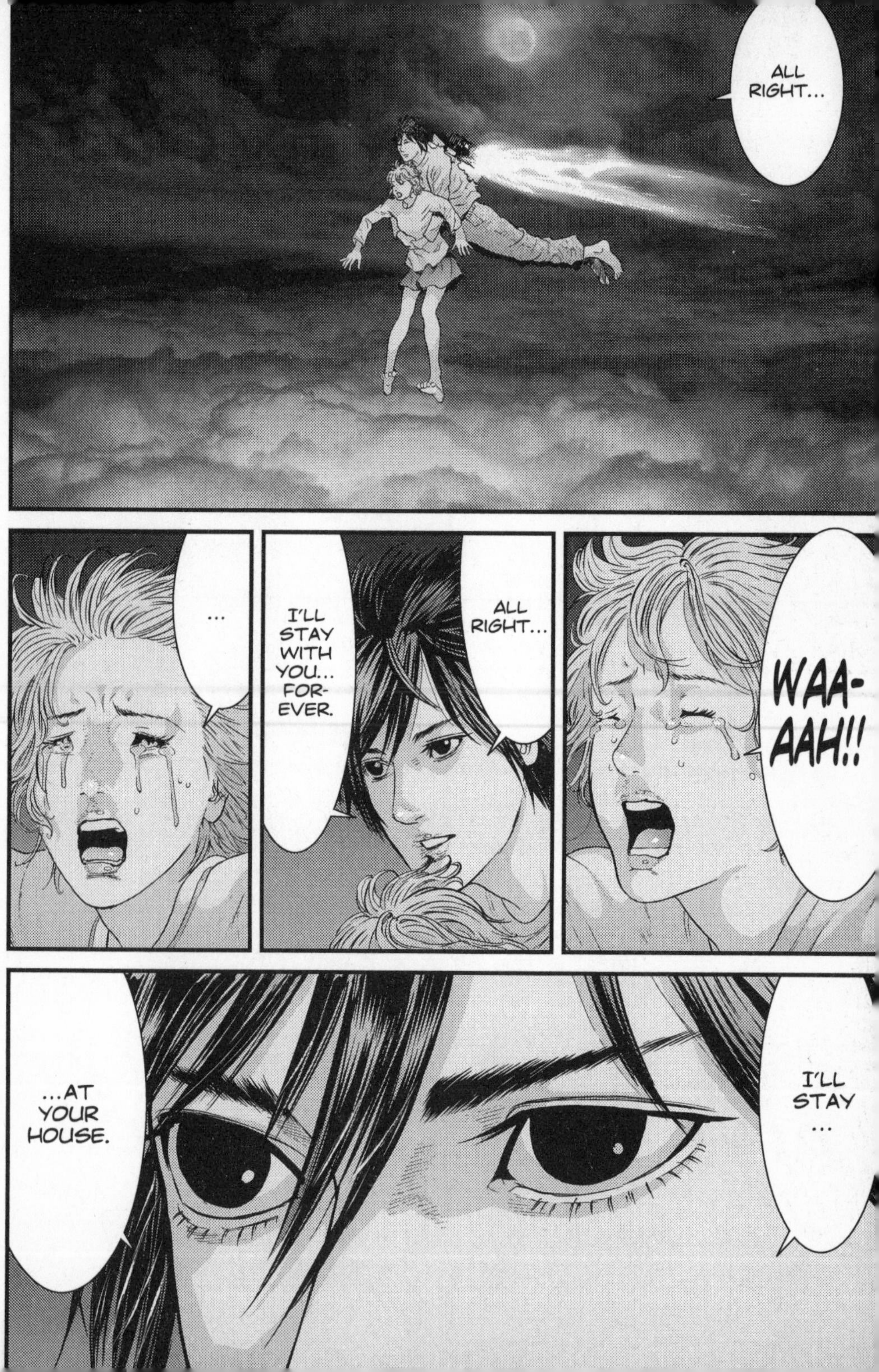
ALL RIGHT…
WAA-AAH!!
ALL RIGHT…
I'LL STAY WITH YOU… FOR-EVER.
…
I'LL STAY …
…AT YOUR HOUSE.

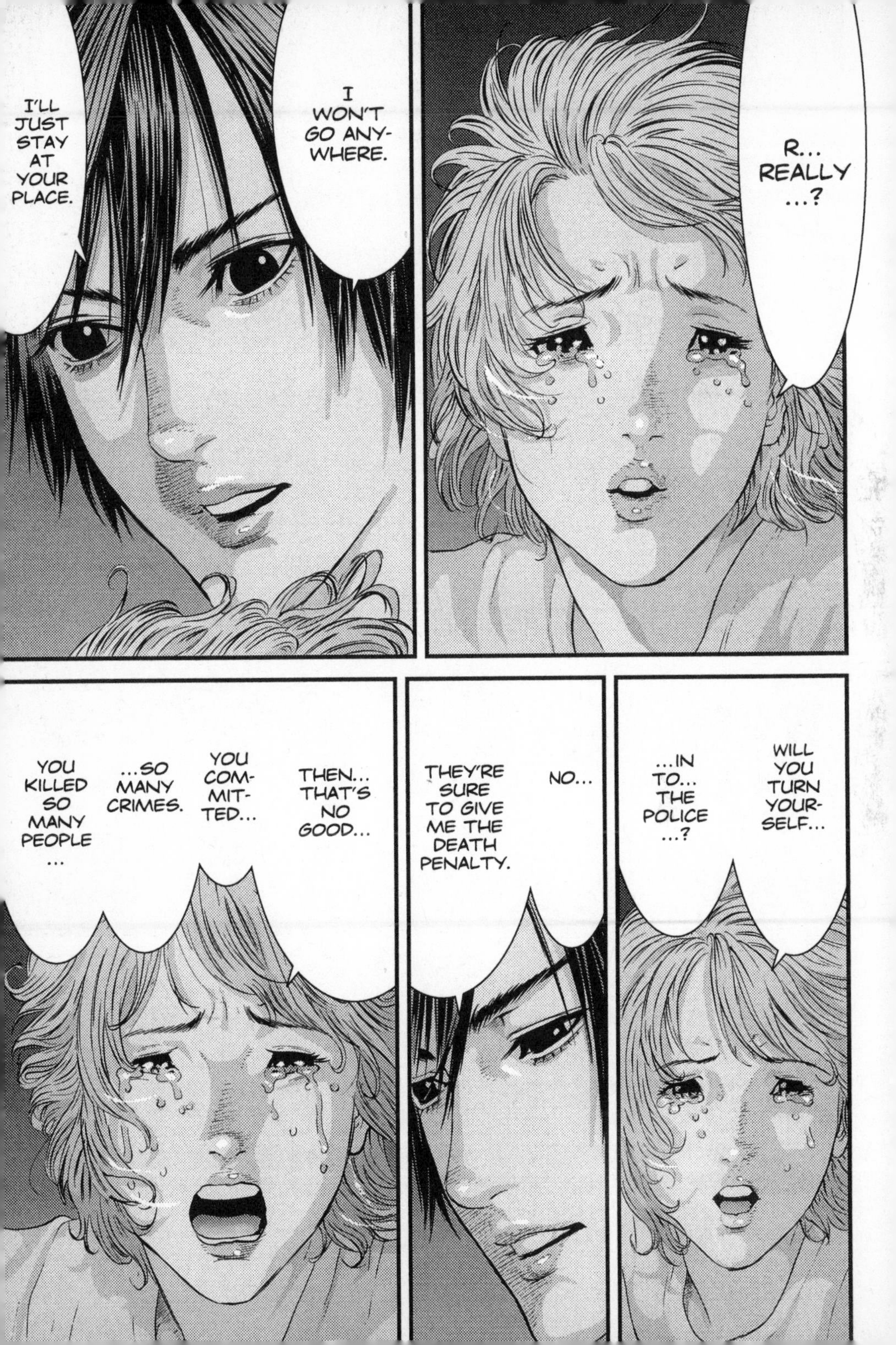
R... REALLY ...?
I WON'T GO ANYWHERE.
I'LL JUST STAY AT YOUR PLACE.
WILL YOU TURN YOURSELF...
...IN TO... THE POLICE ...?
NO...
THEY'RE SURE TO GIVE ME THE DEATH PENALTY.
THEN... THAT'S NO GOOD...
YOU COMMITTED...
...SO MANY CRIMES.
YOU KILLED SO MANY PEOPLE ...

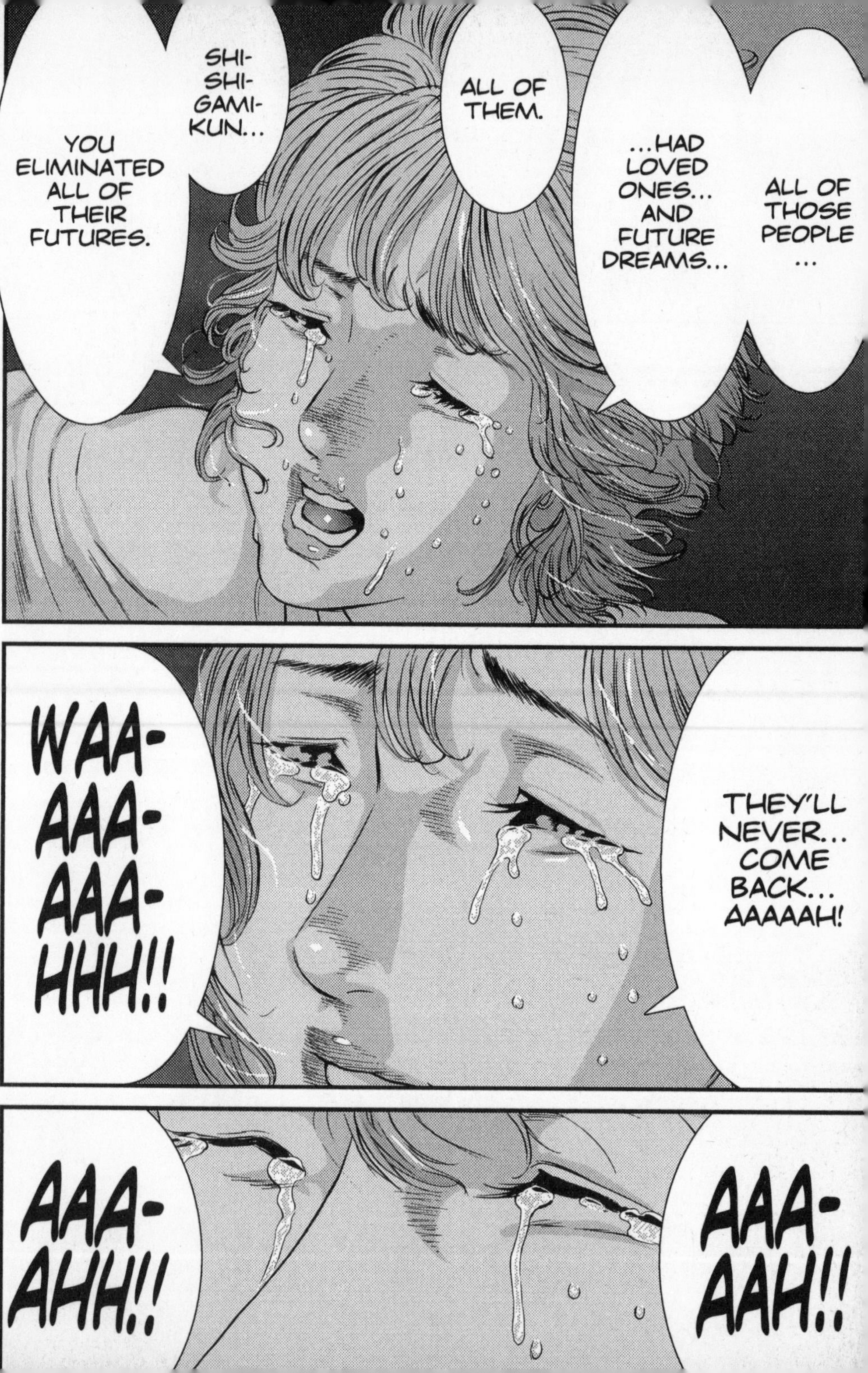
ALL OF THOSE PEOPLE...
...HAD LOVED ONES... AND FUTURE DREAMS...
ALL OF THEM.
SHI-SHI-GAMI-KUN...
YOU ELIMINATED ALL OF THEIR FUTURES.
THEY'LL NEVER... COME BACK... AAAAAH!
WAA-AAA-AAA-HHH!!
AAA-AAH!!
AAA-AHH!!

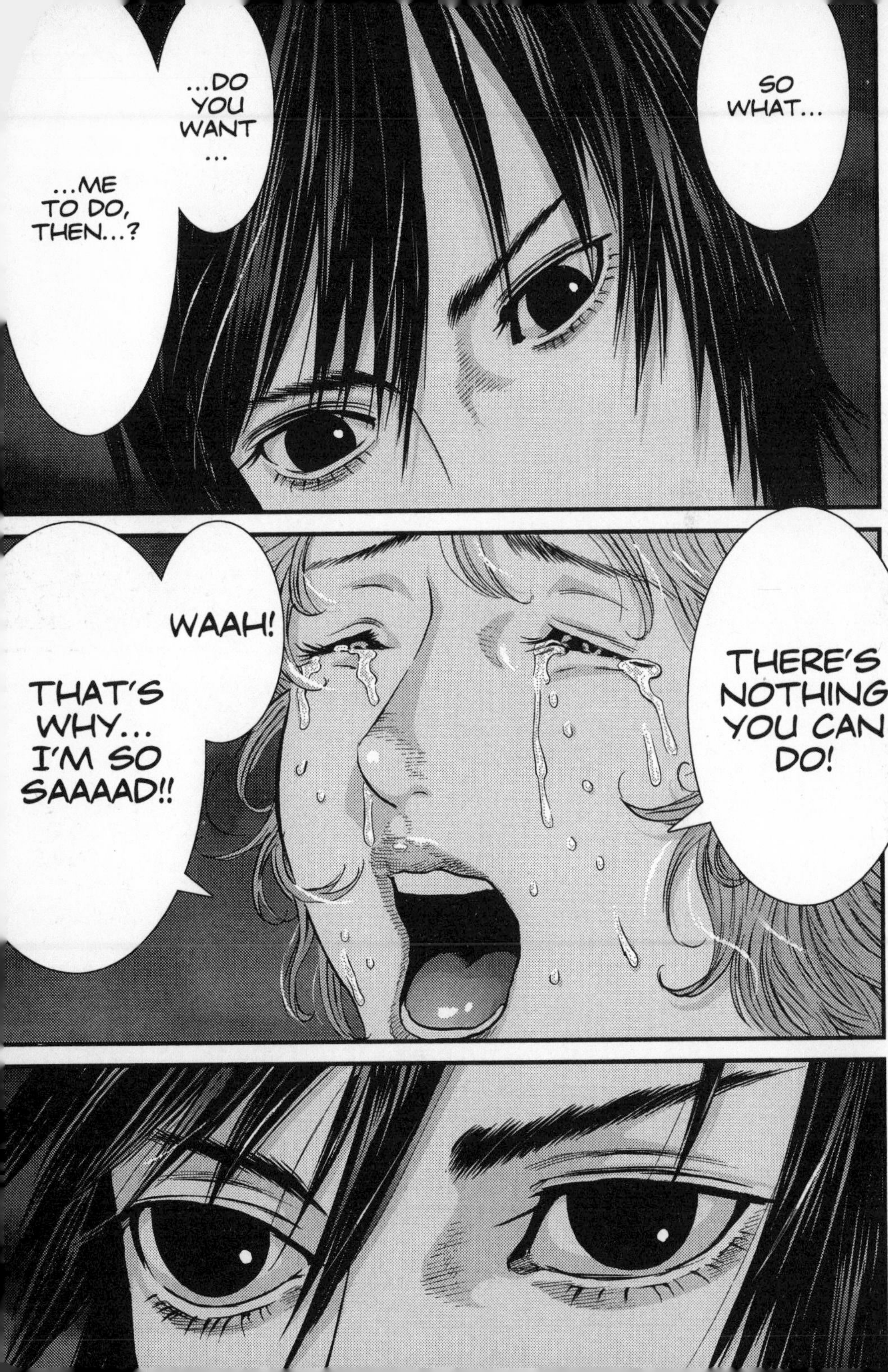
SO WHAT...
...DO YOU WANT ...
...ME TO DO, THEN...?
THERE'S NOTHING YOU CAN DO!
WAAH!
THAT'S WHY... I'M SO SAAAAD!!

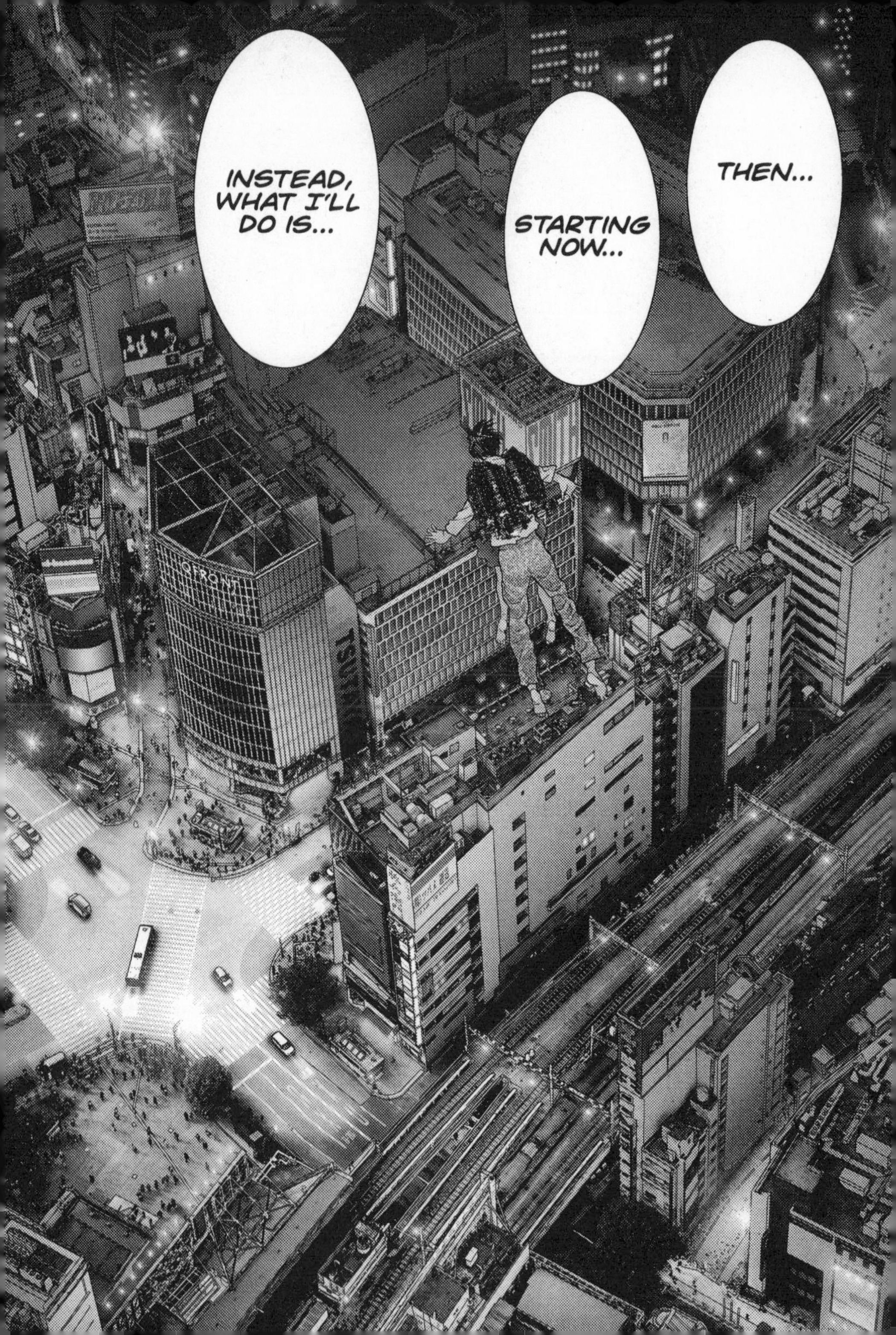
THEN...
STARTING NOW...
INSTEAD, WHAT I'LL DO IS...
QFRONT

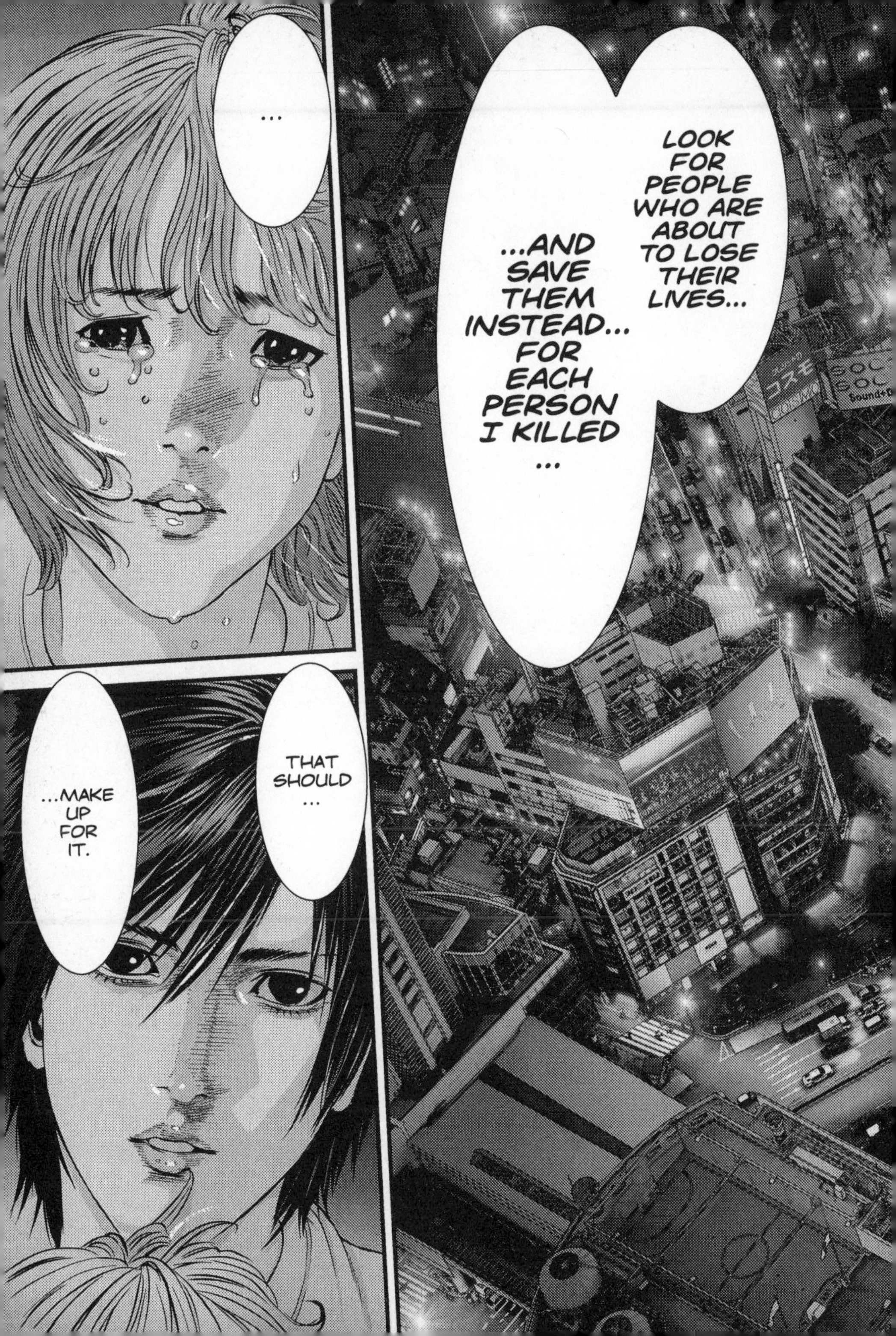
LOOK FOR PEOPLE WHO ARE ABOUT TO LOSE THEIR LIVES...
...AND SAVE THEM INSTEAD... FOR EACH PERSON I KILLED ...
...
THAT SHOULD ...
...MAKE UP FOR IT.

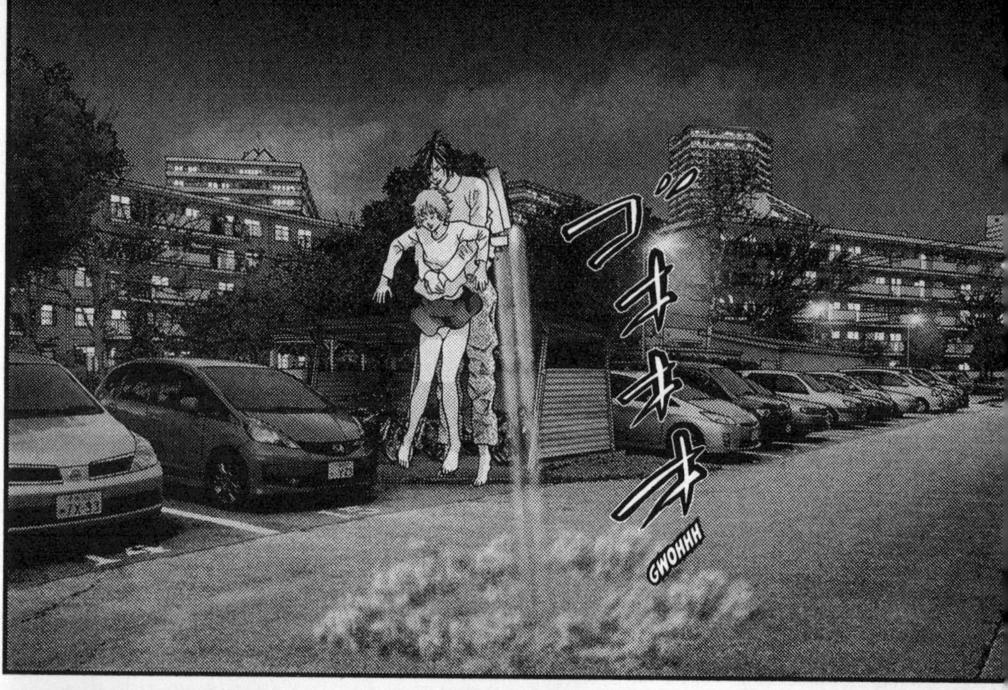
GWOHHH
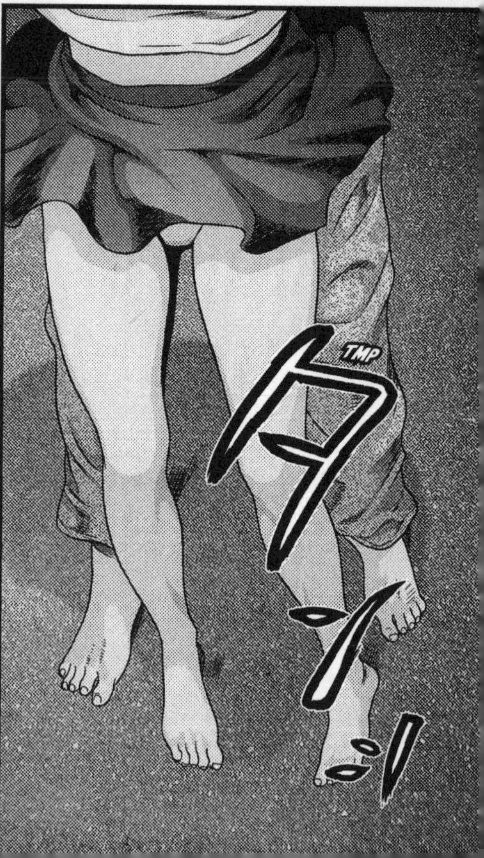
TMP
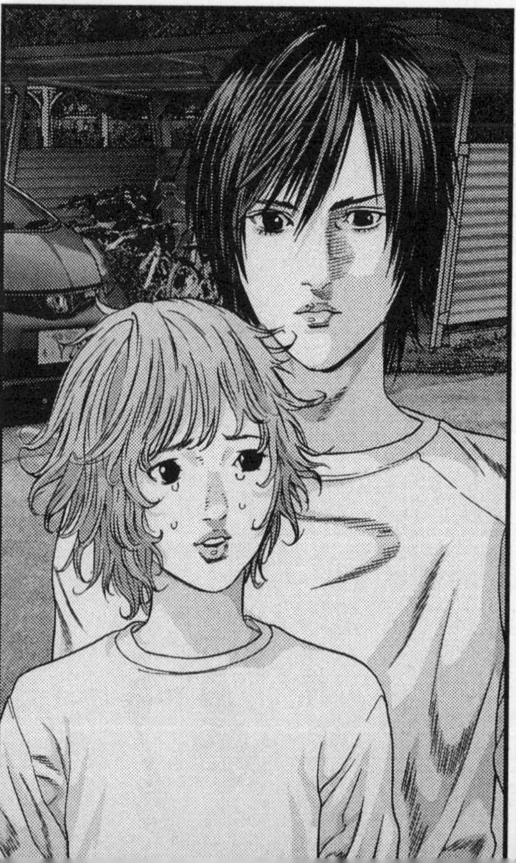

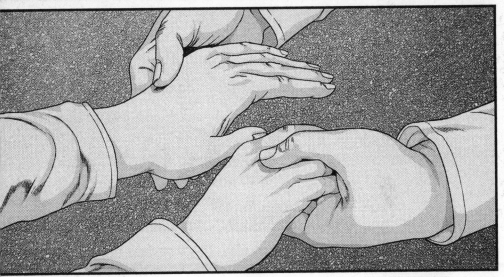

HUH?

...ARE YOURS... BUT...

AND SO...

...ARE SO WARM...

YOUR HANDS...

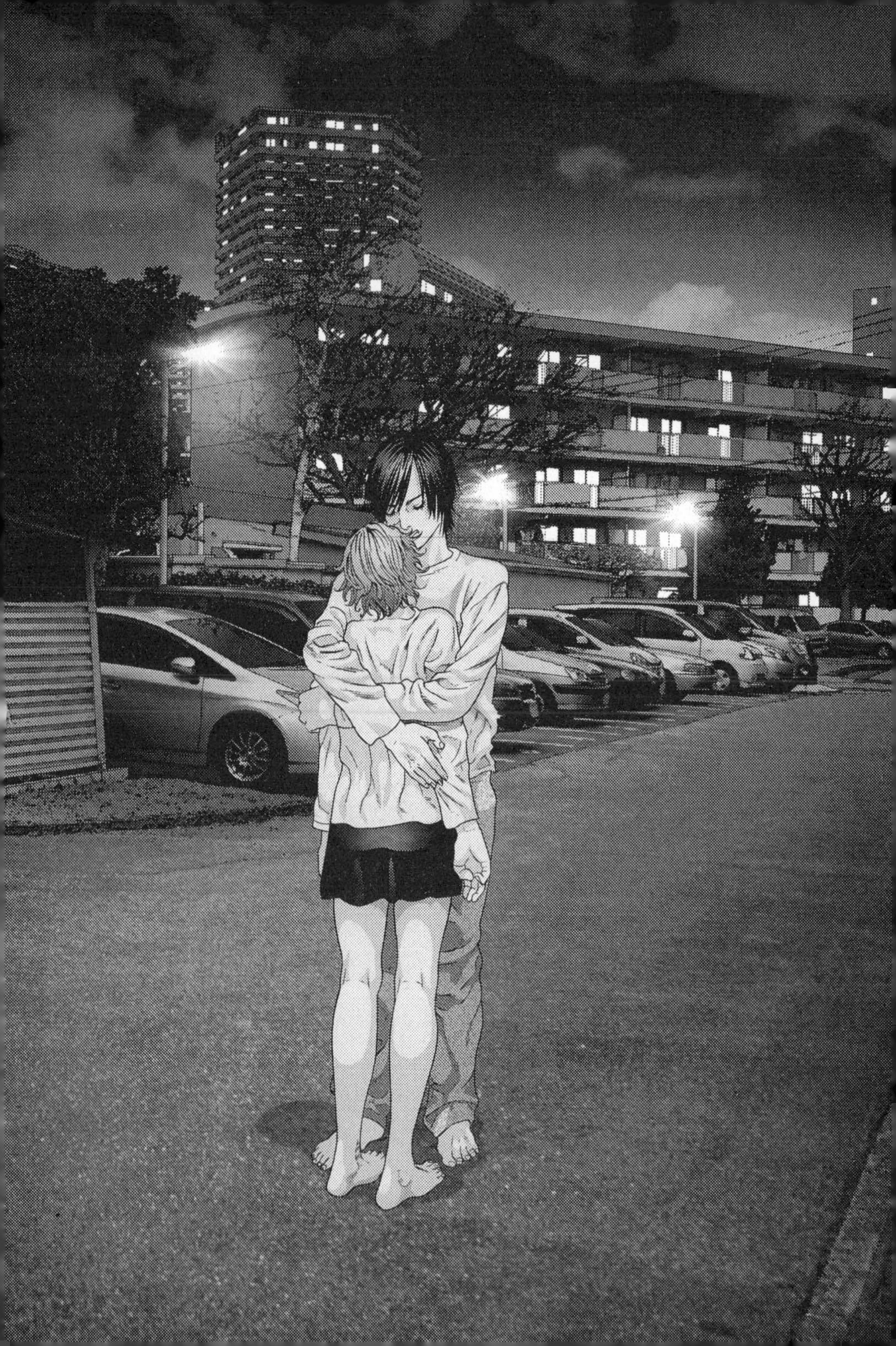

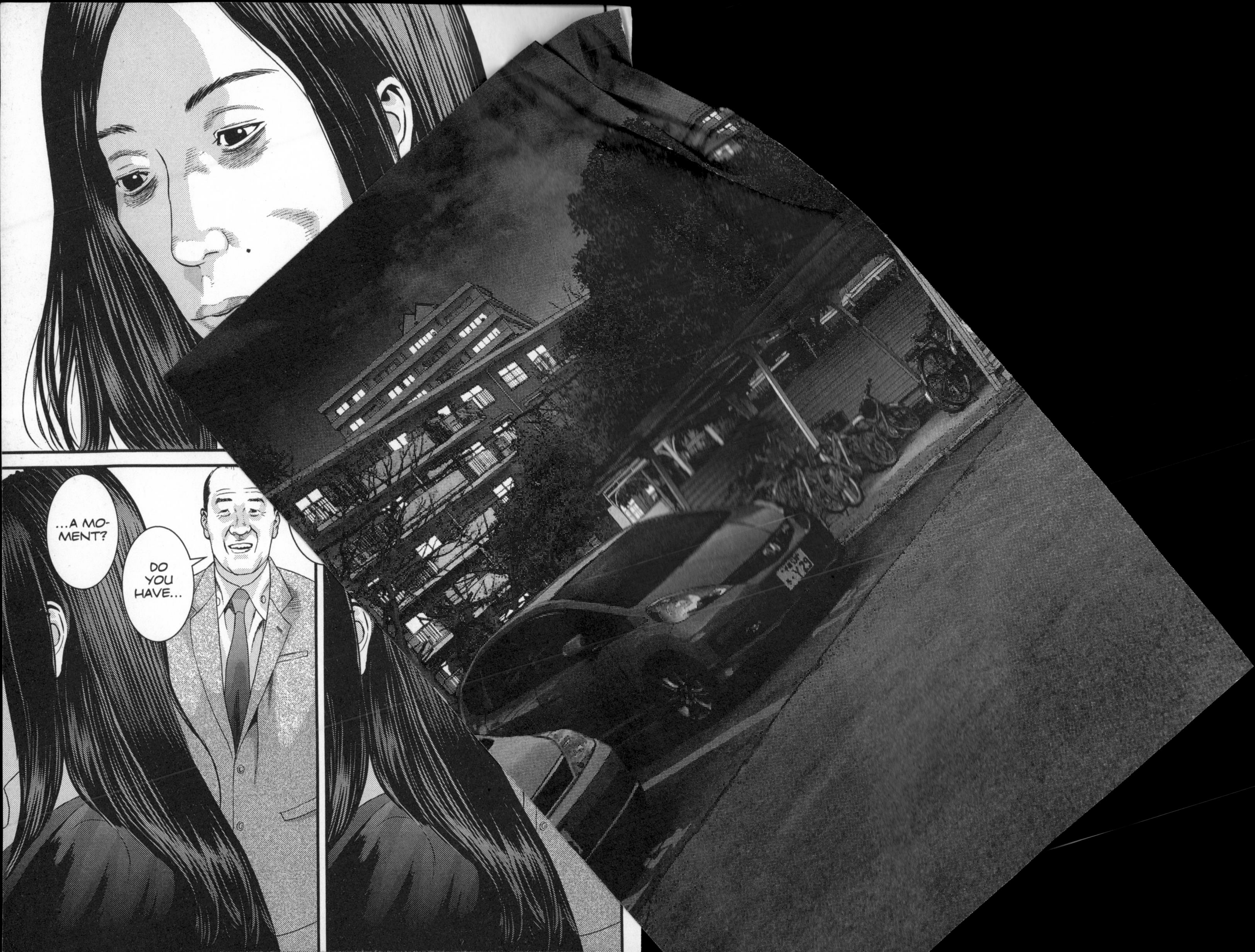
DO YOU HAVE...
...A MO-MENT?

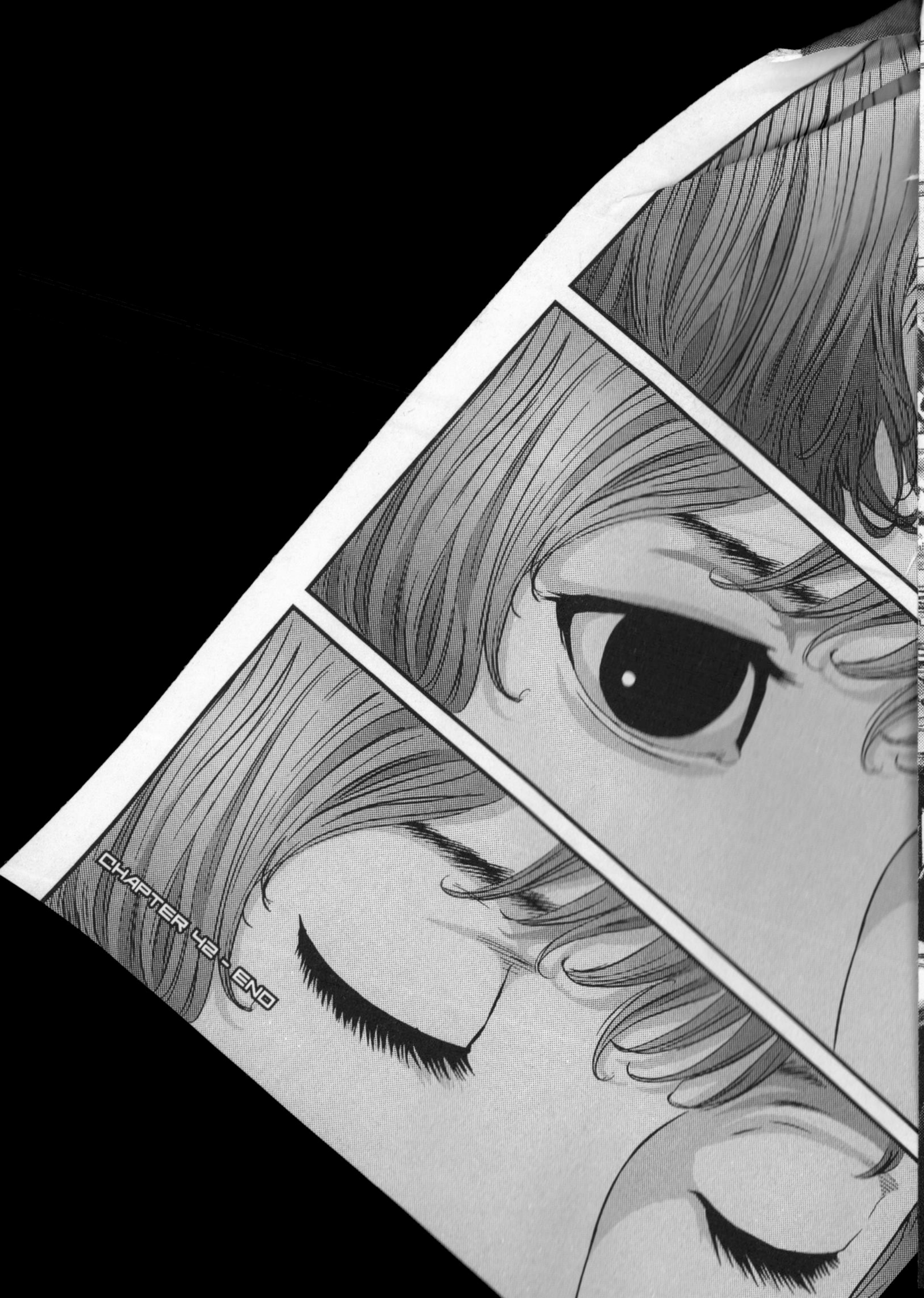
CHAPTER 42 - END

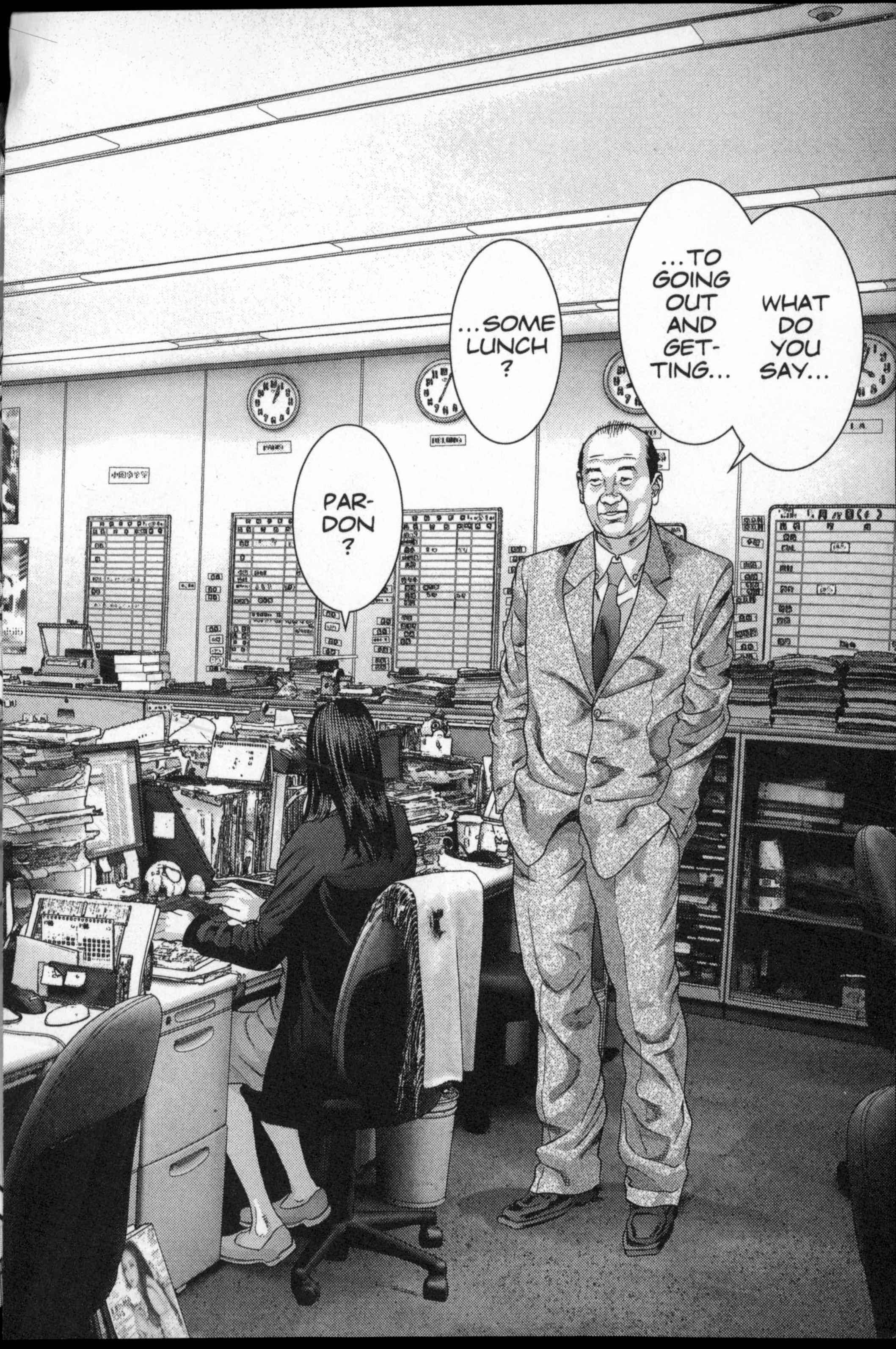
WHAT DO YOU SAY...
...TO GOING OUT AND GETTING...
...SOME LUNCH?
PARDON?

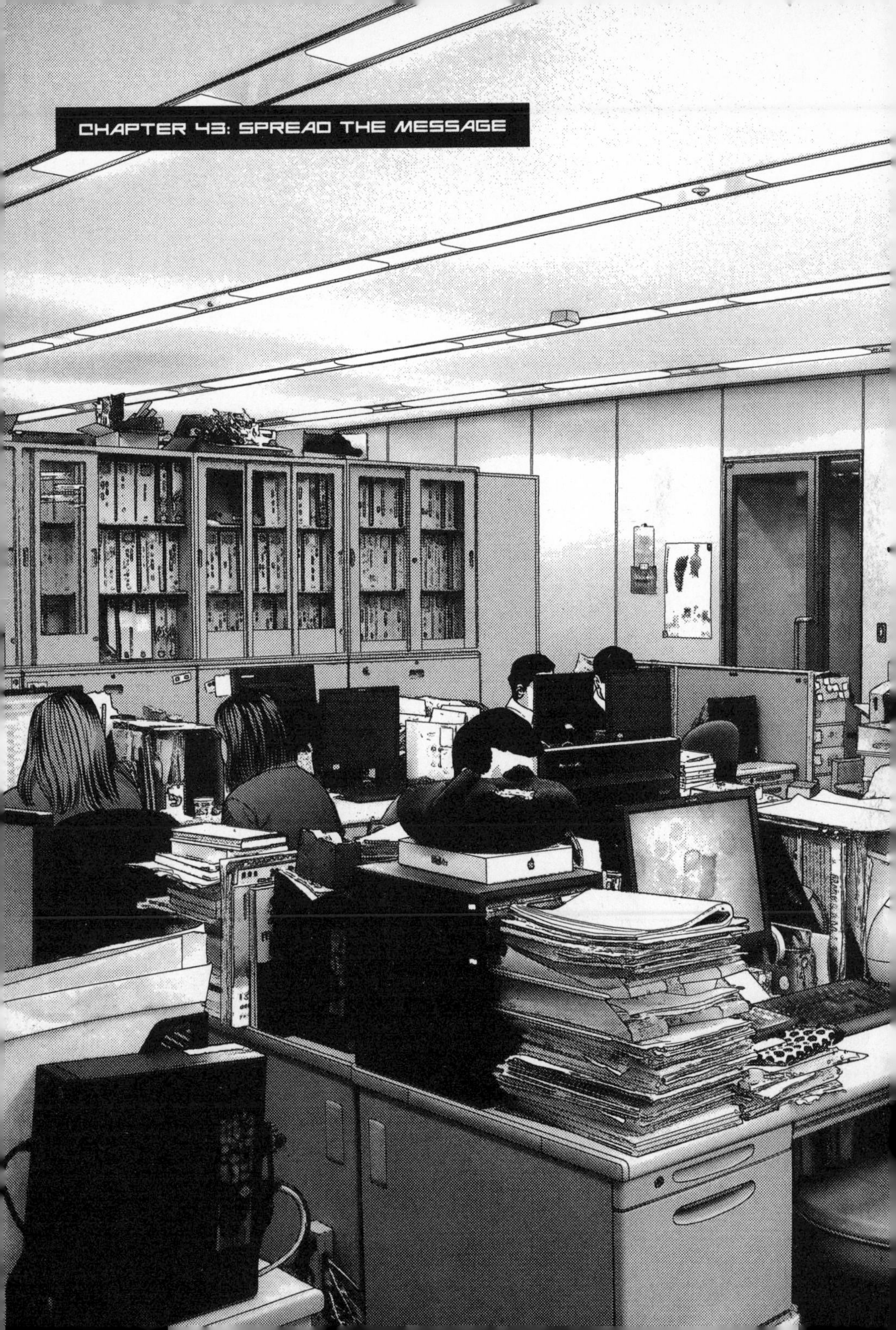
CHAPTER 43: SPREAD THE MESSAGE

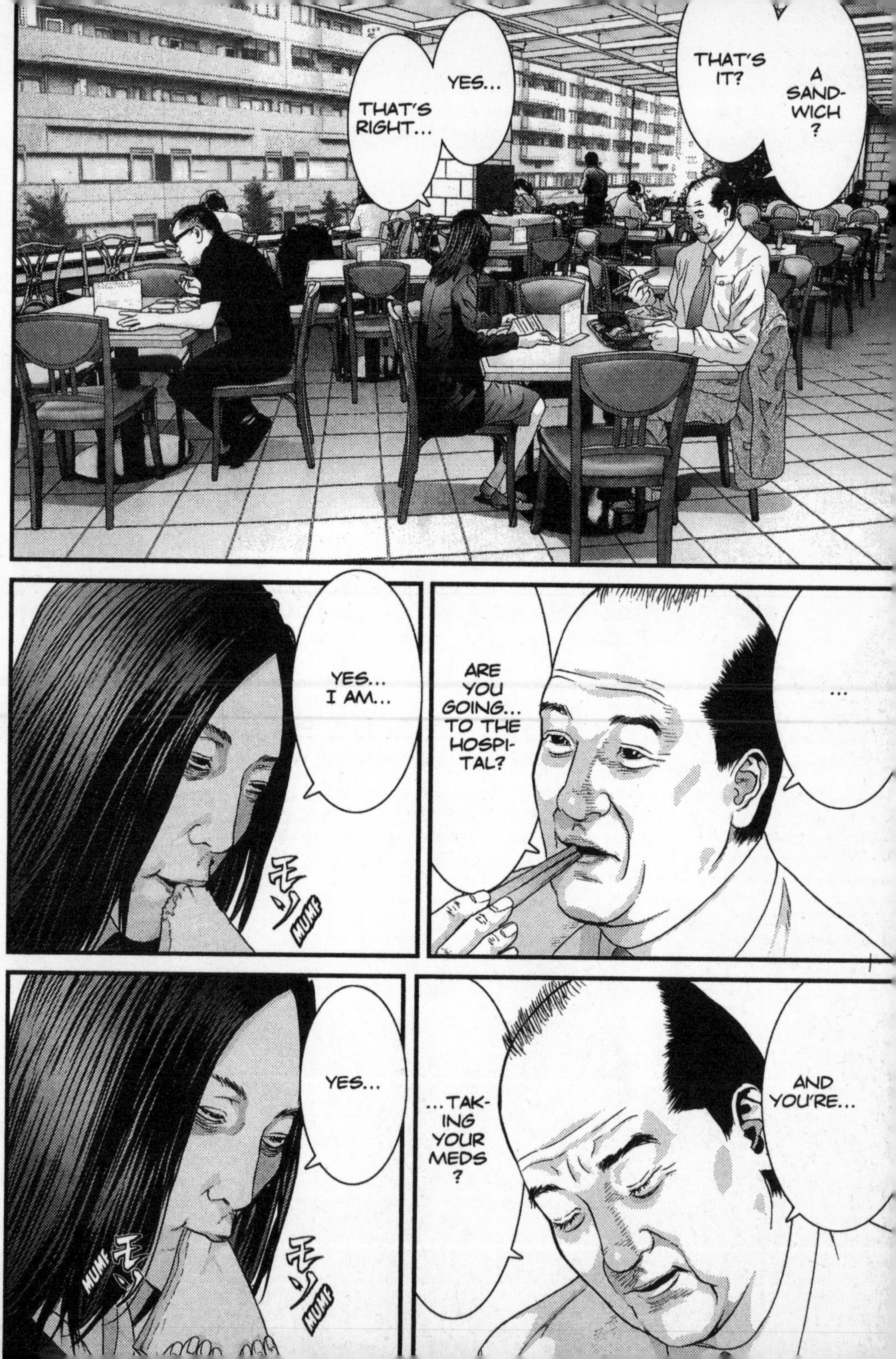
THAT'S IT? A SAND-WICH?
YES... THAT'S RIGHT...
...
ARE YOU GOING... TO THE HOSPI-TAL?
YES... I AM...
MUMF
AND YOU'RE...
...TAK-ING YOUR MEDS?
YES...
MUMF
MUMF

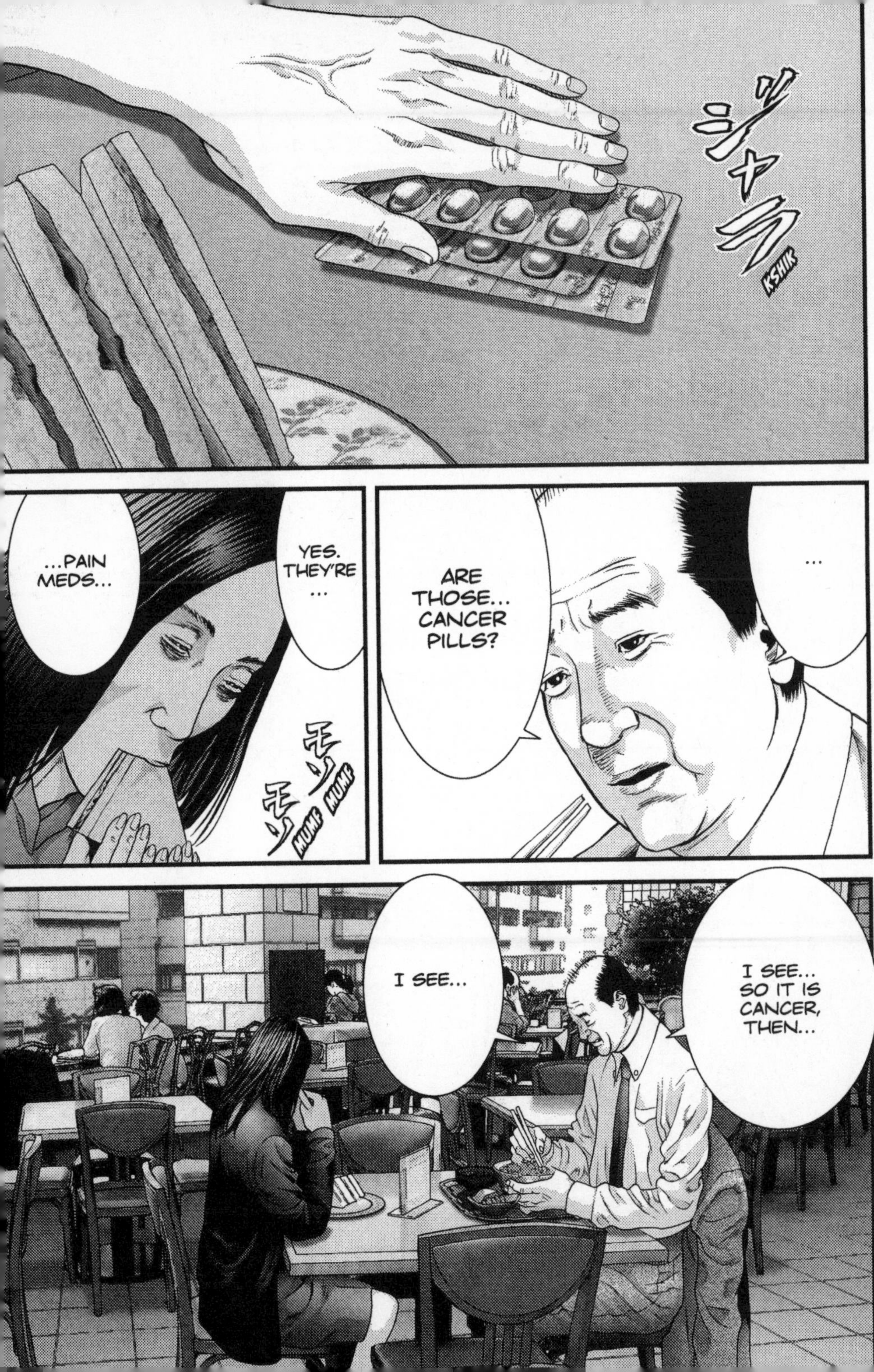
ジャラ
KSHIK
...
ARE THOSE... CANCER PILLS?
YES. THEY'RE ...
...PAIN MEDS...
モソ モソ
MUMF MUMF
I SEE... SO IT IS CANCER, THEN...
I SEE...

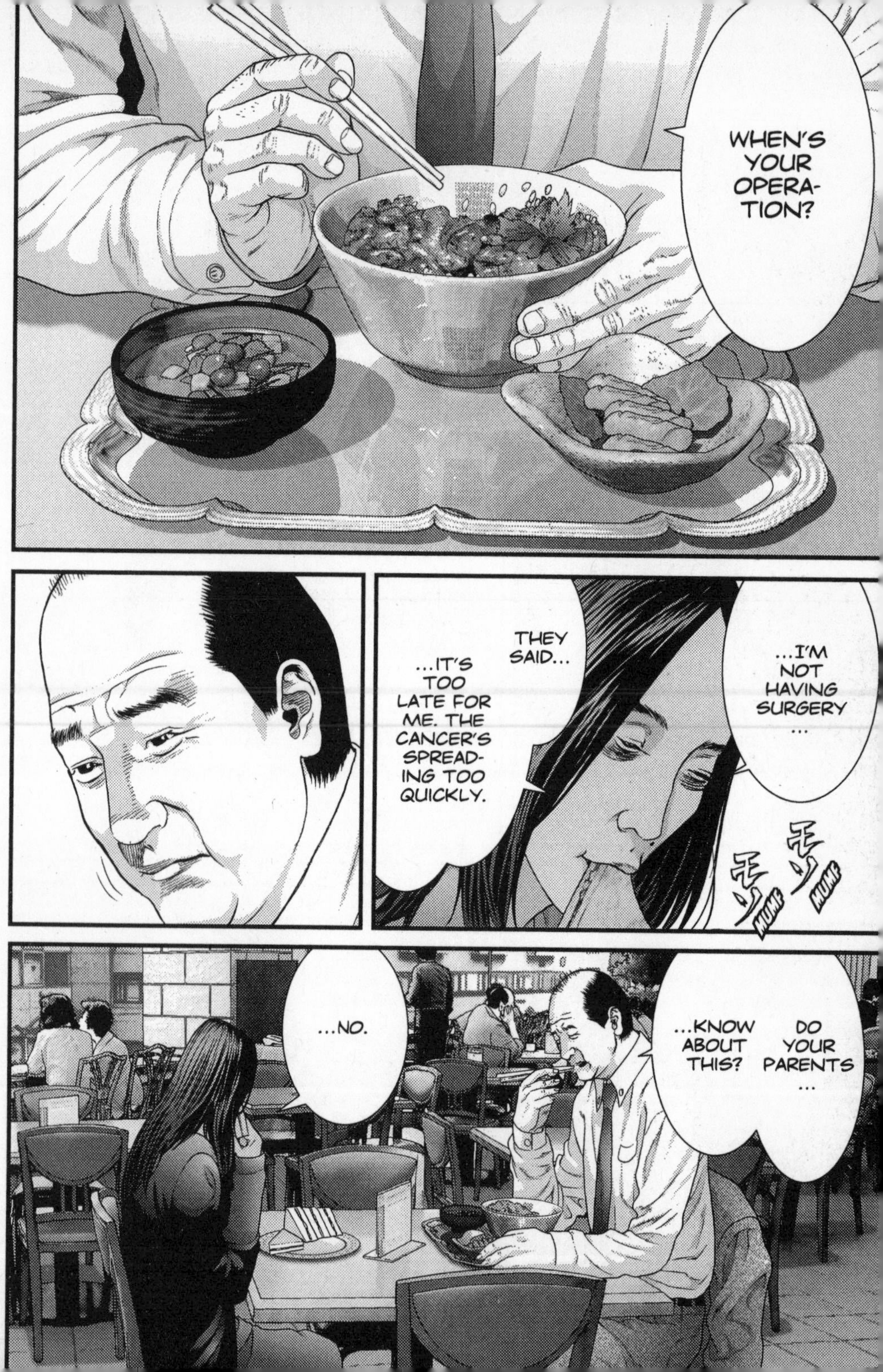
WHEN'S YOUR OPERATION?
...I'M NOT HAVING SURGERY ...
THEY SAID...
...IT'S TOO LATE FOR ME. THE CANCER'S SPREADING TOO QUICKLY.
MUMF MUMF
DO YOUR PARENTS ...
...KNOW ABOUT THIS?
...NO.

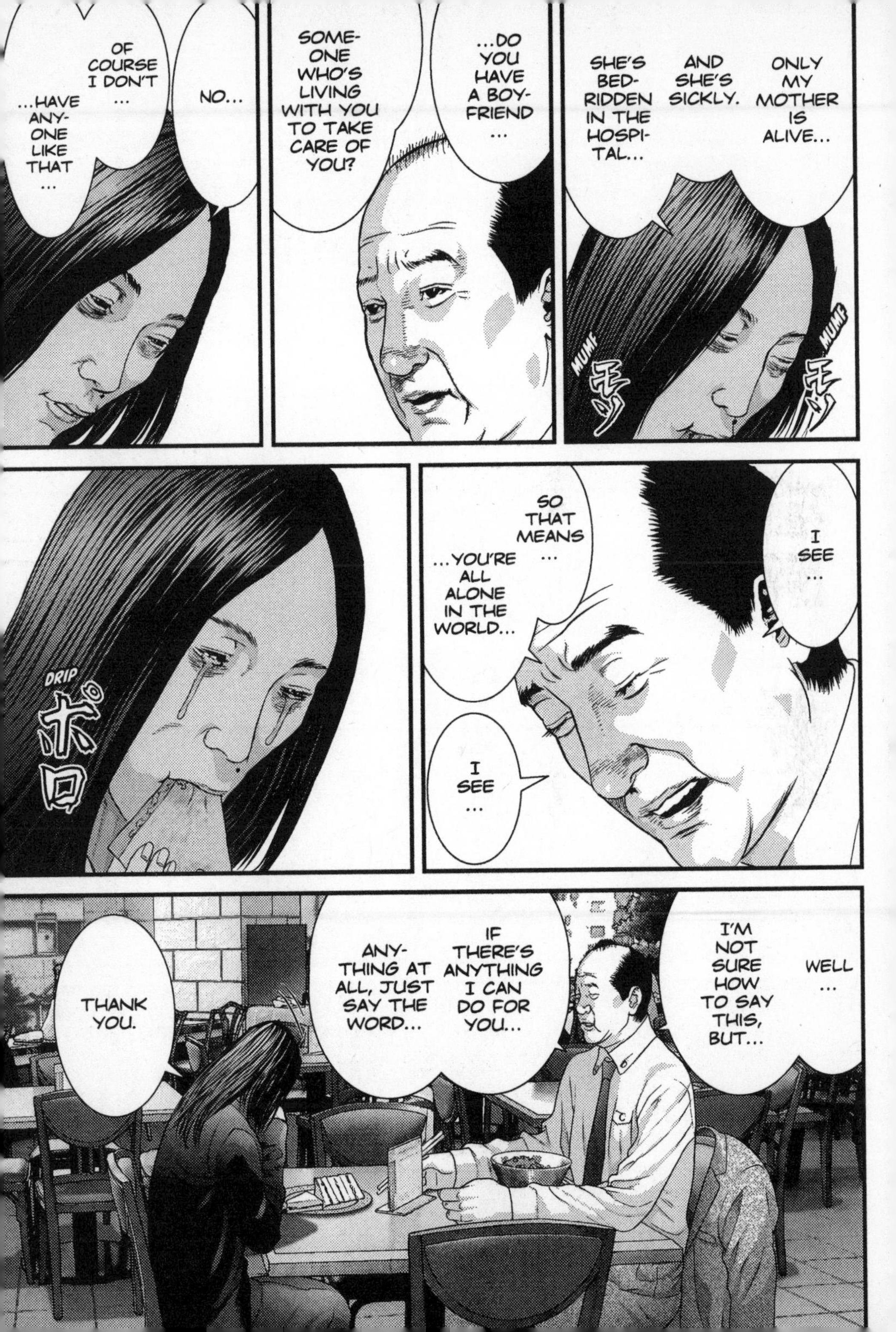
ONLY MY MOTHER IS ALIVE...
AND SHE'S SICKLY.
SHE'S BED-RIDDEN IN THE HOSPI-TAL...
MUMF
MUMF
...DO YOU HAVE A BOY-FRIEND...
SOME-ONE WHO'S LIVING WITH YOU TO TAKE CARE OF YOU?
NO...
OF COURSE I DON'T...
...HAVE ANY-ONE LIKE THAT...
I SEE...
SO THAT MEANS...
...YOU'RE ALL ALONE IN THE WORLD...
I SEE...
DRIP
WELL...
I'M NOT SURE HOW TO SAY THIS, BUT...
IF THERE'S ANYTHING I CAN DO FOR YOU...
ANY-THING AT ALL, JUST SAY THE WORD...
THANK YOU.

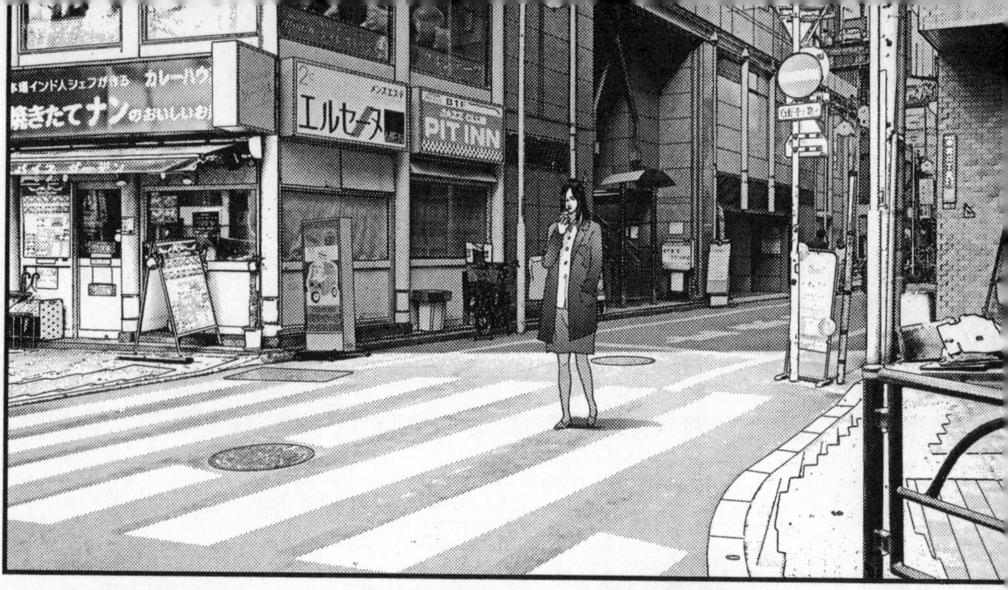
メンズエステ
エルセータ
PIT INN
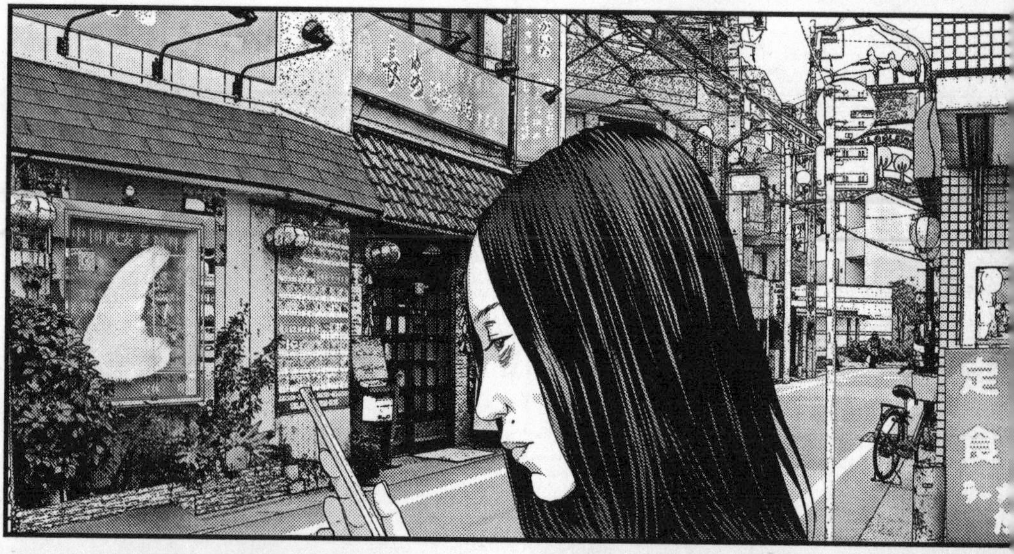
定
食
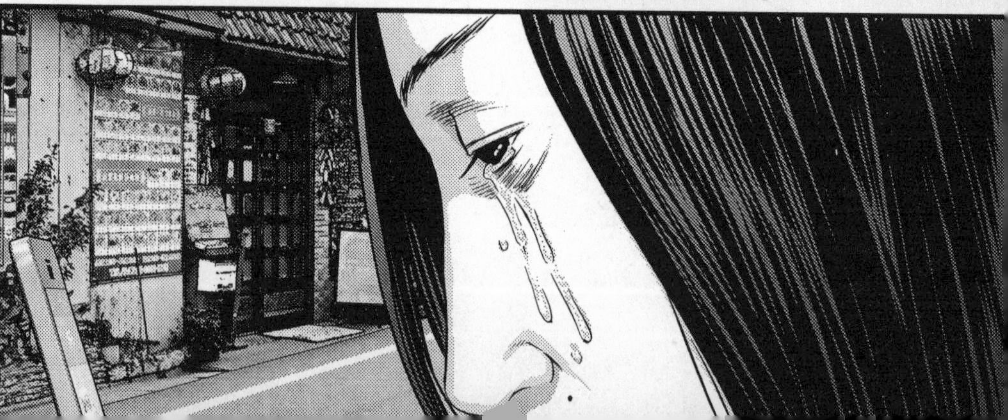

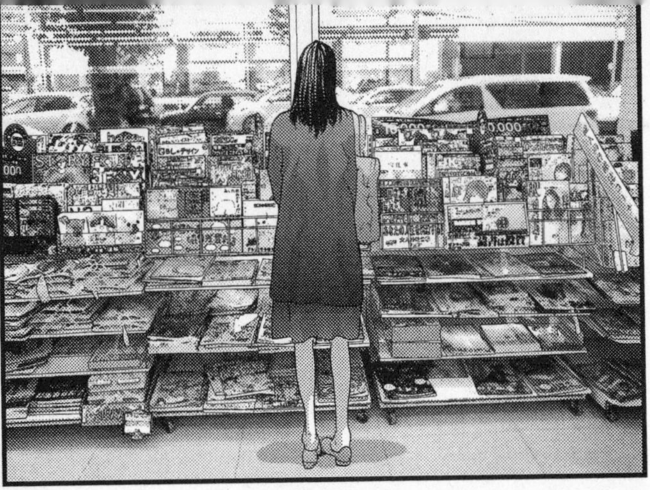
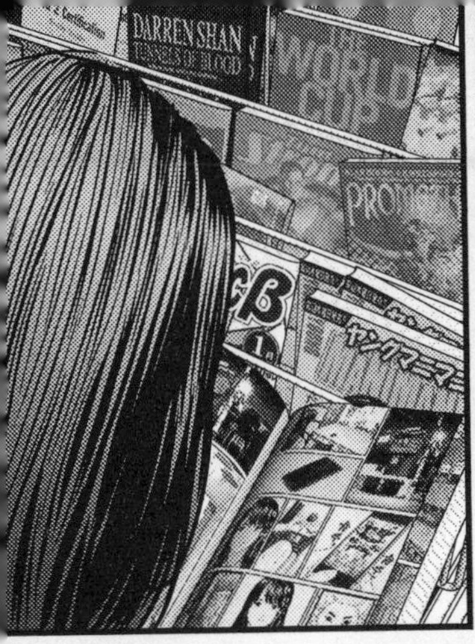
DARREN SHAN
TUNNELS OF BLOOD
WORLD CUP
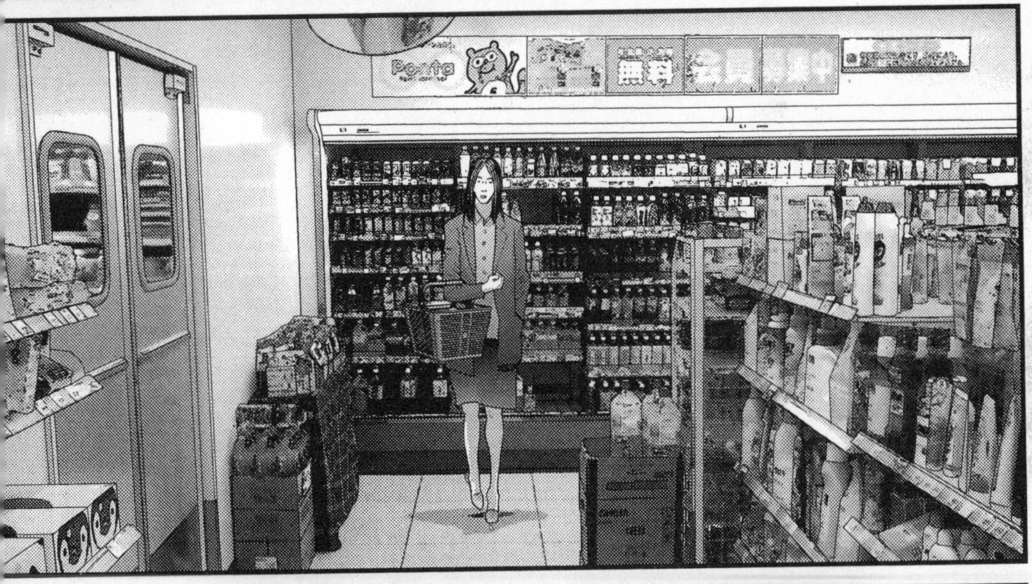
Ponta
無料
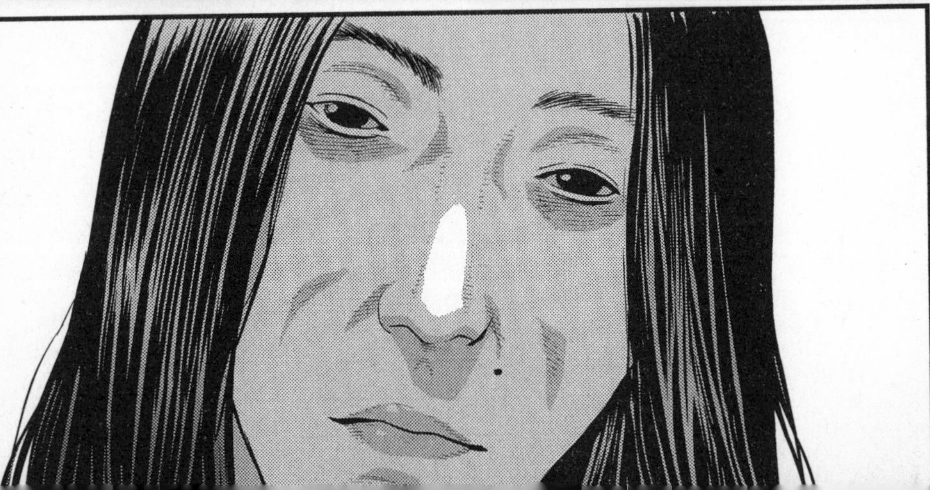

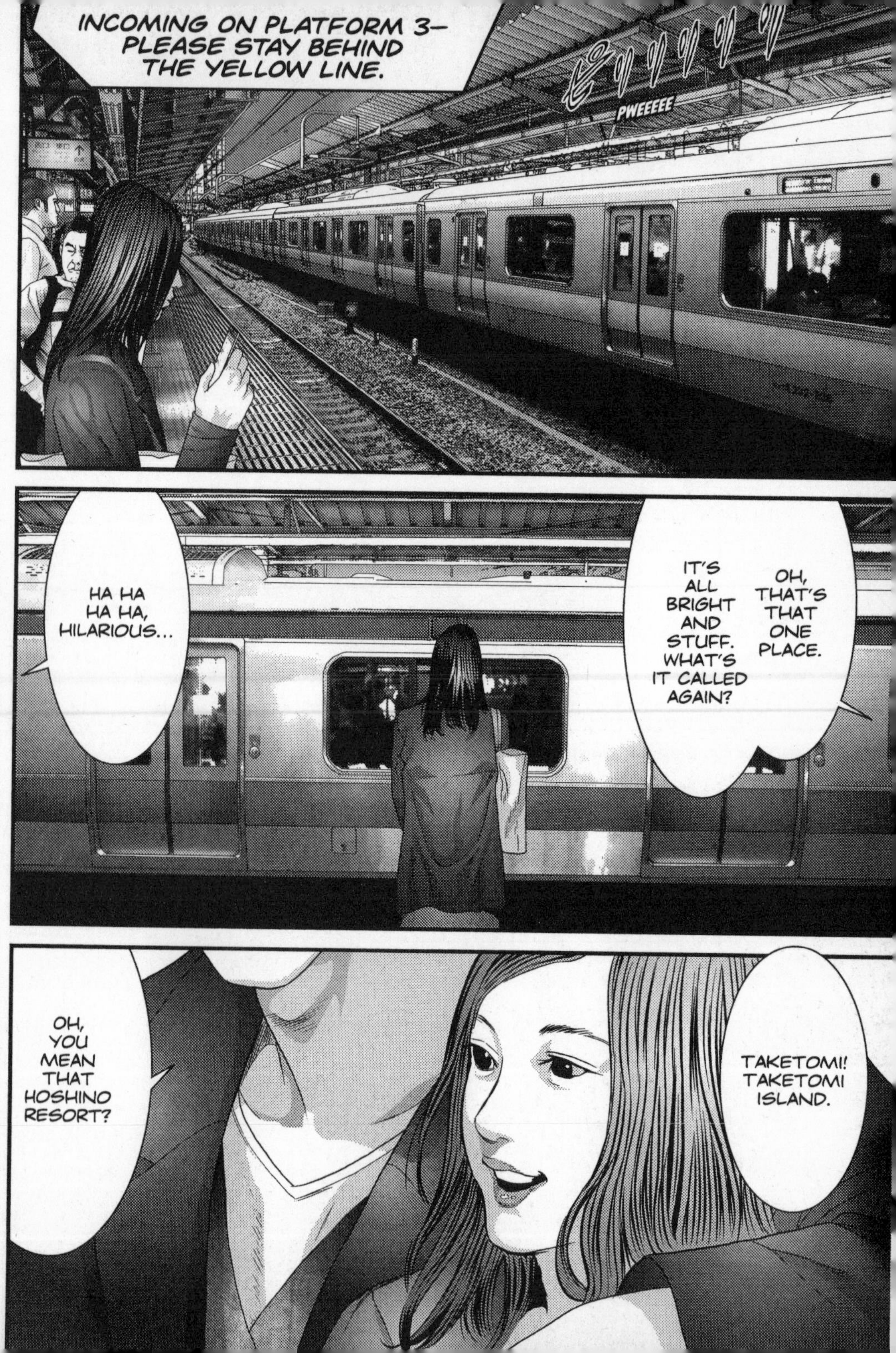
INCOMING ON PLATFORM 3— PLEASE STAY BEHIND THE YELLOW LINE.
PWEEEEE
OH, THAT'S THAT ONE PLACE. IT'S ALL BRIGHT AND STUFF. WHAT'S IT CALLED AGAIN?
HA HA HA HA, HILARIOUS...
TAKETOMI! TAKETOMI ISLAND.
OH, YOU MEAN THAT HOSHINO RESORT?

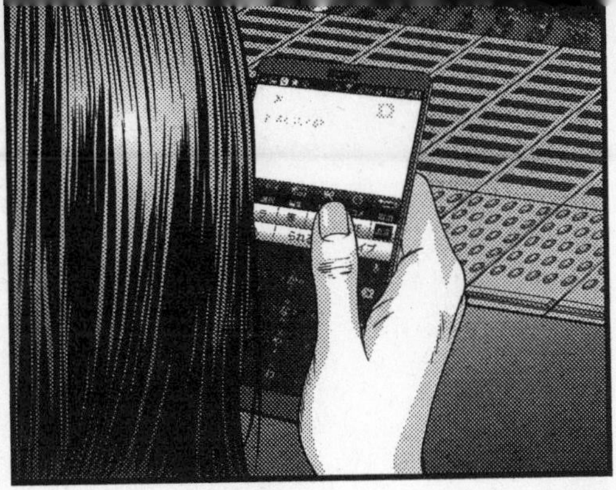
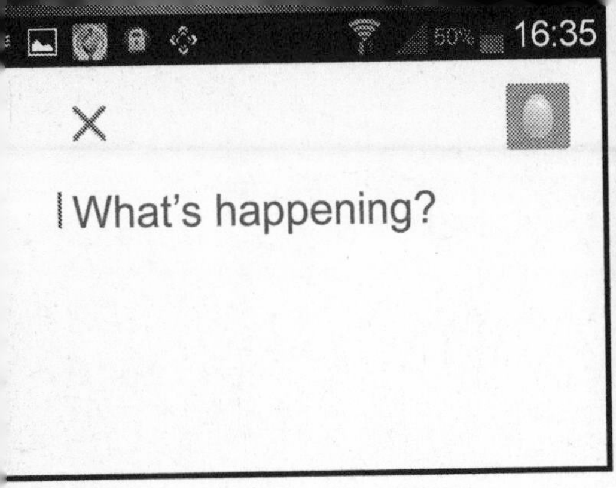
50%
16:35
What's happening?
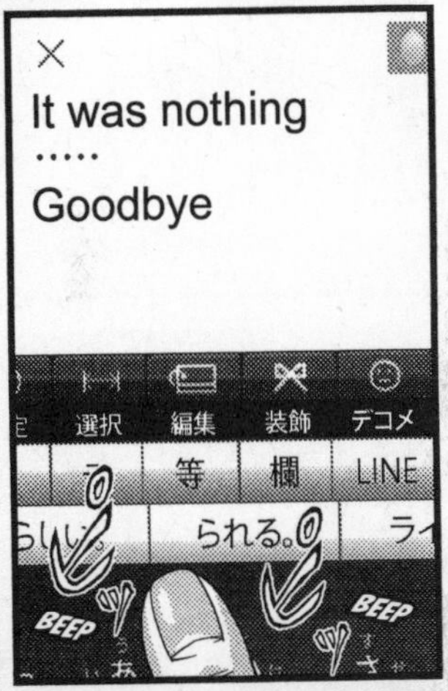
It was nothing
.....
Goodbye
選択
編集
装飾
デコメ
等
欄
LINE
られる。
BEEP
BEEP
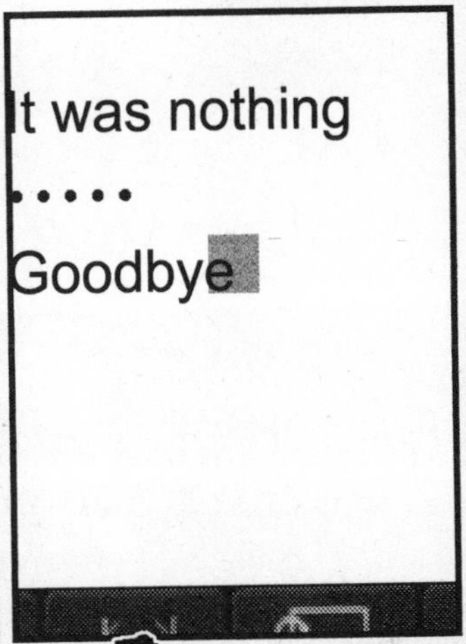
It was nothing
.....
Goodbye
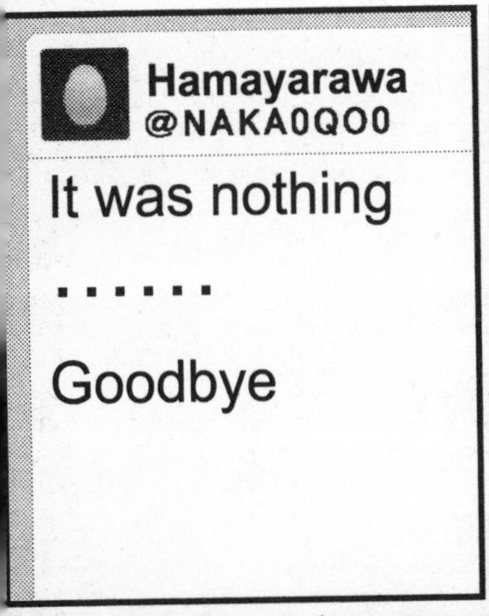
Hamayarawa
@NAKA0QO0
It was nothing
......
Goodbye
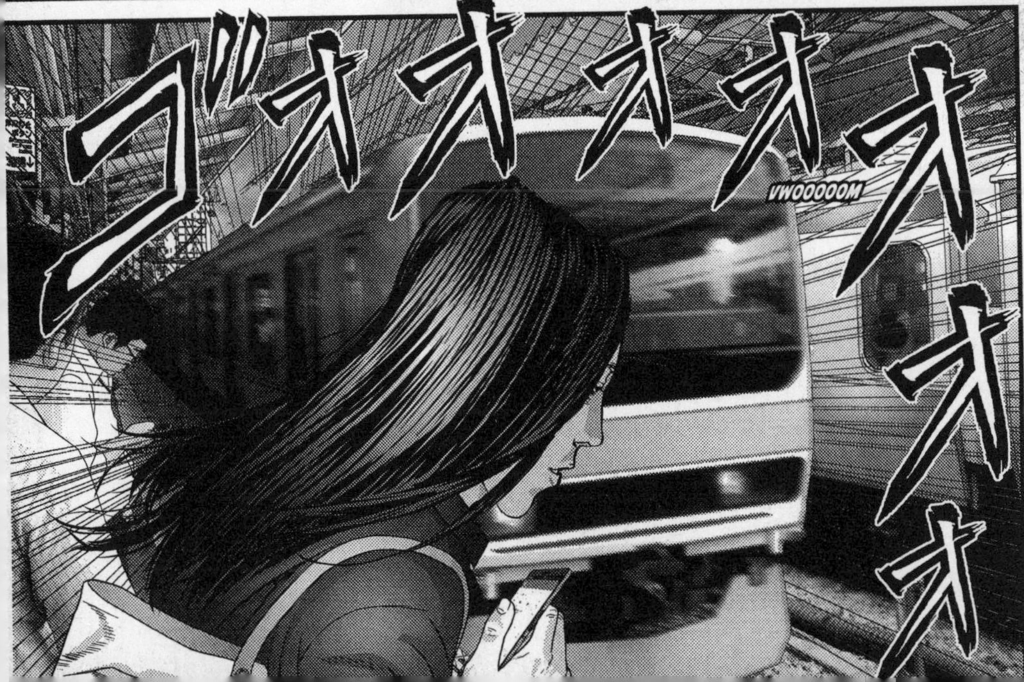
ゴオオオオオオオ
VWOOOOOM

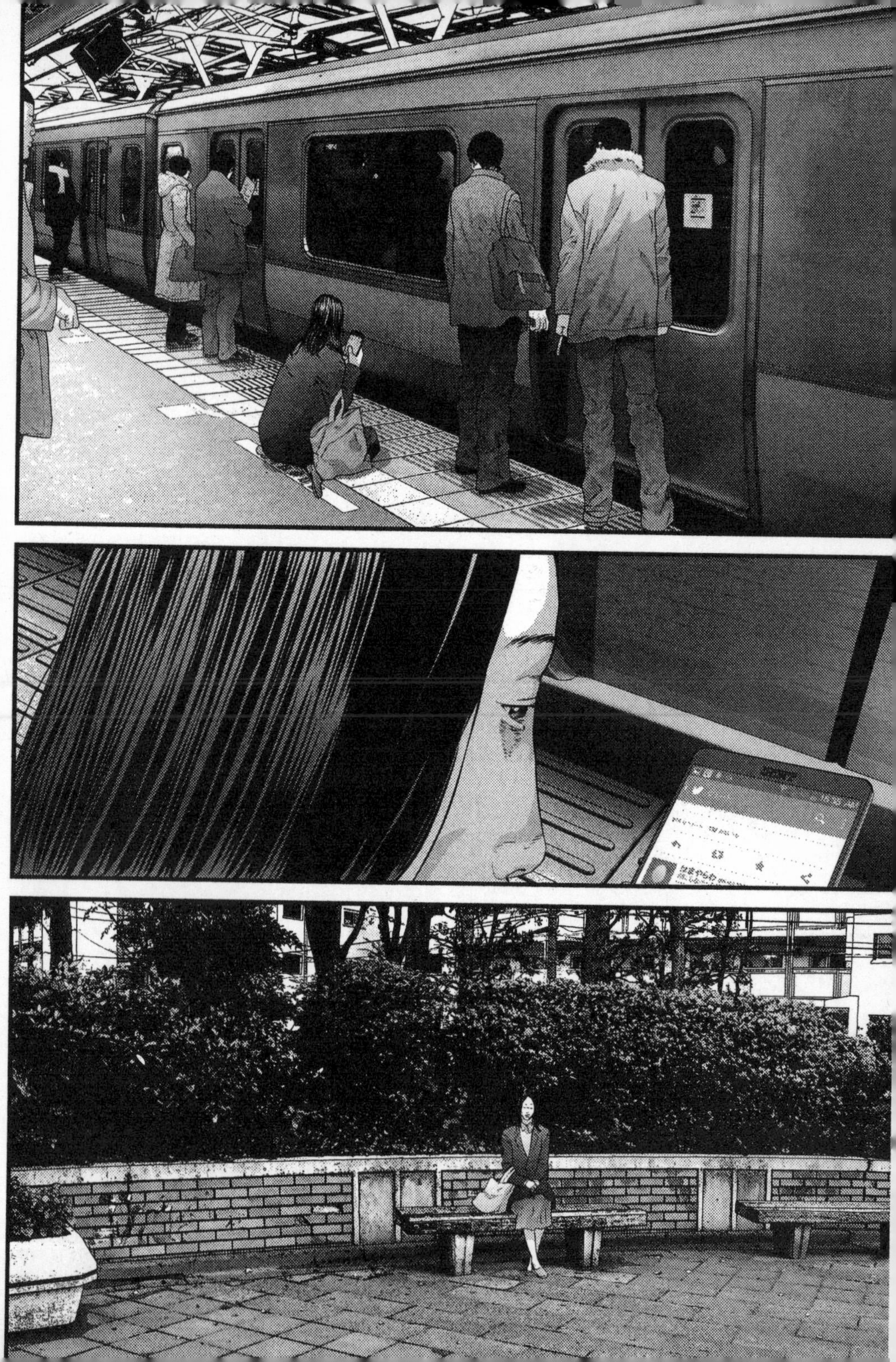

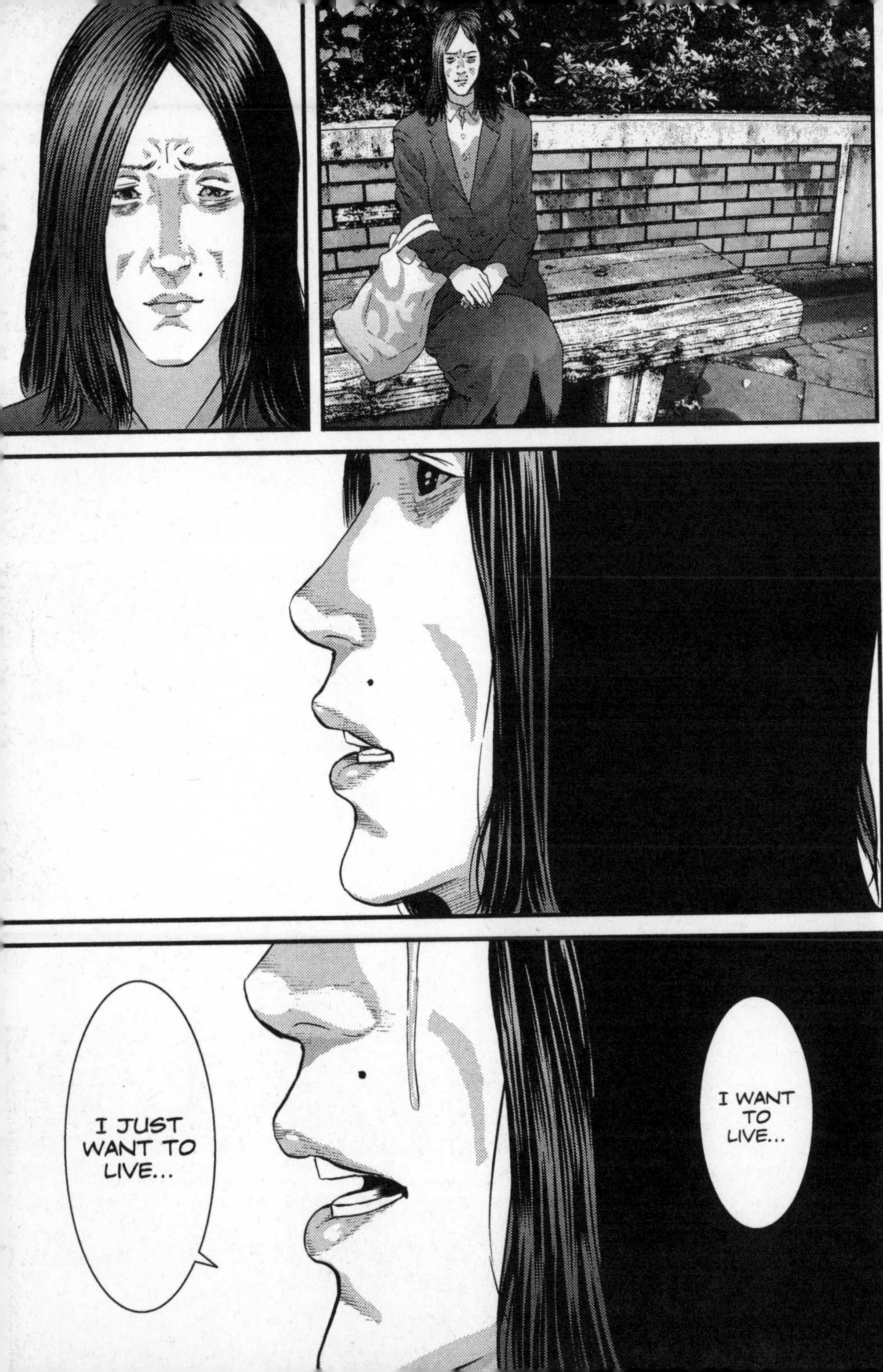
I WANT TO LIVE...
I JUST WANT TO LIVE...

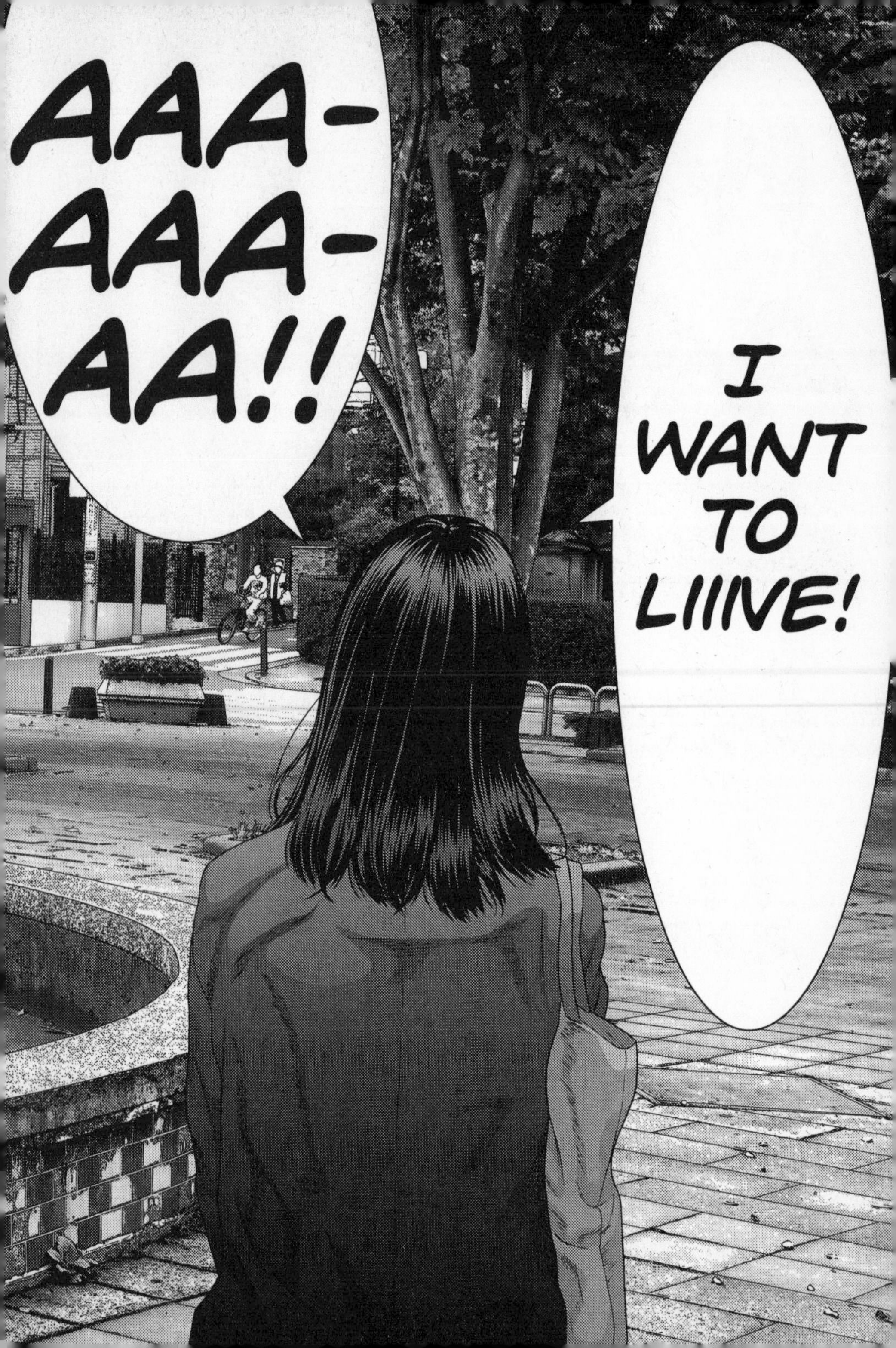
I WANT TO LIIVE!
AAA-AAA-AA!!

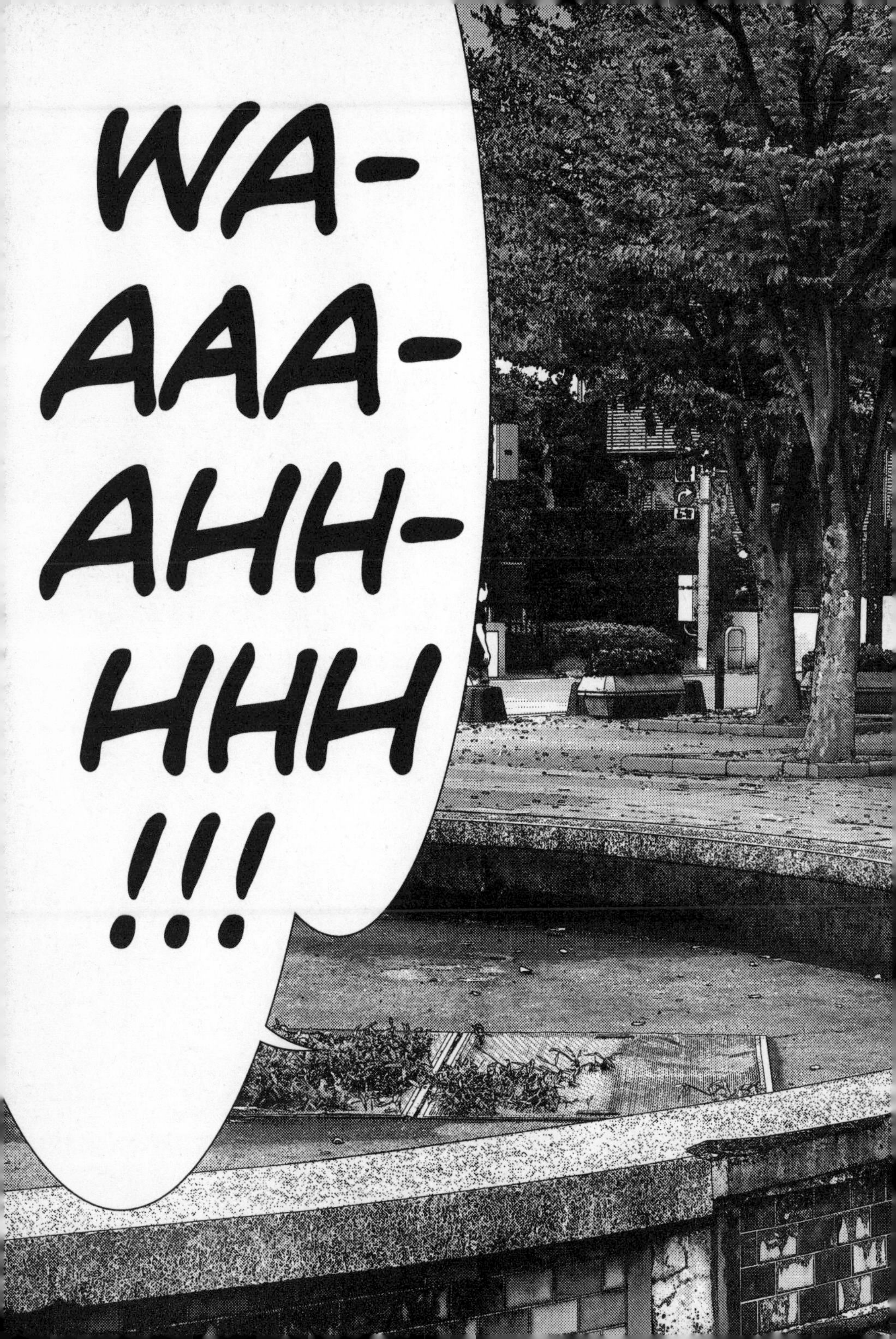
WA-AAA-AHH-HHH!!!

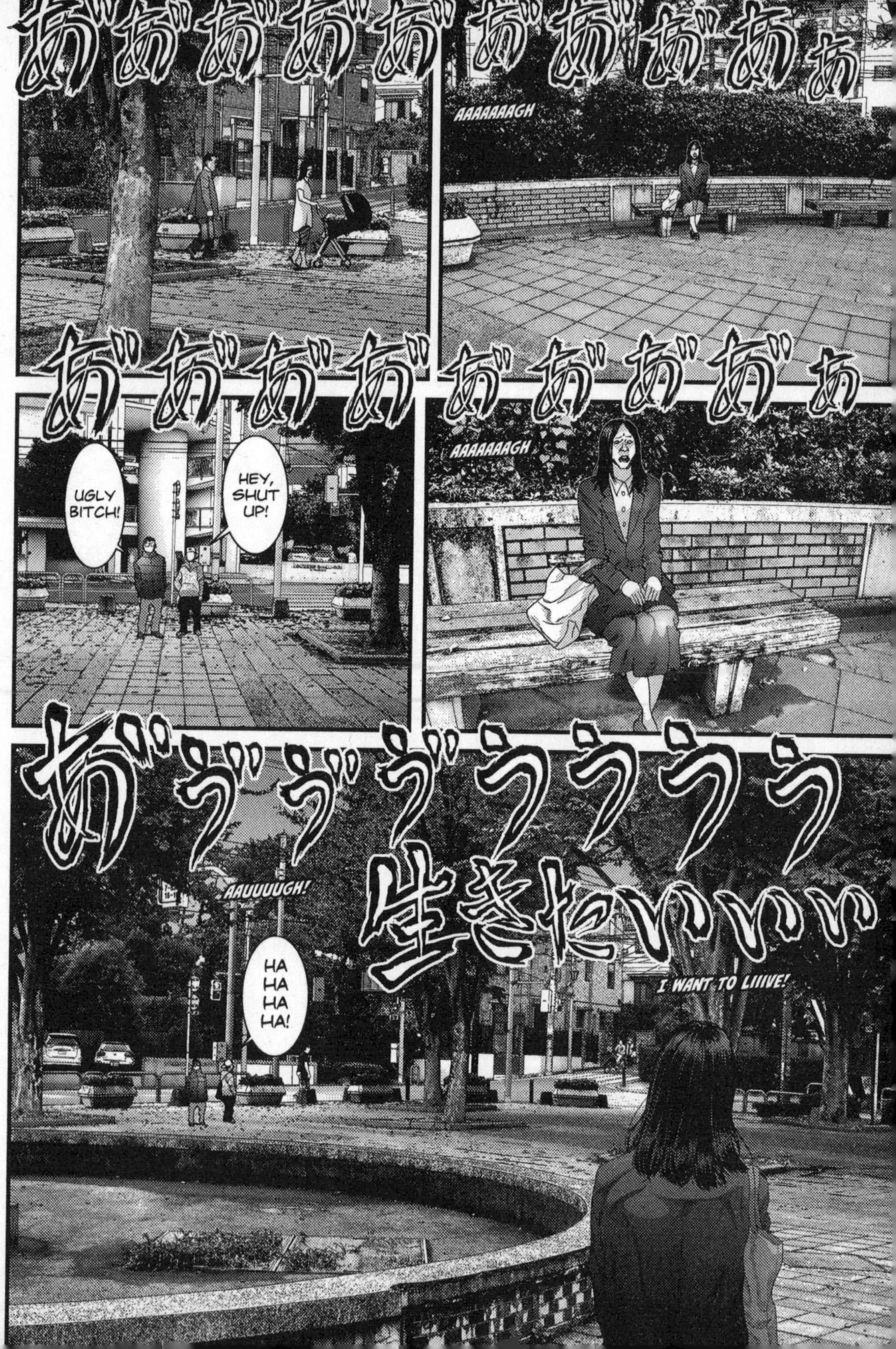
あ゛あ゛あ゛あ゛あ゛あ゛あ゛あ゛あぁ
AAAAAAAGH
あ゛あ゛あ゛あ゛あ゛あ゛あ゛あ゛ぁ
AAAAAAAGH
HEY, SHUT UP!
UGLY BITCH!
あ゛う゛う゛う゛うううう
生きたいいい
AAUUUUGH!
I WANT TO LIIIVE!
HA HA HA HA!

IS THIS A JOKE ...?

WHAT IS THIS?

37% 18:13

Tweets 🔍

cure 1m

Please spread the message.

Message me if you're suffering from an incurable disease or terminal cancer.

There might be a way to help you.

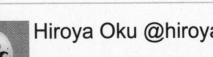

Hiroya Oku @hiroya_oku 20m

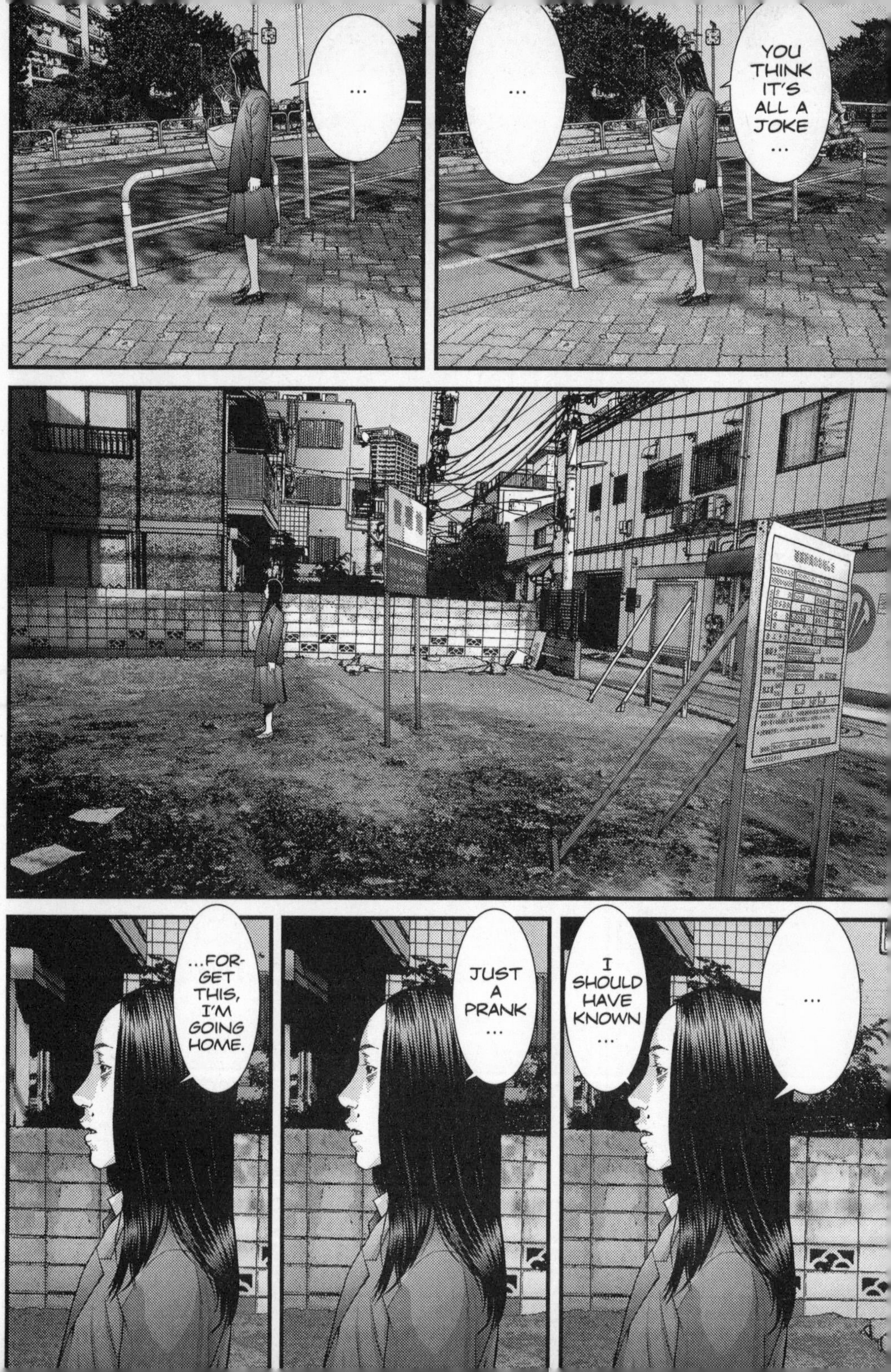
YOU THINK IT'S ALL A JOKE ...
...
...
...
I SHOULD HAVE KNOWN ...
JUST A PRANK ...
...FOR-GET THIS, I'M GOING HOME.

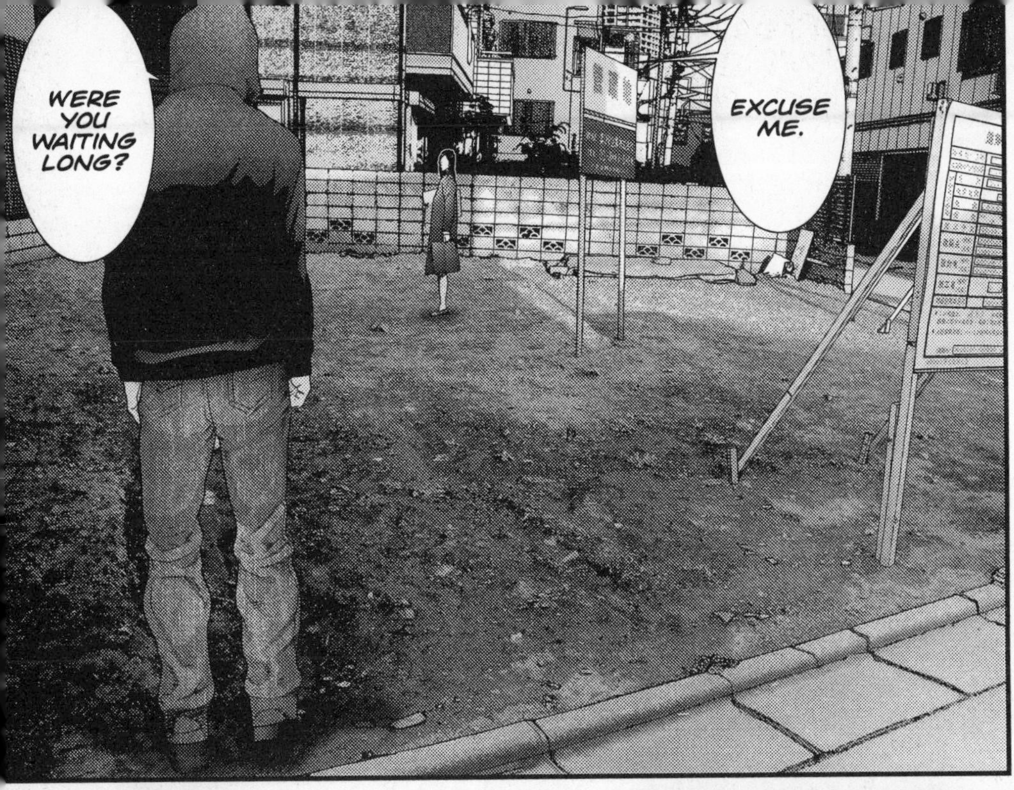
EXCUSE ME.
WERE YOU WAITING LONG?
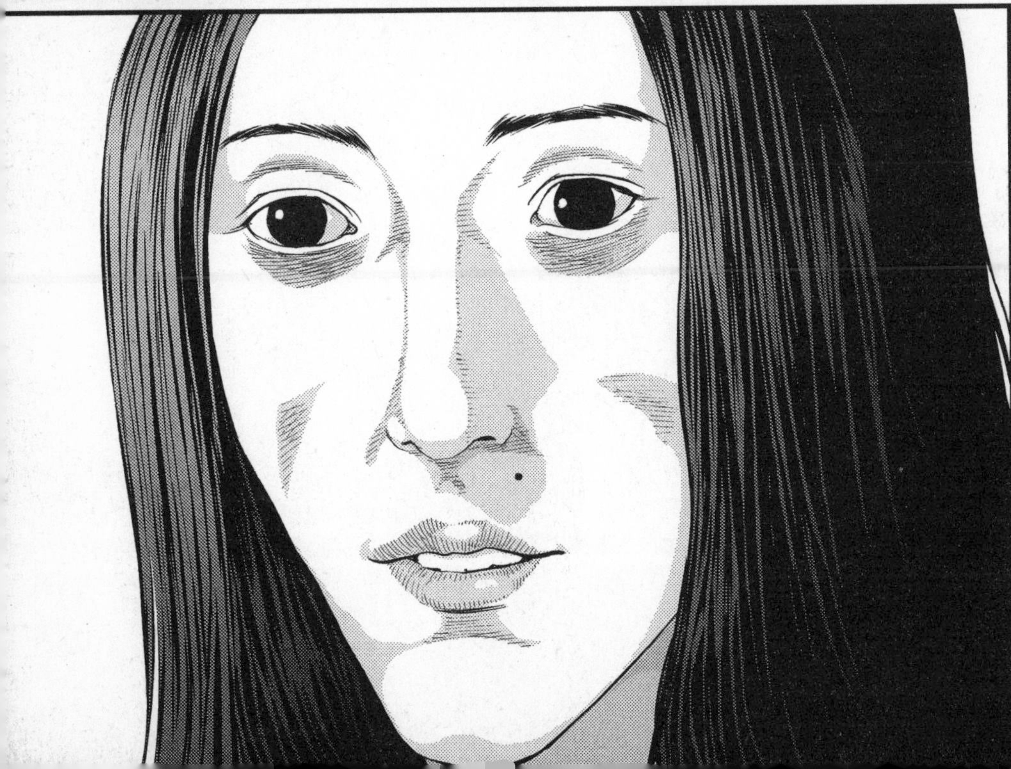

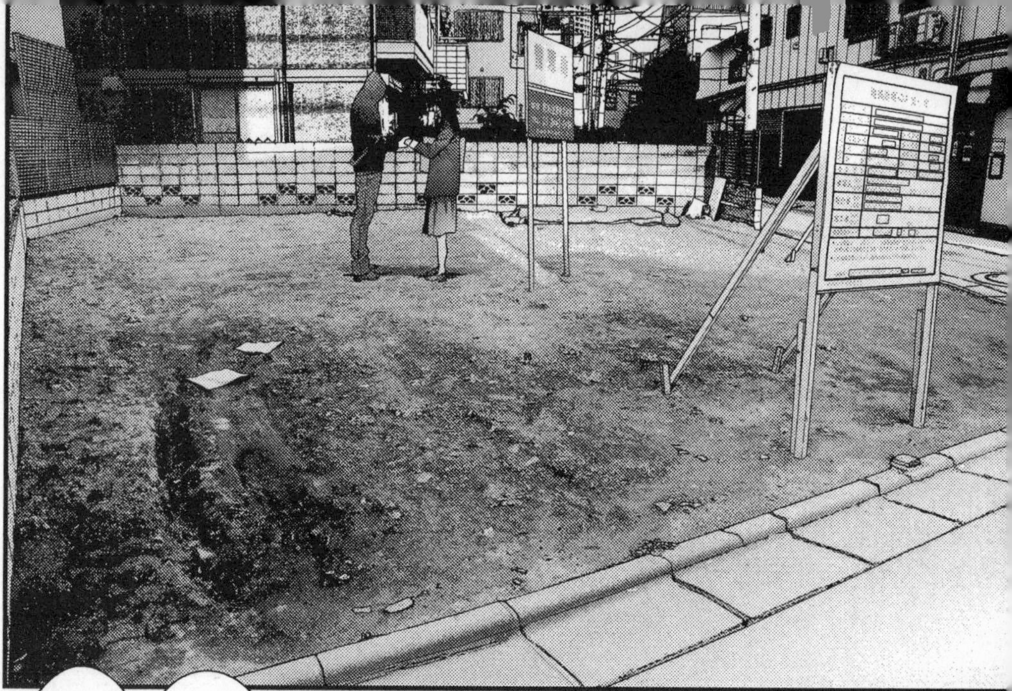
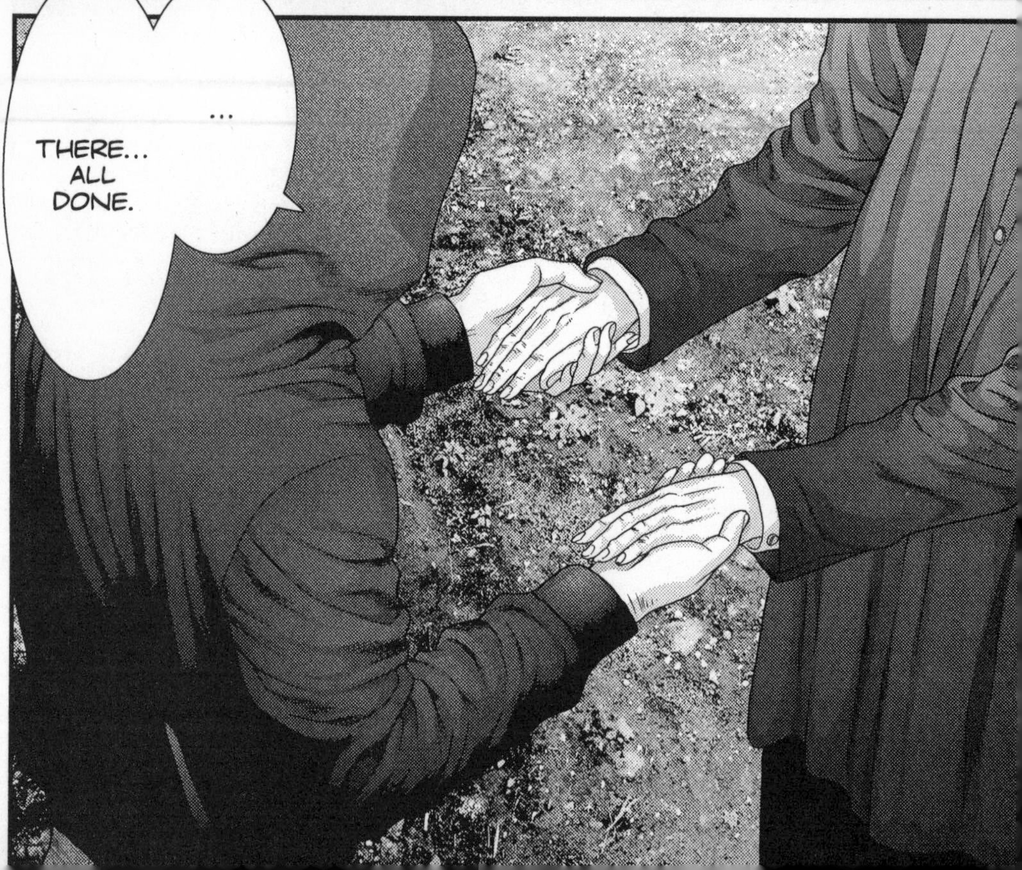
...
THERE... ALL DONE.

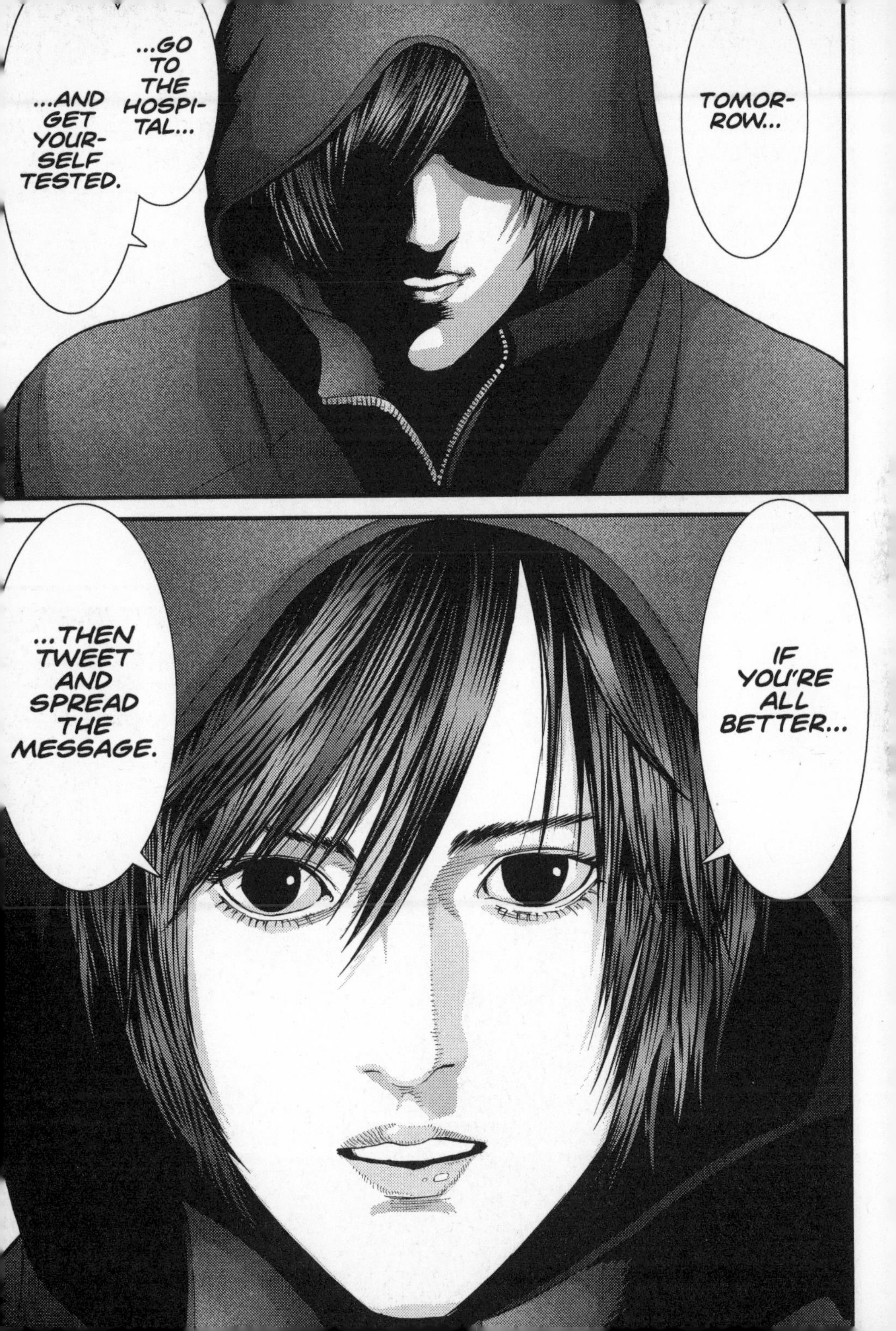
TOMORROW...
...GO TO THE HOSPITAL...
...AND GET YOURSELF TESTED.
IF YOU'RE ALL BETTER...
...THEN TWEET AND SPREAD THE MESSAGE.

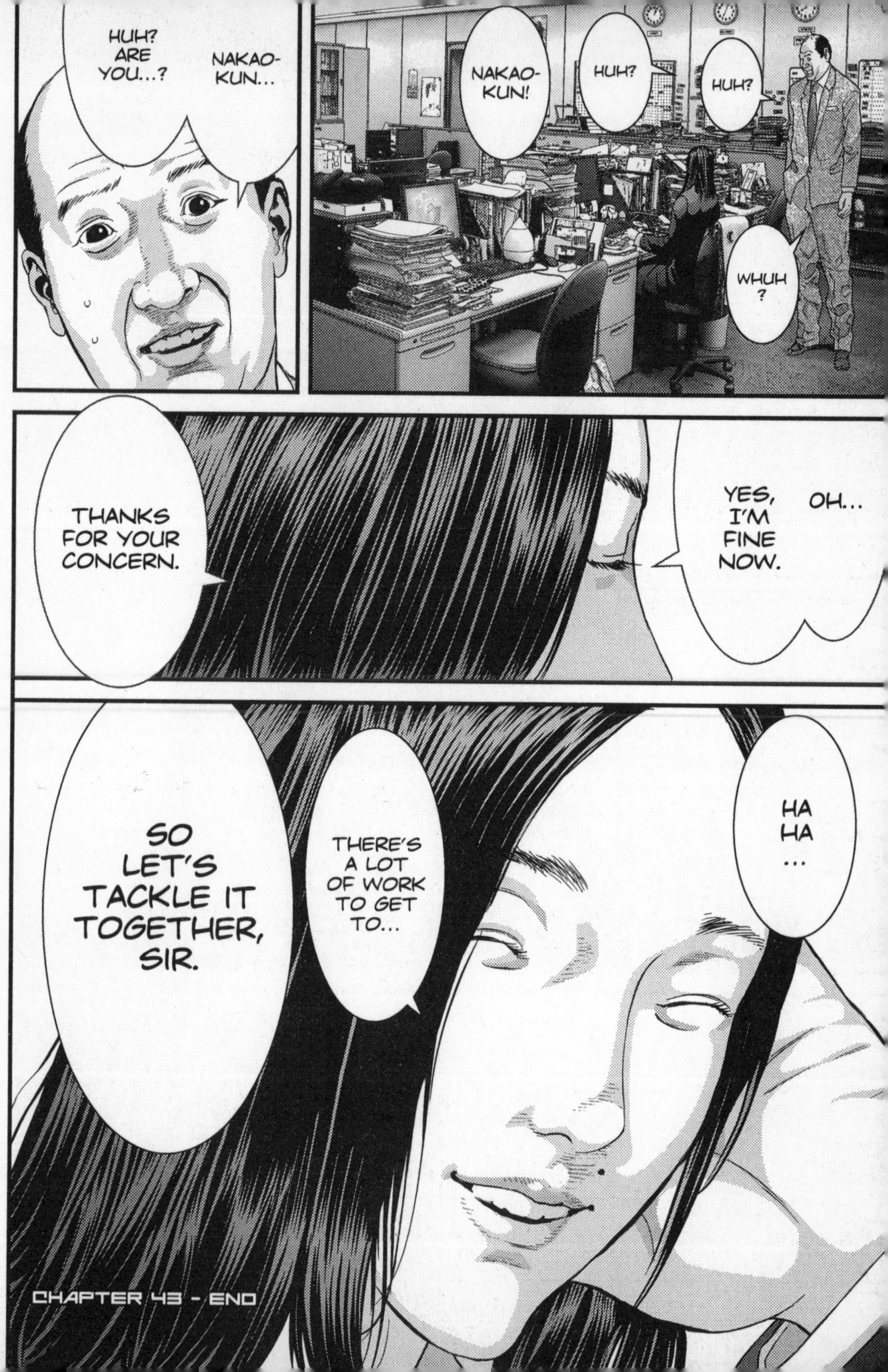
HUH?
HUH?
NAKAO-KUN!
WHUH ?
NAKAO-KUN...
HUH? ARE YOU...?
OH...
YES, I'M FINE NOW.
THANKS FOR YOUR CONCERN.
HA HA ...
THERE'S A LOT OF WORK TO GET TO...
SO LET'S TACKLE IT TOGETHER, SIR.
CHAPTER 43 - END

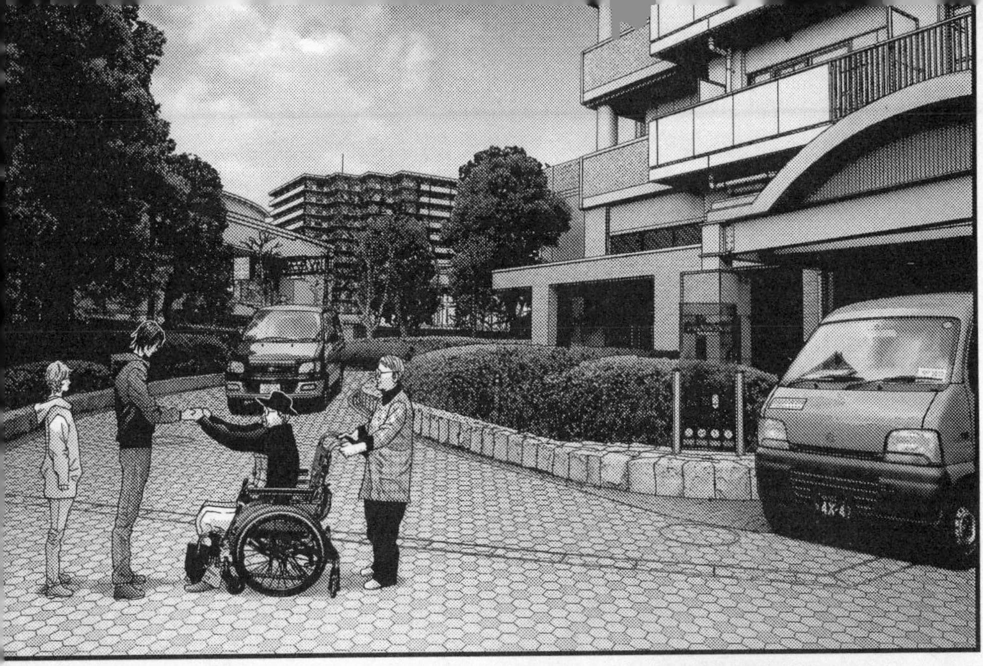
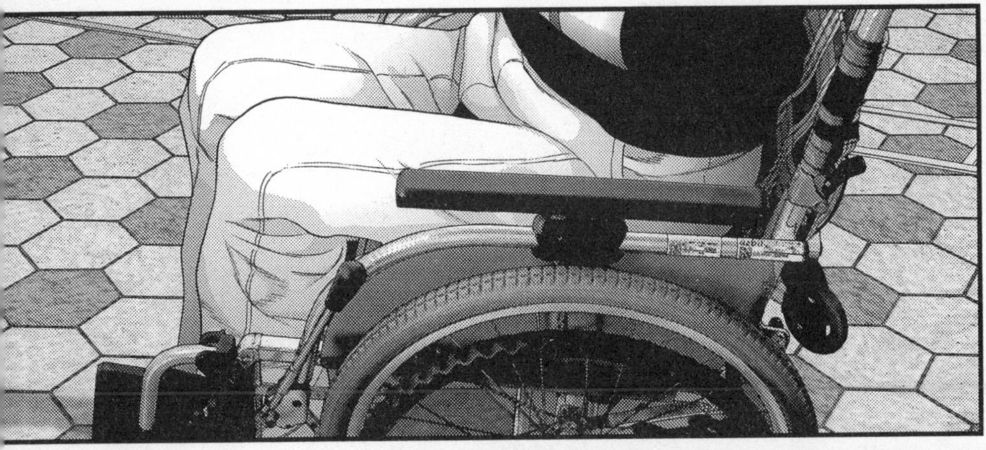
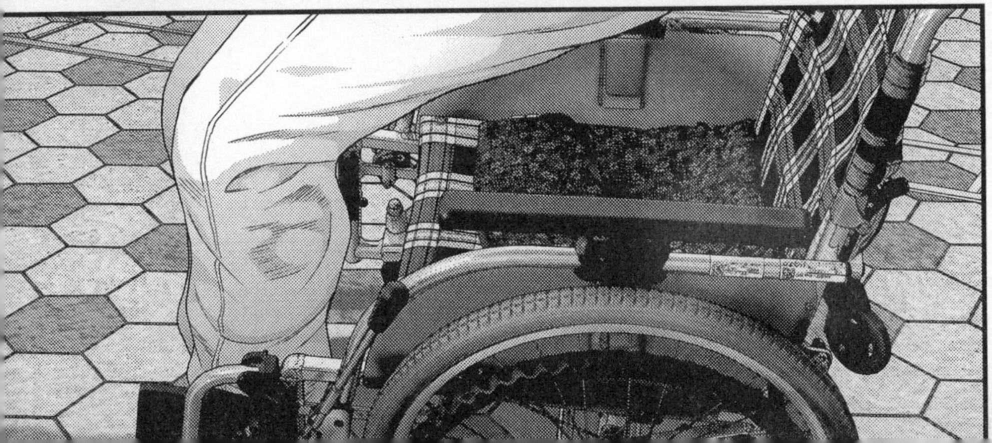

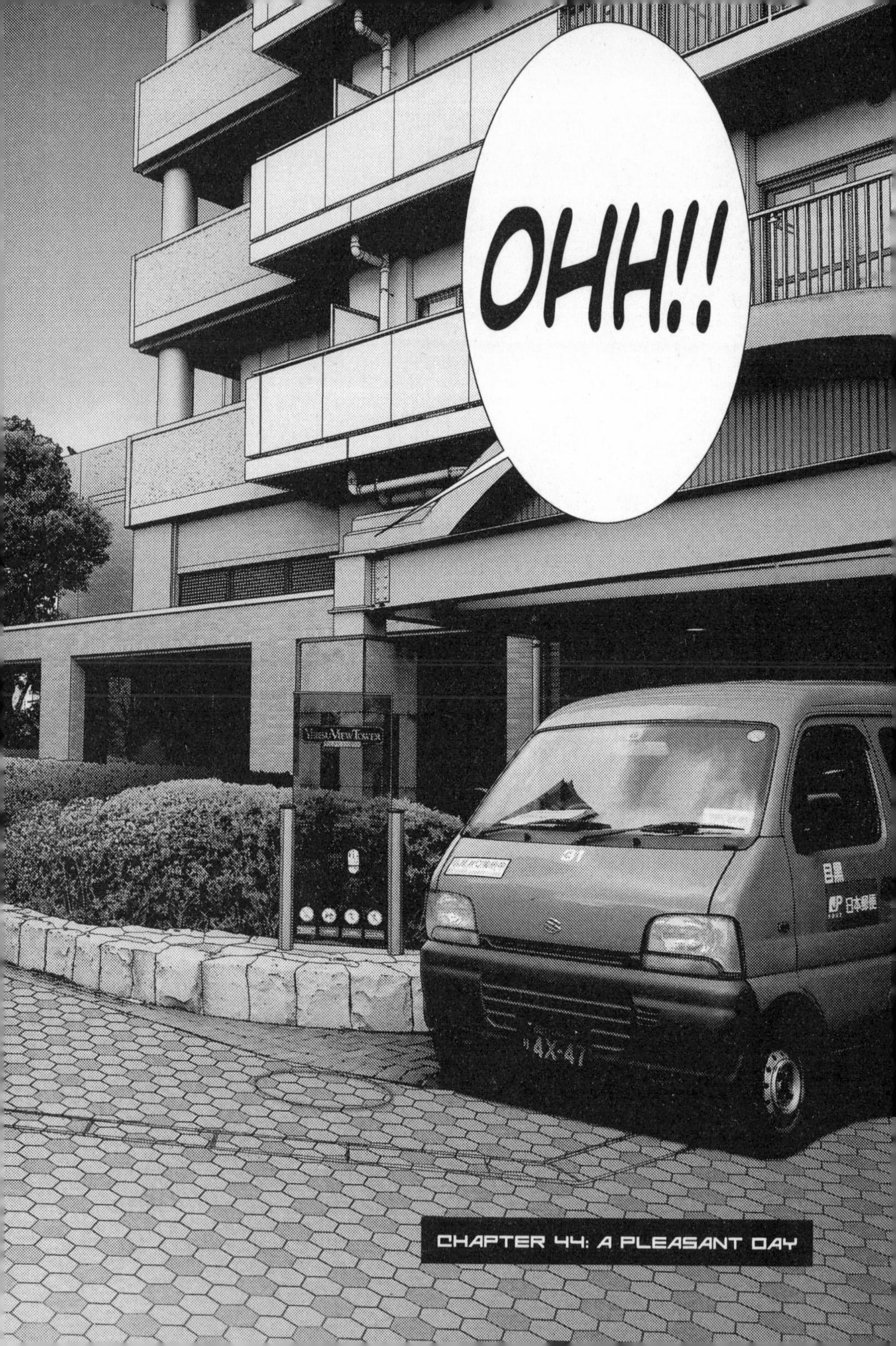
OHH!!
CHAPTER 44: A PLEASANT DAY

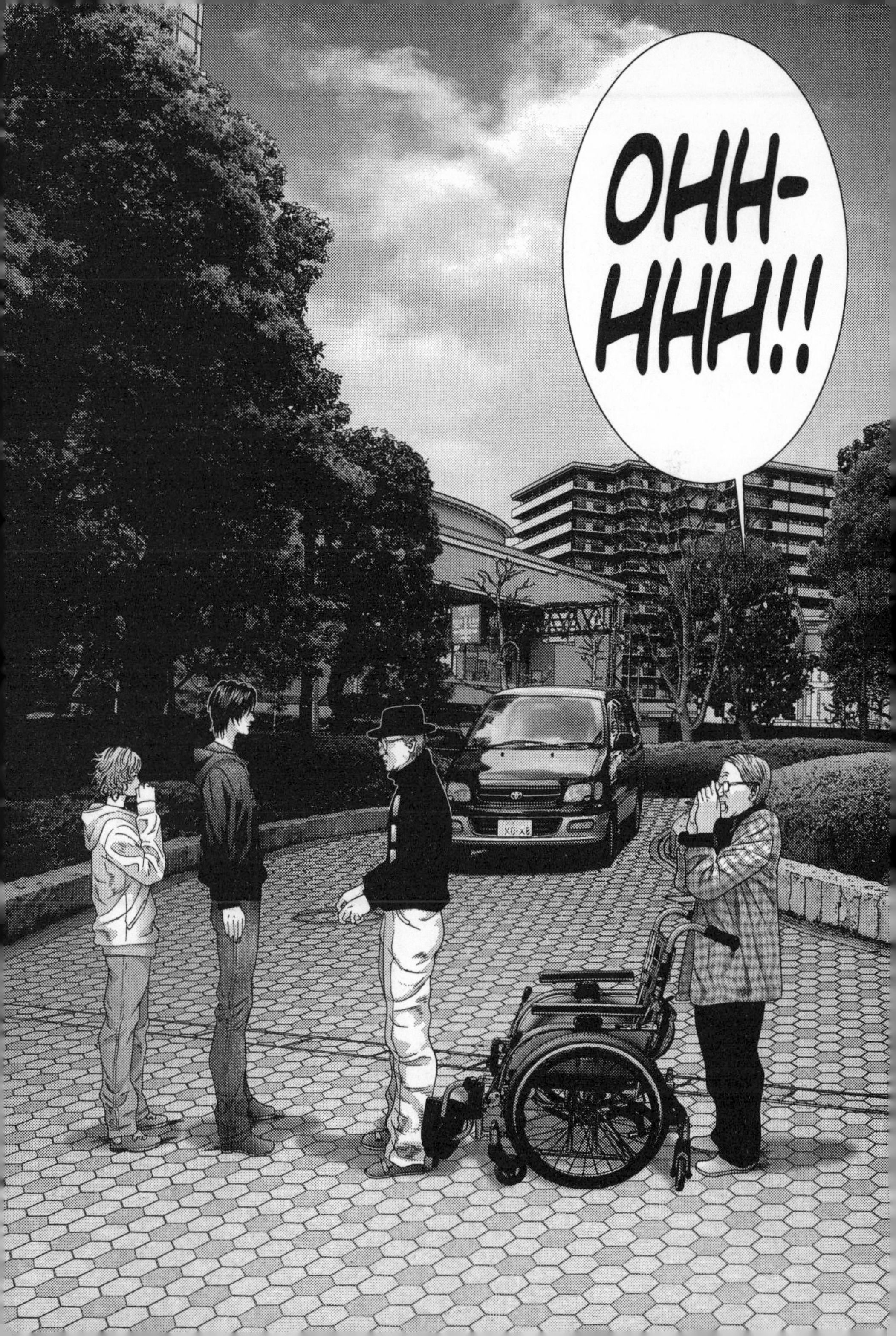
OHH-
HHH!!

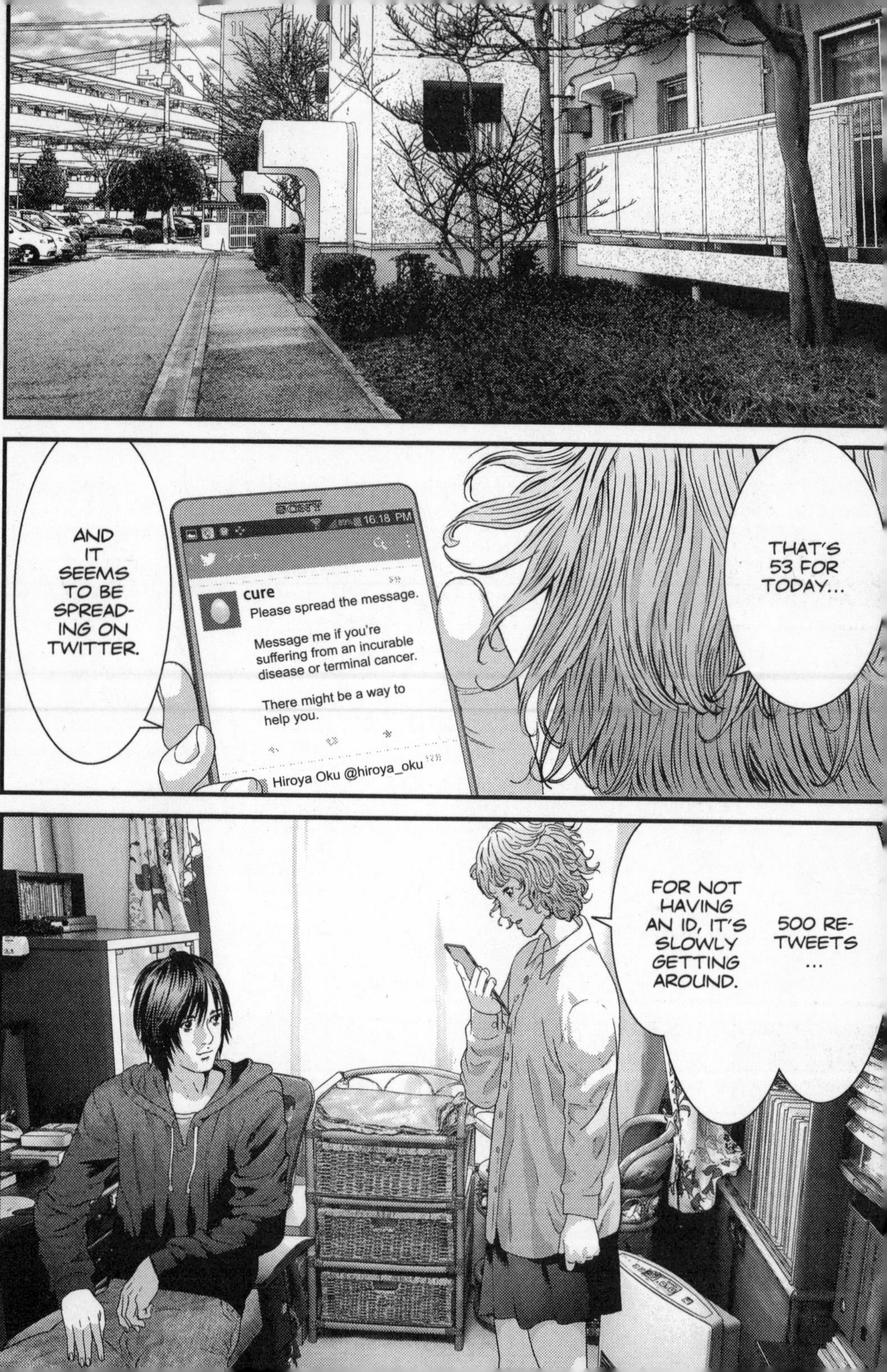
THAT'S 53 FOR TODAY...
SONY
16:18 PM
cure
Please spread the message.
Message me if you're suffering from an incurable disease or terminal cancer.
There might be a way to help you.
Hiroya Oku @hiroya_oku
AND IT SEEMS TO BE SPREADING ON TWITTER.
500 RE-TWEETS ...
FOR NOT HAVING AN ID, IT'S SLOWLY GETTING AROUND.

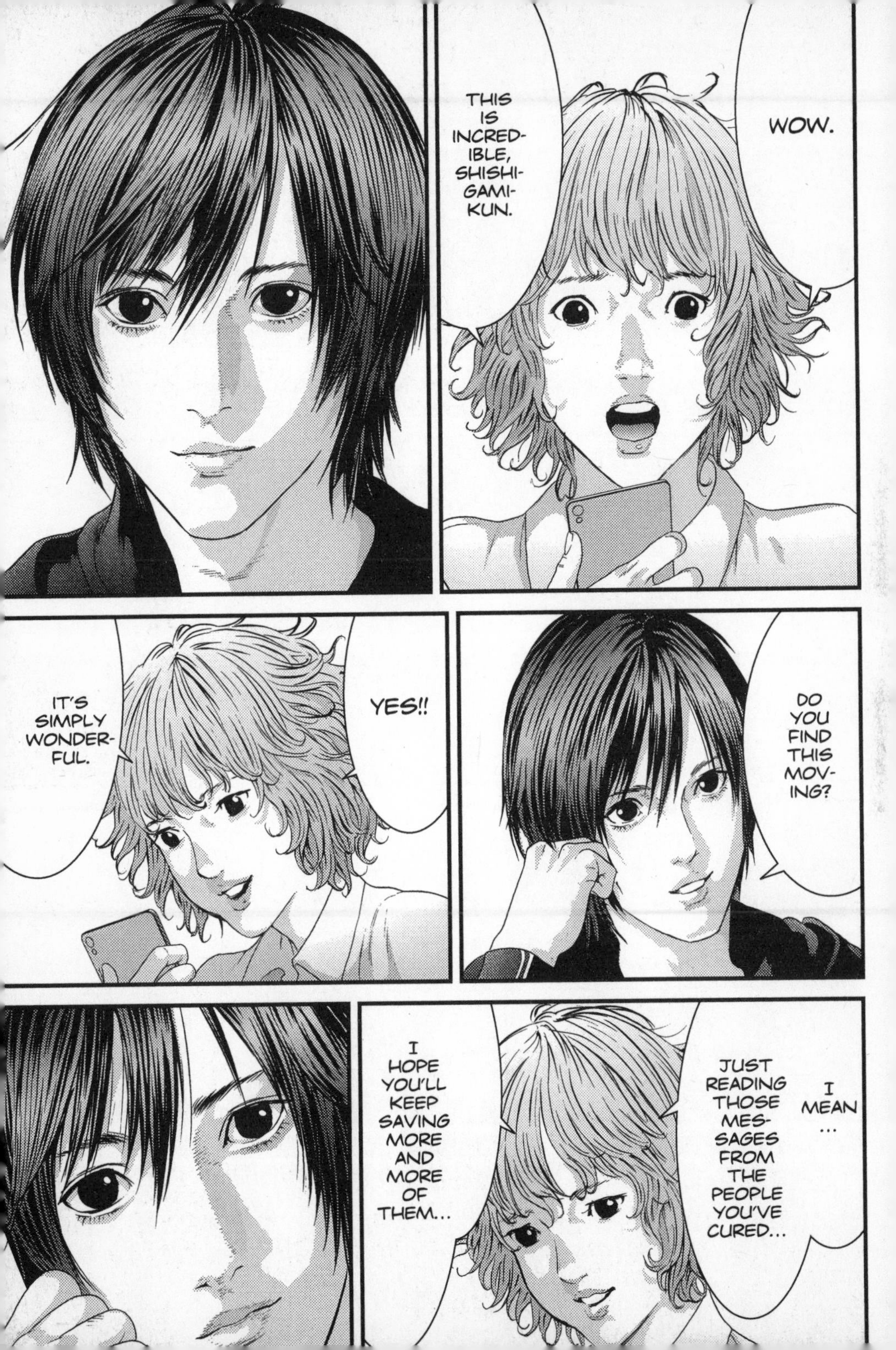
WOW.
THIS IS INCREDIBLE, SHISHIGAMI-KUN.
DO YOU FIND THIS MOVING?
YES!!
IT'S SIMPLY WONDERFUL.
I MEAN...
JUST READING THOSE MESSAGES FROM THE PEOPLE YOU'VE CURED...
I HOPE YOU'LL KEEP SAVING MORE AND MORE OF THEM...

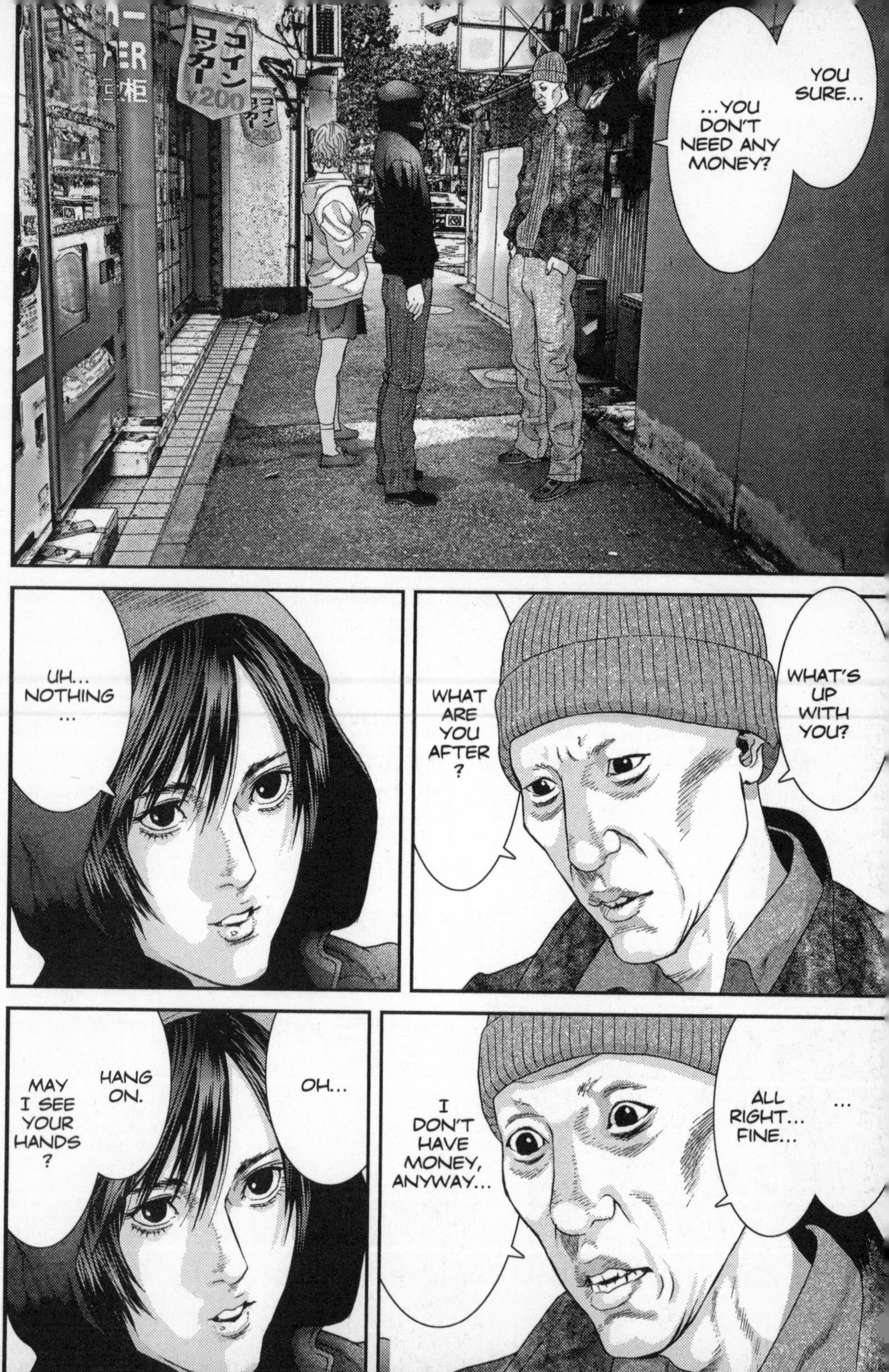
YOU SURE...
...YOU DON'T NEED ANY MONEY?
WHAT'S UP WITH YOU?
WHAT ARE YOU AFTER?
UH... NOTHING...
...
ALL RIGHT... FINE...
I DON'T HAVE MONEY, ANYWAY...
OH...
HANG ON.
MAY I SEE YOUR HANDS?

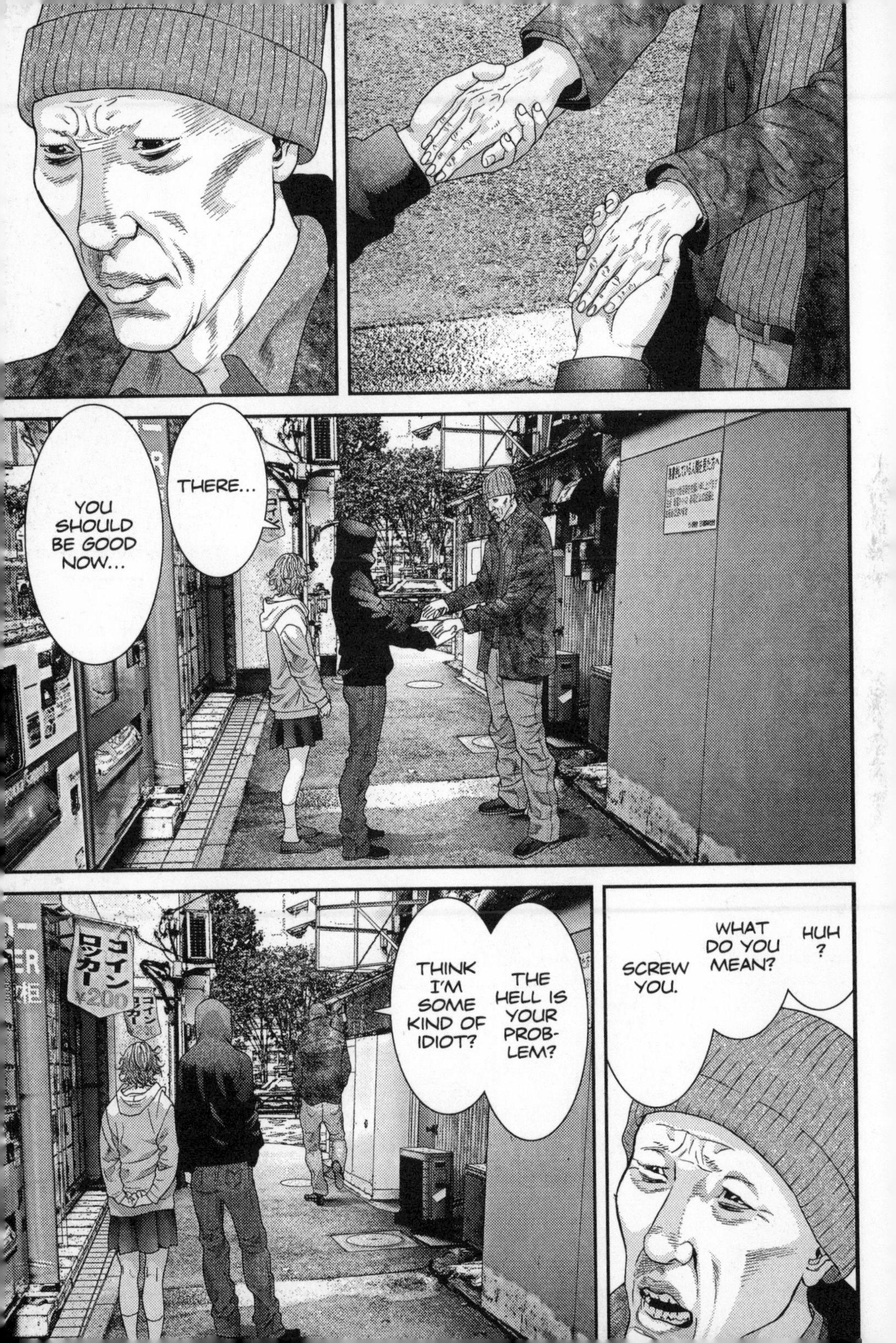
THERE...
YOU SHOULD BE GOOD NOW...
HUH ?
WHAT DO YOU MEAN?
SCREW YOU.
THE HELL IS YOUR PROB-LEM?
THINK I'M SOME KIND OF IDIOT?
コインロッカー
¥200

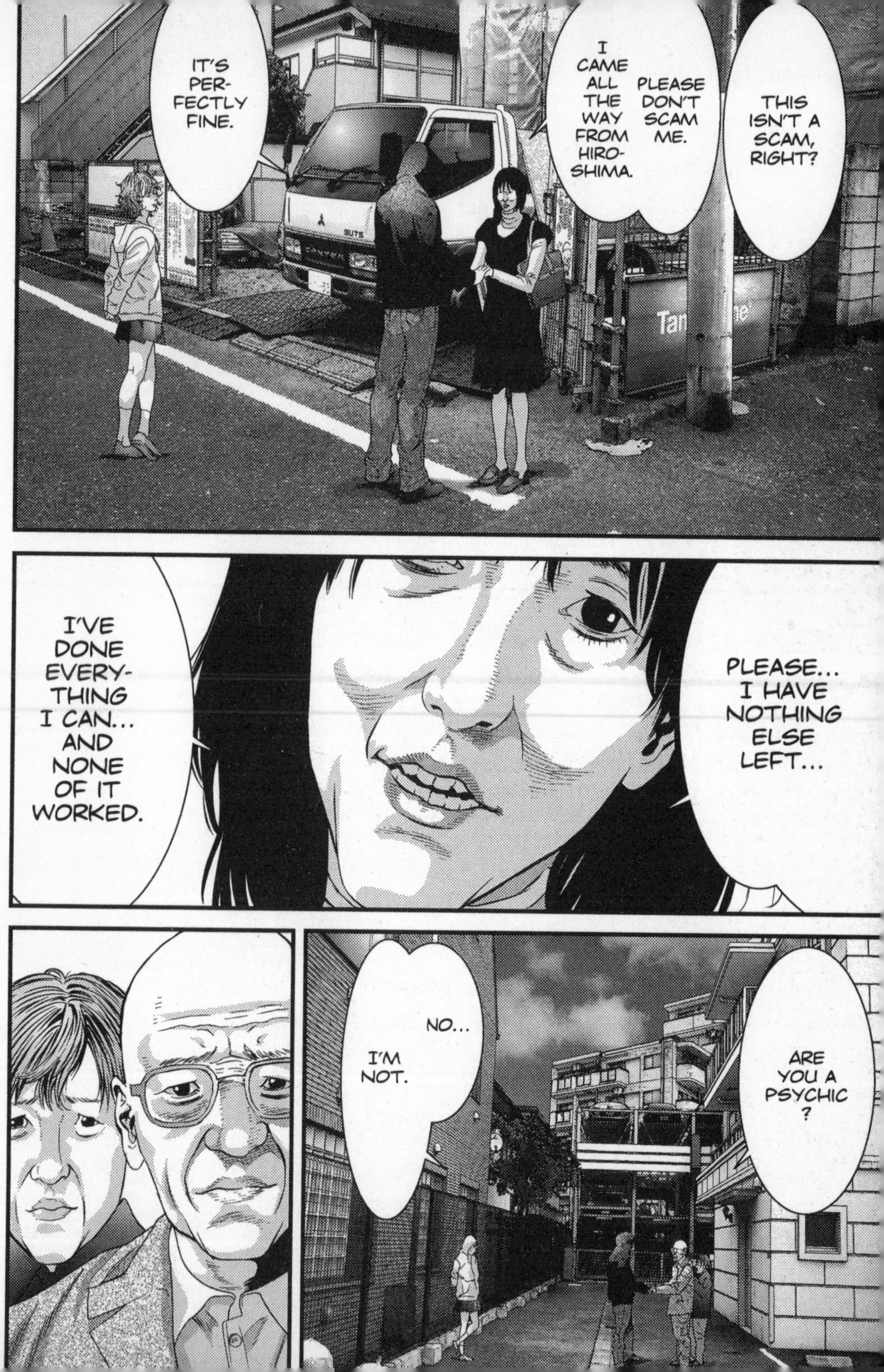
THIS ISN'T A SCAM, RIGHT?
PLEASE DON'T SCAM ME.
I CAME ALL THE WAY FROM HIRO-SHIMA.
IT'S PER-FECTLY FINE.
PLEASE... I HAVE NOTHING ELSE LEFT...
I'VE DONE EVERY-THING I CAN... AND NONE OF IT WORKED.
ARE YOU A PSYCHIC?
NO...
I'M NOT.

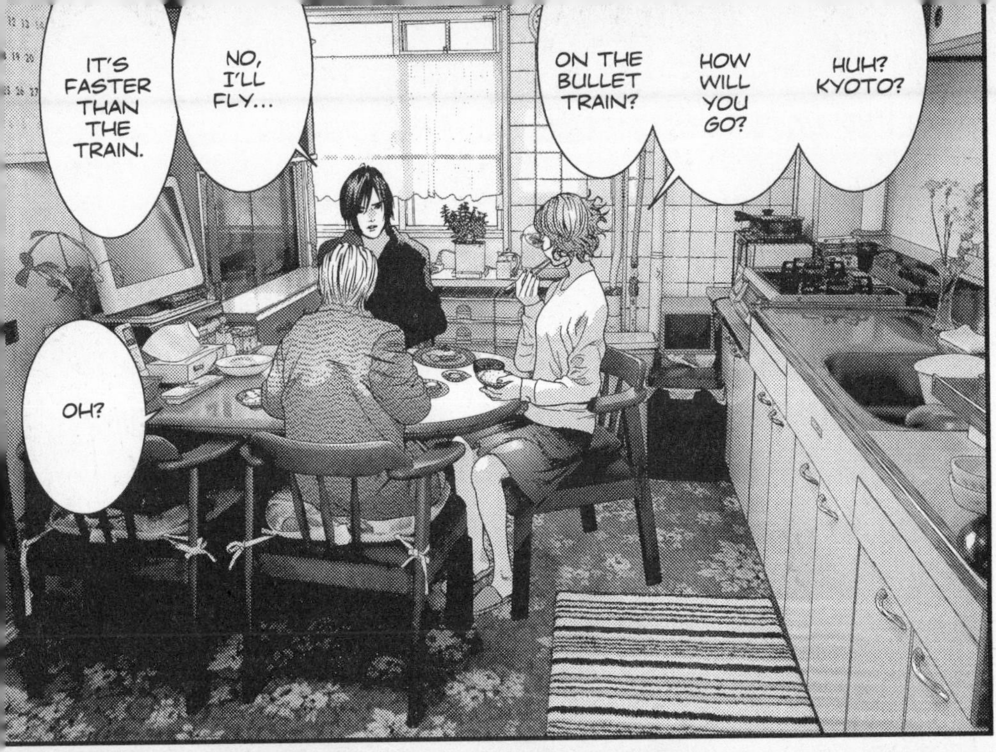
HUH? KYOTO?
HOW WILL YOU GO?
ON THE BULLET TRAIN?
NO, I'LL FLY...
IT'S FASTER THAN THE TRAIN.
OH?

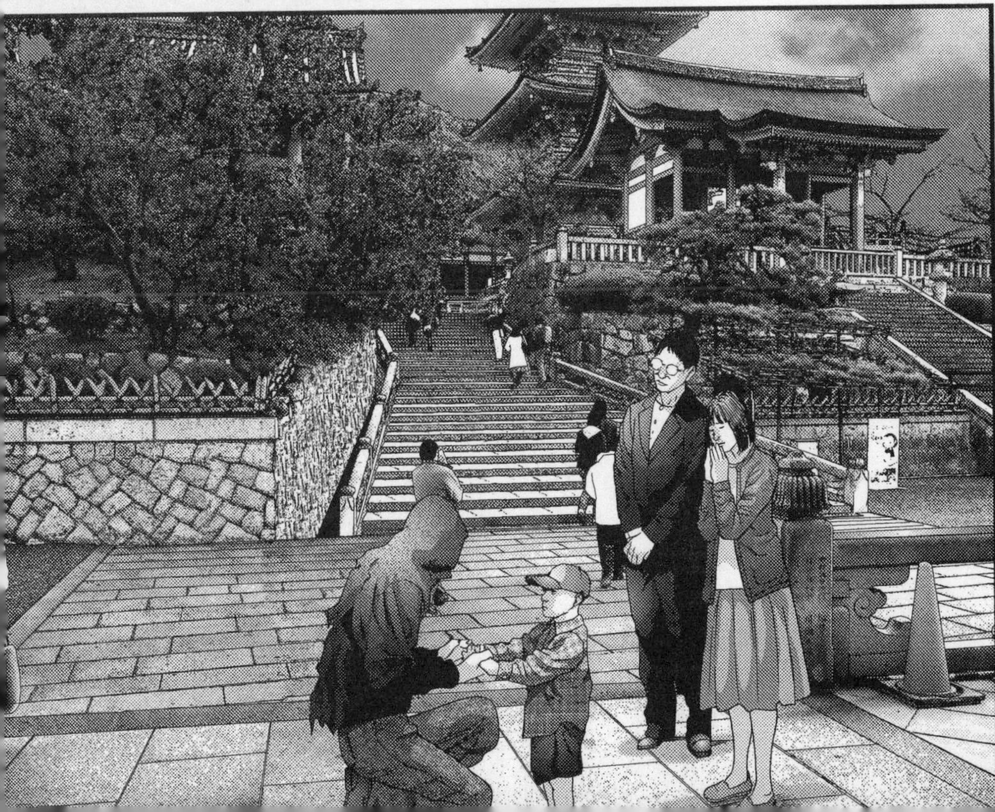

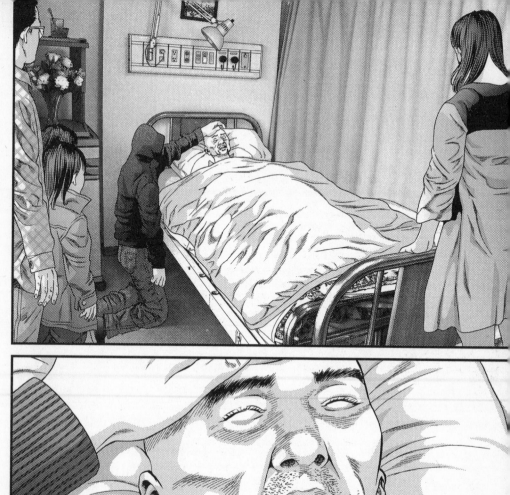

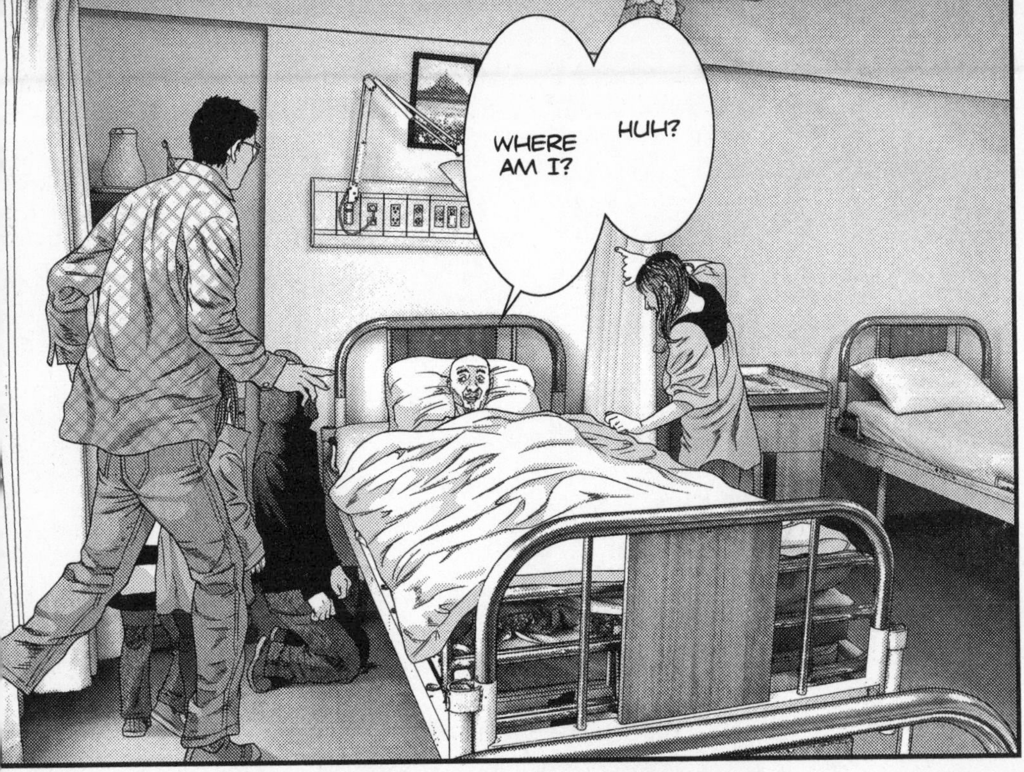
HUH?
WHERE AM I?
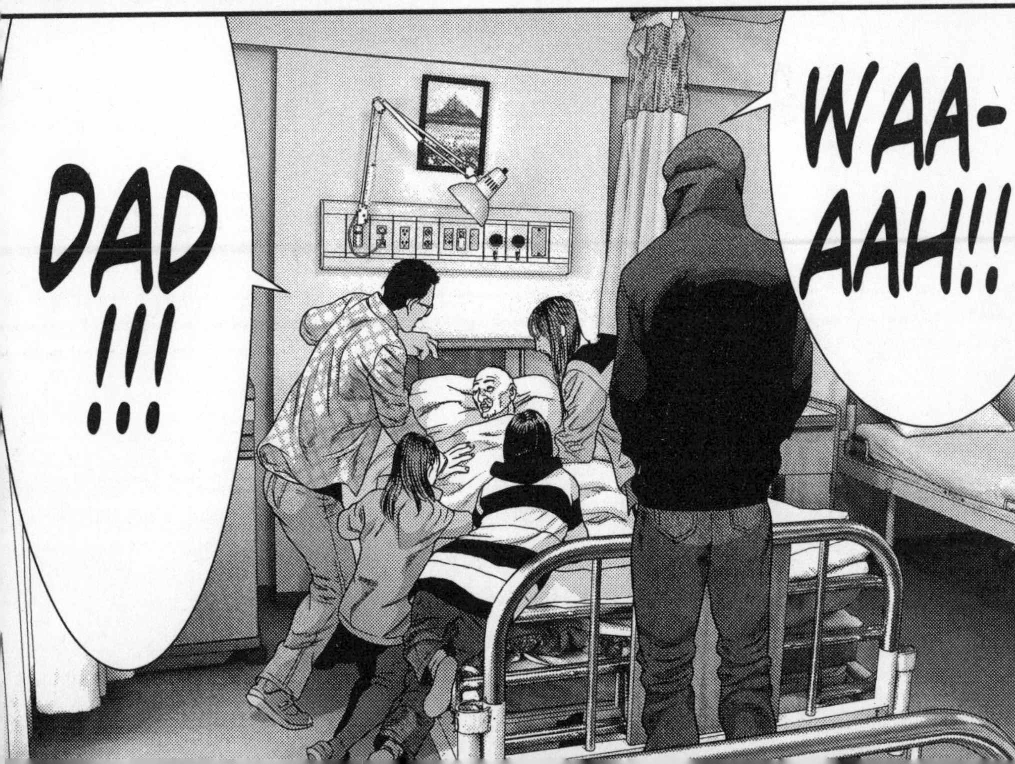
WAA-AAH!!
DAD!!!

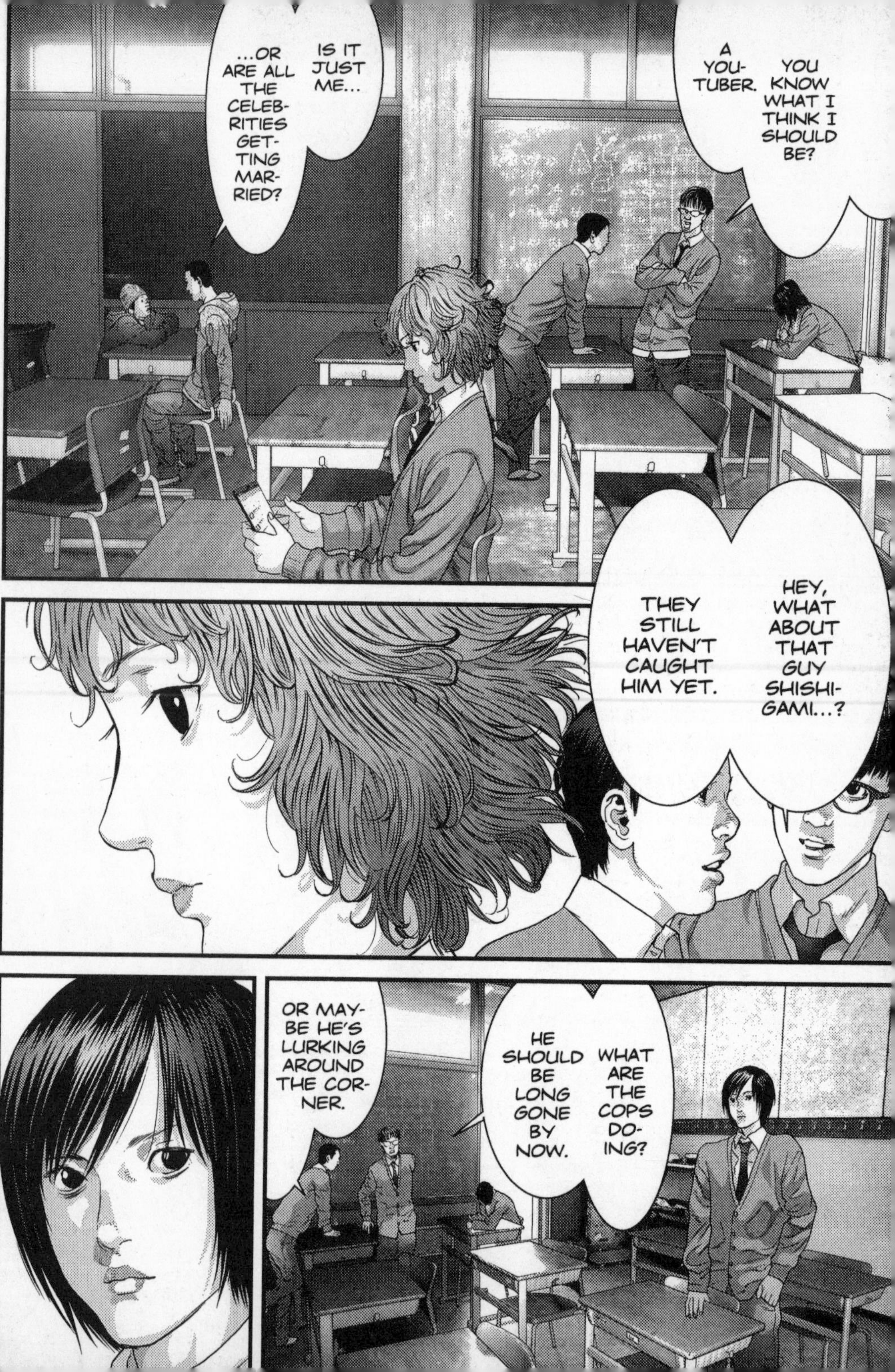
YOU KNOW WHAT I THINK I SHOULD BE?
A YOU-TUBER.
IS IT JUST ME...
...OR ARE ALL THE CELEB-RITIES GET-TING MAR-RIED?
HEY, WHAT ABOUT THAT GUY SHISHI-GAMI...?
THEY STILL HAVEN'T CAUGHT HIM YET.
WHAT ARE THE COPS DO-ING?
HE SHOULD BE LONG GONE BY NOW.
OR MAY-BE HE'S LURKING AROUND THE COR-NER.

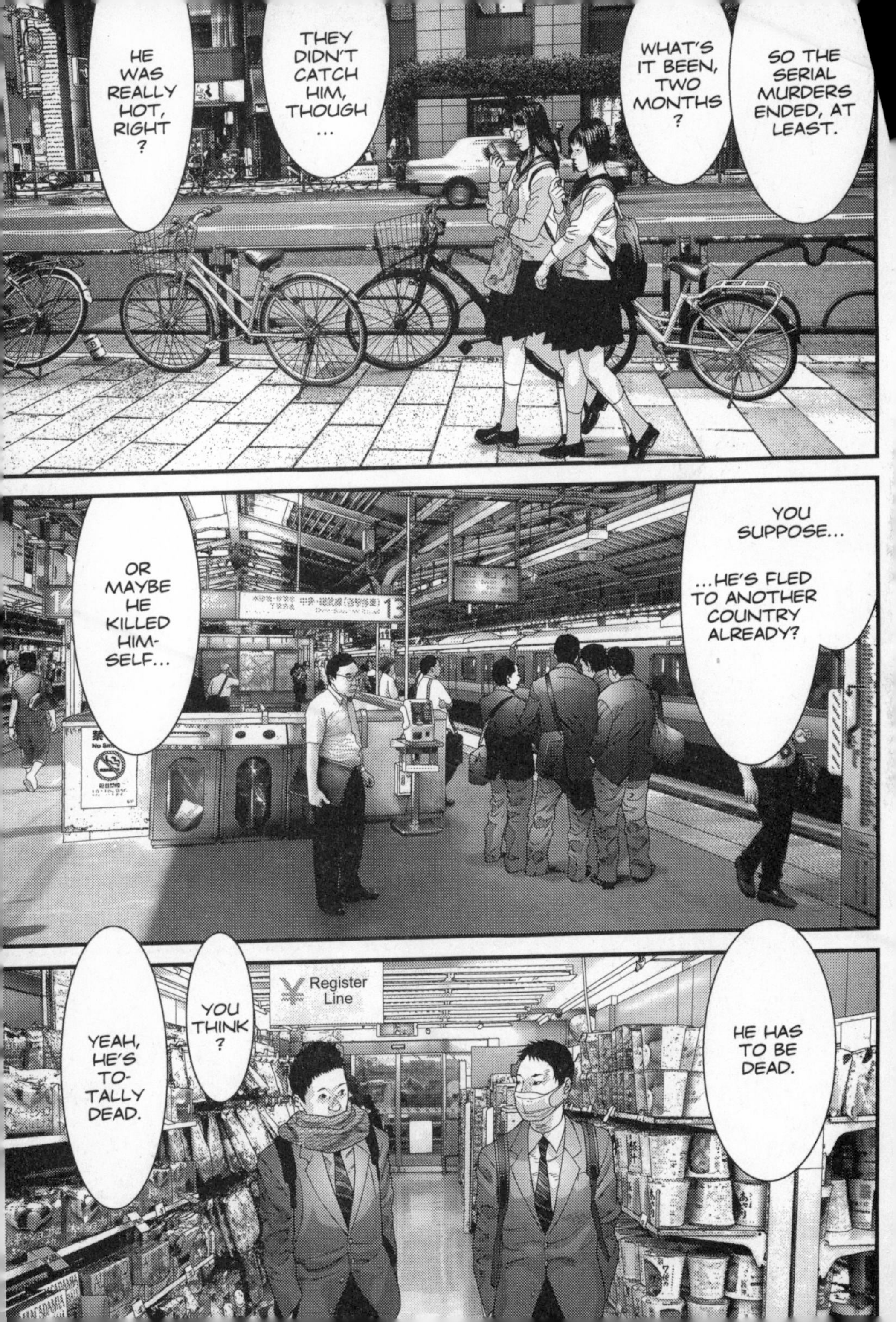
SO THE SERIAL MURDERS ENDED, AT LEAST.
WHAT'S IT BEEN, TWO MONTHS?
THEY DIDN'T CATCH HIM, THOUGH...
HE WAS REALLY HOT, RIGHT?
YOU SUPPOSE...
...HE'S FLED TO ANOTHER COUNTRY ALREADY?
OR MAYBE HE KILLED HIMSELF...
HE HAS TO BE DEAD.
Register Line
YOU THINK?
YEAH, HE'S TOTALLY DEAD.

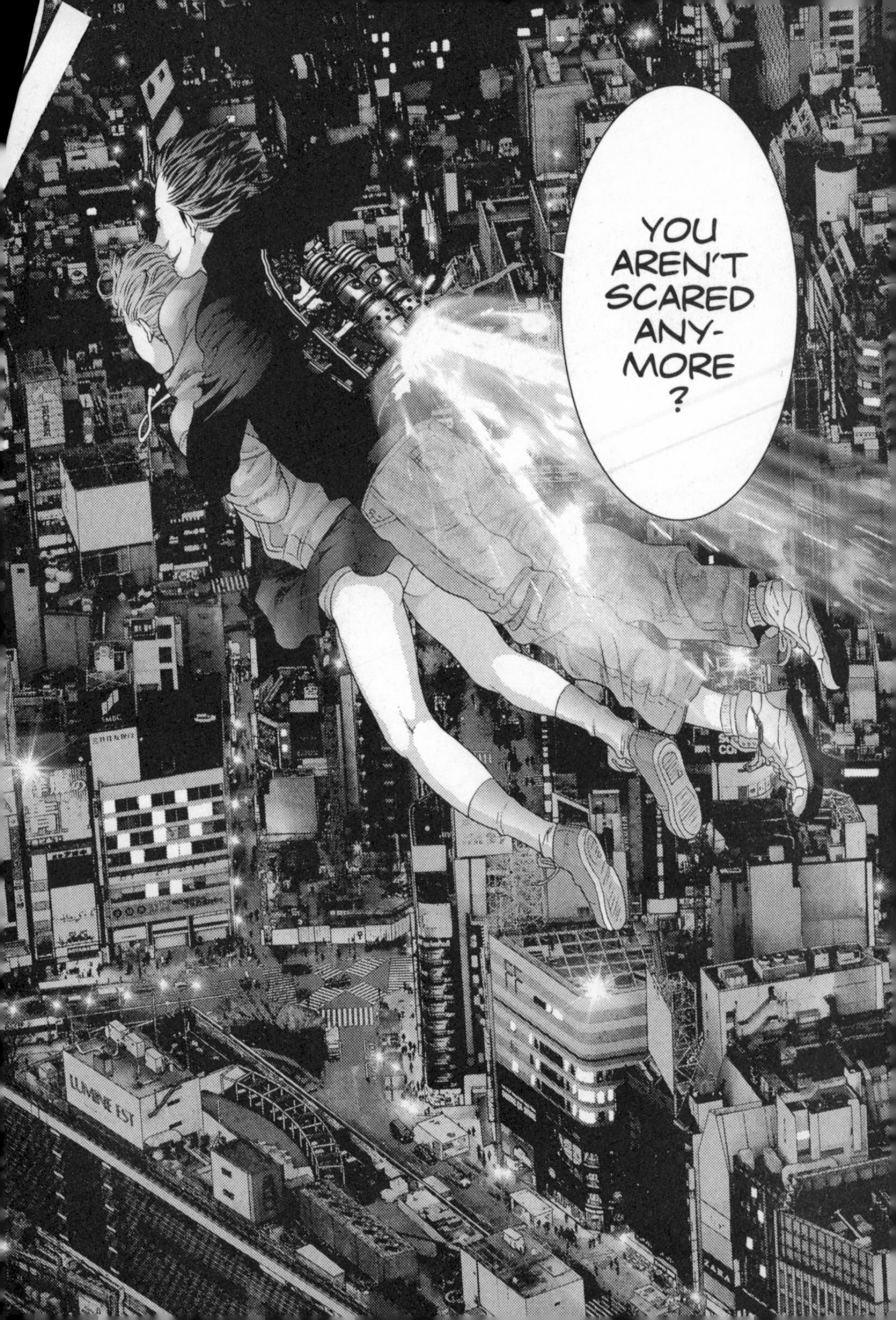
YOU AREN'T SCARED ANY-MORE ?

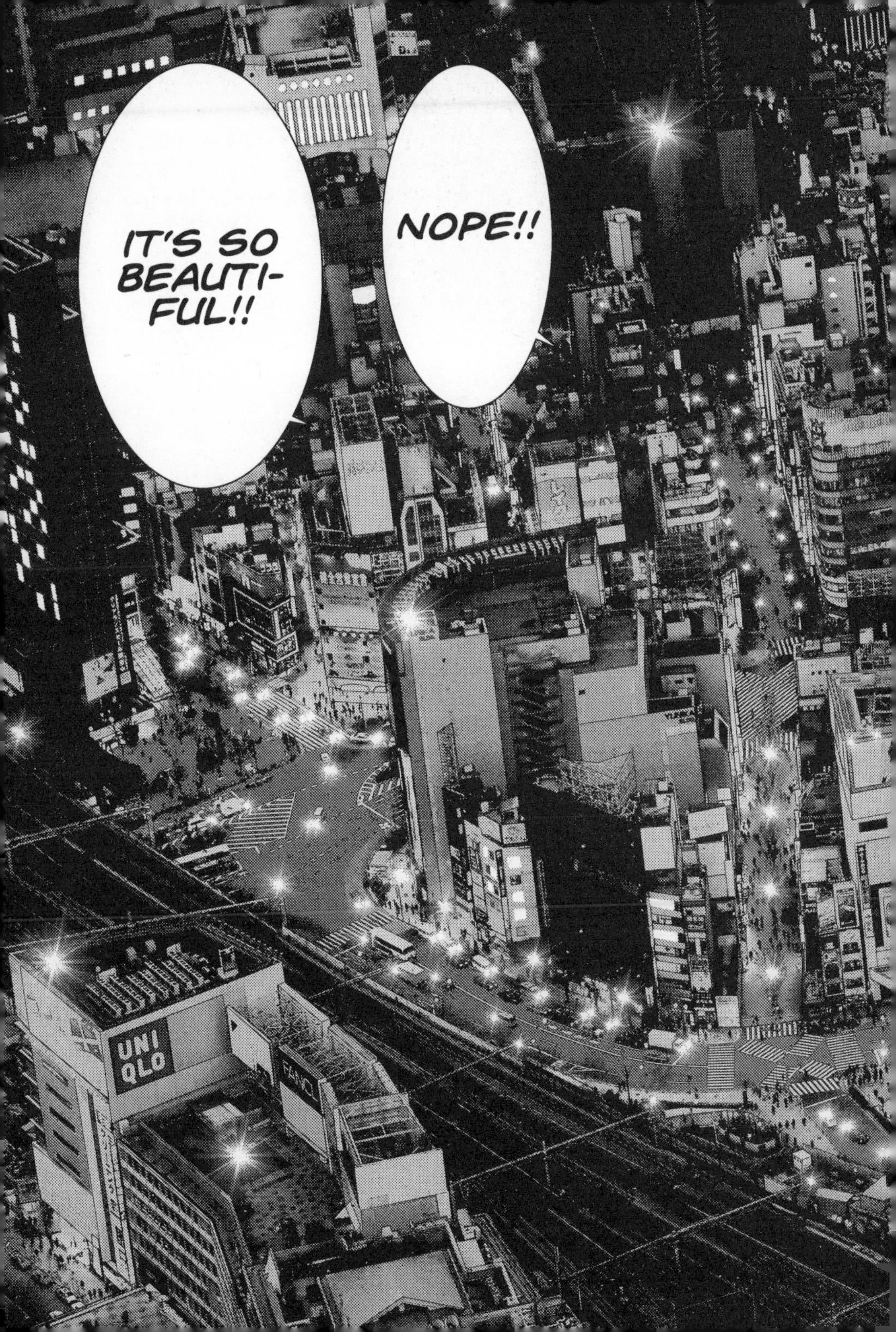
NOPE!!
IT'S SO BEAUTI-FUL!!
UNI QLO
FANCL

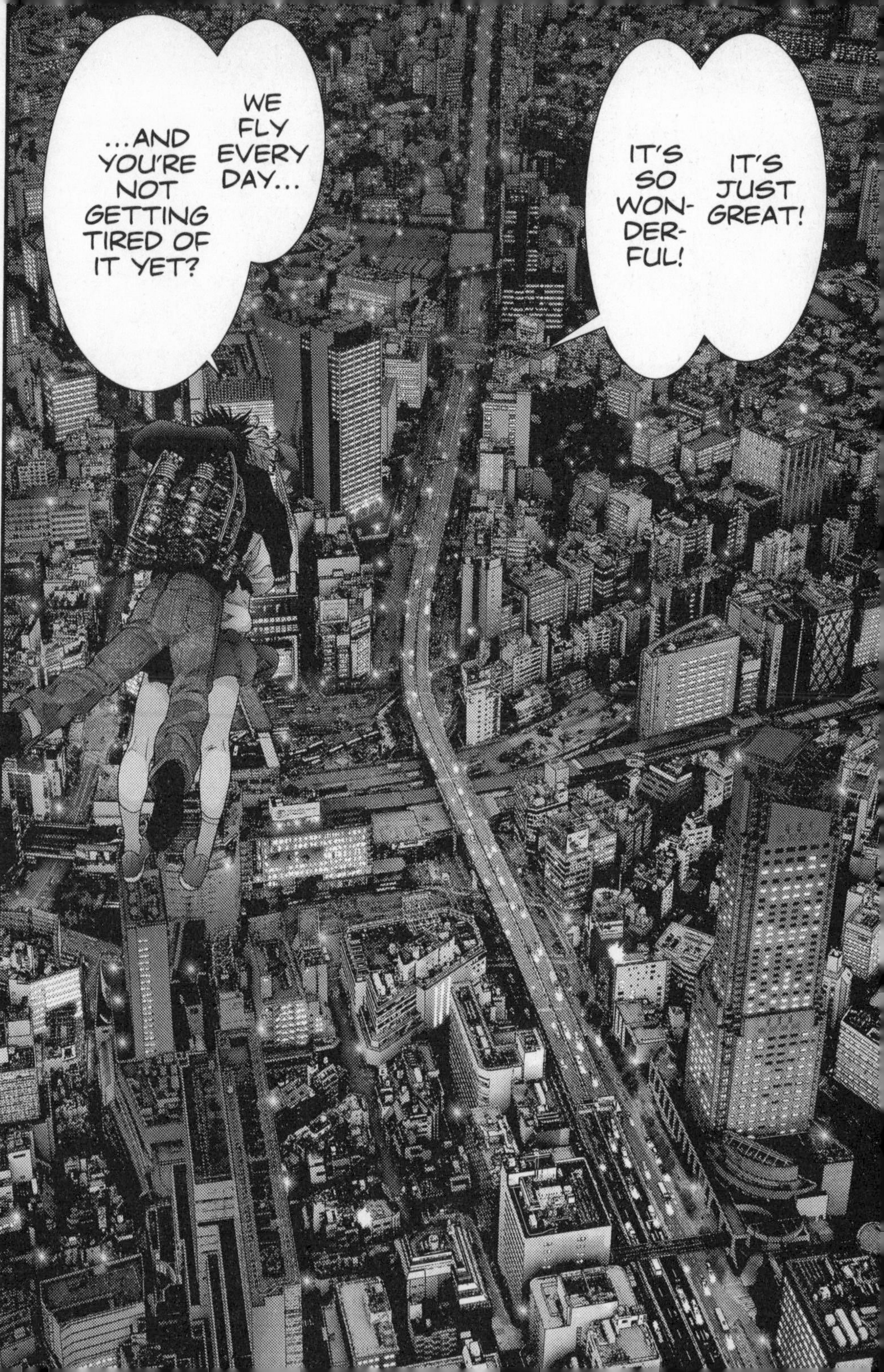
IT'S JUST GREAT!
IT'S SO WON-DER-FUL!
WE FLY EVERY DAY...
...AND YOU'RE NOT GETTING TIRED OF IT YET?

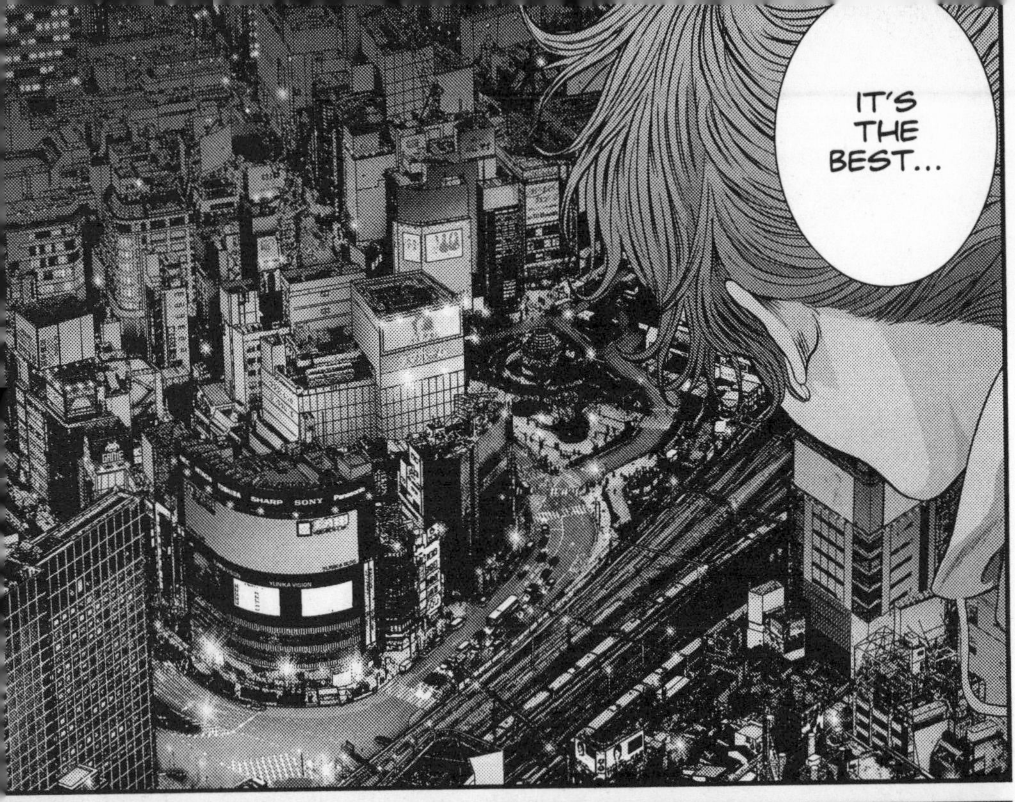
IT'S THE BEST...
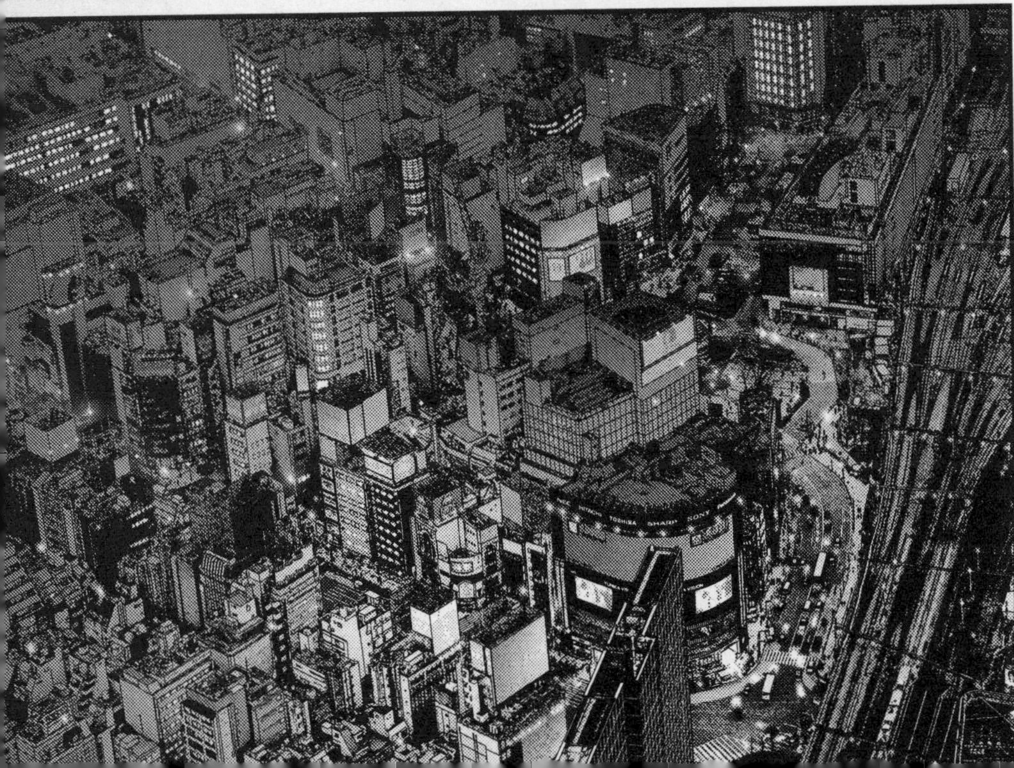

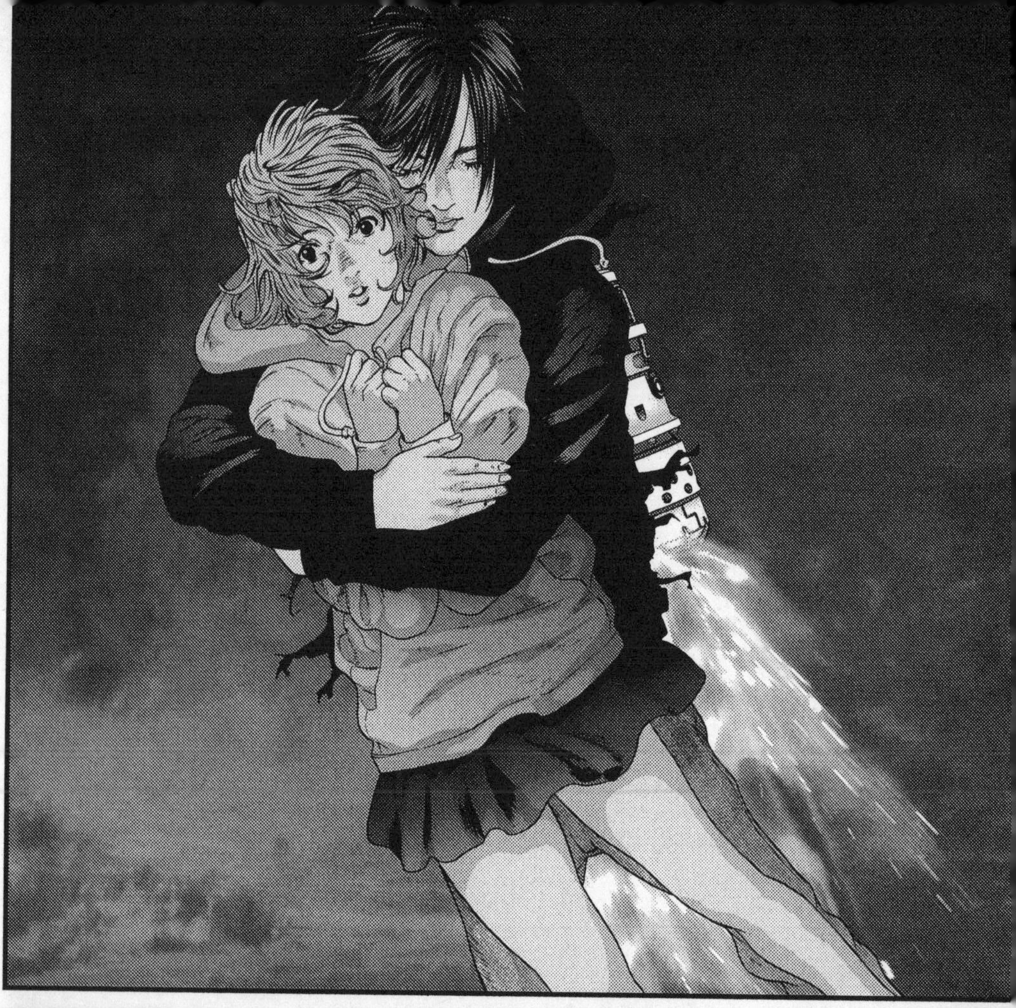

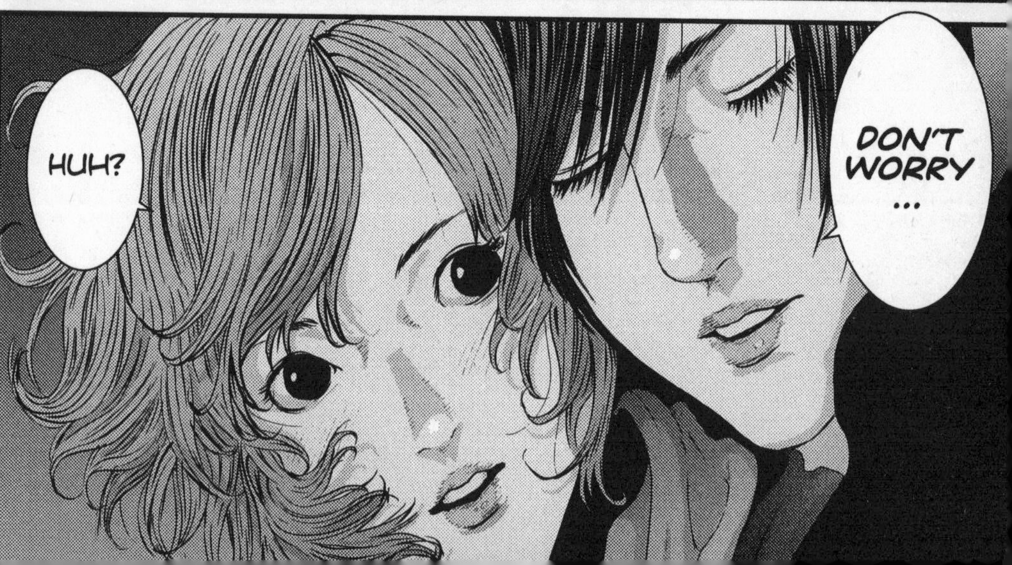
DON'T WORRY ...
HUH?

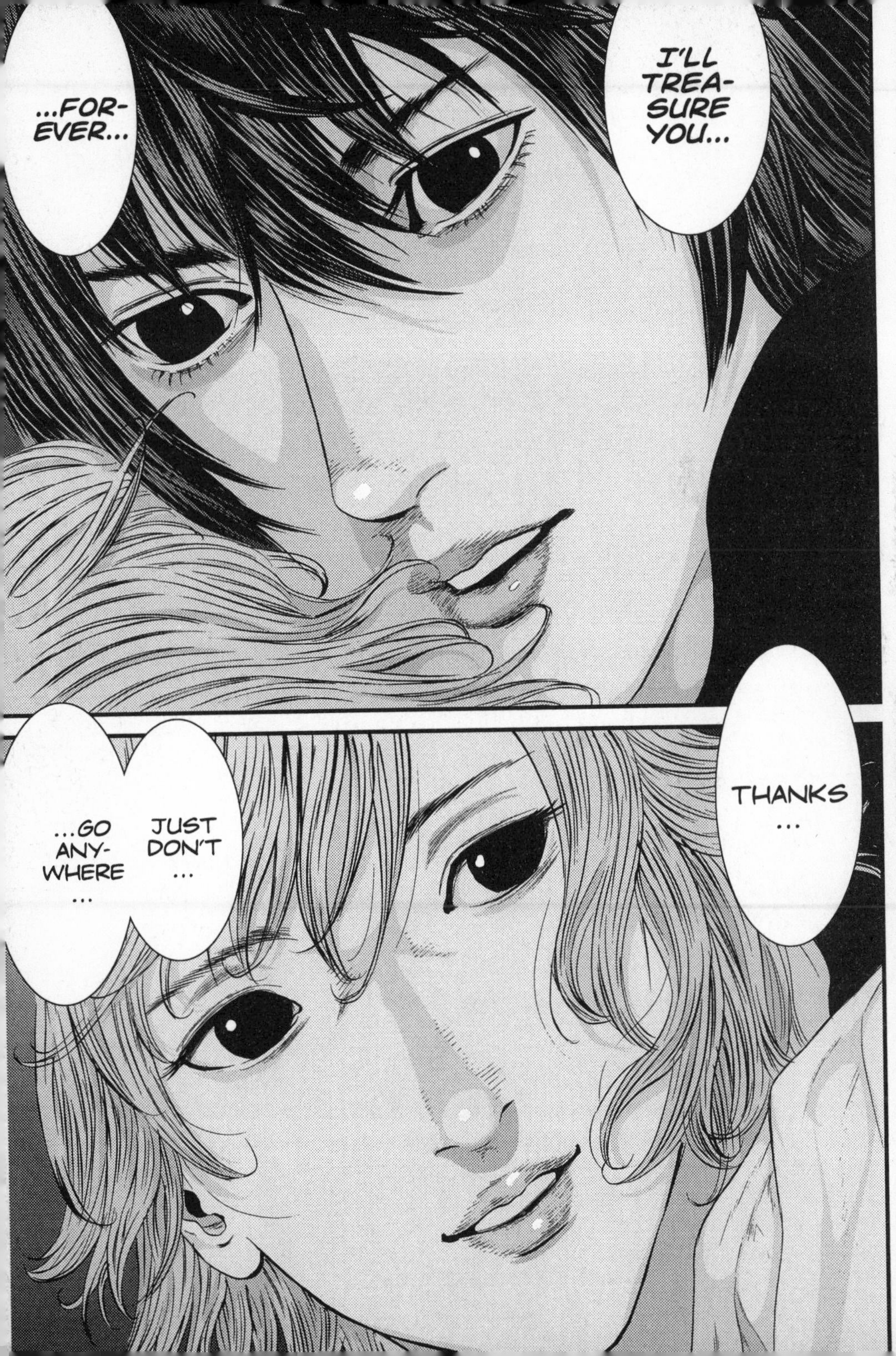
I'LL TREA-SURE YOU...
...FOR-EVER...
THANKS...
JUST DON'T...
...GO ANY-WHERE...

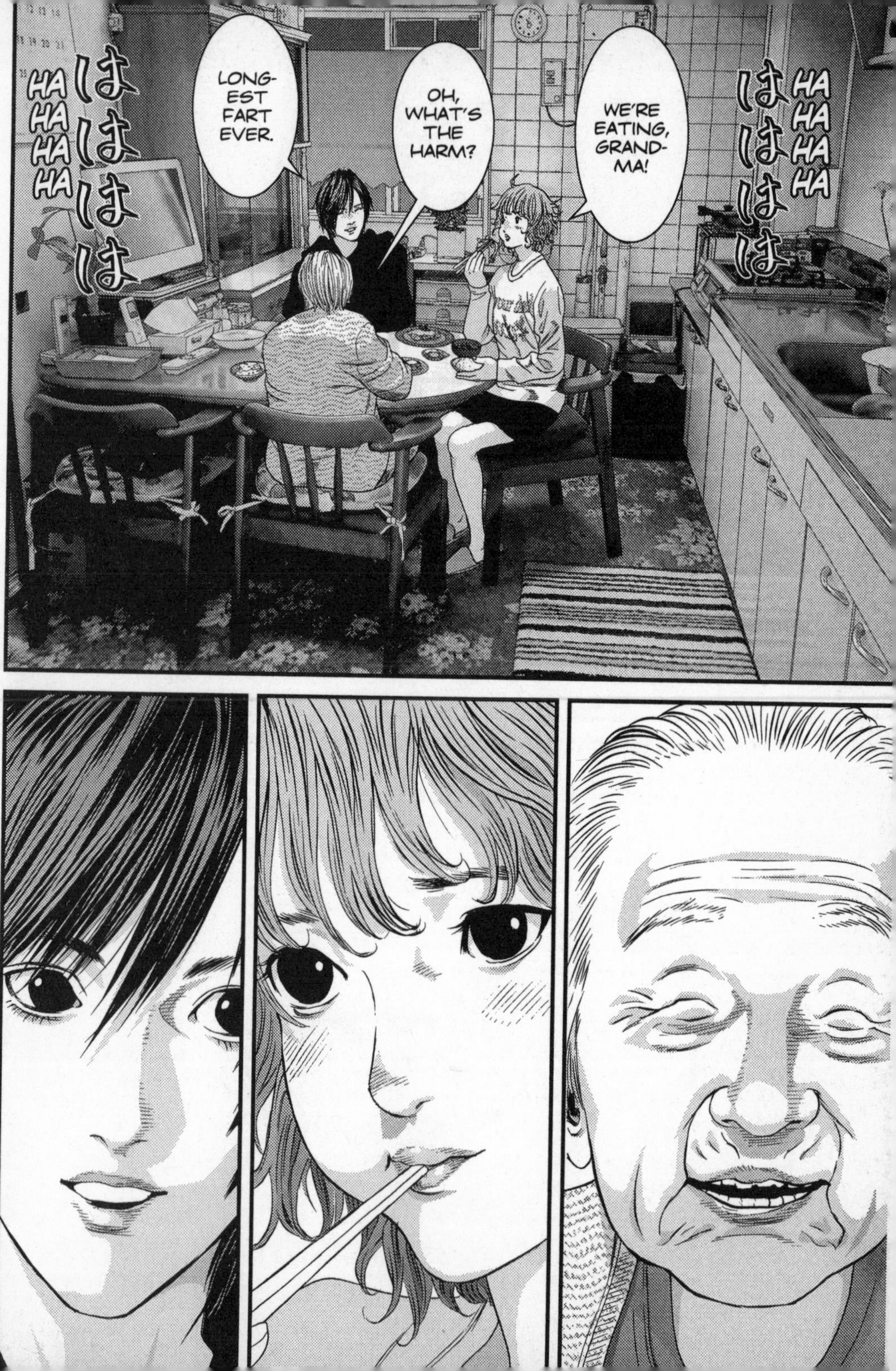
HA HA HA HA
ははははは
WE'RE EATING, GRAND-MA!
OH, WHAT'S THE HARM?
LONG-EST FART EVER.
HA HA HA HA
ははははは

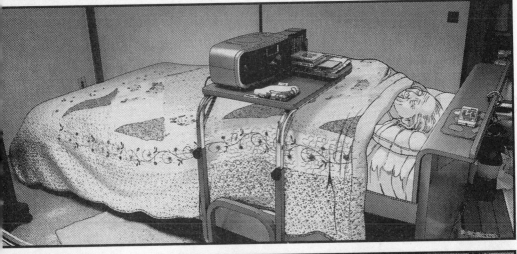

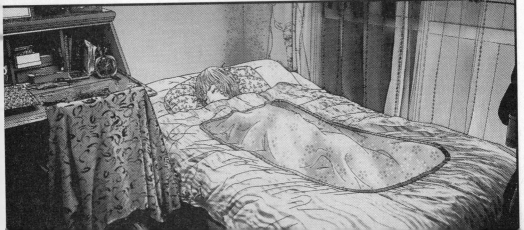

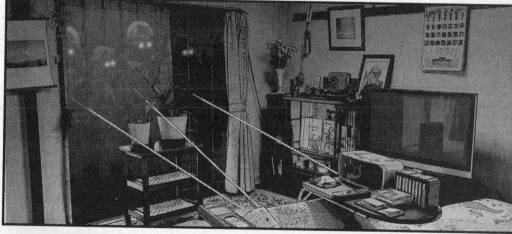

CHAPTER 44 - END

Translation Notes

Daifuku mochi, page 9

A type of mochi (sticky rice cake) that is filled with something sweet; usually anko (red bean paste), but other flavorings like strawberry are common as well.

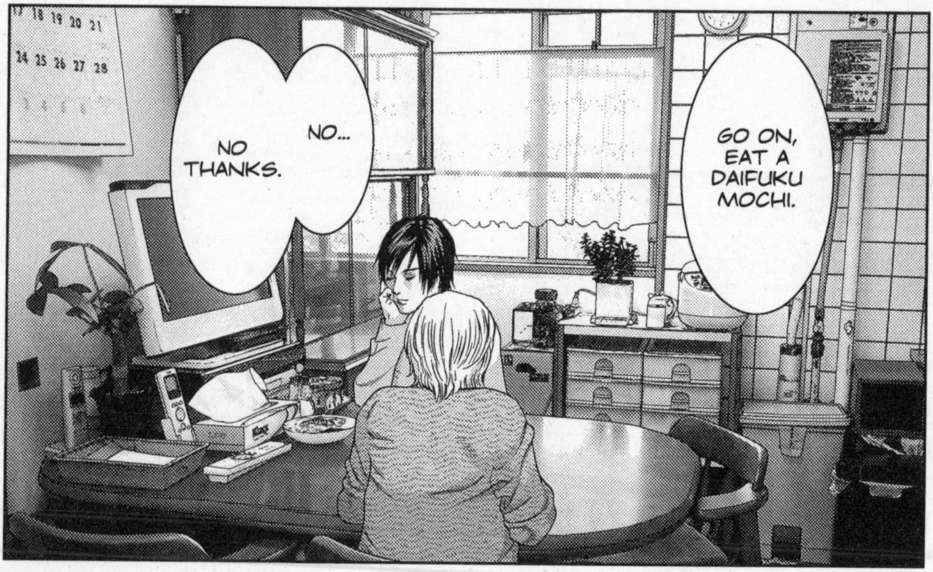
GO ON, EAT A DAIFUKU MOCHI.
NO...
NO THANKS.

TV comedians, page 35-37

The comedians on TV are very clear (non-parodized) depictions of actual, famous comedians seen all over TV in Japan. The two members of the duo Bananaman, Shitara (parted hair) and Himura (with the rounded Beatles bowl cut), are seated on the right end of the row of panels, while next to them with the big smile and closed eyes is the solo comedian Bakarhythm.

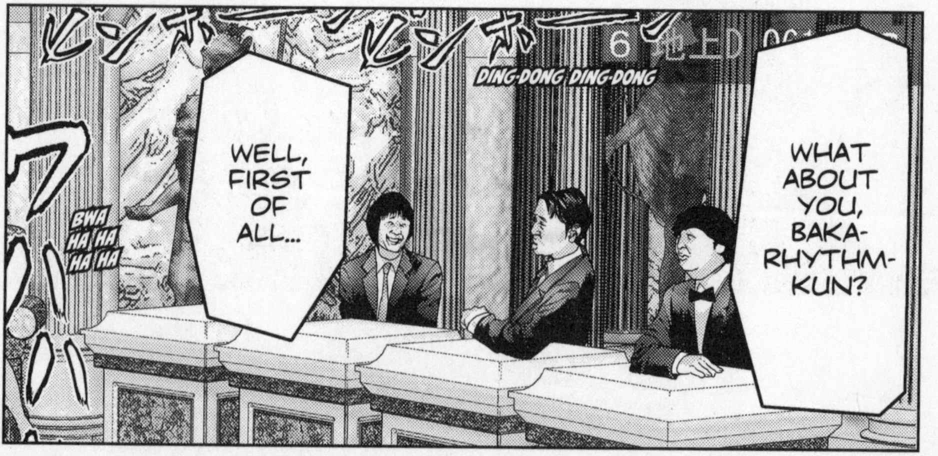
WHAT ABOUT YOU, BAKA-RHYTHM-KUN?
DING-DONG DING-DONG
WELL, FIRST OF ALL...
BWA HA HA HA HA

Becky, page 72

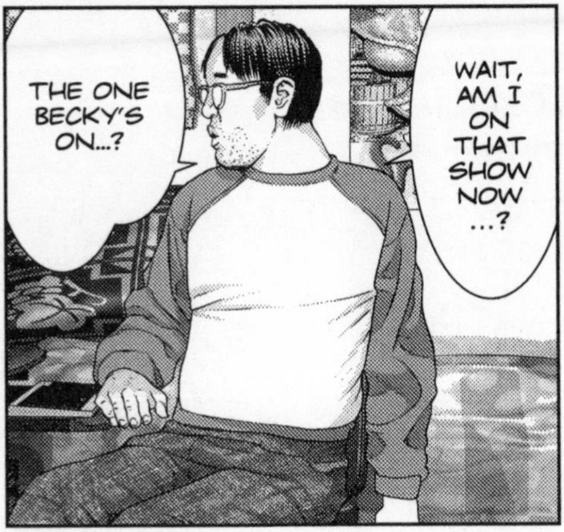
WAIT, AM I ON THAT SHOW NOW ...?
THE ONE BECKY'S ON...?

An extremely popular television personality and actress in Japan, known only by her first name. In addition to her good looks and cheerful personality, Becky is known for being extremely knowledgeable and well-spoken. While there's not enough evidence to tell exactly what show the character is referencing in this scene (as Becky appears on TV constantly), it is most likely the program Monitoring: Human Observation, a hidden-camera variety show in which Becky and the other stars on the show confront their unsuspecting targets with surprising, baffling, or subtle events to see how they react, or if they even notice.

Yakisoba, page 99

Meaning "cooked soba," yakisoba is a common summertime dish of soba (buckwheat) noodles fried in a savory sauce with pork, ginger and chopped nori.

Taketomi & Hoshino, page 156

The island of Taketomi is one of the small subtropical Yaeyama Islands associated with Okinawa, a common vacation destination for Japanese living on the main four islands of Japan. Hoshino Resorts is a company that melds modern resorts with the traditional Japanese inn (ryokan) style, and their recently opened Hoshinoya Okinawa resort is located on Taketomi and features an architectural design similar to traditional Okinawan style.

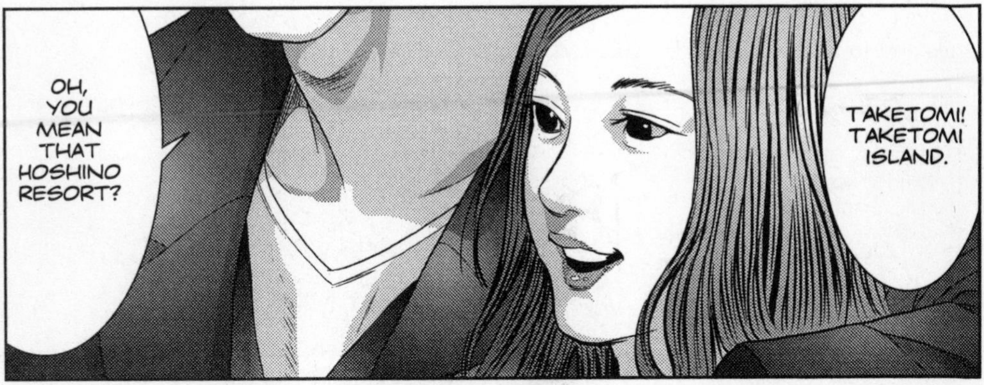
TAKETOMI! TAKETOMI ISLAND.
OH, YOU MEAN THAT HOSHINO RESORT?

A Kodansha Comics Trade Paperback Original.

Inuyashiki volume 5 copyright © 2015 Hiroya Oku
English translation copyright © 2016 Hiroya Oku

Published in the United States by Kodansha Comics, an imprint of Kodansha USA Publishing, LLC, New York.

Publication rights for this English edition arranged through Kodansha Ltd., Tokyo.

First published in Japan in 2015 by Kodansha Ltd., Tokyo, as *Inuyashiki* volume 5.

ISBN 978-1-63236-297-1

Printed in the United States of America.

www.kodanshacomics.com

9 8 7 6 5 4 3 2 1

Translation: Stephen Paul
Lettering: Scott Brown
Editing: Ajani Oloye
Kodansha Comics edition cover design: Phil Balsman